Satire
in Persian Literature

Satire
in Persian Literature

HASAN JAVADI

Rutherford / Madison / Teaneck
Fairleigh Dickinson University Press
London and Toronto: Associated University Presses

Associated University Presses
440 Forsgate Drive
Cranbury, NJ 08512

Associated University Presses
25 Sicilian Avenue
London WC1A 2QH, England

Associated University Presses
2133 Royal Windsor Drive
Unit 1
Mississauga, Ontario
Canada L5J 1K5

The paper used in this publication meets the requirements
of the American National Standard for Permanence of Paper
for Printed Library Materials. Z39.48-1984.

Library of Congress Cataloging-in-Publication Data

Javadi, Hasan.
    Satire in Persian Literature.

    Bibliography: p.
    Includes index.
    1. Satire, Persian—History and criticism.
2. Persian literature—History and criticism.   3. Persian
wit and humor.   I. Title.
PK6425.J38   1988   891'.557'009   84-46118
ISBN 0-8386-3260-2 (alk. paper)

Printed in the United States of America

Dedicated to Nahid
In gratitude for twenty-six years
of pleasant companionship

Contents

Preface

This study began in 1970 when I was teaching Persian literature at Cambridge University. Originally I intended to compile an anthology of Persian satirical poetry on political, religious, and social themes. The book was meant to be used in a course that I was teaching at the time on the social history of Iran. When I had collected some two hundred pieces of poetry, I decided instead to write a history of Persian satire from the classical period to the present. I have continued my work for the past seventeen years while teaching at Tehran University, then the University of California, Berkeley. The first outcome of these studies was an article in Persian entitled "Satire in Animal Fables," which was published in 1974 in the journal *Alefba* (number 4) by my friend, the late Dr. Gholam-Hosain Sa'edi. Under the rigorous censorship of the Shah's reign, *Alefba* was discontinued. I wrote a second article, which was heavily censored, entitled "Satire and Religion" for the Tehran weekly *Negin* (numbers 115 and 116, 1974). This essay was expanded into a small book in Persian that came out in two different editions in 1980 and 1981 in Berkeley and Los Angeles. Having no hope of publishing the book in Iran under the existing harsh censorship, I decided to rewrite it in English; and this book is the result.

So far as I know there has never been a comprehensive study of Persian satire. However, there are studies on individual authors and on various periods, of which the following should be mentioned. E. G. Browne, perhaps, was the first western scholar to take notice of an interesting satirical trend in the poetry and journalism of the Constitutional period (1907-14), and he translated many such poetical pieces in his *Press and Poetry of Modern Persia* (Cambridge University Press, 1914). There have been other works on the subject as well. The Polish orientalist Francizek Machalski devoted one chapter of his *Littérature de l'Iran contemporaine* (Warsaw, 1965, 2 vols.) to "Humorous and Satirical Poetry" of modern Iran. Indian scholar Munibur Rahman published in 1957 a very interesting article entitled "Social Satire in Modern Persian Literature" in *Bulletin of the Institute of Islamic Studies* (Aligarh University). The late Yahya Arianpur in his excellent *Az Saba ta Nima* (Tehran, 1973) devoted a chapter to the satire of the Constitutional period. He extensively discussed Taherzade Saber, Dehkhoda, and Ashraf Gilani. My long-time friend and colleague, Reza Baraheni, an outstanding critic and writer, has devoted two chapters of his *Qissa-nevisi* (Tehran, 1969) to an analytical discussion of the satire of Dehkhoda from the standpoint of style.

9

In recent years two anthologies of modern prose satire have been published in Tehran: *Tanz-avaran-e-Mo'aser-e-Iran* by Bizhan Assadipur and 'Omran Salahi (1970) and *Numune-ha-ye Tanz-e-Mo'aser* by Javahiri Vajdi (1970). I have made use of these anthologies and am grateful to their authors. I have included a recent work on modern Persian prose satire by Jahangir Dorri, *Persidskaia Satiricheskaia Prosa* (Moscow, 1977). With the help of Professor Guitty Azarpay, Near Eastern Studies Department, University of California, Berkeley, I was able to obtain a translation of chapter four, which I incorporated in the section on political satire.

See p. 13

In this study I have not dealt with the nature and definition of satire but have instead devoted two chapters to form and technique. My intention, basically, was to survey the history of Persian satire in its various forms and stages, and at the same time to try to provide a glimpse of the social history of Iran through the eyes of the poets, writers, and satirists who could not tolerate hypocrisy, tyranny, and corruption, and who took issue with the *status quo*. In discussing form and technique I have tried to draw attention to the universality of the subjects as well as to the modes and means used by the representative satirists. I am aware that I have sometimes given too many examples. This excess may be justified by the fact that few of these examples have ever been translated into English, and that those translated have never been collected in one volume. I have tried to model this study upon an excellent work by Matthew Hodgart entitled *Satire* (World University, 1969), which is an analytical survey of satire in western literature.

During this study I was helped by many friends, and I am grateful to them all. First, Mrs. Johanna Domela Movassat, who typed the manuscript and rendered me valuable editorial assistance. Professor Michael Beard of North Dakota University has read the manuscript and made many helpful suggestions. Also I am indebted to my friends Mr. Robert Campbell, Mrs. Susan Sallée, and Mr. Abazar Sepekhri of the University of Texas at Austin, who have helped me greatly in editing and preparing the manuscript for publication.

It is my pleasant task also to thank the friends and colleagues who have provided me with material for various chapters of this study. Mr. Ovanes Ovanesian and Dr. Rezvani, both of Tehran University, have sent me valuable material on the newspapers of the Constitutional period and those of the time of Dr. Mosaddeq. Further, I am thankful to the talented satirist and journalist, Mr. Hadi Khorsandi, who has sent me volumes of his satirical paper *Taghut* (later called *Asghar Agha*). My gratitude is also extended to Mr. Yahya Emami and his son Vahid, of Tehran, who have sent me a stream of Iran's most recent publications and satirical newspapers. I should also like to thank my old-friend Professor Hamid Algar of the University of California, Berkeley, for providing me with numerous additional references and material.

Finally, I would like to thank my wife Nahid, without whose encouragement this study could have not been completed.

Satire
in Persian Literature

1

Definition of Satire

Satire has always shone among the rest,
And is the boldest way, if not the best,
To tell men freely of their foulest faults;
To laugh at their vain deeds and vainer thoughts.

—Dryden, *Essay upon Satire*

The word *satire*, derived from the Latin *satura* ("a mixed food"), has the same meaning in most European languages; when referring to literature, it denotes those writings that have mocking or critical overtones. In Persian, however, as in Arabic and Turkish,[1] no single word is synonymous with this broad concept of satire. Persian distinguishes between two concepts, *hajv* and *hazl*, both of which may be regarded as specialized types of satire. *Hajv* ("invective" or "lampoon") is a form of personal satire. Its intention is rarely social and reformative, and it lacks the directness and irony so integral to most European satire. *Hajv* is simply the opposite of panegyric. *Hazl* ("comical") refers to a more humorous type of satire. It is the opposite of *jedd* ("serious"), although behind the lightness of its form it can and does have serious intent. Sa'di's comment on his own use of *hazl* indicates the double-faced nature of the form:

I have not said this jokingly—let go of *hazl*,
And from it, extract *jedd*.

In recent years the term *tanz* ("mockery") has also been used in Persian for satire, and it is in fact closer to the European expression than either *hajv* or *hazl*. *Tanz* does not refer to a specific form of satire, but rather denotes the satirical quality in a work. Like the European word, it can also refer to any artistic mode. The use of *tanz* has indeed been widely accepted in modern times, but since it was not used extensively in classical times, it has not played so crucial a role in the development of Persian satire as have *hajv* and *hazl*. It is upon the con-

13

cepts of *hajv* and *hazl* that the tradition of Persian literary satire is based.

Let us, therefore, explore the nature of *hajv* and *hazl*. *Hajv*, as we have indicated, conveys scorn and ridicule with a particular person as target. It is a term reserved principally for poetry. The historian Abu'l-Fazl Bayhaqi (996-1077), discussing the struggle for supremacy which began after the death of the Caliph Harun between his two sons Amin and Ma'mun, writes that Grand Vizier Fazl ibn al-Rabi' "told the preachers to vilify [Ma'mun], and ordered the poets to satirize [*hajv*] him."[2]

The tenth-century Iranian poet, Manjik of Termez, likens the pungency of his satire to the sharpness of a sword:

> O, Sir I had no intention of writing a *hajv* on you;
> Except that I wanted to try my talent on you.
> You know a good sword is tried by killing a dog
> And that dog indicates the value of the sword.[3]

This kind of *hajv* in the hands of poets was considered in classical times a particularly potent weapon. Ferdausi (d. 1020 or 1025), whose satire on Mahmud of Ghazna is an excellent example of *hajv*, writes:

> When the poet is offended, he writes *hajv*
> And *hajv* remains up to the day of resurrection.[4]

And there was, unfortunately for the patrons at times, not much practical difference between *hajv* and panegyric. In the courts, the poet would first panegyrize his royal patron. But if his praises went unrewarded, he would threaten to write a *hajv*, and if he were courageous, he would do it. Anvari describes the poet's rather peculiar position of power: "Greedy poets," he says, "write three types of poems":

> One, a panegyric; two, a request;
> And three, if the patron gives,
> Another panegyric; otherwise, a *hajv*.
>
> Of these three, I have written two—
> What the third shall be, is up to you.[5]

The invective power of *hajv* derives, perhaps, from the pre-Islamic Arabic poetic tradition in which *hija* served as a weapon between warring tribes.[6] *Hija* is in fact the Arabic term for *hajv*, deriving from the same verbal root, and it was traditionally employed before a battle when a poet from one tribe would satirize the other tribe, and the rival poet then answer with another *hija*. Some people feared the poet's satire more than the actual killing, because a *hija* would often cause humiliation for a tribe that could not be easily effaced. *Hija*, according to the pre-Islamic Arabs, was answerable either by another *hija* or by the shedding of blood. The power given to this form of satire recalls the ancient Greek and Irish traditions in which invective satire was invested with a magical force.[7] The satirist, it was believed, could drag his victim to the very threshold of perdition.

Time has, of course, erased this magical attribution of power to satire, and offered instead more subtle and indirect satirical modes. As satirists began criticizing whole societies rather than individuals or individual tribes, they began to employ indirect speech in order to guard themselves against the consequences of their attacks. The target of *hajv*, though, is not so broadly social, and thus disguise has never been among its prime considerations. Yaghma of Jandaq (d. 1859), for instance, would abuse anyone unfriendly to him, calling him *zangahbe* ("cuckold") and other degrading names, and making no attempt to be indirect. Qa'ani (1808-54), a poet contemporary with Yaghma, clearly illustrates the nonsocial nature of *hajv*. Qa'ani would praise anyone in the hope of reward, unmindful of his patron's worthiness, and he would at the same time satirize his opponents. Qa'ani's social conscience was not pricked by the sufferings of his countrymen; he had no interest but his own. If he did on occasion write a poem about conditions such as clerical hypocrisy, such poems were exceptions and not the rule. In a typical pompous *qaside*, for instance, he addresses the prime minister, Hajji Mirza Aghasi,[8] with such titles as "the heart of the world," "the soul of the universe," "the perfect man," "the master of the two worlds," "the manifestation of God," and so on. But as soon as Mirza Aghasi was deposed, Qa'ani directed the same epithets to his successor, Mirza Taqi Khan Amir Kabir, Mirza Aghasi becoming at that point a cruel tyrant in the poet's satire. And when Amir Kabir fell out of favor and was deposed, similar titles of praise were again given the new prime minister, Amir Kabir being described as "the family foe," "ill of origin," "of devilish temper," and so on. Compared to such irresponsible satire, the *hija* of the pre-Islamic Arabs is closer to real satire, since it contains a nationalistic or tribal motive and a sense of social obligation, though even *hija* is far removed from the more widely critical sense of European social satire.

Hazl is the opposite of *jedd* ("serious"), and like *hajv* it is applied primarily to poetry. Jorjani defines it in its broadest sense as "a word, the literal or figurative meaning of which is not intended,"[9] and he further defines its sense in his literary terminology as "a poem that lampoons someone or accuses someone of improper speech or action; its content is the opposite of politeness." But even though *hazl* can contain a moral communication, it has traditionally been considered unworthy of literary attention. This neglect may in part result from the fact that in Persian literature *hazl* often consists of humorous poems on sexual subjects, not unlike limericks, automatically excluded, in the Persian mind, from serious poetry. But whatever the cause, we find many references in Persian literature which reduce *hazl* to the level of idle speech or of outright lies. In the dictionary of Dehkhoda,[10] several passages deny that there is any value in *hazl* at all and claim instead that *hazl* is synonymous with "lie" and "libel." Manjik of Termez says, for instance:

> I can't listen to the impossible,
> Lies and *hazl*—
> Writing *hazl* is heresy in Islam.

The puritanical Naser Khosrow (d. 1088) treats *hazl* in much the same way:

> Do not make swearing and lying *(hazl)* your profession;
> Do not sever your origins on purpose.
>
> He has vested his eloquence in writing *hazl*,
> And given this enlightened heart and mind to ridiculous poetry.

Jalal-al-Din Rumi sometimes refers to *hazl* in this derogatory way, too, as when he admonishes:

> Close your corporeal ear to *hazl* and lies,
> That you might see the illumined city of soul.[11]

Rumi, however, more often considers *hazl* a serious genre, the value of which can equal a satirical or critical poem. He tells us, for instance:

> *Hazl* is education; take it seriously,
> And do not be deceived by its outward form.[12]

He also claims:

> Every *jedd* is considered *hazl* by those who write *hazl*;
> Every *hazl* is considered *jedd* by those who are wise.[13]

Between these extremist views of *hazl*, chapter thirteen of the *Qabus-Name* offers, perhaps, the safest estimation. There we are advised, "if you write *hazl*, you must limit it, because humor can humiliate all values."[14]

Hajv and *hazl* thus signify two quite different concepts. *Hazl* is considered, for the most part, a satirical genre less serious and perhaps less reputable than *hajv*—a major concern in its valuation being its inclusion of some degree of *jedd*. And together *hajv* and *hazl* represent the two major streams in the development of Persian literary satire until the Constitutional Revolution. In the Constitutional period, however, the role of satire in Persian literature began to change. Gradually more and more writers and poets felt an obligation to reform society, and an incredible amount of critically satirical poetry and prose appeared. Gradually the need arose for a word to define this new type of satire. The new spirit and the new need are both realized by Taherzade Saber, the great Azerbaijani satirical poet. Dehkhoda says of him, "Saber was not a poet who worshipped fantasy. He never wrote a poem of personal praise or of personal criticism. He did not deal with individual people, but devoted his art to reforming the society and to improving the ethics of the populace at large. . ."[15] Saber hated panegyric and praise, and in answer to people who accused him of not being able to write eloquent panegyric, he would say, "I have no capacity to write panegyric *qaside*; I value my writings of social criticism."[16] By "social criticism" Saber, of course, meant satire, for which he did not have the right word. His lack of the proper literary term is again demonstrated when he writes:

Poetry is a peerless pearl of great price;
I do not debase it by lying or false praise.
I write *hajv*; my words are true
And my language is sweet.
And I give a draught of this drink to people with taste.[17]

For lack of better terminology, Saber uses the word *hajv* to refer to his verse. Modarres-e Tabrizi, who wrote an account of the life of Saber, modifies it by calling Saber's poetry "truthful *hajv*."[18] It was thus to fulfill the need for a new term to describe the new spirit in Persian satire that the word *tanz* came to be used.

Notes

1. In modern Arabic literary criticism, words like *hija*, *fokaha*, and *tahakkom* are used when dealing with satire, each of which requires special definition. In Turkish, *hiciv* and *mizah* are used, both of which also must be regarded as specialized types or subcategories of the broader term *satire*. See Christopher Bürgel, "Lamahat an dowr al-Hija fi al-Adab al-Arabi," *Fekr va Fann* 17 (1980); Ahmad Muhammad al-Howfi, *Al-Fokaha fi al-Adab* (Cairo: Darnihzat, 1967); Zaffer Arikbag and Dündar Akumal, *Turk Edebiyatinda Hiciv ve Mizah Siir* (Istanbul: Aydinlik Basimevi, 1944); Aziz Nesin, *Cumhuriyet Döneminda Türk Mizahi* (Istanbul: Ankara Yayinlari, 1973).
2. Abu'l-Fazl Bayhaqi, *Tarikh Bayhaqi*, ed. Fayyaz' (Mashhad: Mashhad University), p. 32.
3. Mohammad Dabir Siyaqi, *Pishahanqan Shi'ar Farsi* (Tehran: Ketab-ha-ye Jibi, 1972), p. 155.
4. *Shah-Name*, satire on Mahmud, Brokhim edition (Tehran, 1936).
5. Shibli No'mani, *She'r al-Ajam*, trans. (into Persian) Fakhr Da'i-e-Gilani (Tehran: Ibn Sina, 1956), 1:223.
6. See Robert C. Eliot, *The Power of Satire* (Princeton: Princeton University Press, 1972), chapter on the power of *hija*.
7. Archilochus of Paros is an example in point. He was to wed the daughter of a certain Lycambes, but the latter broke his sacred vow. In the terrible violence of his rage Archilochus wrote poems against the father and his daughter and recited them at the festival of Demeter. Lycambes and his daughter hanged themselves out of shame. See also Eliot, op cit., pp. 3-15.
8. See Yahya Arianpur, *Az Saba ta Nima* (Tehran: Shirkat-e Ketab-ha-ye Jibi, 1972), 1:99.
9. 'Ali Akbar Dehkhoda, *Loghat-Name* (Tehran: Sazman-e Dehkhoda), s.v. *hazl*, p. 208.
10. Ibid.
11. Ibid.
12. Ibid.
13. Ibid.
14. 'Onsor al-M'ali, *Qabus-Name*, ed. Amin A. Badavi (Tehran: Ibn Sina, 1956), p. 66.
15. *Loghat-Name*, s.v. Taherzade, p. 101.
16. Ibid., p. 103
17. *Hop Hop Name* (Baku: Azar Nashr, 1962), p. 361.
18. Mohammad 'Ali Modarres-e Tabrizi, *Reyhanat-al-Adab* (Tehran: Ketabfrushi Khayyam, 1954), 4:25.

2

Forms of Satire

Lampoons and satires, that are written with wit and spirit,
are like poisoned darts, which not only inflict a wound,
but make it incurable.

—Joseph Addison

The forms of satire are quite varied. In Latin poetry satire was written in dactylic hexameter. But apart from this kind of verse, which was occasionally imitated by the French and English neoclassicists, there have been no special literary forms particularly associated with satire. Similarly, in Persian literature there is no particular form for satire, though in classical Persian poetry the *qaside* and *qet'e* were often used for the purpose. In this chapter I will try to review the forms and genres of which Iranian satirists have made use.

In traditional Arabic satire, the *qaside* form was often used. The satirical poems of Bashshar ibn Burd (d. 783) and Jarir ibn 'Atiyya (d. 728) may be mentioned as outstanding examples. A similar tradition has passed into Persian poetry, and many panegyrists who wrote *qasides* on various patrons, if a different occasion arose or a reward were not forthcoming, wrote an invective in the same form (*hija*). During the Constitutional Revolution when there was a tendency for satire to be written in a less formal and more idiomatic form, the *qaside* was still used for expressing nationalistic sentiment and censuring those who opposed the revolution. Malek al-Sho'ara Bahar (1886-1951) wrote many *qasides* of such character, some translations of which are included in E. G. Browne's *Press and Poetry of Modern Persia* (Cambridge, 1914).

Here are two examples of the *qaside* form by Sadeq Khan Amiri (Adib al-Mamalek) (1860-1917) and Mirza Abu'l-Qasem Qa'em-maqam (d. 1835). The former was a prominent journalist and a pungent satirist, as well as a poet in both Persian and Arabic. The latter was a famous prime minister, who had a humorous style in his beautifully written correspondence as well as in his poetry. The first poem is about a tyrannical ruler in Khorasan, and the second is a satire

18

on Allah-Yar Khan Asef al-Dowle, who was a general in the Persian army during
the war with Russia in 1826:

> Like a hungry wolf in a flock of sheep,
> Najd al-Saltane has wrought havoc in Khorasan.
> If the state is saved from the grips of Britain and Russia,
> It will not escape the tyranny of Najd al-Saltane.
> If the legendary Rostam comes to him in helmet and armor,
> Before long he will return stripped and naked.
> The governor rushes to invitations like a mountain torrent,
> But flees from guests like the wind from a window.
> No tribal pillager will be like him, neither Shahesvan nor Qashqa'i;
> Neither Sanjabi nor Zangane will be so rapacious.
>
> He gets more interest than there is principal, and more excise than
>   there are goods;
> And he now expects the taxes for the year to come.
> In villages he levies tithes on mushroom, rhubarb and artichoke.
> And in his districts he wants his share of goosefoot and wormseed.
> When a Baluchi comes from the summer quarters,
> He like a flea sticks to his private parts in the hope of
>   getting some yogurt.
> Dull, obtuse, and slow-witted he may be,
> Yet four synonymous foreign words he remembers distinctly:
> "Donnez-moi" in French; "'Itani" in Arabic;
> In Turkish "Ver-mana"; and in English, "Give me"![1]

In the second poem Asef al-Dowle is satirized for his inefficiency and failure
to send the necessary forces, thereby causing the defeat of the Persians. He be-
haved similarly two years later in another war, and Fath 'Ali Shah had him
publicly bastinadoed. Qa'em-maqam, the minister to the Crown Prince 'Abbas
Mirza, whose patriotic and devoted character markedly contrasted with the
cowardice of the general, wrote:

> Before it's too late, flee. It is time to flee away.
> Save your life; it is too dear to throw away.
> It is your life. It can't be easily sacrificed.
> Know what is easy to do and what is hard.
> Cross the river Araxes and hurry away.
> There come the Russians, they will have you at bay.
> O traitor to king, prince and country,
> Do you pay your gratitude thus and flee?
> Amazing it is that with a hundred guns and ten,
> Three times they broke wind which made you gallop away.
> That shying deer who in one day and night reached,
> From the river Zagam[2] to Dizaj,[3] or even beyond,
> Is not fighting a holy war with Russians as his foe,
> But rather he is a new bride gathering her trousseau.
> Why should that hyacinth-like and musky hair
> Be covered with dust? It is a pity and most unfair!

These two poems are fairly late examples of satirical *qasides*, and similar examples are to be found in the works of earlier poets. Such *qasides* are often largely works of social criticism, and only parts of them border on satire. Seyf al-Din Mohammad Farghani (d. ca. 1306), who fled from his native Farghana during the Mongol invasion and lived for the rest of his life in Anatolia, produced numerous *qasides* in which he bitterly criticizes the corruption and cruelty of his contemporary rulers and bureaucrats.[5] Another poet of the same period. Pur-e Baha (d. 1331), in a similar manner devotes some of his *qasides* to social criticism. His poetry is interesting from the point of view of both language and content. It is full of newly acquired Turkish and Mongolian words, and he paints a vivid picture of the social conditions under the descendants of Chengiz Khan. Before Ghazan Khan introduced his tax reform in 1302, such confusion reigned in the Mongol financial administration that every officer, according to his own whim, levied a different tax on the poor subjects. Although in the poem that follows Pur-e Baha praises a famous dignitary, he speaks mainly of the sufferings caused by the special taxes *qalan* and *qopcur*. V. Minorsky, who has translated this long poem into English, notes, "One might think that in his black-and-white ode Pur-e Baha would equally balance the two colors, yet the nature of a born satirist has the upper hand; even in the second part of the poem, addressed directly to 'Ala al-Din Joveini, one finds some barbs hidden among the smiles and roses."[6] Some lines from the poem follow:

> Again the *qopcur* has cast evil and disturbance into the world.
> It has brought forth laments from the old and young.
> The whole world has become scattered and homeless
> Because of the immense *qalan* and endless *qopcur*.
> . . . .
> Like the Sufis who in one breath used to celebrate two festivals,
> Now [the government] imposes *qopcur* twice at a time.
> Who has ever taken the census twice in one year?
> [And yet] in spring *qalan* has been imposed and in autumn *qopcur*.
>
> The people of Jovein have all become homosexuals and self-defilers,
> For every frail infant is assessed with a heavy *qopcur*.
> Sperm in the womb has not yet solidified into an embryo
> When the name of the child has been entered under *qalan* and *qopcur*.
> A boy has not yet been born of his mother
> When they say that *qalan* and *qopcur* should be paid for
> "the celebrations of the circumcision" and "the first cutting
>   of the hair."
> Do women bear twice in a year
> That every six months *qopcur* is imposed on us?
> While a dead man under the sod has become corrupted and decomposed
> His frame is still paying *qopcur* for life.

The *ghazal* as a poetic form has rarely been used in its entirety as a vehicle of satire. However, because of its somewhat incoherent nature, one or several couplets could be satirical without making the whole poem satirical. The *ghazals* of Hafez are good examples in this respect. While pursuing a theme the poet at an appropriate moment makes one or two pungent remarks on the sanctimony or hypocrisy of his contemporaries and then goes back to his original subject. In a similar manner 'Aref-e-Qazvini (1882-1934) wrought his criticism of the government and clerics into his *ghazals*, whose themes are basically patriotic.[8]

After the Constitutional Revolution it was not unusual to find a *ghazal* entirely devoted to social criticism and satire, but this was rare in the classical period. There is one interesting exception to this, however, and that is a *ghazal* by Nizari of Qohestan (d. 1320). Instead of devoting his poem to divine or earthly love, he talks throughout the *ghazal* of the dearness of the price of wheat and complains of the living conditions of his time.[9]

Now we come to *qet'e* ("fragment"), which traditionally was one of the most suitable forms for satirical poetry. Originally it was a detached "fragment" of a *qaside*, but later on it came to be a complete poem. *Qet'e* can be very brief and to the point, thus giving an extra pungency to the satire. It can as easily be expanded to relate a story or incident. Kamal al-Din Esma'il, who was killed by the Mongols in 1237 or 1238, wrote on one of his contemporaries:

> My face shall show no traces of despite,
> Although my Patron speaketh ill of me:
> His praise I'll still continue to recite,
> That both of us alike may liars be![10]

In another poem Sa'di wonderfully describes the devotion of a courtier:

> A man extremely avaricious, so I've heard,
> One morn right early went before Khwarizmshah;
> And seeing him, he bent in two in reverence and
>   straightened up again,
> Rubbing his face into the dust, indeed, before he rose.
> To him, said his son: "Papa mine, fame-seeker!
> Let me ask you a problem, and tell me the answer:
> Did you not say the *qibla* was towards Hijaz?
> [Then] Why do you pray today in this direction?"[11]

The third *qet'e* is by Iraj Mirza (1874-1925), and it is about a certain official who was sent to the United States to recruit some advisors; the result, however, was far from satisfactory:

> May you not benefit from the world, O 'Alai,
> May heaven strike you with a catastrophe!
> We sent you, O Jackass, for a mission;
> But not everything can be justified by a commission.
> In America you were to search for and find
> An advisor both adept and well-refined.
> Then you declared to the asses of that land,
> That for them Iran is a proper grassland.
> You sent a flock of your own kind,
> Especially a tall one with a stubborn mind.

He is mulish, hard-mouthed, restive and vulgar;
Neither does he fear reins nor any fetter.
The asses of our own were well-mannered,
Liked by the nation they were well-accepted,
But the foreigners not only grazed on our grasses,
The sons of bitches excreted on our pastures.[12]

As the repetition of the same rhyme in *qaside* or *qet'e* becomes tiresome, the *mathnavi* comes into use for satirical works of a narrative nature. The *mathnavi* form, which is comparable to rhyming couplets in English, has been employed, until very recently, by nearly all Iranian poets in their narrative poetry. Of the classical poets' works in this form, 'Obeyd-e Zakani's "Cat and The Mice" and Ferdausi's "Braham, the Jew and Bahram-e Gur" should be mentioned; and among the modern poets, "Aref-Name" by Iraj Mirza is a fine example. There are also numerous humorous and satirical stories in the *Mathnavi* of Rumi. The following well-known story about Juhi and his father is not a satirical but rather a humorous tale. Rumi remarks that sinners have "a hundred marks upon themselves, but how should they see them?"[13]

A child was crying bitterly and beating his head beside his
    father's coffin,
Saying, "Why, father, where are they taking you to press
    you tight under some earth?
They are taking you to a narrow and noisome house: there is
    no carpet in it, nor any mat;
No lamp at night and no bread by day; neither smell nor
    sign of food is there.
No door in good repair, no way to the roof; not one neighbour
    to be [your] refuge.
Your body, which was a place for the people's kisses—how
    should it go into a blind and murky house?—
A pitiless house and narrow room, will be lasting nor [your] colour."
In this manner was he enumerating the qualities of the house,
Whilst he wrung tears of blood from his two eyes
Juhi said to his father, "O worthy [sir] by God they are
    taking this [corpse] to our house."
The father said to Juhi, "Don't be a fool!" "Oh papa," said
    he, "hear the marks [of identity]."
These marks which he mentioned one by one—"our house
    has them [all], without uncertainty or doubt.
[It has] neither mat nor lamp nor food; neither its door is in
    good repair, nor its court nor its roof."

As we shall see in the following chapters, the Constitutional Revolution was a turning point in the history of Persian satire. The poets and writers increasingly realized their obligation toward the people and turned away from the court. Persian poetry, which had been basically mystical, didactic, or panegyrical, became more and more concerned with social and national problems. Satire and direct criticism took on a new significance. In a revolutionary age when writers played an important role in the leadership of the movement, new literary criteria were sought. Simpler and much more direct language was needed to suit new and democratic ideas. The language and forms of folk poetry afforded new possibilities particularly.

One of many poetic forms that became popular in this period was the *tasnif*, a popular ballad. Though there are no ancient examples of the *tasnif*, its syllabic system of meter, which is so distinct from the quantitative Persian and Arabic poetry of the Islamic era, might indicate a pre-Islamic origin.[14] After Islam there are a significant number of examples of the *tasnif* in Persian literature, indicating that its simple language and loose structure made it a popular means for criticizing hated oppressors or glorifying national heroes. A British traveler has preserved a *tasnif* about Lotf 'Ali Khan that was very popular in Shiraz some years after that noble prince of the Zand dynasty was treacherously captured and put to death in 1779 by the tyrant Aqha Mohammad Khan-e Qajar.[15] During the Constitutional period the *tasnif* experienced a significant development, and more particularly it became a vehicle of satire. Some years later 'Aref-e Qazvini, who had a talent for music, gave a new dimension to *tasnif*-writing, and both the *ghazal* and *tasnif*, and sometimes a combination of the two, became effective means of arousing popular sentiment. Here I quote a *tasnif*, translated by Browne, signed "Hop Hop" (Hoopoe), that expresses the despair and disillusionment of the people under a government that ignores their grievances:

(1)
"Mother dear, I slept, I saw a vision:
Ramazan was over, Mother dear;
Everyone in clover, Mother dear!
But my dream was a delusion, Mother dear!
All delusion and confusion, Mother dear!

(2)
"Mother dear, I slept, I saw a vision:
The Constitution flourished, Mother dear;
All the poor were housed and nourished, Mother dear!
But my dream was a delusion, Mother dear!
All delusion and confusion, Mother dear!

(3)
"Mother dear, I slept, I saw a vision:
Spacious street and splendid square, Mother dear;
Like a Frankish city rare, Mother dear!
But my dream was a delusion, Mother dear!
All delusion and confusion, Mother dear!

(4)
"Mother dear, I slept, I saw a vision:
The baths were clean and sweet, Mother dear;
'Snap your fingers, stamp your feet,' Mother dear!
But my dream was a delusion, Mother dear!
All delusion and confusion, Mother dear!

(5)

"Weep not, Mother dear, I pray, nor worry:
I will buy you sugar-loaves and sweets untold,
And a pretty out-door mantle stitched with gold,
For when crushed by household care, Mother dear!
You fill me with despair, Mother dear!"[16]

The poets of the Constitutional period employed virtually all the poetic forms in writing on satirical or social topics. Bahar is a remarkable example in this respect and his *Divan* contains numerous satirical pieces written in amazingly different forms and styles. In *The Press and Poetry of Modern Persia*, Browne quotes fifteen pieces of poetry by Bahar, most of which were published in the newspaper *Now Bahar*. In this small collection of mostly satirical poems one finds an interesting array of forms, ranging from the *ghazal* and *qaside* to *musammat*, *mustazad*, and *tarkiband*. These last three are the forms most frequently used by Bahar in this period.

The language used by Bahar and many of his contemporaries is the standard literary language, whereas some other poets like Dehkhoda (1879-1956) and Ashraf Gilani (1871-1934) made use of colloquial and even slang words. This was a bold departure from a poetic tradition that had never used anything but refined language. Dehkhoda was a pioneer in this respect. It is interesting to note that in both his satirical prose and his poetry he chooses a language most appropriate for the occasion and the characters that he is creating, whereas ordinarily, in his other poems, he uses a scholarly and sometimes pedantic language. Here I shall quote two examples by him (both in Browne's translation); one is a poem entitled "The Leaders and the Nation," written in the form of a lullaby. "The leaders" are represented as an ignorant mother, and "the nation" as a sickly child who eventually expires in her arms. In the second poem Dehkhoda, addressing himself through one of his journalist friends in the newspaper *Sur-e Esrafil*, attacks himself for his uncompromising attitude toward the problems of the nation and his relentless criticism:

The Leaders and the Nation

Dust on my head![17] The child has woken up! Go to sleep,
    my pet; the Bogey-man is coming!
Don't cry! The ogre will come and eat you up! The cat
    will come and take away your kiddy!
Oh, oh! What ails you, my pet? "I am hungry" [you
    say]? May you burst! You have eaten all this: is
    it too little?
Get out, dog! Pussy, puss, puss, come here! Hushaby,
    darling! You are my rose! Hush, hush!
"Mamma! I am ready to die with hunger!" Don't cry!
To-morrow I will give you bread!
"O dear, Mamma! My life is ready to leave me!" Don't

cry! The pot is just on the boil!
"O my hand! See, it is as cold as ice!" Fie, Fie my
  Soul! See the breast is dry!
"Why does my head spin so?" [Because] the lice
  are digging holes in your head!
Akh-kh-kh!...What ails you, my Soul? *Haq, haq!* O my
  Aunt! Why are its eyes turned up to the ceiling?
Come here! Alas, see, its body also has become cold!
Dust on my head! Why has its colour turned so pale?
Woe is me! My child is gone from my hands! Alas, alas!
To me there remain but sighs and grief! Alas, alas!

O Kablay

(1)

Rejected by men and by God the Forgiving, O Kablay!
You're a wonderful sample of riotous living, O Kablay!
You're a wag, you're a joker, no end to your fun,
Of living and dead you are sparing of none,
Such a limb of the Devil and son of a gun, O Kablay!

(2)

Neither wizard, diviner nor warlock you fear, O Kablay!
Nor the dervish's prayer, nor the dreams of the Seer, O Kablay!
Nor Shapshal's[18] revolver, nor *mujtahid's* rage:
'Tis hard to believe you will die of old age,
You limb of the Devil and son of a gun, O Kablay!

(3)

Times a hundred I've told you your project will fail, O Kablay!
While half of the nation are wrapped in a veil,[19] O Kablay!
Can Islam in you and your circle prevail?
With fresh words of folly your friends you'll regale,
You limb of the Devil and son of a gun, O Kablay!

(4)

At the heels of the dervish you bark and you bite, O Kablay!
Break the Dominie's windows[20] and let in the light, O Kablay!
While this trumpet[21] of yours doth all secrets proclaim;
Yes, blazon them forth, for what know you of shame?
You limb of the Devil and son of a gun, O Kablay!

(5)

To hell with the folk, if with hunger they pine, O Kablay!
Devil take them, the brutes, since they cannot combine,
  O Kablay!
Since opium hath stolen their courage away,
With your minstrels and singers be merry and gay,
You limb of the Devil and son of a gun, O Kablay!

(6)

In Persia will bribes ever go out of fashion, O Kablay!

Will the *mullas* for justice develop a passion, O Kablay!
From magic and *murshids*[22] can Islam win free?
Bid the dead come to life, for 'twill easier be,
You limb of the Devil and son of a gun, O Kablay!

As an epilogue to the development of satire in Persian poetry, mention should also be made of the advent of modern poetry, which revolutionized not only the traditional form but the subject matter as well. Though the majority of poets were deeply preoccupied with the social and political problems of the country, the unrelenting censorship of the Pahlavi era did not allow them the right of criticism and freedom of expression. Gradually a symbolism of theme and vocabulary emerged. When Nima Yushij (1895-1960) in his poem "Ay Adamha" (O men) describes the agony of a man being drowned at sea to the bystanders on the shore, one immediately discerns the pain of a nation under an intolerable rule. When Forugh Farrokhzad (1935-67) expresses her yearning for a window of light to the outside world, the hard life of an intellectual under a cruel dictatorship can easily be visualized. Words such as "night," "tulip," and "star" are as easy to understand in this context as "the regime" or "martyred guerrilla" might be in an anti-war poem. The following couplet may serve as a brief example:

Every night a star is killed;
And yet this gloomy sky is still filled with stars.[23]

During the 1970s censorship was even extended to words charged with such symbolic meaning. Naturally, under this repressive regime satire could not function openly—in sharp contrast to the freedom that was enjoyed by the poets of the Constitutional period. Furthermore, their journalistic or colloquial language easily lent itself to satire. Blank verse used as a vehicle of satire is seen in "O Bejewelled Land" of Forugh Farrokhzad.

BREVITY IN SATIRE: APHORISM, QUATRAIN, AND EPIGRAM

Aphorism and epigram are the shortest forms of satire, but each is very significant. The former, often prose, embodies a proverbial wisdom, and the latter concisely, pointedly, and often satirically treats a single thought or event in verse. Elements of brevity and wit are common to both forms. As these two elements are among the most important ingredients of humor, it is only natural to find aphorism and epigram used as vehicles of satire.

More than the aphorism, the epigram lends itself to wit and humor. Though originally a poem inscribed on a Greek tomb, before long it became closely associated with wit and satire. Coleridge has described it beautifully:

What is an epigram? A dwarfish whole:
Its body brevity and wit its soul.[24]

In Persian literature, some short *qet'e*, quatrains and single couplets *(tak-beit)* have the character of satricial epigrams. In many quatrains, a point is developed in the first three lines, and the fourth line provides a somewhat unexpected or shocking conclusion. Two examples follow, one from Khayyam and one from Jami:

> In heaven is seen the bull we name Parwin;
> Beneath the earth another lurks unseen;
> And thus to wisdom's eyes mankind appear
> A drove of asses, two great bulls between![25]

Jami wrote the following quatrain on a contemporary poet named Saghari who had accused his fellow poets of plagiarizing his ideas:

> Saghari was saying, "Wherever the plagiarists have seen a fine
> idea in my poetry they have stolen it."
> I have noticed that most of his poems are devoid of ideas:
> Whoever said that the ideas had been stolen spoke the truth.[26]

Very often in a short *qet'e* or quatrain, the humor is built upon a pun, a play on words, or a reference that is difficult to translate. Here are two examples, one from the seventeenth century and the other by a contemporary poet. Mulla Shiri, an Indian poet, criticized Taleb Amoli (d. 1626 or 1627), the poet laureate of the court of Jahangir, in the following *qet'e*

> Day and night our master Taleb[27]
> Is running after worldly pelf.
> As if he does not remember the Prophet's saying:
> The world is a carcass and its seeker *(taleb)* a dog.[28]

The second poem is a quatrain, anonymously published[29] during the early days of the Iranian Revolution when the former premier Shahpur Bakhtiar fled the country. Because he was a good friend of Mehdi Bazargan, who succeeded him, it was believed that the latter might have facilitated his flight. Bazargan is also the name of a checkpoint along the northwestern border of Iran with Turkey:

> He said: "Do you know that Bakhtiar escaped from
> the authorities?
> Radio Iran reported that he escaped from prison."
> "But Khomeini had closed the borders, " I said.
> He said: "Perhaps he escaped from the Bazargan frontier."

"The satiric epigram," writes Matthew Hodgart, "is a kind of anti-lyric; it uses the lyric form and metre, usually associated with romantic love and exaltation, to convey a gross and unromantic message; the ironic tension between form and content produces an effect of surprise." As examples of this kind of shock effect he quotes some Japanese *senryu* that are written in the strict form of *haiku* poetry:

> Zen priests
> Meditation finished,
> Looking for fleas.

> In the whole village
> The husband alone
> Does not know of it.[30]

Hodgart's statement is applicable to aphorisms that are written for a satirical purpose. Maxims and proverbial wisdom can be considered the result of the experiences of many generations, or as representing the values of a certain society on various matters. If the tongue-in-cheek observations of a satirist replace the wise sayings of the past generations, this is bound to produce a shock effect. In Persian literature aphorisms have a long history from the Sassanid period onward, but the most interesting example of the use of this form in the service of satire is *Risala-ye Sad Pand* (One hundred counsels) (1350) of 'Obeyd-e Zakani, one of the finest satirists of the classical era. 'Obeyd in his introduction writes that his work is an imitation of a treatise by Plato, "The Prince of Philosophers, written for the sake of his pupil Aristotle," which was translated "by that unrivalled man of our times Nasir al-Din Tusi from Greek into Persian." Furthermore, the author states that "some other treatises such as *The Book of Counsels* of the just king Anushirvan" were also sources of inspiration to him. After acknowledging such ostensible models, he says that his book will be "a work of sincerity, devoid of the shadows of hypocrisy and affectations, a kind of book which will be beneficial to everyone."[31]

Like many other satiric aphorists, 'Obeyd combines the methods of reduction and exaggeration. Apart from aiming at brevity, he takes a point and strips away its conventional and commonly felt associations. He simplifies in order to generalize, and in doing so he has to dismiss exceptions and special cases. Thus, he tends to exaggerate many points like a caricaturist. For instance, he writes, "Justice bequeaths disaster."[32] Most, if not all, members of the ruling class of 'Obeyd's time (from whom justice might have been expected) seemed to hold to this principle. 'Obeyd's sarcastic and down-to-earth comments often sharply contrast with what is normally accepted. He remarks, "As much as possible, do not speak the truth, so that you may not be a bore and people may not be annoyed with you without a reason." And again, "Engage in ribaldry, cuckoldry, gossip, false testimony, and ingratitude, renouncing the world to come for the sake of this world, and play the tambourine so that you may become dear to the great, and enjoy your life."[33] All these display a strong sense of pessimism toward a society that does not allow anyone but the corrupt and dishonest to succeed. Here are a few more of his ironic maxims:

Do not believe the sheikhs lest you go astray and end up in hell.
Do not lodge next to ascetics if you want to live according to
   your heart's desire.
Do not frequent the courts of kings, and forsake their favors
   so that you may not see their chamberlains.
Do not take lodgings in a street where there is a minaret, so
   that you may be safe from the annoyance of cacophonous
   muezzins.
In this age you cannot find a just governor, a judge who does not
   accept bribes, an ascetic who does not speak hypocritically or
   a chamberlain of good faith.[34]

THE CHARACTER OR TYPE

As indicated in the next chapter, typifications and character sketches are closely
related. The character sketch as a medium of satire has had a long tradition
in Europe, beginning with Theophrastus (ca. 370-286 B.C.). It flourished
remarkably in the seventh century in the works of La Bruyere in France and
Thomas Overbury, John Earle, Bishop Joseph Hall, and Samuel Butler in
England. In Islamic lands Theophrastus was known,[35] but his book *The
Characters* was never translated, nor did it inspire any imitations. Quite
independently of European tradition, a comparable genre developed both in
Arabic and Persian. In both languages some anthologies of stories devote separate
chapters to various classes or types. *Lata'ef al-Tawa'ef* (The witticisms of [various]
classes) by Farkh al-Din 'Ali Safi (d. 1533)[36] is a fine example; it contains
chapters on physicians, astrologers, and misers. Obviously the author does not
differentiate between types and professions. But it should also be borne in mind
that physicians and astrologers were among the traditional butts of satirists and
were often considered "types" rather than professionals.

An Arabic work that concentrates on types rather than professions is *Ketab
al-Bokhala* (The book of misers) by 'Amr ibn Bahr al-Jahiz (d. 869), an interesting
study of the common characteristics and behavior of misers. It is full of humorous
stories and observations:

> There was a man who had attained the utmost limits of avarice
> and ranked as master. Whenever a *dirham* came into his hands,
> he spoke to it, whispered to it, pledged his devotion to it, and chided it
> for having tarried. He used to say, "Through how many parts have you
> passed; from how many purses have you parted; how many humble ones
> have you made great; how many great ones have you humbled! With me
> you may be sure that 'you will neither go naked...nor be exposed to the
> sun.' [*Koran*, XX, 116-117.] Then he would put it in his purse and say to
> it, "Repose, in the name of God, in a place where you will not be slighted
> or humbled and from which you will never be disturbed.[37]

In the *maqame* genre, which was invented, or at least popularized, by Badi'
al-Zaman al-Hamadani (d. 1007) in Arabic literature and imitated in Persian,
one encounters some significant character sketches. Hamadani's principal hero

is a "witty, unscrupulous vagabond journeying from place to place and supporting himself by the presents which his impromptu displays of rhetoric, poetry and learning seldom [fail] to draw from an admiring audience."[38] The second character is a narrator, who continuously meets with the first and relates his adventures in excellent compositions. In fact, these two work closely together and create a market for each other. There are a number of secondary characters that these two meet during their wanderings, and it is by depicting their thoughts and manners that Hamadani gives a fascinating picture of the society of his time. His favorite butts are upstarts, sanctimonious Muslims, and the *judges*, who have no scruples in accepting bribes or in passing unjustified verdicts. The following is a summary translation of the *maqame*, which is a portrait of a parvenu.

Abu'al-Fath al-Eskandari, one of the main characters, describes how he was entertained by a merchant in Baghdad:

> So he wearied me with his wife's qualities until we reached the quarter where he lived, and then he said, "O my master, look at this quarter! It is the noblest quarter of Baghdad. The worthy vie to settle here, and the great compete to dwell here. None but merchants live here, for a man can be judged by his neighbor. My house is the jewel in the middle of a necklace of houses, the center of their circle. How much, O my master, would you say was spent on each house? Make a rough guess, if you don't know exactly.

When they arrive at the house, he comments on the doorway, the door, its latticework, how it was made of a single piece of teak wood, and who the carpenter was. In the house a slave brings them a jug of ice water, the the merchant starts talking about his abilities, and tells him, "Uncover your head! Raise your leg! Bare your arm! Show your teeth! Walk up and down!" Then the comments pass to the jug, which is made of "the best Syrian copper," and then to the water, which is "as blue as a cat's eye, as clear as a crystal rod!" The host continues his pretentious remarks ad nauseam until the guest can no longer bear it:

> So I rose, and he asked, "What do you want?"
> I said, "A need that I must satisfy."
> He said, "O my master! You are going to a privy which shames the spring residence of the emir and the autumn residence of the vizier! Its upper part is plastered and its lower part is white-washed; its roof is terraced and its floor is paved with marble. Ants slip off its walls and cannot grip; flies walk on its floor and slither along. It has a door with panels of teak and ivory combined in the most perfect way. A guest could wish to eat there." "Eat there yourself," I said. "The privy is not part of the bargain.[39]

Qazi Hamid al-Din Abu Bakr of Balkh (d. 1164) imitated the *Maqamat* in Persian, but his work is inferior to its model in scope, finish, ingenuity, and satiric thrust. The style is florid, and the author pays so much attention to his language and literary devices that to attempt to translate a passage from the book would serve no purpose.

Another kind of story with stylistic affinities to the character sketch itself concerns various ethnic groups or the inhabitants of various cities. Such stories, which are often humorous rather than satirical, are very common in Persian literature. Through generalization certain salient qualities come to represent the inhabitants of a region or a city. For instance, the Qazvinis are well-known for their naiveté, Esfahanis for shrewdness, and Rashtis for their tolerant attitude toward a sexual scandal. 'Obeyd-e Zakani who was born in a village near Qazvin related many humorous stories about his own fellow citizens. Here are two short anecdotes by 'Obeyd. One is about a man from Hamadan and the other is about a Qazvini.

A man from Hamadan was going into his home when he saw a handsome young man coming out. He was offended and said: "A curse upon this kind of life. That every day you keep going into the houses of other people. What is the meaning of this? Damn it all, get yourself a wife as we have, so that ten other people will depend on you.

A Qazvini went to fight the heretics[40] carrying a large shield. From the fortress a huge stone hit him on the head, wounding him. He was annoyed and cried out [to the attacker], "Are you blind, man? Can't you see a shield as big as this, so you have to hit me on the head?[41]

'Obeyd also wrote a small treatise entitled "Definitions" that resembles a character sketch. It has been divided into ten chapters, "On the Gentry," "On the Turks and Their Followers," "On the Judges and Their Followers," "Shopkeepers," and so forth, and in each chapter he describes the characteristics of a particular class. One section is translated here:

On the Gentry

Boasting and insolence: The stock-in-trade of the gentry.
Nothing: Their existence.
Hollow: Their civility.
Vanity and folly: Their talk.
Disapproval, greed, malice, and envy: Their characteristics.
The Fool: He who expects any good from them.
The Wretched and Unfortunate: Their attendants.
What is lost: Their generosity.
Non-existent: Their good behavior.
The *'Anqa*[42] of the West: Justice and humanity.
Roguery, violence, hypocrisy, dissimulation and falsehood:
    The ways of the great men.
Lust: Their main ailment.[43]

As a last and modern example of the character sketch in Persian literature, a short piece by Samad Behrangi (1939-68) follows entitled "Aqa-ye Chokh Bakhtiar" or "Mr. Very Lucky." It wonderfully describes the life of an Azerbaijani couple in Tehran during the reign of the former Shah, whose repressive regime had emasculated everyone politically. The couple belong to the Turkish-speaking minority who not only were denied the right of having their own schools and newspapers, but also endured having their accent ridiculed when they spoke Farsi. I am not sure a reader who has not lived under the Shah can fully understand what a wonderfully graphic picture is given of the life of the lower middle-class of Iran at that time:

> His life is like a calm pond. At no price is he prepared to allow a stone to be thrown into that pond and ripple its waters. He is a decent, mild-mannered man unwilling to dispute with even an ant. He gets up in the morning to have breakfast with his wife and child, and then sets out for the office.
>
> He gives a warm heartfelt greeting to even the grocer and the butcher along the way, so that the one will not overcharge for peas, and the other will give him boneless cuts.
>
> His loftiest wishes are to own a car such as a Volkswagen, and to be transferred to Tehran, the capital.
>
> Before he married, now and then he would have a glass of wine, but his wife has forbidden it. He comes straight home from the office.
>
> Now and again in the afternoon, he goes to the cinema with his wife. These two are staunch fans of Iranian films. They maintain that however ridiculous they may be, "After all, they're our country's. Why should we pour our money into the pockets of foreigners?"
>
> His wife tries to dress and make herself up like the actresses in her country's films. She wears high-heeled shoes and a girdle around the house. Their child has been taught only Persian. It seems they are both convinced that speaking Turkish is a mark of an illiterate old crank.
>
> It seems he has no time to read books. As he maintains, impractical, mutually contradictory ideas are found in books; books only produce mental unease. Now and then, however, he enjoys reading one of the weeklies. He even finds it instructive. His wife can make good use of the fashion and cooking sections, and he himself will solve the crossword puzzle and read about the lives of the film stars. In order to be a more cultured person, he sometimes reads "literary and social" books. Both of them are dedicated fans of the radio plays. They generally pass their Fridays sitting in front of the radio. Every week they buy two lottery tickets in hope of winning the Grand Prize.
>
> He accepts religion without question, being unwilling to succumb to doubt concerning the most minute detail of it, but only from the nineteenth to the twenty-first of Ramazan does he fast, or pray.[45]

ANIMAL FABLES

The animal fable has long been a favorite medium of the satirist. From Aesop to La Fontaine to George Orwell, this kind of allegorical approach has been a suitable means for both satire and criticism. At times it was safer to express one's ideas in the disguise of an animal fable. For instance, for the two great nineteenth-century fabulists Ivan Andreyevich and Saltykov Shchedrin, living under the repressive regimes of the Czars, animal fables provided the best way to express criticism and to avoid censorship. George Orwell, living in England, was not restricted by such considerations, yet he portrayed the dictatorship of Stalin and its distortion of the egalitarian ideal of the October Revolution in his *Animal Farm*, which provides a fascinating allegory as a framework for Orwell's story.

Since the very beginning of Persian literature,[46] animal fables have played a very important role. At the dawn of Persian classical literature, Rudaki versified *Kalile va Demne*. Two centuries later 'Attar used the animal fable as a magnificent allegory of the Sufi search for the truth. Rumi in his *Mathnavi* and Sa'adi in his *Gulestan* and the *Bustan* used animal fables to illustrate their respective viewpoints. Two centuries later, this medium was used for an interesting political satire in *The Cat and the Mice* of 'Obeyd-e Zakani. The same tradition is still alive in our own day, in poems such as "Paria" by Ahmad Shamlu and "The Wolves and Dogs" by Akhavan, and the political allegory of Samad Behrangi in "The Little Black Fish."

There are a number of collections of tales, such as *Kalile va Demne, Marzban-Name*, and *Tuti-Name*, that employ animal fables either in the framework tale or in the other stories that are related by various characters or animals. Some such collections derive ultimately from Indian sources. For instance, *Tuti-Name* (The tales of a parrot) by Zia' al-Din of Nakhshab, which was written in the fourteenth century, is based upon an older Persian version that in turn is derived from the Sanskrit in *Suka Saptati* (The seventy tales of a parrot.)[47]

Most of the stories in these collections illustrate a moral point of view, and some criticize social conditions. A point can be made directly or can be suggested by the whole story. For instance, in *Kalile va Demne* a lion, a fox, and a wolf go hunting and kill a deer, a hare, and an ass. The lion asks the wolf to divide them. The wolf says, "The lion gets the donkey, the fox the hare, and I get the deer." The lion is displeased, tears off the wolf's head, and asks the fox to do the dividing. He answers: "It's a simple matter, Your Excellency! You eat the donkey in the morning, the deer at night, and the hare will serve as your lunch." The lion is pleased and asks: "Who taught you such politeness?" The fox answers: "The torn head of the wolf!"[48]

According to the introduction of *Kalile va Demne* the situation under which the stories were written was somewhat reminiscent of the above fable. The philosopher Pilpay is imprisoned because he has criticized the tyranny of Dabshilim, the king of India. He is eventually set free by the king and is ordered to compile a collection of stories on wisdom and moral values. Nasrollah Monshi, the first prose translator of the book into Persian, writes: "This book of *Kalile va Demne* is a compilation of sayings, counsels, and proverbs by the Brahmins and sages of India." Then he goes on to explain the purpose behind the work: "First that they might combine counsel and wisdom with drollery and satire so that the wise will benefit from reading it and the ignorant will regard it as [a collection of] fables."[49]

The fables of *Kalile va Demne* have often been used for didactic ends, but Ibn al-Muqaffa', who introduced them into the Islamic world, seems to have employed them for satirical purposes. A. J. Arberry writes of this first Arabic version: "The stories are a shrewd sometimes caustic commentary on political life under an absolute monarchy, and it is not far-fetched to suppose that the portraits presented are thinly disguised cartoons of the entourage of the Caliph [al-Mansur] himself. The animals are made to deliver themselves of sententious wisdom matured through centuries of Sassanian rule, and the work itself clearly belongs to the 'Mirror of Princes' tradition."[50]

The life and tragic end of Ibn al-Muqaffa' further support this argument. The son of a Persian convert to Islam, he became a prolific translator and polished writer in Arabic prose. In his mid-thirties Ibn al-Muqaffa' incurred the wrath of al-Mansur by including a binding clause in a document drawn between the caliph and his uncle. The caliph entrusted him to Sufyan ibn Mu'awiya, the governor of Basra, for punishment. The governor was one of the dull-witted courtiers who had long suffered from the pointed remarks of the young and witty secretary and held a lasting grudge against him. "The governor had an uncommonly large nose and whenever Ibn al-Muqaffa' visited him, he would enquire, 'How are the pair of you?' On one occasion, Sufyan, trying to be clever, boasted that he 'never had reason to repent of keeping silent,' which drew from Ibn al-Muqaffa' the retort, 'Dumbness becomes you excellently; so why should you repent of it?' Now Sufyan was glad to settle the score once and for all. He directed the furnace to be stoked, then he had the executioner hack off the prisoner's limbs one by one and throw them in the flames, finishing up with his trunk."[51]

An example each from Sa'di's *Gulestan* and from a work by the great scholar of the seventeenth century, Sheikh Baha'i, may illustrate various uses of animal fable in the service of satire in Persian literature. Sa'di's love of animals is an outstanding feature of his work, and he makes numerous uses of them. Sometimes he contrasts their feelings with those of human beings, and sometimes animals serve as masks for various human characters. In one of his poems he describes how the camel is moved to dance by the music of the camel-driver's flute and wonders how some men who dislike music can be less sensitive than a camel. The following fable, derived from a story in the *Gulestan*, belongs to the second category and illustrates the fact that social justice did not exist in Iran, since a man could languish in prison for a long time before proving his innocence:

> I said: "The story of the fox resembles thy case, who was by some persons seen fleeing with much trouble and asked for the cause of his fear replied: 'I have heard that camels are being forced into the service.' They said: 'O fool, what connection hast thou with a camel and what resemblance does the latter bear to thee?' The fox rejoined: 'Hush. If the envious malevolently say that I am a camel and I am caught, who will care to release me or investigate my case? Till the antidote is brought from Iraq the snake-bitten person dies."[52]

"The Cat and the Mice" by Sheikh Baha'i is an imitation of the more famous prototype of 'Obeyd-e Zakani. The cat stands for a fanatical and narrow-minded cleric, and the mouse represents a witty and fairly liberal-minded Sufi. The work, which is commonly attributed to Sheikh Baha al-Din Amoli (d. 1521 or 1522), has also been attributed to the great Shi'ite theologian, Mohammad Baqer Majlesi. The cat has spent some time in the chamber as a student of theology and has gained his favor by catching mice. The student has taught him much about religious cleanliness and the principles of faith. He is now so well-versed in these matters that even his mewing is in exact accordance with Arabic phonetics! Though the mouse is not devoid of theological learning, he is more inclined to mysticism. He has lived several years at the shrine of the great poet Sa'adi and has become well-versed in Sufi lore. In incantations and whirling he follows the dervishes. Now he is a captive in the paws of the cat, so he speaks with great humility to him. The mouse says, for instance: "O king, it is unbecoming of your wisdom and knowledge to have a creature like me as a counselor. But since I must, I tell you that mysticism and piety are characteristics common to all religions, but alas, I don't find them in you."[53] The poems and stories related by the mouse in the praise of Sufism do not convince the cat, however; in the end the cat eats him up. The fable is a satirical picture of the senseless and often-deadly enmity existing in the Safavid period between the Shi'ite fanatics and the Sufis.

IMAGINARY TRAVELS, THE UTOPIAN WORLD, THE WORLD TO COME, AND THE DREAM WORLD

Placing the scene of satire in an imaginary land—in hell or heaven, or in a dream world—is another method of criticizing one's society through the disguise of fictional circumstance. This can be achieved by describing a Utopian society where everything is perfect—in jarring contrast with existing conditions—or by creating a trial in the world to come of the corrupt men and women in the satirist's society. In all these cases the satirist invents a fictional atmosphere that is related to his own society, in either a positive or negative way, but at the same time is so removed from real life that he can express his criticism without directly offending anyone.

Western literature abounds with such satirical accounts that take place in another world. Lucian's The True History (ca. 120 B.C.), one of the oldest examples of this genre, describes a series of impossible voyages—first to the moon, then into the belly of a huge whale where there are great seas and many islands, and finally to the land of the dead. Through these fantastic voyages Lucian parodies both the Illiad and the Odyssey and ridicules the unbelievable tales of travelers. And Rabelais, in the fourth book of Gargantua and Pantagruel (1552), sends his hero through a series of incredible voyages in search of the oracle of the Holy Bottle, situated "near Cathay in Upper India." The inhabitants of these outlandish lands are in fact contemporary Europeans in disguise: one group is called the Papimanes, whose idol is the Pope, and the other is the Papefiques, or the Protestants, who follow tenets just as ridiculous as those of their opponents.

Swift's *Gulliver's Travels* (1726), Voltaire's *Micromegas* (1752), and Samuel Butler's *Erewhon* (1872), whose title is an ironic anagram of the word *nowhere*, are later examples of satiric travelogues. Of the visions of the future Aldous Huxley's *Brave New World* (1932), Ayn Rand's *Anthem* (1938), and George Orwell's *1984* (1949) are outstanding examples. But in classical Arabic and Persian literature there are very few satirical stories set either in an outlandish land or in the world to come; it is only in modern times that such satirical works appear in both languages. The outstanding ancient exception is *Risalatu'l-Ghufran* (The book of forgiveness) by the great Arab poet Abu'l-'Ala al-Ma'arri (973-1057), which is a remarkable example of this genre.

An old man from Aleppo called Ibn Qarih writes a letter to Abu'l-'Ala warning him against the sceptical and atheistic ideas that he had so often expressed. Answering him Abu'l-'Ala writes *Risalatu'l-Ghufran*, pretending that because of Ibn Qarih's pious forebodings he has repented his heretical thoughts. But in reality the book is a bitter satire on the religious zealots who think theirs is the only way to salvation. It is also a satire on the poets who live in their ivory towers and have very little to do with the realities of life. Ibn Qarih, whom the poet sends to visit heaven and hell, meets a group of poets who want to take Abu 'Ali Farsi, the grammarian, to the Divine Tribunal, since he has misquoted some of their verses. Ibn Qarih writes a panegyric on the custodian angel of heaven, but it is of no use—he realizes that poetry cannot open the door of paradise to him. Eventually, when his repentance is verified, through the intercession of Fatima, the daughter of the Prophet, the old man enters heaven.

It is not in heaven but in hell that we meet the most fascinating characters. Ibn Qarih meets Satan, who is being tortured by the guardians of hell, and starts a conversation with him. The questions asked by the devil are too baffling for the old man. He asks: "Why is wine forbidden in this world, but not in heaven?" He asks: "Do men in heaven behave in the same way toward *ghelmans* [angels in the form of young boys] as the men were doing in the two cities [Sodom and Gomorrah]?"[54] Ibn Qarih is outraged and leaves, cursing him. Then he meets Bashshar Ibn Burd, who because of his heretical views is the favorite of Satan among the poets. Ibn Qarih then tells a number of stories relating to the *zindiqs* or freethinkers of Islam, and quoting some of their poetry, he ponders on the nature of their disbelief. Outwardly he condemns their views, but his hope is that at heart they are less heretical than what they express. After paying a visit to Adam in paradise, Ibn Qarih retires to his own palace in order to enjoy the company of an angelic maiden who has been assigned to him. But it is ironic that their amorous dalliance consists of his imagining the love scenes that Imru'u'l-Qais, the great lyric poet who is in hell, has had with his beloved.

An interesting example of this genre in Persian is a novel by Jamalzade entitled *Sara-ye Mahshar* (The plain of resurrection) (1947), which unlike *The Book of Forgiveness* is not confined to men of letters, but rather embraces a large group of people from every walk of life. The writer in his humorous and graphic style describes the positions of various people when they stand before the divine scales upon which their deeds are going to be weighed. As a contemporary Iranian critic writes:

Implicit, however, is a traditional Islamic dogma, which runs through the medieval Persian works that offer counsel to rulers and princes: the dogma that we are answerable for all our misdeeds in this life. So to understand the salient points of this satire, the reader should have a fair knowledge of Shi'a doctrine. But even then he is likely to be confounded by some of the things happening in the heavenly kingdom. We learn, for example, that influential connections, string-pulling, and even bribery play a considerable part in the placement and promotion of the angels and other ministering spirits. The prophets, on the other hand, are dispatched to heaven straight away without any demur or interrogation. Some smart sinners, by reciting an appeasing Koranic verse or an apostolic tradition, are let off lightly; and a great number of people escape the blazing fires of hell by reciting an appropriate line of poetry or even by cracking a joke that amuses God. But, in general, moderation and compromise seem to be the order of the day: moral issues and human values, not the religious dogmas, are the criterion of divine justice.[55]

But religious pretenders and hypocritical mullas are dealt with harshly. One of the most significant stories related here, which was later made into a separate book, is "Ma'sume of Shiraz." The story is based on a well-known quatrain by Khayyam:

> A sheikh beheld a harlot, and quoth he:
> "you seem a slave to drink and lechery;"
> And she made answer, "What I seem I am,
> But, master, are you all you seem to be?"[56]

A sheikh seduces Ma'sume but abandons her to a life of prostitution and misery. One day he publicly rebukes her for being drunk and a streetwalker. But it is the humane poet-philosopher who helps her and now at the day of judgment pleads for an investigation into the case of this fallen maid. The description of the character and appearance of the pretender sheikh is handled with a superb touch of realism and humor.

At the end of the book the narrator meets Satan and discusses with him various spiritual matters. Satan, who is on good terms with God, obtains permission to take him back to earth. Though the narrator is endowed with the gift of eternal life, this proves to be too tedious, and he asks to be allowed to die whenever he wishes.

Another satiric device that is related to the use of a fantastic setting is the introduction of a personality from the past to our own times and the comparison of his ideas and moral views with those of the satirist's own society. Mohammad Muwailihi, a nineteenth-century Egyptian writer, in his novel entitled *The Story of 'Isa Ibn Hisham*, brings one of the characters of the *Maqamat* by Badi' al-Zaman of Hamadan into Egypt at the time of Mohammad 'Ali, where he meets a pasha who has created some charitable foundations. In order to find out about them, the two men go to various government agencies, and thus the writer has the opportunity of criticizing the impact of westernization, corruption, and excessive bureaucracy. Another example is a Persian poem entitled "Rostam-Name" (Book of Rostam) by Bahar. Ferdausi's renowned hero here is a simple farmer in our own world who lives in the province of Sistan. A tax collector who is addicted to opium as well as to bribery ruins his life. The frankness and naiveté of Rostam sharply contrast with the insatiable desire of the official for extortion and repression.

Another work related to the technique is *Khalse* (The book of dreams) by Mohammad Hasan Khan 'Etemad al-Saltane, and though he has only a few satirical passages, its form is interesting. The book, written around 1892, postulates eleven trials of the past prime ministers of Iran, and many of the well-known kings of that country take part in them. A meddlesome mulla asks: "How is it that the ministers are being tried, whereas the orders were issued by the kings who were ultimately responsible for everything?" His friend answers: "The king is the shadow of God, and whoever Divine Providence honors with such favor will be clothed in the robes of honor and sanctity. He cannot be held responsible for all the actions, but rather his only responsibility is in appointing the ministers and the rest is with the latter."[58] The writer is biased in some of his judgments. For instance, because of close family relations with the mother of Naser al-Din Shah, he makes this intriguing woman one of the "great ladies of the world," whereas Amir Kabir, who was her son-in-law and one of the greatest prime ministers of Iran, is severely criticized. Though this great man of Iranian history is forgiven at the end, he is sent to heaven without a "crown" on his head! Another minister, Hajji Ebrahim of Shiraz, who was a notorious traitor and betrayed the gallant Lotf 'Ali Khan of the Zand dynasty, is "crowned and honored."

An imaginary travelogue that became one of the most influential works of the Constitutional period is *Siyahat-Name-ye Ibrahim Beik* (The travel diary of Ebrahim Beg).[59] The author, Hajji Zeyn al-'Abedin of Maraghe (1839-1912), was a prosperous merchant who spent some time as the Iranian vice-consul at Kutaisi in Georgia and eventually settled in Yalta. It was because of the ill treatment he received at the hands of the Iranian consular officers that he took Russian citizenship, but his conscience was never at rest. In 1902 he went to Istanbul, and at the Iranian Embassy he regained his original citizenship. This episode in his life may well serve to illustrate his patriotic attachment to the country of his birth. After many years of long-cherished hopes and expectations, Hajji Zeyn al-'Abedin returned to Iran to find a land wrapped in ignorance and superstitions and devastated by despotism and corruption. Though the characters are given fictional names in the travel diary, it seems to be a record of actual experiences. The book is a bitter satire on the government of Iran and the social conditions of the country; depicted with sobering realism, its object is to awaken Iranians to the deplorable conditions and to bring about reform.

The son of a well-to-do Iranian merchant, Ebrahim Beg is born in Egypt, and in order to comply with the will of his deceased father, he visits the country of his origin. Accompanied by his tutor, Uncle Yusef, he describes his adventures in various parts of Iran in the first volume of his diary. Between what he hopes to see and what he does see, between his ideals and the stark realities of life, there is a staggering contrast. Ebrahim Beg lashes out in every direction at government officials, clerics, judges, and almost everyone who fails in his duties to the general public. The second volume deals with the return of Ebrahim Beg to Egypt, his love affair there, and his death caused by his disappointment over his country. The third volume is the dream Uncle Yusef has of Ebrahim Beg's journey to heaven and hell. This part obviously is modeled on *The Book of Forgiveness* or *The Divine Comedy*, with the difference that Ebrahim Beg deals only with Iranians in the other world.

The two following passages are from the first and second volumes and describe Ebrahim Beg's stay at Ardabil in northwest Iran:

On the fourth day I saw people running left and right and from every direction they were shouting, "It is a holy war!" I said to myself, "What is this new game? With whom are they fighting a holy war?" I got up to see what was happening. Uncle Yusef clung to me saying, "I won't let you go. You might get hurt." "Let me see what is going on," I said, and freeing myself from him, I ran ouside. Upon inquiry I found out that a certain Sheikh Saleh, donning a winding sheet and brandishing a sword, had come out and declared a holy war. More than two thousand townspeople had gathered around him. I don't know what one of the government officials had done to displease his Reverence, but he was ordered to be dragged from his house. Then the poor man was beaten in such a way that he fainted. Some were saying that he had died, but according to others he was still alive, "but he will die." I thought, "Good God! What chaos is this. Is there no government in this land? Is there no authority? How can a mulla beat a government official to death, could the authorities not protest? I was told that it had been a few years since the return of his Reverence from the Holy Places[60] and the closing of the other clerics' shops.

Outside his house, with whomever he is, he does not eat anything but barley-bread and vinegar, but in his own private quarters he has the best food.

"When in private many other things they maintain."[61]

What is non-existent in Iran is law and order. Therefore, no one knows his duties, whether he be the governor or the governed, the subject or the official. There are no schools, no proper taxes. But there is bribery, despotism, and extortion. The cities are in ruins, the plains are uncultivated, the water in the gutters has gone bad, and because of its smell it is hard to walk along the streets. The beggars have become ministers, the ministers have become beggars, the affairs are not in the hands of the experts. Continuous snatching, plundering, dragging away, and forcing one's way are the order of the day.[62]

The travelogue form is also the basis of an interesting poem by Zabih Behruz

(1889-1971). It is one of the rare examples in which the traditional Me'raj-Name, or the account of Mohammad's journey to heaven, is parodied. Inspired by the first verse of Sura Al-Isra (17) of the Koran, the accounts of this ascension describe how God carried His servant from the Sacred Mosque at Mecca to the Mosque of Aqsa in Jerusalem, and from there as far as the Seventh Heaven where the Prophet is admitted to ecstatic contemplation of the Divine Essence. From the earliest times of Islam, this Night Journey has given rise to popular stories in Arabic and then in other languages of the lands of Islam. These stories, which have gradually become part of Muslim eschatology, through mystical, theological, and literary elaborations, have always been treated in a very spiritual and esoteric manner. Behruz treats the whole account very lightly and humorously. By bringing down to the level of everyday life an ascension that has always been regarded as highly spiritual and beyond this world, he creates a human and profane atmosphere that reflects his own ideas about this particular episode:

> One night God, who had created everything and had nothing to do, commands the angel Gabriel to go and fetch his favorite Prophet Mohammad. Descending to earth on his heavenly steed, Gabriel comes to the house of the Prophet, who is fast asleep. Gabriel taps him on the shoulder, but the Prophet, thinking that it is his youngest wife 'Ayesha trying to wake him up, says, "Please, dear 'Ayesha, let me sleep this one night."

The whole journey to the Seventh Heaven, the angels standing in two lines to applaud the Prophet, and many other details are humorously described. The Prophet is about to be admitted to the presence of God, where no one has ever been accepted, when an uproar and bustle is heard. A star has gone out of its orbit, and God has to attend to it. Mohammad, accompanied by Gabriel, returns to his home, missing this very rare occasion of being admitted to the presence of God. The whole journey lasts but a moment.[63]

Notes

1. *Divan-e Adib al-Mamalek* (Tehran: Armaghan, 1934), pp. 454-55.
2. Zagam is a river near Ganja in the Caucasus.
3. Dizaj is a city in Iranian Azerbaijan. In this line there is a clever pun that cannot be reproduced on *se tiz* ("three winds") and *setiz* ("struggle" or "fight").
4. 'Abbas Eqbal, ed., *Mirza Taqi Khan Amir Kabir* (Tehran: University of Tehran, 1961), pp. 118-19.
5. For various examples of such *qasides*, see Zabihullah Safa, *Tarikh-e Adabiyat dar Iran*, 3, Pt. 1 (Tehran, 1984), pp. 86-95; and also my article in *Ayandeh* (Tehran), "Tanz va Intiqad-e Ijtima'i dar Adabiyat-e Farsi pish az Mashrutiyat," 7, Nos. 9-10 (1982): 661-68.
6. Viladmir F. Minorsky, *Iranica, Twenty Articles by V. F. Minorsky* (Tehran: Tehran University Press, 1964), p. 299.
7. Ibid., pp. 299-300.
8. See Munibur Rahman, *Post-Revolution Persian Verse* (Aligarh: Institute of Islamic Studies, Aligarh University, 1955), pp. 52-53, 55, and 59.
9. See *Kolliyat-e Nazari* in *Farhang-e Iran-Zamin*, ed. G. Baradin (Tehran, 1958), 5: folio 178B.

10. E. G. Browne, *A Literary History of Persia* (Cambridge: Cambridge University Press, 1924), 2:82.

11. *The Bustan of Sa'adi*, trans. G. M. Wickens (Toronto: University of Toronto Press, 1974), p. 168.

12. *Divan-e Iraj Mirza*, ed. M. J. Mahjub (Tehran: Nashr-e Andisheh, 1964), p. 153.

13. *Mathnavi*, trans. R. A. Nicholson (London and Leiden: Gibb Memorial Series, Messrs, E. J. Brill, 1925-40), 2:383-84.

14. See Munibur Rahman, *Post-Revolution Persian Verse*, pp. 109-26; and Yahya Arianpur, *Az Saba ta Nima*, 2:151-68.

15. Edward Scott-Waring, *A Tour to Shiraz* (London: T. Cadell & W. Davies, 1802), pp. 53-54.

16. E. G. Browne, *The Press and Poetry of Modern Persia* (Cambridge: Cambridge University Press, 1914), pp. 233-34.

17. *Khak be saram* if loosely translated, means "woe to me!" or "botheration take me." The translation of this very colloquial poem is extremely difficult, and Browne has added numerous footnotes to it. The beauty of the original poem lies in the fact that it has been written in the language in which an Iranian mother talks to her child. For the originals of this and the following poems see *Az Saba ta Nima*, 2:92-94. Cf. E. G. Browne, *The Press and Poetry of Modern Persia*, pp. 249-50.

18. *The Press and Poetry of Modern Persia*, pp. 181-82. Concerning Shapshal Khan, the Russian agent provocateur, see E. G. Browne, *Persian Revolution* Cambridge: Cambridge University Press, 1910), pp. 105, 170-71, 198-202, and 418-20.

19. I.e., the women.

20. The Turkish word *kaghizluq* means a window covered with paper instead of glass.

21. This is an allusion to the paper *Sur-e Esrafil* ("Trumpet of Israfil") in which this poem appeared.

22. Spiritual guides.

23. This poem I believe is by Mohammad Zuhari. I couldn't find a source for this well-known line, and thus have quoted it from memory.

24. Herbert V. Prochnow, *A Dictionary of Wit, Wisdom and Satire* (New York: Harper & Row, 1962), p. 88.

25. E. H. Whinfield, trans., *The Quatrains of Omar Khayyam* (London: Trübner & Co., 1883), p. 252.

26. Browne, *A Literary History*, 3:512.

27. *Taleb* means "a seeker."

28. Shibli No'mani, *She'r al-Ajam*, Persian translation, 4:160.

29. This poem is probably by the famous satirist Hadi Khorsandi.

30. Matthew Hodgart, *Satire* (New York: McGraw-Hill, 1969), pp. 162-63.

31. *Kolliyyat-e 'Obeyd-e Zakani*, ed. Parviz Atabaki (Tehran: Iqbal, 1962), p. 204.

32. "The Ethics of the Aristocrats," Ibid., p. 172.

33. "Risale-ye Sad Pand," *Kolliyat-e 'Obeyd-e Zakani*, p. 207.

34. Ibid.

35. He is mentioned by Ibn al-Nadim in *Al-Fihrist* and Qifti in his *Tarikh al-Hukama*, ed. Julius Lippert (Leipzig: Dieterichische Verlagsbuchhandlung, 1903), p. 106; cf. Dehkhoda under "Theophrastus."

36. Ahmad Golchin Ma'ani, ed. (Tehran: Iqbal, 1962).

37. Quoted in Bernard Lewis, *Islam from the Prophet Mohammad to the Capture of Constantinople* (New York: Harper & Row, 1974), 2:261.

38. R. A. Nicholson, *A Literary History of the Arabs* (Cambridge: Cambridge University Press, 1969), p. 328.

39. Quoted in Bernard Lewis, *Islam*, 2:263 and 268.

40. By the "heretics" 'Obeyd means the Assassins or Isma'ilis, the followers of Hasan Sabbah, who terrorized many parts of Iran in the twelfth and thirteenth centuries. Their last strongholds were destroyed by Hulagu in 1257. Qazvin was the main base for the campaigns against the Isma'ilis.

41. 'Obeyd'e Zakani, *Kolliyat*, p. 268. There is an interesting imitation of 'Obeyd's "Definitions" by Shari'at-madar-e Tabrizi, entitled *Me'rat al-Bolaha* (The mirror for the fool), published in 1889 and 1902; reprinted by Mahmud Kartira'i in his edition of the *'Aqa'ed al-Nesa* (Tehran: Athar-e Iran, 1970).

42. A mythical bird like the phoenix.

43. 'Obeyd, *Kolliyat*, p. 317.

44. Author of sentimental pulp fiction.

45. Quoted from an unpublished translation by Robert Campbell.

46. On this subject see my article, "Tanz va Enteqad dar Dastan-e Heyvanat," *Alefba* 4 (1974):1-22.

47. A large number of these tales have found their way into European literature through either Arabic or Persian translations. After *Kalile va Demne* was translated into Arabic from the Pahlavi, two Persian versions were made by Nasrollah Monshi in 1143-45 and Hosein Va'ez Kashefi (d. 1505). The latter, entitled *Anvar-e Soheili* was translated into French in 1642 as *Le Livre des Lumières*, which in turn was used by Jean de La Fontaine in his *Fables*. See my "Persian Influence on English Literature, Oriental Tales," *Indo-Iranica* 25, no. 2 (June 1972).

48. Abu'l-Ma'li Nasrullah, *Kalile va Demne*, ed. M. Minovi (Tehran: Offset Publications, 1964), pp. 86-87. This story has been versified by Rumi in the first volume of the *Mathnavi*, trans. James N. Redhouse (London: Trübner & Co., 1881), 1:218-77.

49. The work was originally derived from two Sanskrit books: *Panchatantra* (Five stages for becoming learned) by Vishnu Sarma, written probably in the fifth century B.C., and another collection entitled *Hitopodesa*. Many years later the whole book came to be known as *Pilpay*, which means "a man of learning."

50. A. J. Arberry, *Aspects of Islamic Civilization* (Ann Arbor: University of Michigan Press, 1971), p. 74.

51. Ibid., p. 73.

52. *Gulestan*, trans. Edward Rehatsek (London: George Allen & Unwin, 1964), p. 91.

53. *Kolliyat-e Asha'r-e Farsi va Mush va Gorbe-ye Sheykh Baha'i*, ed. Mehdi Tohidipur (Tehran: Ketabfurushi Mahmudi, 1957), p. 92.

54. *Risalatu'l-Ghofran*, ed. Dr. 'Aiysha 'Abdul-Rahman Bint al-Shati (Dar al-Ma'arif, 1965), p. 309.

55. Hasan Kamshad, *Modern Persian Prose Literature* (Cambridge: Cambridge University Press, 1966), p. 98.

56. *The Quatrains of Omar Khayyam*, p. 317.

57. *Khalse ya Khab-Name*, ed. Mahmud Katira'i (Tehran: Tahuri, 1969).

58. Ibid., p. 17.

59. Hajji Zeyn al-'Abedin, *The Travel Diary of Ebrahim Beg*, ed. Baqer-e Mo'meni (Tehran, 1974).

60. Two cities in Iraq—Kerbela and Najaf, where Imams Hosain and 'Ali are buried—are called the Holy Places.

61. This is a well-known line from Hafez. Cf. Chapter 4, "Satire and Religion." *Siahat-name-ye Ebrahim Beg*, ed. Baqer Mo'meni (Tehran, 1974), pp. 129-30.

62. Ibid., 2:34.

63. The *Me'raj-Name* of Zabih Behruz along with his *Gand-e Badavar*, a parody of the *Gulestan*, were completely published for the first time in 1985 by Mard-e Amruz Publications (apparently in Germany).

3

Techniques of Satire

Satire should, like a polished razor keen,
Wound with a touch that's scarcely felt or seen.

—Mary Wortley Montagu,
To the Imitator of the First Satire of Horace

The literary forms used by the satirist are very numerous, but the techniques are fairly limited. The main techniques of satire can be divided into five different categories: (1) the technique of reduction, (2) the method of exaggeration, (3) parody, (4) the use of irony or the ironic situation, and (5) the humorous or derisive use of the exact words of a person who is satirized.

THE TECHNIQUE OF REDUCTION

By reducing the status and dignity of the person being satirized the satirist aims at his degradation or devaluation. Cartoonists very often make use of this method. The physical belittling, for instance, of a candidate for public office, in front of the towering figure of his rival, can indicate either lack of support or his shrinking popularity among the public. The satirist or cartoonist may pick up one salient characteristic or aspect of his victim and make it the representative feature of that person. In this case, a person is reduced to one particular trait or feature that is exaggerated in a ridiculous manner. According to Matthew Hodgart the reduction may first be accomplished on the level of plot and will almost always be expanded to the level of style and language. He cites *Gulliver's Travels* as a classic example of a reductive plot and says: "The changes of scale in Books I and II first represent the political scene in England as the absurdly trifling antics of the Lilliputians, and then the narrator's countryman appears to the giant king of Brobdingnag as 'the most contemptible

43

race of little odious vermin that nature ever suffered to crawl on the face of the earth.' "[1]

Reduction can work on a number of other levels. Hafez, criticizing the parvenus of his time, sees two reasons for their showing off: their acquiring a Turkish slave and their riding a mule instead of their old donkey, which was the normal means of transportation:

> O God, put these upstarts back on their donkey,
> Since all their airs come from a Turkish slave and a mule.[2]

'Obeyd-e Zakani in an interesting little anecdote strips Sultan Mahmud of Ghazna of his regal pomp and trappings by revealing his early sex life. Even in a conservative society like Iran a man loving a young boy was not considered disrespectable—the love of Mahmud for the young Ayaz has become proverbial—but being loved by a man as a young boy would have been a disgrace:

> Sultan Mahmud attended the sermon of a certain preacher and took Talhak,[3] the court jester, with him. When they arrived, the preacher was saying that whenever a man had made love with a young boy, on the Day of Judgment they would put the boy on the neck of the homosexual to be carried across the narrow bridge of Sirat to Paradise. Sultan Mahmud was terrified and began to weep. Talhak told him, "O Sultan, don't weep. Be happy that on that day, you will not be left on foot either."[4]

Animals are often used in conjuction with the method of reduction. The animal fable may be used as a kind of disguise to express what cannot be expressed openly, and the satirist in comparing humans and animals may show that despite much ado about human's being civilized, he in many ways can be more bestial than any ferocious animal. For instance, driven by his religious or political convictions he will exterminate millions of men, women, and children and commit atrocities that no animal can rival. Mirzada 'Eshqi (1893-1924), the revolutionary poet who was assassinated by the secret police of Reza Shah, had an extremely pessimistic view of his contemporaries and expresses it in a poem entitled "In Criticism of Mankind," of which the following few lines may serve as an example:

> In the view of the wise man of the West,
> The initiator of new ideas, Darwin:
> From the ape nature took away a tail,
> And then called him derisively a man.
> If humanity is proved by the lack of tail,
> I am ashamed of my manhood, looking for a tail.
> I wish I were an ape like my ancestors,
> Living at ease in a forest deep.
> Why was I created a man?
> Why was I fashioned in this vein?
> If I were a gnat in the air
> Or a camel grazing on the plains,
> If I were a blunt-toothed jackal

Or a wolf in utmost distress
It would have been better than to be a man,
The most harmful kind of animal.[5]

The poet then compares humans with various animals such as the fox and the scorpion and concludes that man is more harmful than any of them. 'Eshqi also despairs of his own countrymen because he is not like them and wants to tell the truth, so he ends up being an outcast. In animal fables human's similarities to some animals are often exploited. The cunning of a fox, the sloth or dirtiness of a pig, and the stupidity of a bear are proverbial. Sometimes this kind of characterization is utilized in full. In "typification," or the creation of types, the balance of human disposition is broken down such that one quality becomes dominant; the result is that a person becomes one-dimensional.

The use of animal characterisitics for satirical purposes has been common in the modern literature of Iran. 'Eshqi in the last few months of his life published a satirical paper entitled *Qarn-e Bistum* (The twentieth century), which had been discontinued a few years earlier and very probably was one of the reasons for his assassination. At that time a republic was being proposed for Iran, and 'Eshqi, who suspected a British hand behind the whole plan, bitterly attacked the newspapers that were supporting this idea. In the satirical poems that he published the opposition papers were identified with and characterized by various animals: *Nahid, Tajaddud, Kushesh, Setara, Golshan, Jarchi* as a viper, owl, mouse, dog, donkey, and cat respectively. Some years earlier, from 1909 to 1911, a satirical paper was being published in Tabriz entitled *Hasharat al-'Arz* (The insects of the earth), which represented the ruling class and the opportunists in power in the form of insects emerging from their holes when the time was most appropriate. Abu Turab Jali (b. 1909 or 1910),[6] one of the poets with leftist leanings whose political poetry gained popularity before the 1953 *coup d'etat* of the Shah, wrote a poem entitled "Housecleaning." The poet likens the Iranian ruling class to a large number of malicious vermin who are nesting under the rug of the room; one must remove the rug and sweep them out. Each species, such as cockroaches, bedbugs, and earthworms represents a special class in the governmental hierarchy of Iran.[7]

In the reductive technique the satirist may go one step further and make his characters not only animals, but animals who lack all traces of individuality or freedom. Eugène Ionesco in *The Rhinoceros* (1960) beautifully describes the various forms of collective hysteria that have resulted from totalitarian rule and continuous indoctrination. The whole population of a town has turned into rhinoceroses who do exactly as they are told. However, there is one character, Bérenger, who is not changed. He is left to resist and criticize. He says, "I'm staying that way until the end. I'm not capitulating."[8]

In Rand's *Anthem*, Huxley's *Brave New World*, and Orwell's *1984* the situations are very similar. In these stories the heroes do not want to submit to the ways of life and values that have been forced upon them—they are fighting for their humanity and individuality. The first book is pro-technology; its hero is banished from society for the "sin" of reinventing the lightbulb. The last two view technology as a threat and suggest that, while industrialization and mechanization have long been seen as a means to prosperity, this may not be so. It is ironic to think that both may further inhibit our freedom.

Charlie Chaplin in his great film satire *Modern Times* (1936) criticizes the dominance of the machine over man and the effect of technology and mass production on life. The opening scene epitomizes the film: sheep go down a gangway and are then replaced by workers who hurriedly enter a factory. In another scene Charlie is fed by a machine in the most ridiculous way in order to save working time. He becomes so accustomed to fastening the bolts in the assembly line that he follows an elderly lady on the street, trying to fasten the buttons on her dress.

The great Czech satirist Karel Čapek developed this theme further in *R.U.R. [Rossum's Universal Robots]* (1921); it was this play that for the first time gave the world the word *robot*. This brilliant vision of the mechanized future reflects the concerns of the writer about modern barbarism—the worldwide lack of regard not only for the individual, but also for the entire human race in the face of dangerous technology that science has placed in its possession. Čapek, who throughout his life was obsessed with the idea of mechanized subhuman beings, produced in 1936 yet another fascinating satire on the subject entitled *War with the Newts*. This is the story of a great number of "sly, clever creatures who were first trained by man for various uses, and who, finally, turned into a mob without a soul or morals but with dangerous technical skill, and plunged the world into ruin."[9] This work could not have been more prophetic, since already the dreaded shadow of Hitler's Nazism was steadily enveloping Europe.

There are a number of recent Persian counterparts to such satirical works. Very similar to *The Rhinoceros* is *Khar* (The ass) (1983), a play by Parviz Sayyad.[10] After the revolution in Iran a couple have lost their jobs because of their lack of cooperation with the authorities. When the husband goes back to his official post and tries to justify whatever the government does, he appears to his wife as a man with the head of an ass. The frantically frightened wife speaks to her father, brother, her former lover, who is a writer, and to the family lawyer and doctor, but whoever tolerates the governmental wrongdoings assumes the same asinine form in her eyes. Meanwhile the husband argues that an ass is a very gentle and harmless animal, much better than many vicious men. In the end the wife submits and joins the others and appears with the head of a donkey. In the last act of the play, the husband takes away his ass mask, confessing that despite his defense of his position he cannot bear it any longer.

Not being reduced to the level of an animal, but rather being forced to the state of total submission is displayed in the play of Gholam-Hosain Sa'edi entitled *Mah-e 'Asal* (The honeymoon) (1978).[11] Influenced by the theater of the absurd, the play shows how the Savak used to intimidate people into collaboration. While on their honeymoon a young couple are told by an official, who phones them, that they have to accommodate a "guest." Soon afterward the "guest" arrives—an old woman dressed totally in red. When the couple disobey her, two men arrive at the apartment and beat them into submission. The presence of the ever-intruding old woman becomes so intolerable that eventually the young couple give in and follow her instructions. At the end of the play the couple, who have come to look very much like the old woman, receive instruction from a "voice" to go to a certain house as "guests." The metamorphosis is complete, and two independent-minded persons have become virtual robots.

An example of a different kind is a short story by Feridun Tonkaboni that criticizes senseless industrialization and the subjugation of man to machine. The writer wakes up one morning to find himself in a society where the Paikan car company has monopolized everything and everyone. The story is called "The Year 1388," which corresponds to the year 2009 in the Christian calendar. In the Iran of 2009 Paikan cars and soccer games have become national obsessions; even foreign tourists before entering the country have to change their cars to Paikans because no other cars are allowed in many public places. The satire in the story is manifold. On the one hand it demonstrates the irrational subjugation of man to machine and its tragic consequences; on the other it ridicules the claims of progress and advancement in Iran as well as the senseless fascination with westernization. It should be remembered that in the last years of the Shah's reign this car, whose engine and parts were provided by Hillman of England, became the symbol of national pride in Iran. A well-known and often- repeated advertisement declared: "The day that every Iranian has a Paikan" would be the zenith of prosperity. It is against this background that the craze for Paikan cars is ridiculed as a symbol of an artificial industrialization.[12]

THE TECHNIQUE OF EXAGGERATION

This technique, which can be used in association with the reductive method, represents a person by highlighting his or her most ridiculous characteristics. This is the technique of caricature in which personal features or ideas may be magnified and humorously exaggerated. Max Beerbohm, one of the greatest satirists of the century, writes: "The perfect caricature must be an exaggeration from top to toe. The whole man must be melted down, as in a crucible, and then from the solution be fashioned anew. He must emerge with not one particle of himself lost, yet with not a particle of himself as it was before. The most perfect caricature is that which . . . with the simplest means most accurately exaggerates . . . the peculiarities of a human being, at his most characteristic moment, in the most beautiful manner."[13]

One of the methods related to this technique is to exaggerate a trivial manner and discuss it in a dignified manner. If the imitation of a certain style is also involved, the work becomes a burlesque, which will be further discussed in the section on parody. The following excerpt from *The Clouds* by Aristophanes may serve as an example. The play is a fascinating satire on the teachings of the sophists. Strepsiades is a roguish old peasant who has come to learn the Socratic manner of argumentation so that he may silence his creditors. He loudly knocks at the door, disturbing one of the students of the academy:

Student. [within.] Damn it! Who's knocking?
Strepsiades. Pheidon's son, Strepsiades, of Cieynna.
Student. A dolt, by Zeus, for kicking the doors so very unsubtly. And causing my mental conception to miscarry!
Strepsiades. Forgive me; I'm only a country yokel. But tell me what your conception was.
Student. Against the rule, except to students.
Strepsiades. It's all right to tell me. I've come to the Think shop to be a student.
 . . .

Student. Chaerephon asked [Socrates] whether gnats, in his opinion, hummed through the mouth, or through their tails.
Strepsiades. And what did he say about the gnats?
Student. He declared that the gnats entrail is small; the breath therefore proceeds through it with violence toward tail. Hence the rump resounds with the force of the blast.
Strepsiades. So rump of the gnat is a trumpet! Thrice-blessed for his analysis![14]

One of the clerics of the Qajar period in Tabriz uses the same technique to satirize the vanities, pretension, and fanaticism of his confreres. Hojjat al-Islam Nayyer (d. 1894) is the author of a long poem entitled "Fasfat' ul-Fasil" (The big wind), which has never been published.[15] The poem is in Arabic, but very often Persian and Turkish words and phrases are humorously interwoven into it. Some of the arguments in the poem remind one of the discussions that Saint Augustine had with his disciples, asking how many angels could sit on the head of a pin. The ulema of Tabriz have gathered to tackle the most serious theological questions:

They differed on the excrement of Jinns;
Most of the experts considered it unclean.

Some of the disputants say that since the Jinns (genies) are invisible, nothing can be done if they make us and everything around us unclean by their drop-pings. A fierce fight ensues between the proponents on every side of this absurd idea. The poet, treating many such ridiculous discussions, takes on the famous theologians of Tabriz one by one, and with a wickedly unsparing sense of satire exaggerates their personal characteristics and dissects them by describing their most ridiculous beliefs.

PARODY

Parody is imitation with the intent to criticize. To impersonate a famous model is not necessarily satirical. Without any intention of ridiculing, a talented actor may imitate the speech and gait of his original so well that the audience cannot tell them apart. "But," as Gilbert Highet puts it, "when [one] exaggerates the faults and underscores the foibles of his victim, so that the audience sees something new and ridiculous, or contemptible, or hateful, in the character of the person mimicked, and laughs with a certain malicious delight, and thereafter admires the original a little less than it did before seeing that cruel portrait— then the act is parody, and the effect it produces is the effect of satire. It is the difference between a portrait and a caricature. Both resemble the subject; but one is intended to reproduce the most central and typical features of its model, and the other (however delicately) to distort, to belittle, to wound."[16]

Thus in parody imitation is combined with exaggeration or reductive technique. It may be exercised on the two different levels of form and content. The parodist's intent may be to ridicule the literary style of his model or simply to use that model as a vehicle to satirize a certain person or subject. In literary parodies if a low and rather vulgar language and the imagery are used the result will be called "travesty," whereas a dignified and sometimes high-flown style will be called "mock-heroic."

In Persian literature, though all these types exist, the terms describing them are used very indiscriminately. Three words, *javab*,[17] *nazire*,[18] and *naqize*,[19] are used for parody. The first often means an answer to a poem criticizing the poet. One example was quoted in the last chapter by Kamal al-Din Esma'il of Isfahan (d. ca. 1237), and another example comes from the pen of Abu 'Ala of Ganja, who was the father-in-law of the famous poet Khaqani (d. 1199). The enmity between the two gave rise to a series of bitter invectives. One of the few translatable ones follows:

> Thy verse, Khaqani, deeply I admire,
> Yet one small hint to offer I desire;
> Mock not the man whose years outnumber thine:
> He may perchance [thou know'st not], be thy Sire![20]

Not very different from this form is the *naqize*, which originated in Arabic literature. Traditionally an Arab poet would write a panegyric (*qaside*), which often praised his own tribe; as a result he would sometimes be challenged and satirized by a poet from a rival tribe, who would compose a *naqize* in the same style and meter. R. A. Nicholson, who discusses the famous examples by al-Akhtal, Jarir, and al-Farazdaq, translates the plural *naqa'iz* as "flytings,"[21] i.e., disputes or exchanges of personal abuse in verse form. On the whole this genre is more invective than parody, challenging and answering a previous attack; and notable examples are provided by Suzani, Khaqani, and Ghaza'iri.[22]

The term *nazire* is more widely used. Two well-known examples are by two poets of the fifteenth century: Abu Ishaq of Shiraz, whose *divan* is entitled the "Treasure of Appetite," and Nezam al-Din Mahmud Qari of Yazd, who is known as the "Poet of Clothes." In dealing with their respective subjects, food and clothing, both poets humorously parody many well-known lines from both contemporary and ancient poets.

According to Browne, Abu Ishaq was an admirer and disciple of the well-known Sufi master of the town of Mahan in Kirman, Shah Ne'mat 'ullah Vali, but he could not restrain himself from parodying the mystical rhapsodies of the master "in profane poems addressed to various culinary delicacies." Ne'mat 'ullah's poem contains these lines:

> We are the pearls of the shoreless Ocean; sometimes
> We are the Waves and sometimes the Sea;
> We came into the world for this purpose, that
> We might show God to His creatures.

Abu Ishaq parodied this as follows:

> We are the dough-strings of the bowl of wisdom;
> Sometimes we are the dough and sometimes the pie-crust;
> We came into the kitchen for this purpose, that we might
> Show the fried meat to the pastry.[23]

A recent example of political parody is written in imitation of a famous ghazal of Hafez that begins:

> I say it openly and am delighted with these words;
> I am a slave to love and free of the two worlds.[24]

An anonymous poet, who was imprisoned by the Shah, wrote a long ghazal in imitation of the verses making the Shah the speaker:

> I say it openly without sorrow and woe
> I am a slave to Carter and free in what I do.
> Don't complain, O people, if I waste your oil,
> If I don't he will make me his spoil.
> Don't shout or cry as I have no fears,
> Though your clamors may reach the spheres.
> Let the country lie in ruins through my tyranny,
> As I am happy in this palace, in tyrannical luxury.
> Scion of Churchill I am and raised by the CIA's hand,
> Though I was born in an Islamic land.
> On the tablet of my heart there is nothing but "autocracy";
> What can I do? Nothing else my master has taught me.
> Like Death incarnate above the people I stand;
> Though at the door of foreigners I hold a humble hand.
> Whoever speaks of justice, I am bent on his destruction;
> Though I know at the end [in]justice will bring my ruination.[25]

After the revolution of 1979, when a totalitarian theocracy replaced a totalitarian monarchy, the same method of parodying well-known verses was often adopted by the satirists who had fled Iran. The following is an imitation of a quatrain by Omar Khayyam, which appeared anonymously in the weekly

Ahangar in Exile (London, 3 October 1982):

> Like a madman I will forsake mankind,
> Leaving good and bad as well as sea and land behind.
> To show the people what destruction I can summon,
> Around my head the turban of the sheikh I'll wind.

Among the classical poets of Iran Ferdausi is the poet most often imitated by the satirists. In the third chapter of his *Ethics of the Aristocrats* 'Obeyd-e Zakani changes the famous battlefield episode between Rostam and Human into a scene of homosexual debauchery in which the two heroes take turns complying with each other's desires. *The Cat and the Mice* of 'Obeyd (to be discussed as political satire in chapter five) is perhaps the best-known mock-heroic poem in Persian literature. Though it is not in the same meter as *Shah-Name*, in many respects it imitates the work of Ferdausi.

When Muhammad 'Ali Shah was ousted in 1909 the *Shah-Name* served as a model for many mock-epic poems in which the Shah and his generals boasted of their valor but were ultimately defeated by the Constitutionalists. The famous Azerbaijani satirist 'Ali Akbar Saber, in a poem unmistakably entitled "Shah-Name," describes how a royalist general invades Tabriz and is ignominiously defeated by the hero of the revolution, Sattar Khan. The poem, which is an admirable imitation in Azari Turkish of Ferdausi's style, presents a ridiculous picture of a general who tries to justify his defeat.[26] In another poem Ashraf Gilani makes the former Shah express his desires in a more colloquial vein. The poem, written in the *qaside* form, is an imitation of the heroic *rajaz*, but it does more than depict the Shah's bravado; it reflects the passionate feelings of the poet:

> I am that famous, shameless libertine
> Whose days and nights were passed twixt sleep and wine!
> Although my belly daily larger grows,
> My strength is waning like the melting snows.
> Could I to Tehran once an entrance gain
> Its people butcher-like I'd cleave in twain,
> And its inhabitants, both great and small,
> With shot and shrapnel I would dose them all!
> As for the Regent[27] off his head should go,
> Who caused my projects to miscarry so;
> And with my pen-knife out the eyes I'd bring
> Of Sultan Ahmad Shah, the reigning king;[28]
> Out of Sardar-i-As'ad's heart I'd take,
> And the Sipahdar into mince-meat make;
> The Parliament with cannons I would shake,
> For freedom's balm to me's a poisoned snake;
> And, by my worthless Northern Friend's advice,
> I'd crush the folk, as though they were but lice;
> The Deputies to one long rope I'd tie,
> And topsy-turvy turn the Ministry.
> Now in the dust my head is bowed, and I
> Glide like a serpent from the Nation's eye.

. . . .

Should Tehran once again become my share
Not one of all its people will I spare.
Of grocer, baker and of caterer,
Of druggist, butcher and of fruiterer,
Townsman and peasant, toilers without rest,
Of aged men and children at the breast,
Of blacksmith, joiner, carpenter therewith,
Of draper and of pedlar and goldsmith.
The blood in such wise on the earth I'll shed
That it shall form a sea with waves of red!
But cruel fate has tied my hands, alack!
And fortune sinister doth break my back!
I'm poor, I'm poor, I'm poor, I'm poor indeed;
I have not, have not, have not, aught I need!
O belly, belly, belly, belly mine,
'Tis you who cause me thus to grieve and pine!
To thee, Bahadur, greetings do I send;
Where art thou? Help me, O my trusty friend!
Sardar Muhiyy, I hear, hath marched from Ray,
And wends towards Mazandaran his way.
This time, for all my bulging paunch, I feel
That on the gibbet I shall dance a reel!
With empty purse and brains of sense bereft,
I've neither foot to fly nor refuge left![29]

Still another example of the mock-heroic style is found in *The Book of Fleas* by Bahar. It was written while he was imprisoned during the reign of Reza Shah. The poet describes his fight during the night with various vicious insects that infest his cell. By exaggerating their stature and capability, he gives a heroic dimension to the battle, which on the one hand is humorous and on the other is tragic as it reflects the hardships of a political prisoner.[30]

One final aspect of parody concerns the degree of faithfulness with which the imitations follow the originals. Sometimes the tone and the general contour of a certain literary style are desired. For instance, *The Book of Fleas* and the poem on Muhammad 'Ali Shah by Ashraf Gilani do not mimic specific episodes of *Shah-Name*, but rather bear a general resemblance to the style of Ferdausi. In some other parodies exact parallelism with the original is needed; remembering the original enhances the effect of the parody. A famous homily by Sana'i begins:

O Lord, I sing thy praise since thou art God Almighty;
I will follow no path except what thou doth show'st me.[31]

A contemporary poet, Abu-Qasem Halat, closely imitates the poem and often adopts the exact lines, but changes "God" to "Bribery," which has come to be the Omnipotent Lord of many lands:

Bribery, I sing your praise, as you are the Lord of every land;
Yours is no place special, yet you are in every hand.

You are not virtue, yet virtue-like you lead men to redemption.
You are not the Prophet Khizer, yet like him you lead men to salvation.
Outside you are all fears, but inside full of confidence;
On the face you are apprehension, but in truth all assurance.
If you are revealed, you are toil and pains;
But remaining in secret, you are all charm and grace.
You are that legendary Rostam all might and influence;
You are that renowned Hatem all generosity and benevolence.
You are a sweet potion, yet you turn poison if failed;
You are poison turning sweet, if your art is displayed.
You bind everyone, though you are neither a lasso nor a chain;
You color everyone, though you are neither a paint nor a stain.
Shed your light on me, as you sun-like shine bright;
Bear me on your wings, and carry me to fortune's sight.
   This servant of yours is all praise for you;
So that from the bounds of poverty you save me too.[32]

IRONY

Irony is yet another tool in the hands of the satirist. The word is derived from the Greek *eironia* ("dissimulation") which in turn comes from *eiron*, meaning "one who says less than he means." It is a form of "speech in which the real meaning is concealed or contradicted by the words used; it is particularly employed for the purpose of ridicule, mockery or contempt, frequently taking the form of a sarcastic phrase."[33] One of its earliest usages was "Socratic irony," a technique in which one pretends ignorance as a method of dialectic in order to defeat one's opponent. Another form of irony is "dramatic irony," which increases the intensity of a dramatic situation. Here the spectators are usually aware of the real situation, but the character through his words and actions belies it. The classic example is Oedipus's unwitting condemnation of himself in Sophocles' *Oedipus Tyrannus*.

In Persian literature "Socratic irony" (Tahhakiem-e Soqrati) is translated as "Socratic dissimulation" or "feigning ignorance" (Tajahil-e 'Arif). Rashid al-Din Vatvat (d. 1182), a well-known poet and literary critic, discusses this under the heading of "the learned feigning ignorance."[34] "Ironic situation" or "dramatic irony" is often described as "the play of fate" (*bazi-ye charkh*)[35] or "the play of destiny" (*bazi-ye sarnevesht*). In ordinary speech *kenaye* ("sarcastic remark") and *ta'ne* ("bitter taunt") are used for irony. Many poems of Hafez have a delicate twist that brings to mind this definition of irony by E. P. Whipple: "Irony is an insult conveyed in the form of a compliment."[36] Here is an example by Hafez in which he criticizes the preacher of the city:

"It is unlawful. Drink not wine," the Sheikh sarcasticly said.
"'To be sure. I won't listen to any ass," I replied.[37]

In another poem Hafez once again turns to the subject of religious hypocrisy and uses subtle irony:

> People say: "The preacher of the town is an angel";
> I wholeheartedly agree with them. He is not a human being.[38]

Irony can be purely verbal, or it can be created by juxtaposing two different situations; then it is called "ironic situation." In a short story entitled "The Tail of the Cat" a contemporary satirist named 'Abbas Towfiq presents two incidents side by side without any authorial comment. In the first part an old egg-seller is knocked down by the car of the director general of a government office who is returning drunk from a late-night party. Seeing the official plate of the car, the policeman on the scene begins to blame the poor old man and kicks him away. In the second part of the story a cat's tail is caught under the bicycle wheel of a young baker who is going to work, and the same policeman arrests him for hurting the animal. Here is part of their dialogue:

> "You pimp, you have run over the cat and are trying to get away?"
> "I have not killed a man."
> "You bastard! You think a cat is less than a person? Do you think that you are living in Africa and you can do whatever you like to animals? Don't you know that in this country we have the SPCA? Don't you listen to the radio?

> Crush not yon ant, who stores the golden grain:
> He lives with pleasure, and will die with pain."[39]

> "By God, officer, I am innocent. It was the cat who jumped from the gutter into the road in front of me."
> "You bastard! How did he know that an idiot like you is riding a bike? How could I answer the authorities that on my beat a poor cat has been run over by a bicycle? Let's go, I'm going to take you in."
> [Pleading] "Can't you overlook it this once!"
> "Get going, you son of a bitch. How can I overlook the law? I have to take you to court so that when they give you four years, you'll know that even running over a mosquito should be punished, let alone a cat!"
> "But . . ."
> [Ashgar's eyes brighten and his speech softens.] "But, what?"
> "But can't you do something not to take me to court? The truth is that I am very afraid of it."
> "Then, I have to administer the law myself!"
> "Very well, officer."
> "Then give me 40 tomans as your fine and get lost."
> "But, officer, it was only the tail of a cat . . ."
> "O.K. Then 20 tomans."
> "Please, have pity. I don't have it."
> "You talk too much. 10 tomans."
> "By God, I don't have it! My wage for two days is 10 tomans!"
> "Well, 5 tomans, not a penny less!"
> "By God, I don't even have 5 tomans."
> "You bastard! You haven't got a penny in your pocket and you want to fight the law? Let's go, you murderer! . . ."[40]

THE USE OF THE SUBJECT'S OWN WORDS

People expect greatness and wisdom from their leaders, whose statements consequently should be wise and impressive. But being human, they make mistakes and utter a great deal of nonsense (as does everyone else in his or her life). The sycophants who usually gather around powerful leaders try to deify them and make their everyday utterances memorable maxims. The satirist may pinpoint such words, and by putting them in a relevant framework, create a ridiculous picture of a certain leader. Or, as statesmen seldom fulfill their early promises, the satirist achieves his end by contrasting the statesman's words and actions. The satiric effect may also be created by quoting exact words but taking them out of context. On the whole, this technique is aimed at demonstrating the contradiction that often exists between what leaders promise and what they actually do, or to show how their tenets are at variance with the common beliefs of the people.

An interesting example of this technique is *An Evening with Richard Nixon* by Gore Vidal.[41] Apart from Nixon, the play's "characters" includes Dwight Eisenhower, John F. Kennedy, Spiro Agnew, Lyndon Johnson, Barry Goldwater, Nikita Khruschev, and other well-known personalities. All of the statements by Nixon and most of those of the others are derived from their interviews and speeches, and all of the sources are documented at the end of the book. According to Vidal, "much brooding on the national amnesia" led him to write this play. He explains, "I decided that I would put in a single *two-hour entertainment* the thirty-seventh president's career, using his own words and those of others. At the end of this narrative, it won't be possible for anyone to say, 'Oh, I'm sure he never said that about China, or Truman, etc.' " In fact, a strange discrepancy often exists between what Nixon said and what he did. In the play Nixon says, "The three passions of Quakers are peace, civil rights, and tolerance. That is why, as a Quaker, I can't be an extremist, a racist, or an uncompromising hawk." He claims that he has "never engaged in personalities in campaigns," but he does everything to discredit a political rival, Helen Gahagan Douglas, even accusing her of being a Communist. When the French leave Vietnam he says, "We stand firm for the right of all the South Vietnamese people to determine for themselves the kind of government they want"; but as soon as it becomes clear that Ho Chi Minh will win the election, he changes his mind. What Gore Vidal brings out so wonderfully is that politicians often speak out of expediency rather than conviction, and Nixon is an arch-politican.

Turning to Persian literature, one finds a particularly interesting example of this technique in the satirical essays of Dehkhoda entitled *Charand Parand*. Some of the great clerics of Iran played an important role in the Constitutional Revolution by firmly supporting the national cause. In the last years of his reign, three of the ayatollahs residing in Iraq wrote letters to Mohammad 'Ali Shah and urged him to respect the wishes of the people by abandoning his autocratic ways. He wrote a letter to the three clergymen, saying that the nation supported him wholeheartedly and that only a few foreign agents and godforsaken constitutionalists were stirring up trouble. He called them "heretics" and said that his only aim was to save Islam from them. His letter was even more incongruous considering the fact that these clergymen were among the leaders of the revolt.

Dehkhoda writes a very short introduction and then quotes the royal letter verbatim, arguing that whatever the king does is the best of its kind—even his nonsense tops all other nonsense. The letter is so ridiculous that it serves as an unconscious self-parody. I translate here only the introduction of the satirist:

> O scholars of Iran, you have been reading the *Charand Parand* [Non-sensical talks] of Dakhou[42] for the last one and a half years, and you know what they look like, but now read the following royal letter and see if I have ever written, or you have ever read, anything like it. If so, you, like Dakhou, will believe in this [old] saying that "The king's words are the king of words."

Akhavan Thaleth, the contemporary Iranian poet, using the same method, has chosen some very amusing passages from the diaries of Naser al-Din Shah, which were the result of several royal trips to Europe. Though the satirist occasionally adds a few comments here and there, the writings of the king constitute the bulk of the satire:

> Sunday, ninth of Rajab...
>
> Today before noon, accompanied by Ostad Hosain, the chief masseur, and other workers of the royal bath we went to a [public] bath in Paris the capital of France. We had heard many wonderful things about the baths here, yet neither in the dressing room nor in the bath chamber was one Parisian to be seen. As we wanted to speak with the natives of France, we necessarily spoke a few words in French to the royal interpreter. The foolish fellow gets a handsome salary from us as well as his fief and appanages, yet he does not know the French for hair-remover, pumice stone, headrest-towel and even massage. In short we had heard that men and women together here take a bath and that neither the emperor, nor the government nor the clergy raise any objections. We had also heard that eight or nine year-old children in France fluently speak French without stammering or with a foreign accent, which they say we have. We wanted to see all these things for ourselves to find out if they were true or if the royal interpreter had lied to us, making up all these fabrications.
>
> Anyway in our bath chamber there was not one French man, woman or child, young or old. It seems that our servants—the Prime Minister, Ra'is al-Mamalek Sepah-Salar and Hajji Emam Jum'a, who had been included in our sun-glorious retinue, let no one in, fearing some harm to our blessed and auspicious being. Master Hosain the Masseur gave us a thorough massage while we were giving him some orders in French. The poor man was bewildered and kept looking at us in amazement, and this amused us. In fact it was a very good massage. Then we lay down, that is to say that they informed our Majesty that as usual we took a short nap, about three or four hours, though we never realized it.
>
> The royal interpreter did not know what the "nap in the bath" is called

in French. May the plague take him—he is not worth the salary he gets. Foolish ignoramus! On this account we called him names. Especially in the dressing room of the bath, in front of some of the workers we called him in French and Persian "ignoramus and good-for-nothing fellow," so that he might be punished. The poor soul became very distressed and ashamed, and tried to support his argument that such a word does not exist in French with the confirmation of the attendant translator, viz. Mo'addab al-Saltane, Monsieur Richard Khan, and swearing by God and the Prophet that this is the truth. After a great deal of amazement and with the emphatic remarks of Monsieur Richard Khan we came to accept this to some extent. But how is this possible? With so many inventions and so much progress, the steam engine, the airplane, etc., they don't have a word for the afternoon nap in French? If it is as the royal interpreter says and Monsieur Richard Khan, who himself is a native of France . . . , it must be an imperfect language.

In short, the purpose was to have an auspicious and good bath. When we came out and looked at ourselves in the large mirror for awhile, in truth, we were pleased with ourselves . . . .[43]

Notes

1. Matthew Hodgart, *Satire*, p. 115.
2. *Divan-e Hafez*, ed. Mohammad Qazvini (Tehran: Zavvar Publications, n.d.), p. 135.
3. Talhak (or Talkhak) was the jester of Sultan Mahmud the Ghaznavid (d. 1030). Later on his name as Dalqak came to mean *jester* in Persian.
4. 'Obeyd-e Zakani, *Kolliyyat-e*, p. 264.
5. *Kolliyyat-e Mosavvar-e 'Eshqi*, ed. 'Ali Akbar Salimi (Tehran: Amir Kabir, 1956), pp. 395-96.
6. For some of his poems see Hosain Kuhi Kermani, *Bargi az Tarikh Mo'aser-e Iran ya Ghogha-ye Jumhuri* (Tehran, 1951), pp. 147-60.
7. See Munibur Rahman, *An Anthology of Modern Persian Poetry* (Aligarh: Institute of Islamic Studies, Muslim University, 1958), 1:156-58.
8. Eugène Ionesco, *The Rhinoceros*, tr. Derek Prouse (New York: Grove Press, 1960), p. 107.
9. Karel Čapek, *War with the Newts*, tr. Lewis Gannelt (New York: Bantam Books, 1964), p. xii.
10. (Los Angeles: Publi-Print, 1983). The play was performed by Parviz Sayyad and Mary Apik in August 1983 at Montgomery Theatre, San Jose, California. It was also performed in Los Angeles one month earlier.
11. Gholam-Hosain Sa'edi (Gowhar-e Morad), *Mah-e 'Asal* (Tehran: Ketab-ha-ye Jibi, 1978).
12. For this story see *Anduh-e Setarvan Budan* (n.d.). The story was written in 1968. See also Tonkaboni's other story entitled "Machine-Mobareze ba Bisavadi" ("Literary Machine"), a satire on the Shah's campaign for literacy published in the collection of stories entitled *Setare-ha-ye Shab-e Tire* (Tehran, 1978), pp. 71-93.
13. Edgar Johnson, *A Treasury of Satire* (New York: Simon & Schuster, 1945), pp. 628-29.
14. *The Complete Plays of Aristophanes*, ed. Moses Hadas (New York: Bantam Books, 1962), p. 106.
15. There is a manuscript of the poem at the National Library of Tabriz.
16. Gilbert Highet, *The Anatomy of Satire* (Princeton: Princeton University Press, 1962), pp. 68-69.
17. See Browne, *Literary History*, 2:81.
18. Ibid., 3:344-45.
19. Ibid., 2:82.
20. Quoted in Ibid.
21. Nicholson, *Literary History*, p. 239. See Muhammad Qazvini, *Yaddashtha* (Tehran: Tehran University Press, 1968). There is an unpublished work on "Naqize va Naqize-Sazan" by Mehdi Akhavan-i-Thaleth, of which a chapter was published in *Ettela'at* (1976). See also the intro-

duction to the *Naqa'iz Jarir wa'l-Akhtal* by 'Abd al Majid al-Muhtaseb (Cairo: Dar al-Fikr, 1972).

22. See Mohammad Dabir Siyaqi, *Ganj-e Baz-Yafte* (Tehran: Ketabfrushi Khayyam, 1965), pp. 19-20.

23. Browne, *Literary History*, 3:345-46. "When subsequently Sayyid Ni'matu'llah met Abu Ishaq, he said, 'Are you the dough-strings of the bowl of wisdom?' To which the latter replied, 'Since I am not in a position to talk about God [Allah], I'll talk about God's bounty [Ne'matu'llah].' "

24. *Divan-e Hafez*, op cit., p. 216.

25. The title of the poem is "A Personal Account of the Yazid of Our Time." The poem was copied and circulated privately during the revolution.

26. *Hop Hop Name*, (Baku: Azermashr, 1962), p. 167.

27. Abu'l-Qasim Khan Nasir al-Mulk, elected Regent on the death of his predecessor, 'Azd al-Mulk, on 13 September 1910.

28. He succeeded to the throne on 18 July 1909 upon his father's deposition.

29. Quoted in E. G. Browne, *Press and Poetry*, pp. 244-46.

30. M. Bahar, *Divan-e Malek al-Sho'ara Bahar*, (Tehran: Amir Kabir, 1956), pp. 290-92.

31. *Divan-e Sana'i*, ed. M. Mossaffa (Tehran: Amir Kabir, 1957), p. 742.

32. Abu'l-Qasem Halat, *Divan-e Khurus-e Lari* (Tehran: Talar-e Ketab, 1983), p. 394.

33. *Encyclopaedia Brittanica*, 13th ed., s.v. "Irony."

34. *Hada'eq al-Sehr* (The garden of magic), ed. 'Abbas Eqbal (Tehran, 1929), p. 58.

35. See the poem of Hafez in chapter 4, "Satire and Religion," pp. 62-63.

36. E. P. Whipple, quoted in Herbert V. Prochnow, *A Dictionary of Wit, Wisdom and Satire*, 1964, p. 143.

37. *Divan-e Hafez*, Anjavi's edition (Tehran: Javidan, 1986), p. 204.

38. This poem is not in the Qazvini edition; it is in a lithographed edition of *Divan* (no date) printed in Bombay.

39. A famous line by Ferdausi quoted in the *Bustan* of Sa'di, chapter 2, story 29. The translation of the poem is by Sir William Jones, and it has been quoted by A. J. Arberry in his *Classical Persian Literature* (London: George Allen & Unwin, 1958).

40. Persian text quoted in *Tanz-avaran-e Amrouz-e Iran*, ed. B. Asadi and A. Salahi (Tehran: Athar-Iran, 1970), pp. 64-65.

41. Gore Vidal, *An Evening with Richard Nixon* (New York: Random House, 1972).

42. This was his pen name. See chapter 6, "Political Satire."

43. Akhavan Thaleth, *Behtarin-e Omid* (Tehran: Athar-e Iran, 1969), pp. 84-86.

4

Satire and Religion

Going from the King to the Priest was as if
For fear of the snake I ended up in the dragon's mouth.

—Naser Khosrow

Religious satire may originate from three different forms of criticism: first, an atheist or agnostic may direct it toward a religion; second, a religious zealot may criticize the devotee of a different sect or faith; and third, a believer in a certain sect or faith may criticize his own coreligionists for their moral laxity or for another, similar, reason.

Obviously, satire of the first category was rather difficult to write under both Christianity and Islam, up to very recent times. Writers and poets such as Omar Khayyam and Abu'l-'Ala al-Ma'arri, who could not accept the traditional values without questioning them, were exceptions in their own ages. Even in the nineteenth century in a democratic country like England, FitzGerald found in Khayyam a convenient way of voicing his own agnosticism. At the time of the publication of Darwin's *The Origin of Species*, when Matthew Arnold heard the "long, withdrawing roar" of the "Sea of Faith," Khayyam seemed like a safety valve for an age that was rather reluctant to express its own religious doubts. E. B. Cowell, FitzGerald's Persian teacher and friend, was so disturbed by the popularity of *The Rubaiyyat* that he regretted until the end of his life having introduced the old sceptic of Nishapur to FitzGerald.

The second category embraces intolerant believers of all creeds. An extremist who is convinced that his religion is the only true religion will not tolerate any other belief. Such fanaticism has engendered many tragedies and has cost many innocent lives. Sultan Mahmud of Ghazna not only fought holy wars with the heathen Indians and plundered the wealth of their temples, but he also did the same to his own countrymen on the pretext that they were Shi'ites and Qarmatis. The author of *Mujmal al-Tawarikh wa al-Qisas* writes that when Mahmud came to Rey "he ordered many gibbets to be erected and crucified many leaders of Dailam and had fifty Kharvar [15 tons] of the books of the renegades [Shi'ites], Ismailis and philosophers burned under their gibbets."[1]

In the third category of religious satire, criticism is directed at the sanctimonious politicians and clergy who have made religion a means of achieving and maintaining of power. This, along with the last-mentioned category, is in reality nothing but taking advantage of the credulity of people and a misusing of religious authority for selfish and worldly ends. In Islam the simplicity and piety of the four early caliphs was soon replaced by the Umayyad dynasty's courtly life, which was an imitation of the Byzantine and Sassanid courts. The Abassids subsequently followed much the same pattern, and before long no traces of piety or simplicity were left in the lives of Islamic rulers. Gradually theologians such as al-Ghazzali, Mawardi, and Ibn Majeh, by drawing upon such traditions as "the faith and state are twins," invested the ruler of the time with a spiritual stature. Later on, dynasties such as the Fatimids in Egypt, the Ottomans in Turkey, and the Safavids in Iran considered themselves the rightful successors of the Prophet and family. Of course, direct criticism of such personalities was hardly possible. Instead, the hypocrisy of lesser dignitaries of the faith became the prime target of the satirist. Sa'di aptly describes the whole group of such clergy in a well-known couplet:

> They teach the people to abandon the world
> While they themselves hoard silver and gold.[2]

I

Omar Khayyam and Abu'l-'Ala al-Ma'arri, as important practitioners of agnostic satire, deserve detailed consideration. Though the *carpe diem* philosophy of Omar Khayyam does not exactly correspond with the bitter pessimism of Abu'l-'Ala toward life, nonetheless they have many features in common, especially on the subject of religion, and a brief comparison of them will not be inappropriate.[3]

There are several main points in the philosophy of Omar that are voiced again and again in his poetry. He does not deny the existence of God, but he is not satisfied with the explanations given by major religions on the subject of man's relationship to God, the reason for his creation, and the day of judgment. He regards man as:

> . . . a child made with wit profound,
> With tokens of the Maker's favour crowned;
> Yet the world's potter takes his masterpiece,
> And dashes it to pieces on the ground![4]

The Sufis believe God is the only real agent—"Fa'el-e Haqiqi"; the world is not free from this rule for a single moment. According to Khayyam, God contrives every action of man and besets his way with snares, yet man is called the sinner. Omar admits his doubts about the world to come and criticizes those who talk with unshaken certainty of what will happen:

> They preach how sweet those Houri brides will be,
> But I say wine is sweeter—taste and see!
> Hold fast this cash, and let that credit go,
> And shun the din of empty drums like me.[5]

Khayyam regards hell as "a fire enkindled of our griefs" and heaven as "but a moment's peace, stolen from our woes."[6] Similarly, from doubt to faith, from life to death, there is but a "breath" or a moment, and a whole life consists of this "precious breath." He suggests, therefore, "enjoy while you may." In Omarian *carpe diem* doctrine the wine becomes a symbol for all the pleasures of life, even those that are forbidden by Islam. It also becomes a symbol of defiance to all religious hypocrites whose actions and declarations offer an obvious discrepancy:

> O Mufti, you go more astray
> Than I do, though to wine I do give way;
> I drink the blood of grapes, you that of men:
> Which of us is the more bloodthirsty, pray?[7]

Or:

> They, who of prayer-mats make such great display,
> Are fools to bear hypocrisy's hard sway;
> Strange! under cover of this saintly show
> They live like heathen, and their faith betray.[8]

Omar symbolizes through wine and wine-drinking his defiance of the sanctimony and hypocrisy of the religious of his age in innumerable quatrains, many of which have a satirical or sarcastic tone. Some Persian scholars such as Mohammad 'Ali Forughi and Jalal Homa'i do not consider them "genuine works of Khayyam." Quoting a well-known *ruba'i* in which the poet wishes his corpse to be washed with wine, wrapped in vine leaves, and buried under the threshold of the tavern, Homa'i says, "Such a poem can only come from the pen of a nonchalant drunkard, not that of Khayyam."[9] Obviously, such bacchanalian chants are disturbing to an orthodox mind that considers Omar a thoughtful and respectable philosopher. But this kind of bacchanalism and revolt is at the heart of Omar's poetry.

Poems with similar themes are too numerous in collections of Khayyam's work to be included here. Furthermore, some of them are to be found even among the oldest sources that mention Khayyam and his poetry. Some of such quatrains are also attributed to poets other than Khayyam. This shows that many other poets shared Khayyam's views. For instance, the following quatrain is attributed to Omar, and it is also included in the *divans* of both Anvari and Kamal-e Esfahani:

> Though I drink wine, I am no libertine,
> Nor am I grasping, save of cups of wine;
> I scruple to adore myself, like you;
> For this cause to wine-worship I incline.[10]

Similar criticisms of pretentious ascetics and men of religion very often can be found in the works of other poets. Hafez says:

> Hypocrisy is lawful, but wine unlawful.
> O what a religion! And O what a way![11]

Though in his nonpoetic works Khayyam tries to conform to the formal religion of the age, occasionally he cannot restrain himself from criticism of his contemporaries. "If they see that someone is in search of truth, trying to avoid falsehood, deceit, imposture and pretension, they will ridicule and humiliate him."[12] But in his quatrains he emerges as the Khayyam that we know, with his doubts and uncertainties, absorbed in the mysteries of life and fate, and critical of the hypocrisy and show of saintliness of his contemporaries.

Though more scholarship has been lavished on Khayyam than on any other Persian poet, he is still one of the most controversial figures in the literature of Iran. The absence of an authentic and definitive manuscript of his *Rubaiyyat* makes it a hard task to decide on both the number and the authenticity of his quatrains. The number of quatrains in various manuscripts varies from around 150 to 1,200, and one has to weed out the dubious poems by checking them against a handful of the most reliable quatrains found in old sources about Khayyam.[13] Interestingly enough, these quatrains, which are used as key-quatrains to show Khayyam's thoughts, represent a harmonious and integral way of thinking. There are a few pious poems addressing God, but they do not contradict the others, and they show Khayyam to be more of a doubter than a disbeliever. "The portrait of [Khayyam] which outlines itself from this selection does not, indeed, differ very much from the one familiar to us through the version of FitzGerald. We see that FitzGerald, for all the liberties he has taken with the original, has grasped with a sure psychological and aesthetical instinct the true kernel of the 'Omarian poetry.' "[14]

It is interesting to note that, although some sources have tried to present Khayyam as a devout and God-fearing Muslim, others have criticized him for his sceptical views. The earliest note of criticism comes from his great contemporary Abu Hamid al-Ghazzali, who writes about Khayyam, "His doubts reflect his own state. He is bewildered and lays blame sometimes on the world and sometimes on the heavens or fate, and occasionally negates everything. If he speaks, he utters dark and confused words. But a believer is never in doubt."[15] It seems that during his lifetime Khayyam's quatrains, containing his most heartfelt sentiments, were kept within the circle of his intimate friends, as there are very few contemporary references to them. About seventy years after the death of Omar, another great theologian, Fakhr-al-Din Razi, quoting one of the quatrains of Khayyam, criticizes him for his scepticism.[16] Qifti, who died in 1273, has a still more scathing statement to make. "The latter Sufis have found themselves in agreement with some of the apparent senses of [Khayyam's] verse, and have transferred it to their system and discussed in in their assemblies. . . ; though its inward meanings are to the [Ecclesiastical] Law stinging serpents, and a combination of rife and malice."[17] This statement explains why most of the *Rubaiyyat* manuscripts are inflated by the mystical quatrains of several Sufi poets, and why some translators (like Nicholas and Omar Ali Shah) have tried to give a mystical interpretation of the *Rubaiyyat*.

Interestingly enough, the farther we get from the time of Khayyam the more the stories about his scepticism appear, and the more the seemingly Khayyamian quatrains are attributed to him.[18] It seems likely that, apart from the erroneous attribution of several quatrains by other hands to Khayyam, some brother sceptics have expressed their own feelings in quatrains that passed under the name of Khayyam. The body of such quatrains existing in Persian literature is so large that one can suggest Omarian tradition was followed by many later poets, who often preferred to remain anonymous. Even the stories made up about the life of the poet of Nishapur indicate a similar device. In one of them the wind breaks Omar's jar and spills his wine. The tipsy poet angrily rebukes God, saying, "I drink wine, and You behave like a drunkard!" Divine wrath blackens the face of the blasphemous poet. The quatrain that the story puts in the mouth of the miscreant poet and secures for him God's favor is good-humored and in keeping with the Omarian philosophy:

> Was e'er man born who never went astray?
> Did ever mortal pass a sinless day?
> If I do ill, do not requite with ill!
> Evil for evil how can'st thou repay?[19]

The famous Arab poet, Abu'l-'Ala al-Ma'arri (973-1057) is also worthy of a close examination. He is a great poet and thinker whose impact was great not only on Arabic literature, but also on Persian literature. Surely, the blind genius of Ma'arri, who was known throughout the Islamic world and whose works R. A. Nicholson puts on a par with the *Divine Comedy* and *Paradise Lost*, must have served as a model for many sceptics and freethinkers in Iran.

In many ways Ma'arri was much in advance of his time. His courageous criticism of religious and political men makes one wonder how he could survive in an age of fanaticism and absolute belief. He did not deny the existence of God, but he scorned all religious institutions. For him religion is "a fable invented by the ancients" in which men believe through force of habit and education, never stopping to consider whether it is true. He bitterly lashes out at unscrupulous people who prey upon "human folly and superstition"[20] and make religion a means of their worldly ambition. Islam is neither better nor worse than any other creed:

> Hanifs[21] are stumbling, Christians all astray,

Jews bewildered, Magians far on error's way.
We mortals are composed of two great schools—
Enlightened knaves or else religious fools.[22]

Ma'arri questions many teachings of the major religions and only agrees with them on a few points. Using his remarkable gifts of wit, satire, and epigram, he lashes out at various creeds and sects. With incredulity he questions the Islamic law that punishes a theft exceeding one-quarter of a dinar by cutting off the thief's hand, while the compensation for the loss of a hand under other circumstances is put at five hundred dinars:

Why for a quarter do they amputate a hand
Five hundred serve to compensate?
Such contradictions silent awe compel.
Lord God, deliver us from the Fires of Hell.[23]

In many respects Abu'l-'Ala resembles Khayyam, though he has a darker and more pessimistic view of life and humanity. Both were accused of heresy for their liberal and often critical views of religion and their condemnation of the pretensions and follies of the religious. Abu'l-'Ala refers again and again to burial, the separation of the members, the mixing of the body with the earth, which reminds one of the potter in the *Rubaiyyat* who fashions cups and jars of the clay of the dead. Like Khayyam, Ma'arri regards the accounts of resurrection and paradise as "old wives tales," and sorrowfully he asks:

Has ever a dead man risen from the grave
To tell us what he has heard or what has passed?
Are you forsaking the cash of wine of this world
For the credit of milk and wine to come?[24]

A deep cynicism overshadows human fate in the work of both poets, yet the difference is that Khayyam wants to make the best of his time while he is alive. Abu'l-'Ala, being a blind and lonely man, doubly felt the sense of confinement in this world. The Omarian outlook toward life is more moderate and acceptable, but both poets have many views in common. As a last example, let us quote two more poems by them, both of which similarly condemn the pretentious and sanctimonious of their time. Omar writes:

These fools by dint of ignorance most crass,
Think they in wisdom all mankind surpass;
And glibly do they damn as infidel,
Whoever is not, like themselves, an ass.[25]

Abu'l-'Ala says:

Animals are void of reason
To shed light over them or reason for them.
Men of wisdom are so proud of themselves

As if they are prophets for common folk.
This group is hypocritical and that slow-witted.
If piety is dependent on obtuseness and inanity
Asses are amongst the most pious.[26]

Occasionally one comes across blasphemous poems whose writers were not necessarily unbelievers or agnostics. It seems that such poems were written in a mood of agnosticism that many people at one time or other encounter in their lives. Naser Khosrow (1003-88), the famous Isma'ili propagandist, poet, and traveler, whose faith no one can doubt, has some such poems in his *Divan*. Some Iranian scholars have tried to argue that these poems are not from the pen of Naser Khosrow.[27] But such thoughts can occur to a pious person too, and these poems could be their results. They were not removed from the *Divan* in later years. Here is only a short part of E. G. Browne's translation of this long *qaside*:

O God, although through fear I hardly dare
To hint it, all this trouble springs from Thee!
Hadst Thou no sand or gravel in Thy shoes
What made Thee suffer Satan willingly?
'Twere well if Thou hadst made the lips and teeth
Of Tartar beauties not so fair to see.
With cries of "On!" Thou bid'st the hound pursue:
With cries of "On!" Thou bid'st the quarry flee![28]

In modern times similar points of view can be seen in the works of Iraj Mirza and Sadeq Hedayat. The former was bitterly opposed to the clerics who used Islam as a means to further their worldly ambition:

O God, how long will I be silent?
I see all this coming from You.
Every particle in the world dances to Your tune,
Every trick comes from the hands of You.
Why do You meddle in our affairs?
Why don't You leave all of us alone?
Wealth and poverty are in Your hands;
You give glory and send humiliation.
You have created these *Akhunds* and *Mullas*;
You have disrupted our sweet dreams.
Had You nothing else to do
To create Satan with so much ado?
Why wherever You noticed an evil custom
You chose it for us the Muslims?
What is the difference between "Monsieur" and "Agha"?
Why is that one on the shore and this one drowning?
Are there not enough trappings to Mohammad's religion?
Is it not time for removing them all?
Come and take off this bell from our neck—
From this burden relieve us all.[29]

A younger contemporary of Iraj Mirza, Sadeq Hedayat (1903-51) is even more bitterly critical of religious extremism. Hedayat belonged to that group of Iranian intellectuals who, being extremely proud of their pre-Islamic heritage, held Islam responsible for whatever unpleasant things happened in Iran. One can detect at the bottom of the feelings of Hedayat an Aryan chauvinism defying the so-called Semitic cultural supremacy. In his novels and short stories he often paints bitterly satirical pictures of the Iranian clergy and of hypocritical Muslims. In one of his least-known short stories, whose title might be translated as "The Islamic Mission into the European Countries," he depicts a religious rogue who goes to preach Islam to Europeans but, after many acts of incredible hypocrisy, ends up opening a liquor shop in Paris. Hedayat's satirical language and talent for story-telling are remarkable, but his antagonism to his subject is such that the desired effect on the reader cannot be produced.

In a short play entitled *Afsane-ye Afarinesh* (The legend of creation), which was published in Paris in 1946, Hedayat's satirical picture of the scene of creation reminds one of the courts of despotic kings of the East. The names tend to be derogatory: "Khaliqoff,[30] Gabriel Pasha, Michael Effendi, Mulla Izrail, Israfil Beik, Monsieur Satan, Daddy Adam and Mommy Eve." After being expelled from heaven Adam is not at all displeased and says, "Though the life here is full of struggle, it is much better than the boring and tasteless life in heaven. I was being suffocated there." Eve seconds him: "It was really a blessing that they kicked us out of heaven. At least here nobody watches us and we are free."[31]

The chief difference between the writings of Hedayat and the poems of Khayyam or Abu'l-'Ala is that the latter two classical writers question many vital issues out of real agnosticism but are nonetheless believers in God, while Hedayat is not a believer and chides the devotion of the religious with a peculiar disdain. Therefore, his views lack the depth and breadth of those two great poets.

II

Satire arising from religious feuds between Muslims might have as many as four different aspects: first, criticism of the followers of other religions by the Muslims; second, scathing remarks exchanged between adherents to Greek philosophy and staunch believers in the *Shari'a*; third, similar exchanges of criticism (often with fervent religious overtones) between the nationalistic followers of the Shu'ubiyya movement and their opponents; and fourth, the mutual criticism of members of various Islamic sects. Obviously we cannot review the whole range of the history of Islam in Iran, so we will confine ourselves to a few examples from each category.

One of the most interesting examples of the Muslim attacks on other religions is to be found in the *Shah-Name* in the story of the king, Bahram Gur, and Lunbak, the water-carrier, perhaps the only satirical story in the whole book. Though presenting a fairly stereotypical picture of the Jews, Ferdausi's delineation of the characteristics of a wealthy miser is interesting. Bahram on a hunting expedition hears of the hospitable and generous Lunbak, and of the knavish Braham, a wealthy Jewish merchant. After arranging that no one should buy water from Lunbak, Bahram goes to the water-carrier and tests his generosity and hospitality under very dire conditions. But when Bahram, posing as one of his officers, goes to stay with Braham, the merchant sets many conditions before eventually allowing Bahram Gur to spend the night in his courtyard. The wealthy Jew eats a sumptuous dinner, but instead of food gives Bahram pieces of "good advice." As the king has promised to make amends if his horse does any damage to the house of his host, in the morning he is forced to remove the refuse of his horse, for which he brings out a costly silken handkerchief. Taking the droppings he flings them into a ditch. Braham, seeing this, leaps into the ditch and secures the handkerchief. Returning to his palace Bahram summons both the Jew and the water-carrier and bestows the wealth of the former on the latter. He only gives four drachmas to Braham, but he is certain the old miser will use this capital to amass another fortune.[32]

The depiction of the Jews in such a stereotypical fashion was not uncommon in Persian literature. In Persian proverbs, at least, the Jews have always been associated with wealth and miserliness. In the Middle Ages, they, like other minorities, did not take part in the politics of the Islamic world, but rather engaged in trade and certain other professions, sometimes becoming physicians to Muslim emirs. Only during the Mongol period was there an exception. The Jews, along with the followers of other creeds, tried to convert the Mongols, who were pagans, to their own respective religions and thus gain power. During the reign of Arghun (1284-91), a Jew by the name of Sa'd al-Dowle became his all-powerful minister, a situation unacceptable to the Muslim public. A poet from Baghdad bitterly criticized Sa'd al-Dowle for his various acts of repression, and thus concluded his poem:

> The Jews of this our time a rank attain
> To which the heavens might aspire in vain.
> Theirs is dominion, wealth to them doth cling,
> To them belong both councillor and king.
> O people, hear my words of counsel true:
> Turn Jews, for heaven itself hath turned a Jew!
> Yet wait, and ye shall their torments cry,
> And see them fall and perish presently.[33]

Expressing views differing from those of the *ulema* on matters of faith was considered heresy, and Islamic philosophers, who were influenced by the Greek tradition, were often the subject of criticism. Though Greek philosophy had an invaluable impact on the development of Islamic philosophy, its great exponents, such as Avicenna (980-1037) and Farabi (870-950) were often vilified by the conservative and the faithful. Avicenna, on being accused of laxity in matters of faith, defends himself in one of his quatrains:

The heresy of a man like me is no easy matter.
A faith stronger than mine could not exist.
In the world there is no man like me;
And he a heretic, so there no Muslim does exist.[34]

Abu Hamid al-Ghazzali (1058-1111), Ibn Ghilan of Balkh, and Fakhr al-Din Razi are only three of many theologians and orthodox writers who criticized the philosophers. Most of their criticisms were directed against Avicenna and his teachings. The sharp-witted and learned al-Ghazzali, in his *Tahafut'l-Falasefe* (The mistakes of philosophers), criticizes those who were trying to combine the Koranic teachings with the ideas of the Greek philosophers. He writes with sarcasm, "Hearing high sounding and ponderous names such as Socrates, Hippocrates, Plato and Aristotle and a list of their much-vaunted sciences such as geometry, logic, natural sciences and theology have dispelled their reason and have led them to heresy."[35] Some poets attacked the philosophers in a similar vein. Ferdausi, reviling "the philosopher who speaks in vain," asserts that he would never follow the path of philosophy.[36] Khaqani goes even further and in a bitter invective says that "philosophy is the quagmire of misguidance for you; nay, don't set foot in it." He concludes:

Do not lay the Greek brand [of philosophy] on the hips
of the noble Arabian steed of faith.
Do not put the lock of Aristotelean logic
at the door of the best nation.
Do not lay the worn out design of Plato
on the best cloth of brocade.[37]

Similarly, Sana'i, being a devout Muslim, was opposed to the liberal-minded adherents of the Greek school of thought. In one of his *qasides* he writes:

O vile-tempered philosopher, because of your indolence for praying,
How long will you debase yourself with Greek thought?
How long will you forsake the sincerity of Abu Bakr
And the wisdom of 'Ali for the ways of Pharaoh and Haman?
It is not wisdom to read philosophy to become perfect;
Wisdom is to have a soul yearning for the Prophet.[38]

The Shu'ubites were otherwise known as "Ahlal-Tasviye" (people of Equality), because they contended for the equality of all Muslims without regard to distinctions of race. They invoked the Koranic verse that said, "The most virtuous of you is the dearest to God,"[39] and the words of Mohammad, in his farewell speech, that "no Arab surpasses a non-Arab except by piety." At the beginning, the Shu'ubites defended all non-Arabs against the view that the Arabs enjoyed a unique and incomparable excellence because of their language and race. However, the movement later tended to become an expression of Persian nationalism. Some Persian poets writing in Arabic ended up boasting of their descent, culture, and language in a way that was similar to the Arabs. The Shu'ubiyya movement was also responsible for many vituperative poems. In this connection reference should be made to Bashshar ibn Burd (killed in 783); Ishaq Karami, the poet of the court of al-Mutawakkil; and Mahyar-e Dailami (d. 1051).

Bashshar's father, the descendant of a noble Persian family of Tokharistan, was brought as a slave to Iraq. Bashshar, who may have had leanings toward Zoroastrianism, did not conceal his strong national sentiments. A poet of great significance in Arabic literature, he gave new depth and originality to his poetry by combining his Persian cultural heritage with a talented use of Arabic. While revealing the wealth of his cultural heritage, he bitterly rebukes the "upstart" Arabs for their arrogance and pride. In the *Kitab-al-Aghani* we read that one day a Bedouin Arab meets Bashshar. Knowing that he is a non-Arab (*Mawli*), the Bedouin asks how Bashshar could write poetry. Bashshar becomes angry and recites the following poem extemporaneously:

> To the proud Arab, boasting of his descent,
>   I will tell who he is and who I am.
> Now that you have covered your nakedness with furs
>   and have become a companion to the nobles,
> O Shepherd's son, whose father knew nothing
>   but the herd, deceive not yourself.
> Remember the time when helpless with exhaustion,
>   you and your dog drank the water of a foul ditch.
> Now you demean the *Mawli*, and your debased [background]
>   does not allaow you to know him truly![40]

In another poem he writes:

> Is there no one to impart my words to all the Arabs?
> To those who live and those who rest under the ground?
> To say of what noble descent I come,
> My grandfather was Khosrow [Anushirvan],
> My father was Sasan, and my uncle the Caesar of Rome.
> What crowned forefathers did I have!
> The haughty warrior for whom everyone would kneel
> When walking to his glorious seat,
> Clad in sable robes.
> Seated behind the curtain, the attendants would
> Rush to him with cups of gold.
> He would never drink from the cups filled
> With milk of cow or camel.
> He would never drink such milk
> Drunk by the bedouins from small leather sacks.[41]

Bashshar, after depicting the hardships of the life of the nomadic Arabs, contrasts them with the culture and the life of the Sassanid Persians. He enumerates the glories of the Iranian race, among which are overthrowing the Umayyad dynasty and restoring power to the "Family of the Arabian Prophet."

The most outstanding example of the Shu'ubiyya movement in Persian poetry is to be found in Ferdausi's *Shah-Name*. Toward the end of the book, as he describes the fall of the House of Sassan, Ferdausi often cannot hide his deep sense of sorrow at the loss of past national glories:

> From drinking camel milk and eating lizards,
> The Arabs have advanced to such an extent
> That they lay claim to the throne of Iran.
> Curse be upon thee, O world, curse!

Satirical writings that were produced as a result of disagreement and animosity existing between various Islamic sects naturally should be mentioned here. The history of such conflicts in Iran is so elaborate and extensive that even a summary cannot be attempted. From the advent of Islam until the Mongol invasion, numerous sects sprang into being, such as Khawarij, Shi'ites, Mu'tazilis, Hululie, Mobayyeza, Muhamare, Hulmaniye, Keysanieye, Isma'ili-ye, Qarameteh, and Sunnites.[42] After the Mongol invasion, with a few exceptions, the more heretical sects disappeared, and the conflict was centered on the major sects of Islam. When in the sixteenth century the Safavid kings imposed Shi'ism on Iran, the old conflicts found new forms among the various schools of thought in Shi'ism. It was quite an imposition, as all the while a "hate triangle" among Sufis, fundamentalists, and philosophers continued. Sa'eb, a sixteenth-century poet who found no sense in sectarian feuds, summed up such hostiility::

> The talk of heresy and faith ends ultimately in one point.
> The faith is the same, each sect a different joint.[43]

Obviously, there was no end to religious pamphleteering, and a few examples will suffice. In 1177, during the Seljuq period, Shehab al-Din Tavarikhi, a convert from Shi'ism to Sunnite Shafe'ism, wrote a book whose translated title is *Some Audacities of the Shi'ites*, in which sixty-seven examples of their "audacities" are enumerated. He says, "Shi'ism is inspired by Zoroastrianism," and "it is the vestibule to heresy." 'Abdu'l-Jalil of Qazvin, one of the great Shi'ite preachers, answered him in a work entitled *Some Fallacies of the Sunnites on the Subject of Some Audacities of the Shi'ites*, which is commonly called *Kitab-al-Naqd*. 'Abdu'l-Jalil launches his polemics in an eloquent, witty, and sometimes satirical way. He bitterly criticizes the Sunnites, and especially the "Mushshabaha,"[44] and accusing them of a blind and illogical adherence to predestination and to the traditions of the Prophet. He regards them, in their ignorance, as the enemies of the household of the Prophet.

Of the numerous examples of intersectarian criticism mentioned above, only three have been translated, here two by Naser Khosrow and one by Sana'i. In the first poem, Naser Khosrow ridicules the four main Sunnite schools for their laxity in allowing the playing of chess, drinking of wine, taking of opium, and homosexuality, respectively:

> Shafe'i said: "Playing chess is not unlawful.
> Do not cheat for the Imam has ordered you to be truthful."
> But Hanifeh has even a better idea on wine:
> "If it's boiled, drink it, for it is not unlawful!"

The Hanbalites say: "If stricken with grief
Take bhang and stroll gaily!"
If you follow the fourth jurist, Malek,
He will prescribe for you cohabitation with a young boy!
Take bhang, drink wine, lie with fair ones and gamble,
Truly Islam has been perfected by these four Imams![45]

A second poem, apparently scoffing at the idea of resurrection, is in fact a criticism of the people who believe in the resurrection of the body rather than the soul:

Some luckless wretch wolves in the plain devour;
His bones are picked by vulture and by crow.
This casts his remnants on the hills above;
That voids its portion in the wells below.
Shall this man's body rise to life again?
Defile the beards of fools who fancy so![46]

Two centuries later Naser al-Din Tusi (1201-74), the great Shi'ite philosopher, theologian, and scientist, who as minister to Hulagu Khan was instrumental in bringing to an end the line of Isma'ili rulers in Iran, answered him in the following quatrain:

Shall this man's body rise to life again
When thus resolved to elements? I trow
God can remake as easily as make:
Defile the beard of Nasir-i-Khosrow![47]

And Sana'i illustrates in this poem the blind hatred existing between the Sunnites and Shi'ites:

Common folk were beating a Shi'ite out of hatred and for
the sake of faith.
A passer-by joined them and beat him even more severely.
I asked: "If they were beating him on account of his heresy
and beliefs,
Then why did you, cruel of heart, hurt him two hundred times
more? What was his crime?"
He said: "I have no idea of his crime. But I followed the
Sunnites and beat him for the reward of God!"[48]

III

In the third kind of religious satire the coreligionists of the satirist become his targets. Persian literature abounds with this kind of satire, and in a broader sense this category can be subdivided into criticism of the pretentiously religious and criticism of Sufis, whether by outsiders or by themselves. It is therefore necessary to discuss the social significance of the Sufi movement in Iran.

Although it is imposible to simplify a movement with a millennium of history behind it into a few major trends, it is nevertheless clear that one of the main

characteristics of Sufism was its censure of religious fanaticism as well as its tolerance of other creeds. The spirit of religious tolerance can be seen in many Persian
masterpieces of Sufi literature. Rumi (1207-73) in his *Mathnavi* equates ignorance
and fanaticism with inexperience and lack of understanding. He likens a person
with such qualities to an embryo, who is nourished only by blood before he
is born. In a parable God speaks to Moses, saying, "We behold the inner self
and the state of mind. Not the clamour and the outside."[49] Another wonderfully expressive story in the *Mathnavi*, by comparing them to human languages,
sums up the poet's ideas about warring sects. Four men—a Turk, a Persian, a
Greek, and an Arab—have some money, and all want to buy some grapes. They
are asking for the grapes in their own tongues, and because they cannot
understand one another, they are fighting bitterly. A man who knows all four
languages comes and puts a stop to their quarrel. Some Sufis even went so far
as to communicate with the Creator even through inanimate beings. Of course,
this is not to say that every Sufi enjoyed such a breadth of intellect or had
similarly tolerant attitudes toward other creeds. For some, fundamentalism and
traditionalism were of the highest importance. However, it is a significant fact
that in the Middle Ages and at the time of the Inquisition in Europe such
tolerance and breadth of view was relatively common among the Sufis.

Similarly, a symbolic vocabulary of a somewhat profane nature was yet another
sign of the defiance of sanctimony and pretension. The symbolism that starts
with 'Attar in Persian Sufi poetry makes use of words that were peculiar to pre-
Islamic Iran, Zoroastrianism, Christianity, and some other creeds: the temple
of the Magi, the cup of Jam, the Magi, his novice, the old man of the tavern,
the synagogue, monastery, churchbell, special Christian girdle (*zonnar*), Christian
boy, idol, idol-worshiper, wine, and drunkard. This kind of symbolism might
be related to *Shathiyyat*, a very interesting and significant word in Sufi terminology. It is an outwardly blasphemous expression whose inner meaning is in
accordance with the faith (*Shari'a*). *Shathiyyat* is often used for the expressions
uttered by the Sufis when they are in an ecstatic mood.[50] All of this means that
a Sufi does not content himself with the outward paraphernalia of the formal
religion, but rather that he strives for higher and more transcendental values.

The Sufi interpretations of the *Koran* and of the *hadith* (traditions of the
Prophet) were in many ways different from those of other Muslims. Similar
differences existed on many issues of secondary importance. For instance, *sema'*
(music and dance) was regarded as unlawful by the *Shari'a*, whereas many Sufis
looked upon it as a necessary means of elevating the soul and achieving the
desired state of mind or mood (*hal*) for worship. But the Sufis' main objection
was to those people who attached a great deal of importance to the outward
trappings of religion, forgetting about its essence. Though it may not be
universally so, it is true to say that most of the Sufis bitterly complained of hypocritical sheikhs and sanctimonious clerics.

In the *ghazals* of Hafez (d. 1389) a combination of mystical disdain for pretentious religiosity and social criticism is expressed in extremely subtle ways. In 1357

when Shah Abu Ishaq Inju, the liberal-minded and poetic patron of Hafez, was put to death, a totally different type of ruler followed him: Mobar'ez al-Din Mohammad was exceedingly cruel, and his narrow-minded asceticism was exactly what Hafez most hated in his contemporaries. Mobar'ez al-Din had no sooner taken possession of Shiraz than he closed all the taverns and won the title of *mohtaseb* ("chief of police" or "the constable" in Browne's translation) from the wits of Shiraz as well. Hafez refers to those days of oppressive restrictions in one of his *ghazals*:

> Though wine gives delight and the wind distills
>   the perfume of the rose,
> Drink not wine to the strains of the harp,
>   for the constable [*mohtaseb*] is alert.
> Hide the goblet in the sleeve of the patch-work cloak,
> For the time, like the eye of the decanter, pours forth
>   blood.
> Wash the wine-stain from your dervish-cloak with tears,
> For it is the season of piety and the time of abstinence.[51]

Looking back with nostalgia at earlier years, Hafez hopes that at least asceticism will not be synonymous with hypocrisy:

> They have closed the doors of the wine-taverns; O God, suffer not
> That they should open the doors of the house of deceit and
>   hypocrisy!
> If they have closed them for the sake of the heart of the
>   self-righteous zealot,
> Be of good heart, for they will reopen them for God's sake![52]

In another piece the poet directly addresses the preachers:

> The preachers who on the pulpit such righteousness display,
> When in private many other things they maintain.
> I have a question to the scholar on his studies bent
> Why those preaching repentance, seldom repent?
> As if they do not believe in the Judgment Day
> That in the work of God they cheat and play.[53]

At the time Hafez was writing, however, most of the Sufis had long since lost the purity and sincerity of their early predecessors. As with any other movement, Sufism lost, with time some of its altruistic aspects. Sufi masters began to appear who greatly valued their venerated position in society. The number of martyrs such as Hallaj or Sohravardi who died for their ideas dwindled, and the persecution of the Sufis by the zealots considerably lessened. In the time of Hafez, of course, as in all ages, true and false Sufis existed side by side, and it is to the latter group that his criticisms were directed. At the beginning of a famous *ghazal* he scoffs at the hypocritical Sufi who has become a common trickster instead of trying to learn about the secrets of the "Unseen":

> The Sufi has laid his trap and opened up his kit;
> He has begun his schemings with the juggling heavens.
> The play of the wheel will break the egg in his hat,
> For he has offered trickery to the people of the secret.[54]

In another line Hafez censures the Sufis who put on their special cloaks (*'khirqas*) but are unable to exorcize the demon of selfishness from their souls:

> God disdains this cloak a hundred times
> That in each sleeve lodges a hundred idols![55]

Even poets more devoted to Sufism than Hafez often criticized the ways of some of their less-truthful brethren. Rumi, who calls them "time-servers,"[56] includes several stories about their greed in the *Mathnavi*.[57] Jami (1414-92) in his *Selselatu'l-Zahab* (Chain of gold) relates a humorous story entitled "In Criticism of Pretenders to Sufism Who Forsake the Essence and Stick to the Outward Show." He describes a homosexual sheikh who enthusiastically greets a young and handsome novice in the hope of fulfilling his lewd desire under the garb of spiritualism.[58] Another delightful satirical picture in the same work describes the sudden arrival of a certain emir to the monastery (*Khaneqah*) of a sheikh. As soon as the news is whispered to the sheikh the scene changes. He and his disciples create a scene of incredible ecstasy: one weeps loudly, the other chants an incantation, and a third beats himself senseless and falls to the ground at the feet of the emir.[59]

'Obeyd-e Zakani (d. 1371), the greatest satirist of Iran, has his own views on both Sufis and the zealots. In two hilariously ridiculous letters he parodies the style of two Sufis writing to each other.[60] His *Resale-ye Delgosha* has many humorous anecdotes on the two groups. Someone asks a preacher to define Islam. He replies, "I am a preacher. I have nothing to do with Islam!"[61] Zakani's "Definitions" on the subject are pertinently witty:

The Sheikh:	Devil.
The Devils:	His followers.
Hypocrisy:	What he says about the world.
Temptation:	What he preaches about the world to come.
Nonsense:	What he says about philosophy.
The Sufi:	A freeloader.
Bhang:	That which fills the Sufi with ecstasy.
The Haji:	One who swears falsely by the Ka'ba.[62]

'Obeyd contends that many believers, who have no real respect for it, use religion as a means of amassing wealth. He divides society into two groups: first, the common people who "have suffered so much from hunger and oppression that they remember neither God nor the Prophet";[63] second, the rich and powerful who indulge so much in pleasure that they hardly think of religion. 'Obeyd in his *Ethics of Aristocrats* has a section on the beliefs of the great men of his age, which are in sharp contrast with those of the past:

The Adopted Principle

When the great and sagacious men, whose existence honors the face of the earth, thought a great deal on the human soul, its origin and destiny, and weighed the beliefs and habits of the great men of the past, they ultimately rejected the body of these beliefs. They say: "It has been revealed to us that the rational soul has no value by itself and that its existence is dependent upon the body's existence and its extinction upon the body's destruction." They also maintain: "What the prophets have said concerning the rational soul, that it never diminishes or increases, and that after departure from the body it will subsist through its own essence, is impossible. Likewise the idea of resurrection is an absurd supposition. Life is the outcome of the harmony of bodily elements, and when the body decays the man is destroyed forever. What are considered to be the joys of Heaven and the sufferings of Hell exist in this world. As the poet says:

> He who has been given, has been given here,
> He who has been given naught,
> "Tomorrow" they've declared his lot.[64]

So their minds are necessarily quite undisturbed by the revival and resurrection, future ordeal and punishment, closeness or distance [from God], Divine wrath or favor, perfection or imperfection; and as a result of such convictions they would spend their lives in seeking after lust and sensual delights. They say:

> You who result from four and seven[65]
> And suffer from seven and four,
> Drink wine for I've told you thousands of times,
> There is no return, when you're gone, you're no more.[66]

They often have the following quatrain inscribed upon the coffin of their forefathers:

> Beyond this rotary vault, there is no arch or mansion.
> Except for you and I none has wisdom and perception.
> You that have thought in nothingness is something,
> There is nothing in it; you this thought must shun.[67]

And it is because of this belief that they do not have the least consideration for the life, property, and honor of the people:

> For him a cup of fire-colored wine
> Is dearer than the blood of one hundred brothers.

Indeed they are great masters of success, and what was veiled and hidden for many thousands of years in spite of men's purification of the intellect and soul, was easily revealed to them.[68]

The emergence of the Safavid dynasty at the beginning of the sixteenth century was not only a turning point in the political history of Iran, but was also extremely important in the religious history of that country. Shah Esmaʻil (1487-1523), a young Sufi leader whose fanatical followers almost worshiped him, created a theocracy in which Shi'ism became the source of nationalism in Iran. He ruthlessly persecuted the believers of other Muslim sects and created a predominantly Shi'ite state, which was in fact an island in the sea of Sunnite Islam. Strangely enough, although the old Persian empire was revived approximately within its old boundaries after almost eight and a half centuries, it was religion more than language and race that accounted for this new sense of nationalism.[69]

The Safavi kings, by reason of their political aims and strong antagonism toward the Ottoman sultans, greatly encouraged the propagation of the Shi'a doctrine and its principles. It was the age of great theologians and divines rather than outstanding poets and mystics. Strangely enough, even though the Safavids were the descendants of a great Sufi, they "employed every kind of severity and vexation, whether exile, expulsion, slaughter, or reprimand, slaying or burning many [Sufis] with their own hands or by their sentence."[70] The Safavi kings preferred that the poets write panegyrics to the Prophet and the Imams instead of writing qasides about the kings. The result of this dire religiosity was that many poets left for the courts of Delhi or Istanbul, and most of the Sufi khaneqahs were closed. In the place of poets, philosophers, and Sufis there arose theologians who, despite their intellectual abilities, were harsh, dry, and fanatical.

It is obvious that in an age of overriding preoccupation with religion, clerical hypocrisy could not be absent. Though there are occasional satirical pieces on the subject in the Safavid period, the number of such works considerably increases during the Qajar period, and more particularly toward the end of the nineteenth and beginning of the twentieth centuries. Sa'eb of Isfahan (d. 1669 or 1670), who after spending some time in India became the poet laureate of Shah Abbas II, was an outspoken poet. Though one of the greatest poets of the period, he is mostly known and remembered for his tak-beits, or couplets, some of which have become proverbs. The following two examples dwell on the appearance of the pretentious clergy (often the favorite butt of satirists):

> If hugeness of turban is an indication of learning
> The dome of the Shah's Mosque would be the greatest of scholars.
>
> Let not, O Sa'eb, the ascetic's turban pass with you for learning,
> For, as in a dome, hollowness of the head creates much echo.[71]

Religious satire sometimes is to be found in the most unlikely places. Mohammad Hashem Asef wrote a history entitled Rostam al-Tavarikh, which begins with the last years of the Safavid dynasty and ends at the time of Karim Khan, who died in 1779. The whole work is a wonderfully satirical and at the same time quite realistic sketch of the history of this period. It has many passages that depict the hypocrisy and greed of the clergy serving the kings, a topic to be discussed at some length in the following chapter.

Celebrations of Muharram and mourning for the death of Imam Hosain, the grandson of the Prophet, who was martyred with many of his family and followers in Kerbela, were part of the Shi'ite tradition, celebrations which continued to be practiced in Iran. But if commemorations were not celebrated with sincerity and devotion, they provided a suitable topic for the satirist. E. G. Browne quotes a passage from a curious little book by Turki of Shiraz entitled *Kitab al-Sufra fi zammi al-Riya* (The book of the table, censuring hypocrisy) "in which the ostentation of the host and the greed of the guests is satirized with some pungency":

> Now hear from me a story which is more brightly coloured
>   than a garden flower,
> Of those who make mourning for Hosain and sit in assemblies
>   in frenzied excitement.
> . . . .
>
> In every corner they prepare a feast and arrange a pleasant
>   assembly;
> They carpet court-yard and chamber, they bedeck with
>   inscriptions arch and alcove;
> They spread fair carpets, they set out graceful furnishings;
> A host of gluttonous men, all beside themselves and
>   intoxicated with the cup of greed,
> On whom gold has produced such an effect that,
>   like the stamp on the gold,
> It has set its mark on their foreheads, making enquiry about
>   such assemblies.
> One of them says, "O comrades, well-approved friends,
>   versed in affairs,
> I and Hajji 'Abbas went yesterday to the entertainment of
>   that green-grocer fellow.
> In that modest entertainment there was nothing but tea
>   and coffee,
> And we saw no one there except the host and one or two
>   *rawza-khwans*.[72]
> To sit in such an assembly is not meet, for without sugar and
>   tea it has no charm.
> God is not pleased with that servant in whose entertainment
>   is neither sherbet nor sugar.
> But, by Him who gives men and *jinn* their daily bread,
>   in such-and-such a place is an entertainment worthy of kings,
> A wonderfully pleasant and comfortable entertainment, which,
>   I am sure, is devoid of hypocrisy.
> There is white tea and sugar-loaf of Yazd in place of sugar,
> And crystal *qalyans* with flexible tubes, at the gargle of which
>   the heart rejoices.
> The fragrance of their tobacco spreads for miles, and the fire
>   gleams on their heads like [the star] Canopus.
> No water will be drunk there, but draughts of
>   lemon, sugar and snow.
> One of the reciters is Mirza Kashi, who, they say,
>   is the chief of *rawza-khwans*.
> Another of them is the rhapsodist of Rasht,

who is like a boat in the ocean of song.
From Kirman, Yazd and Kirmanshah, from Shiraz,
  Shushtar and Isfahan,
All are skilled musicians of melodious and charming voices:
  they are like the kernel and others like the shell.
In truth it is a wonderful entertainment, devoid of hypocrisy:
  by your life it is right to attend it!"
When the friends hear this speech with one accord
  they assemble at that banquet.[73]

Yaghma of Jandaq (1782-1859), who is chiefly known for his abusive and obscene verses, was not on good terms with fanatical clerics. Once fearing for his life and facing excommunication by a powerful clergyman, Mulla Ahmad Naraqi, he vowed to be a devout Muslim. But his repentance was nothing but pretension. He writes:

By pretending Islam I saved my neck from the Sheikh of the city;
What could I do but show tolerance with such an infidel?[74]

In another poem Yaghma describes a dream in which he sees Imam Hosain complaining about a notorious mulla:

I saw in a dream the martyr of Kerbela
Whose tears poured forth in profusion.
I said: "O master, in whose grief
Every eye will weep till the Day of Judgement,
We cry for your sake,
But why are your eyes scattering pearls?
Is Ibn Ziyad[75] again in arms against you
Or the wicked Shemr[76] in your pursuit?"
He said: "I am not complaining of the foes,
My days are darkened by the friends.
Particularly, an ass who kicks and brays
In assemblies every morn and night.
From pulpit to pulpit he continues
To humiliate the House of the Prophet.
He follows my poor family
Like a plunderer after the booty;
Now placing them in Kufa, and now in Syria.
Sometimes he says that 'Abedin[77] is a slave
And sometimes he claims that Fateme[78] is a bondsmaid.
His hatred against us is as deep-rooted
As the fight between Russia and England."
. . . .

I asked: "May I be your sacrifice,
Who is that wretch to tyrannize you so much?
The son of what whore is he?
What lecher has sired this cuckold?
What is his name and what his profession?"
The Imam heaved a deep sigh and said:
"He is Mulla Hasan, the pea-roaster!"[79]

One of the most remarkable pieces of satire on hypocritical clerics is written by Qa'ani (d. 1853 or 1854), a famous poet of nineteenth-century Iran. Qa'ani, who shared the views of Yaghma on hypocritical clerics, in an incredibly vivid description pictures a preacher who comes to a mosque to perform the Friday prayer. His appearance is deceivingly impressive, but his sermon, and particularly his similes, are absurd and far-fetched:

> Yesterday a preacher came to the Friday Mosque,
> Whose garments were all snow white from head to toe.
> A yellow rosary he had in hand of the Holy Clay,
> And a *mohr*[80] for prostration heavily made of the same.
> The sleeves of his robe were protruding left and right
> Like an elephant who brandishes his tusks.
> The tail of his turban rested upon his shoulder
> Like the extending horizons under the dome of the sky.
> On his forehead a scar was left by cupping,[81]
> Though he proudly passed it for a sign of prostration.
> As for his eyes, one was watching the right, the other the left
> To see who was greeting him from the rich or poor.
> Like a tight-rope walker he moved
> With dignity, harmony, and grace.
> Coming into the public view, he renewed his ablution
> In full accordance with the Shi'ite formula.
> From the pond he rinsed his mouth and washed his hands,
> To such an extent that I cannot do justice to full details.
> Then he went to the first row at the gallery of prayers
> To recite the *Koran* and shake and wave his head.
> Hardly had the public prayer come to an end
> When like a monkey to the pulpit he jumped.
> Then with his head, beard, nose and lips
> Many coquettish gestures he displayed, and thus his sermon
>   began:
> "O folk! Who has sharpened the spikes of the thorn?
> Who has made the dung of goats so round on the road?
> Who has given that heavy mace to the poppy?
> Who has fashioned the stature of the pine tree so comely?
> To the neck of the tulip who has fixed ruby buttons?
> To the head of the narcissus who has placed a saffron fringe?
> In short, be scared of the Day of Reckoning
> And seek to learn of the horrors of that day,
> Those scorpions and snakes whose dreadful stings
> Are sharper than spears and swords.
> That fiery mace which beats the sinner down
> In the hands of the angels who come to the grave."
> The audience wept because of that horrifying sermon;
> Whereas I laughed and laughed with a flushing face.
> But my laughter was for the sake of God;
> Because that sermon was all lies and hypocrisy.[82]

The Constitutional Revolution at the turn of the century brought a new flourishing of religious satire. A new age of freedom was ushered in, with the writers and poets feeling an obligation to reform their readers. In this way politics and social problems dominated Persian poetry. One has to search for such poems in the poetical works of the earlier periods, whereas the poems of the Constitutional period were rarely otherwise. The growing familiarity with western democracy and a sense of admiration for the advances of the West, combined with the advent of journalism in Iran had brought about a great change in Persian literature, of which satire was only one aspect.

Iranian clergy greatly contributed to the Constitutional Revolution. Some, like Jamal al-Din Esfahani and Theqat'ul-Eslam, died for the cause of freedom, and others, such as Mulla Kazem Khorasani, Seyyed Mohammad Tabataba'i, and Malek al-Motakallemin were considered to be the bulwarks of the movement. There were, however, some reactionary clerics, such as Sheikh Fazl 'ul-Allah Nuri and Mir Hashem Davachi, who looked upon the whole movement with suspicion and called it a "heresy." Such men, as well as many fanatical and superstitious Muslims, not only opposed a new parliamentary system, but also opposed any change that questioned their old values. This extended to many other domains such as the system of education, hygiene, the emancipation of women, and the publishing of newspapers. Naturally such men became the subjects of bitter satire by many poets and writers.

Some of the religious satire written in the period immediately before the Constitutional Revolution falls into the category of socio-political satire, which is discussed in later chapters. Here we will concentrate on religious satire from the turn of the century onward, discussing first the Azerbaijani poet, Saber, who exercised a great influence on Iranian satirists. Ali Akbar Saber (Taherzade) (1862-1911) was born into a typically religious family in Shamakhi and suffered at the hands of fanatical Muslims early in his life. Saber draws a very humorous and true-to-life picture of his contemporaries, bringing into focus a great number of ridiculous religious and superstitious beliefs. The satirical poems of Saber, mostly published in the journal *Mulla Nasr al-Din*, angered many dignitaries and clergy. Mohammad 'Ali Mirza, when he was the crown prince and resided in Tabriz, was so irritated by the criticism of the paper that he ordered its issues to be confiscated at the border. Some clergymen of Tabriz, as well as others in Najaf called it a "misleading paper," and others even regarded its "heretical" writings as more dangerous than the "sword of Shemr" (the murderer of Imam Hosain). Jalil Mamad Qoli-zade, the editor of the paper, had to find lodging in the Georgian quarter of Baku out of fear of the fanatics. Saber in one of his famous poems addresses himself to his fellow-citizens, saying that he is a true believer in God and the Prophet. But he pointedly adds that his Islam, or his Sufism is very different than theirs in that it lacks the trappings of superstition and demagogy.

Saber has no objections to Islam, but he opposes the superstitions, hypocrisy, and sanctimony that have destroyed its image as a benign and tolerant religion. In the following poem he gives an account of the beliefs of a fanatic who is opposed to modern ways of life and who does not even care for a religious morality. It is entitled "Questions and Answers":

> "My friend, in what state is your glorious city today?"
> "God be blessed, it's the same as it was in Noah's day."
> "Have you new schools for the young of your country to learn in?"
> "No, we've only Madrassahs, which stand since the year Adam was
>   born in."
> "Do the citizens in your land read newspapers every day?"
> "Some literate madmen do, but I don't, I must say."
> "Now tell me, my friend, are there libraries in your town?"
> "Young people opened a few, but we turned them upside down."
> "Are the hungry helped in your country by other men?"
> "God sees their sufferings himself—why should we help
>   them, then?"
> "Do you take care of widows and women. that are in need?"
> "To the devil with them—can't they marry again, indeed?"
> "Is the need for unity talked about in your land?"
> "Yes, it is, but for eloquence's sake, you must understand."
> "Is the nation split into Shi'ites and Sunnites still?"
> "What do you mean? For such words, young man, you ought to be
>   killed."
> "Well, there is nothing else I can say to you, so good-bye."
> "Good riddance! I wish you to fall in a pit and die!
> Just look at him! Look at his face—what a loathsome sight!
> The way he talks! Why, he can't even put his cap on right!"

In another poem a father is introduced who is opposed to the western style
of education, imagining it will endanger the principles of Islamic faith:

> If the child is mine, I don't want him in school;
> Leave me alone, don't trouble me anymore!
> Though the poor wretch is eager to be learned;
> He tries hard to be accomplished and informed,
> But all this is the manner of the infidel
> It is harmful to the Faith, I don't want him in school!
>
> He is too young to distinguish between good and evil
> He does not know that education is to no avail.
> Like other kids he is not beguiled with nice words
> He wastes his life, I don't want him in school.
> Leave me alone, don't trouble me anymore![84]

In the world that Saber depicts it seems that no sense logic exist, that vanity
and selfishness prevail. Superstitious beliefs have become religious convictions.
For instance, when anyone sneezes once or any odd number of times, any
undertaking decided upon at that moment is doomed to fail. In a poem entitled
"The Odd Sneeze"[85] this leads to the most ridiculous situations. In another
poem a religious zealot is glad that the newspapers have been closed down so
that he will not hear the chatterings of the "heretics" anymore.[86] In still
another poem a wealthy Hajji slaughters a sheep on the Feast of Sacrifices[87] in
order to give away the meat as alms. He puts aside a big chunk of meat plus

the sheep's head, legs, heart, and liver to be used in his own household and sends the other parts to his brothers and sisters on various pretexts. He does not even want to give the sheep's skin to the school so that the students can have something to sit on. Although the poor avidly watch the scene, they only get the most useless parts as alms.[88]

Ashraf Gilani has translated or adapted most of the poems of Saber into Persian and published them along with many other satirical poems in his journal, Nasīm-e Shomal. In a poem which is a close imitation of Saber, Ashraf describes one of the ulema who looks back with nostalgia to bygone times when their "wise sayings" were rules; no one opposed them, nor was there any sign of revolt. But now everyone has become a heretic, a Babi, or a Constitutionalist, with no regard for the clerics. Throughout the poem he reiterates:

> What a wonderful time had we!
> What good company and rules had we![89]

This recalls a similar refrain in Saber's poem:

> What a wonderful time was it
> When the people of the country were all ignorant.[90]

Ashraf Gilani in one of his poems shows his great admiration for the advancement of the West and criticizes the conservatives at home who are untouched by the spirit of the twentieth century. Clearly, this poem, written in the earlier decades of the century, is in sharp contrast to the present prevailing anti-West feelings in Iran:

> O Ferangi,[91] we are Muslims, heaven is for us;
> In the world to come, rest and ease, Houris and Peris[92] are for us.
> O Ferangi, unity, science and industry are yours;
> The means of empire, war and strife are yours;
> But envy, greed, hatred, resentment and enmity are ours;
> Sound sleep, pleasure, rest and ease—these are ours.
>
> O Ferangi, all those beautiful buildings are yours;
> The opening of factories and marvellous inventions are yours;
> Writing politely with words well-chosen are yours;
> Misplaced ignorance, hue and cry, abuse and slander are ours;
> Sound sleep, pleasure, rest and ease—these are ours.
> . . . .
> O Ferangi, men of war on the sea are yours;
> Railroads and fast-traveling on the land are yours;
> Flying in zeppelins in the sky are yours;
> On the earth indolence, ignorance and misery are ours;
> Sound sleep, pleasure, rest and ease—these are ours.
> . . . .
> Sheikhi[93] and Babi belong to us, Peter the Great and Napoleon
>   to you;
> Dahri[94] and Sufi belong to us, schools and laws to you;

Robes and turbans are for us, airplanes and ships are for you;
Get lost O foolish man! Illusion belongs to you, truth to us;
The garden of Paradise, Houris and Peris, rest and ease are for us.

I have heard that Hosein the knight of Kurdistan,[95]
Departed from Isfahan and conquered Hindustan.
How could Europe have heroes great like him?
Rostam and Gudarz[96] the valiant *Pahlavans*[97] are ours;
Sound sleep, pleasure, rest and ease—are all ours.

Though outwardly Muslims, inwardly infidels we are;
Deniers of the truth, enemies of the faith and forgetful of the
    world to come.
We consume endowed property as if it were mother's milk for us.
Talk of magic signs and sessions with the clergy are ours;
The garden of Paradise, Houris and Peris, rest and ease are ours.[98]

One of Ashraf's contemporaries was 'Ali Akbar Dehkhoda (1879-1955), whose pungent essays opened a new chapter in Persian satire from the point of view of style and technique. Dehkhoda wrote about such social problems as drug addiction, ignorance, superstition, the hoarding of wheat, and corrupt and tyrannical officials. In his later essays he vehemently attacked the sanctimonious clerics whose influence and practices brought Islam into decline. Being so critical of the backwardness of the Muslims and holding some *ulema* responsible was a dangerous task requiring uncommon courage. In one essay he wrote:

> If you tell an Iranian Muslim, "O man of faith, wipe your nose or clean up your ears. . . ," even such simple things will be hard for him to do. But if you suggest, "O Seyyed, turn into a prophet; Your Excellency the Sheikh, become an Imam; Your Reverence the Hujjatul-Islam, become a vicegerent to the Imam," looking at you in amazement, immediately our master will assume a sad mood, his voice will become soft as a whisper and he will pretend that his chest has become a target for the shafts of mischief-makers and dissidents of our time or of those from whom the truth has been veiled. All the particles of his being are now ready to receive the revelation, except that at first he hears a voice as soft as the treading of an ant or the buzzing of a bee, but in a few days time he sees [the angel] Gabriel in all his celestial glory!
>
> Strange to say, though the advantages of Islam are as clear as the daylight to all of the world, and though there are many explicit Koranic verses and revealing traditions putting an end to the line of Prophets and announcing the cessation of revelations, and though believing in these is part of our faith, yet all these apocryphal prophets, false Imams, and lying vicegerents leave the whole world aside and choose to bless only the land of Iran, which is the center of Islam with their existence. . . .[99]

Dehkhoda then goes on to describe how in the past few decades numerous men have claimed to be the vicegerents to the hidden Imam and, announcing their imminent Messiahlike appearance, have given themselves incredible titles such as "Eternal Beauty," "The First Point," and "Pre-Eternal Morning." Nowhere in the "mountains of America"[100] or the "villages of Europe" are such men suffered to appear, nor does their nonsense find such wide currency. Dehkhoda maintains that lack of proper public education on religious matters combined with the ambition, love of position, and greed of some of the *ulema* are responsible for the decline of Islam.

This essay created such a furor of protest from the clerics that Dehkhoda had to write another one[101] to defend his point of view. This letter, which does not have a satirical tone, is purposefully written in a ponderous and scholarly style, and it displays his extensive knowledge of Islamic theology and tradition. Although Dehkhoda managed to escape the wrath of the faithful, he did not stop criticizing them. In several of his poems he returns to the subject of religious pretension. "Perhaps It Is a Cat," in language full of detailed mannerism, describes an old zealot coming from the public bath early one morning, when in the dim light the hem of his robe suddenly touches a stray dog. Knowing that from the touch of this unclean animal one needs cleansing and ablution, he keeps on insisting to himself, "Surely it was a cat!"[102]

An even more strained relation existed between Iraj Mirza (1874-1925) and some of the clerics of his time. Indeed, several times because of his satirical verses on the clergy and other controversial subjects his life was endangered and his *Divan* proscribed. Furthermore, he was considered to be a freethinker, and, upon his death, was denied burial in a Muslim cemetary.[103] Iraj Mirza, who is essentially a satirical poet, covers a wide range of social probblems in simple and witty diction that comes very close to ordinary speech. The emancipation of women, hypocrisy of the clerics and statesmen, self-flagellation, and the inflicting of wounds upon oneself in Muharram processions are among the most-discussed topics in his *Divan:*

> On the portal of a caravanserai
> A fresco painting of a woman was on display.
> The turbaned scholars heard the news
> From a source trustworthy and true.
> They exclaimed: "Woe to the faith!
> Men have seen a female face unveiled."
> Faith and peace were fleeing fast
> Like lightning when the faithful arrived.
> One fetched some soil and the other water;
> They fashioned for her a veil of clay.
> Chastity which was going with the wind
> Was saved only with a handful of dust.
> When the religion of the Prophet
> Was out of danger, they went home and slept in peace.
> Due to this negligence of great magnitude
> The savage folk were restive as roaring lions.
> They would have torn the garb of chastity
> Of that woman unveiled and open-faced.
> Her lovely lips they would suck
> Delightfully like sugar candies.
> In short the population of the whole city
> Would be drowned in the sea of sin.

The gates to heaven would be closed
Everyone would be packed to hell.

. . . .

This is why in the eyes of God and men
So honored are the students of the faith.
With scholars great as these
Of the country's progress why should we despair?[104]

Iraj was one of the most outspoken critics of the clergy's misuse of power. Many of his contemporaries shared his views and expressed them to various degrees also. We should bring this chapter to a conclusion by mentioning two very different figures in modern Persian history: Malek ul-Sho'ara Bahar, a poet of great satirical talent, and Dr. 'Ali Shari'ati, a revolutionary writer on the subject of Islam, who occasionally took issue with the more rigid views of the *ulema.*

Bahar (1886-1951), the most eminent poet of his time, combined a classical style with a responsiveness to contemporary thought and problems. He touches on most of the topics that concerned Iraj, though his diction is much more polite and restrained, and he is not at all a freethinker. Bahar is a Muslim intellectual who deplores superstition and hypocrisy replacing the high ideals of Islam. Being a great defender of the cause of freedom and justice, he writes, "Imam Hosain died to defend his just cause, and to set an example for you in the struggle against tyrants. Having expectations from the Sheikh and Mulla of the town is a fruitless hope, prepare yourself for the fight. Why are you beating your head with a sword? Brandish it against the enemy and revive yourself."[105] He repeats the same idea in a poem whose title has a double meaning. "Man Bakiam" means "I am weeping" as well as "With whom am I talking?" The poem, which was written on the occasion of the mourning processions in the month of Muharram, takes note of the fact that everyone is weeping in memory of the tragic death of Hosain in Kerbela. At the same time it questions the value of such ridiculous acts as self-flagellation and the infliction of wounds upon oneself:

One group of Iranians are faithless rogues and thieves;
And the other beat themselves and cut themselves, I am weeping.
I say strike the neck of the tyrant with this sword,
But Satan says cut yourself with it; with whom am I talking?[106]

In another poem entitled "Hell," Bahar gives a terrifying and yet humorous account of hell as imagined by religious zealots. According to them, interestingly enough, out of the whole population of the world, only Shi'ites enjoy the possibility of going to heaven; of those only a very few chosen Shi'ites indeed:

Except for the *ulema,* that fiery abyss
Will engulf the rest of the world.
Except for the Shi'ite, whoever believes
In God will be lodged in hell.
And among the Shi'ite, whoever is dressed
In Western attire, and has a tie,

His silk-soft body will roast in fire.
One who works for the state,
His soul   will be consumed behind his desk in hell
One who is elected and talks of the Constitution,
On the day of reckoning in hell will hold office.[107]

During the Pahlavi era the power of the clergy underwent a transformation.
The dictatorial regimes of Reza Shah and his son greatly curtailed clerical power,
and as the westernization of Iran persisted, there was less reason to blame the
clergy for social problems for which they had no blame. Though the satirical
writings on sanctimony and similar matters continued, especially in the novels
of Hedayat and Jamal Zade, the government rather than the clergy was held
responsible for the shortcomings. Furthermore, in the last few years of struggle
for the revolution, the *ulema* attained a leading role in the movement of the
Iranian people. This caused the memory of many corrupt clergy who had mis-
used their authority to be tarnished. During the revolution in Iran Islam became
a rallying point for various political groups that eventually ousted the shah. As
Iran became a theocratic state, the hope of establishing a true democracy faded
for many intellectuals, and once again the bigotry and corruption of the clerics
became the most salient topics for Iranian satirists. This will be discussed in a
latter chapter. Here one more example should be given which belongs to pre-
revolution Iran.

Dr. 'Ali Shari'ati (1934-1977) was one of the leading exponents of Islamic revolt
in Iran. His short satirical piece belongs to the third category discussed in the
present chapter, and his point of view is interesting since Shari'ati is opposed
to excessive westernization on the one hand, and to a rigid fundamentalism on
the other.

Dr. Shari'ati, a Sorbonne-educated sociologist who spent more than a year
in the shah's jails, more than anyone else was responsible for propagating Islamic
tenets among the Iranian youth. A prolific writer, he preached a tolerant and
progressive Islam, and he often clashed with the views of the traditionalists. He
was not a satirist, but he very often criticized those whom he thought failed
to carry out their social responsibilities.[108] He gave fresh and often liberal
interpretations to various Islamic tenets, and hence he found several rigid clerics
opposing him. A certain Mulla Hosaini Milani wrote a book, whose title in
translation is *What the Doctor Says* in which he bitterly criticized Shari'ati for
saying, among other things, that music is not forbidden in Islam. At one point
Shari'ati had expressed his dismay at the fact that during the pilgrimage to Mecca
each Muslim sacrifices one sheep, and that the number of the slaughtered animals
is so great that the carcasses are buried by bulldozers, without being properly
packed and utilized. Al-Hosaini al-Milani had answered that sacrificial meat could
not be given to just anyone, and particularly not to those Sudanese whose
forefathers had sung and danced in the mosque of the Prophet during his lifetime.
Here is a passage from Shari'ati's answer:

I am thankful to his Eminence Al-Hosaini al-Milani for both answering me and providing me with the reason and origin of this theological judgments (i.e. those of Christian Bustani and the Sunnite Bukhari and Muslim!).[109] Firstly, he states that since some Sudanese were thieves and played music, Shi'ites can give their sacrificial meat to heretics or bury it in the ground rather than give it to the Sudanese. Secondly, because fourteen hundred years ago some Sudanese artists used to frequent the Prophet's Mosque in Medina and entertain the Prophet and his wife, today Sudanese people should be punished! Thirdly, the Shi'ite Hajji who sacrifices a sheep in Mecca should carry out a historical research, concerning the starving black who has come to get some of the meat for his wife and children, in order to find out the latter's relationship to the minstrels who sang and danced fourteen centuries earlier in the Mosque of the Prophet and are mentioned in the Encyclopedia of al-Bustani. If by means of historical documents and established proof, and through biographies and genealogies . . . this poor starving wretch proved to the Iranian Hajji that he has not descended from them, then he will be allowed to cut a piece from the carcass of the sheep. . . . But if the evidence was not enough, or it proved that he is one of the descendants of the Sudanese minstrels, then he should be driven away. He is worse than a heretic and an unbeliever, and for the sake of this unforgivable sin he and all his should die of hunger!

Of course, my problem is solved, and at that in a very philosophical way! However, there is another problem. If a sin is so horrendous that the whole race of the sinner is condemned by a theological judgment forever, and becomes a race of pariahs . . . how is it that in the age of the Prophet, nay in the very Mosque of the Prophet, it took place? And, not only did the Prophet not drive them away, nor did he stop their action which took place openly, but rather, taking his wife on his shoulders,[110] he went and listened to the music of the Sudanese. If I, under any circumstances and for any motivation, had quoted this story from Bukhari or Muslim, what would the learned Mr. al-Hosaini al-Milani have done to me? He would have accused me of being a Sunnite, a propagator of dancing in Islam, and he would say that I have no respect for His Holiness the Prophet and his Mosque, which was the place of divine revelation. And he would say that according to me the Prophet of Islam was shouldering his wife like a hippie of the new wave and went to listen to and watch a musical and dance program. God be praised that I did not quote this, but rather that it is quoted by the learned Mr. al-Hosaini al-Milani, the great religious personality, and that it is quoted as a historical and rational proof of the judgment of the Shi'ite clerics.[111]

Notes

1. Quoted in Sa'id Nafisi, *Pur-e Sina* Tehran: Danish, 1955), p. 162.
2. Sa'di, *Gulestan*, ed. M. J. Mashkur(Tehran, 1965), p. 83
3. See Badia' al-Zaman Foruzanfar's article on the relationship of Omar and Abu'l-'Ala in *Majalle-ye Daneshkade-ye Adabiyyat-e Tabriz*, numbers 8 and 9,   1948, pp. 1-29.
4. *The Quatrains of Omar Khayyam*, p. 194.
5. Ibid., p. 74. Cf. FitzGerald's *Rubaiyyat*, 2d ed., 13.
6. Ibid., p. 62.
7. Ibid., p. 206.

8. Ibid., p. 96.

9. Jalal Homa'i, *Tarab-Khane*, ed. Yar Ahmad Tabrizi (Tehran: Anjuman-e Athar-e Melli, 1963).

10. *Quatrains of Khayyam*, p. 226.

11. Hafez, *Divan*, ed. Abu'l-Qasem Anjavi Shirazi (Tehran, 1967), p. 145.

12. Khayyam, *Algebra*, ed. Gholam-Hosain Mosaheb (Tehran: Anjuman-e Athar-e Melli, 1938), introduction.

13. One of the most reliable MS is that of the Bodleian Library (dating from the fifteenth century), which has 158 *ruba'is* and was one of the main sources of FitzGerald. The discovery and purchase of two seemingly very old MMS by Chester Beatty and Cambridge Libaries in the 1940s created a sensation among Omarian scholars, but eventually both copies proved to be forgeries. A recent carbon-14 test on the Cambridge MS showed it to have been fabricated within the last century.

14. Arthur Christensen, *Critical Studies in the Rubiayat of 'Umar-i-Khayyam* (Copenhagen: A. F. Host, 1972), p. 53.

15. Quoted by Esma'il Yegani, *Hakim Omar Khayyam va Roba'iyyat-e-u* Tehran: Anjumdu-e Arthar-e Meli, 1963), p. 29 from a MS of the *Maqalat-e-Shams-e* Tabrizi in Istanbul University, number 6790.

16. *Resale fi al-Tanbeih 'ala al-Asrar . . .*, ca. 1202, MS 1933, in As'ad Effendi Collection, Suleimanieh Library, Istanbul.

17. Browne, *Literary History*, 2:250.

18. See my *Persian Influence on English Literature* (Calcutta, 1983), pp. 48-49.

19. Winfiend, *Quatrains of Khayyam*, p. 226.

20. Nicholson, *Literary History of the Arabs*, p. 318.

21. *Hanif* here is synonymous with "Muslim."

22. Nicholson, *Literary History of the Arabs*, p. 318.

23. I. Goldziher, *Deutschen Morgenländischen Gesettshaft* 29 (1875): 637-38, quoted by E. G. Brown in *A Literary History of Persia*, 2:292.

24. Omar Furukh, *'Aqa'id-e Falsafi Abu'l-Ala, Filsuf-e Ma'arra*, trans. Khadiv Jam (Tehran: Ketab-ha-ye Jibi, 1963), p. 291.

25. Winfield, *Quatrains of Khayyam*, p. 106.

26. Omar Furukh, *'Aqa'id-e Falsafi Abu'l-Ala*, pp. 411-12.

27. See *Divan-e Naser Khosrow*, ed. S. H. Taqi-Zade (Tehran: Chapkhane-ye Gilan, 1956), pp. 366-67. Cf. this poem with the poems on pp. 70 and 71. See also the comments on the above-mentioned poem of Mojtaba Minovi, who does not regard it as a genuine work by Naser Khosrow.

28. Browne, *Literary History*, 2:243.

29. Iraj Mirza, *Divan*, ed. Mohammad Ja'far Mahjub (Tehran: Amir Kabir, 1964), pp. 82-83.

30. The Persian word for *creator* plus a Russian suffix.

31. Sedeq Hedayat, *Afsane-ye Afarinesh* (Rome: Intisharat-e Babak, n.d.), p. 32.

32. See *Shah-Name*, trans. Arthur George Warner (London, 1915), 3:17 ff.

33. Browne, *Literary History*, 3:32 (quoted from *Tarikh-e-Wassaf*).

34. *Pur-e Sina*, p. 46.

35. *Tahafut'l-Falasefe*, ed. Suliman Dunia (Cairo, 1955), p. 32, quoted by A. J. Arberry in *Revealation and Reason in Islam*.

36. A.A. Dehkhoda, *Lughat Name*, "B", under "Bisar grey".

37. *Divan-e Khaqani*, ed. Mohammad 'Abbasi (Tehran: Amir Kabir, 1957), p. 156.

38. *Divan-e Sana'i*, ed. M. Mosaffa (Tehran: Amir Kabir, 1957), p. 247.

39. *Koran*, 49:12.

40. *Kitab-al-Aghani* (Cairo: Bulaq, 1868), 3:33.

41. *Kivan-Bashshar Ibn Burd*, ed. Mohammad al-Taher Ibn 'Ashur (Cairo, 1950), 1:377-79.

42. For an account of some of these sects see Browne, *Literary History*, 1:xxx.

43. The Persian text is quoted in Browne, *Literary History*, 4:271. The translation is mine.

44. Mushshabaha was a sect whose followers compared God's actions with human ones. They claimed that the *Koran* is eternal with all its letters, accents, and written signs.
45. *Divan-e Ash'ar-e Naser Khosrow*, ed. Nasrullah Taqavi (Tehran:'Elmi, 1925-28), p. 505.
46. Browne, *Literary History*, 2:243.
47. Ibid.
48. The Perisan text is quoted by 'A. A. Dehkhoda in his *Amthal va Hekam* (Tehran: Amir Kabir, 1960), 1:338.
49. *Mathnavi*, 2:138.
50. See Abu al-Mafakher Bakharzi, *Owrad al-Ahbab va Fosus al-Adab*, ed. Iraj Afshar (Tehran: Tehran University publications, 1966), p. 59.
51. Browne, *Literary History*, 3:277.
52. Ibid., p. 278.
53. *Divan-e Hafez*, p. 135.
54. Ibid., pp. 90-91.
55. Ibid., p. 342.
56. *Ibn al-Vaqt.*
57. *Mathnavi*, book 2, story 4.
58. *Silsilatu'l-Zahab* in *Haft-awrang*, ed. Murtaza Mudarres Gilani (Tehran: Amir Kabir, 1959), pp. 126-27.
59. Ibid., pp. 22-23.
60. *Kollliyyat-e 'Obeyd-e Zakani*, pp. 310-11.
61. Ibid., p. 287.
62. Ibid., p. 317.
63. Ibid., p. 270. This is the answer of Mowlana 'Azud al-Din to someone who asks, "How is it that in the days of the Caliphs many people claimed to be God or Prophets, but they don't claim it anymore?"
64. I.e., there is no future life.
65. Mankind was believed to be the product of the four elements and the working of the seven heavens.
66. This quatrain is by Omar Khayyam, *Rubaiyyat* (Lucknow, 1894-95), number 723.
67. This quatrain is also attributed to Khayyam.
68. *Kolliyyat-e 'Obeyd-e Zakani*, pp. 162-63.
69. Shah Esma'il and his opponent Sultan Selim the Grim were both of Turkish extract and both spoke Turkish. Only the former's *Divan* is in this language, though, the latter preferring to write in Persian. Cf. Browne, *Literary History*, 4:12-15.
70. Ibid., 4:27.
71. For more examples see Mortaza Ravandi, *Tarikh-e Ejtema'i-ye Iran* (Tehran: Amir Kabir, 1977), p. 454.
72. The professional reciters or rhapsodists employed on these occasions.
73. Quoted in Browne, *Literary History*, 4:184-86. The original Persian text was lithographed at Bombay in 1891-92.
74. Bastani Parizi, *Khatun-e Haft Qal'e* (Tehran: Ketabfrushi Dehkhoda, 1965), p. 350.
75. 'Obeidallah Ibn Ziyad was the governor of Basra, and he was sent by Yazid, the Umayyad Caliph, to confront Hosain, the son of 'Ali, who had been invited by the people of Kufa.
76. In the battle which took place at Kerbela (10 October 680) Hosain and all his followers were massacred. Shemr was the general who killed them.
77. Zayn ul-'Abedin, the son of Hosain, was ill and did not take part in the fighting. He was captured with the women and children and later freed by Yazid.
78. Fatame, the daughter of the Prophet and the mother of Hosain. But here it seems the reference is to the daughter of Hosain, who had the same name.
79. *Divan-e Yaghma-ye Jandaqi* (Tehran, 1866), p. 334.
80. The rosary and *mohr*, a piece of clay, are specially made from the earth of Kerbela, where Hosain fell.

81. An artificial scar was formed by cupping *(hajame't)* to increase the venerability of the person by suggesting that his forehead bears the trace of constant prostration in prayer.

82. *Divan-e Qa'ani*, ed. Mohammad Javad Majub (Tehran: Amir Kabir, 1957), pp. 322-23.

83. Dorian Rottenberg, trans., *Azerbaijanian Poetry*, ed. Mirza Ibrahimov (Moscow: Progress Publishers, 1969), p. 225. Cf. *Hop Hop Name*, p. 104.

84. Saber, *Hop Hop Name*, p. 239.

85. *Azerbaijanian Poetry*, p. 226.

86. Saber, *Hop Hop Name*, p. 48.

87. Observed on 10 Zihajjah.

88. Saber, *Hop Hop Name*, p. 117.

89. Ashraf al-Din Gilani, *Kitab Bagh-e Behesht* (Tehran, n.d.), pp. 176-77.

90. Saber, *Hop Hop Name*, pp. 129-31. Cf. Ashraf, *Bagh-e Behesht*, p. 176.

91. *Ferangi* originally meant *from France*; now, *European*.

92. Originally *ghelman* (plural of *gholam*, "boy")—fair young men in paradise who will take care of the pious women of Islam.

93. The Sheikhi sect was founded by Sheikh Ahmad ibn Zain al-Din al-Ahsa'i (d. 1827 or 1828); see Browne, *Literary History*, 4:402-3, 410-11. The Babi sect was founded by 'Ali Mohammad of Shiraz, styling himself the "Bab" (d. 1850); see Browne, *Literary History*, 4:149-54, 420-23.

94. *Dahri* is a materialist.

95. Hosain Kurd is the hero of an adventure story that was once very popular in Iran.

96. Rostam and Gudarz are heroes of ancient Iran whose deeds are recorded in the *Shah-Name*.

97. A *pahlavan* is a warrior, a knight.

98. Translated from the Persian text given in *Javedane Seyyed Ashraf al-Din Gilani*, ed. Hosain Namini (Tehran: Kitab Farzan, 1984), p. 299.

99. 'A. A. Dehkhoda, "Zuhur-e Jadid" ("new appearance"), in *Sur Esrafil* (20 June 1910; Year 1, Number 4). Published by Inlisharat-e Rudaki (Tehran, 1982), p. 40.

100. It seems that Dehkhoda did not know about Joseph Smith and the Mormons.

101. See Yahya Arianpur, *Az Saba ta Nima*, 2:84-86.

102. Dehkhoda, *Amthal va Hekam* (Tehran: Amir Kabir, 1960), 1:300-304.

103. M. Ishaque, *Modern Persian Poetry* (Calcutta, 1943), p. 19.

104. Iraj Mirza, *Divan*, p. 172.

105. M. T. Bahar, *Divan-e Malek ul-Sho'ara Bahar* (Tehran: Amir Kabir, 1956), pp. 387-88.

106. Ibid., p. 389.

107. *Divan-e Malek ul-Sho'ara*, 1:164.

108. For some of Shari'ati's views see *On the Sociology of Islam: Lectures by Ali Shari'ati*, trans. Hamid Algar (Berkeley, California: Mizan Press, 1979) and *Marxism and Other Western Fallacies: An Islamic Critique*, trans. R. Campbell (Berkeley, California: Mizan Press, 1980).

109. In Islam, after the *Koran*, the traditions of Mohammad are considered to be the most important guide for the faithful. Muslim (d. 874) and Bukhari (d. 870) have collected the most authoritative and ancient of the traditions, and both of their collections bear the same title, *al-Sahih*. Al-Hosaini quotes them, as does a Christian scholar of recent times, Al-Bustani, to repudiate Shari'ati.

110. 'Ayesha, the youngest wife of the Prophet, was ten or eleven when he married her. Because of her reddish hair he used to call her "my little red one" and was extremely fond of her.

111. 'Ali Shari'ati, *Shi'a*, volume 7 of *Collected Works* (Solon, Ohio: Hosainieh Ershad, 1979), pp. 317-19.

Mulla Dopizeh, the writer of satirical definitions that are published with the works of Obeyd-e Zakani. A seventeenth century Indian cartoon. *Fogg Museum, Harvard University.*

A bowman with narghile, a seventeenth-century Iranian cartoon. *Fogg Art Museum, Harvard University.*

A satirical drawing from the late nineteenth century. Holy men boiling an egg during the fast. *From Persian Meniature Painting by Laurence Binyon.*

№36. ٣٦

Superstitious veneration of a *Mulla*. From *Mulla Nasreddin* 36 (7 October 1907).

دستورالعمل حادن سيّد محمديزدى بجاعت اخته که مشروطه طلبان ما خفوز رسانند

Seyyed Muhammad Yazdi teaching the *Jinnis* how to overthrow the constitution. *From the illustrated comic weekly, Azerbaijan 17 (11 October 1907).*

قوی گلسونلر : داللهی بو کتاب ایله اونلارک جوابینی ویره بیلهرم ٠

"Let the Russians come, I will answer them all by this book" (i.e., the *Koran*). *From Mulla Nasreddin, 17 (1909).*

Saber and the people of Shirvan. "By God I am a true believer, o people of Shirvan!"
From Hop Hop Nama.

A religious dispute. *From* Mulla Nasreddin. Reproduced from 'Ali Akbar Dehkhoda's *Lughat-Nama* (Under Taherzada Saber).

5

Socio-Political Satire in Classical Persian Literature

> Why should we fear; and what? The laws?
> They all are arm'd in virtue's cause;
> And aiming at the self-same end,
> Satire is always virtue's friend.
>
> —Charles Churchill, *The Ghost*

Throughout Persian history, except for the short period of the Constitutional Revolution and one or two others such as early Islam, freedom of expression was impossible in any sense we would recognize. In the classical (pre-Constitutional) period, emirs and kings, exercising an absolute power over their subjects, would not tolerate the criticism to which free expression would have inevitably given rise. Sa'di with his characteristic humor and realism illustrates the point:

> Contradicting what the Sultan would say
> Is to waste your life in this way.
> Should the prince say "It is night" amidst noon-day,
> Declare that you behold the moon and stars.[1]

Thus the relationship of the court poet to his patron was that of courtier to ruler. When the emir was angry or upset, the poet's duty was to appease him with extemporaneous poetry. Sultan Mahmud, for instance, while drunk, once cut his beloved Ayaz's hair. The next day he was so upset that no one dared speak to him. But 'Unsuri, the poet laureate, changed the royal mood with but one spontaneous quatrain. The author of *Qabus-Name*, a prince himself and well versed in the courtly tradition, writes that "the poet has to know the nature of his patron and to know what pleases him, so that he may praise him in a way that he will be pleased."[2] Of course, not all poets were writers of panegyric; some indeed were opposed to the life a panegyric poet led. Ibn Yamin (d. 1367 or 1368), who is noteworthy for his magnanimous attitude, writes:

> By traversing the long road of hope you'll
>   never get rich,
> Save only if you tarry on the threshold of
>   contentment.
> Go, get yourself a pair of oxen and a field
>   for sowing—
> Call one of them Emir and the other call Wazir.
> And if this doesn't yield you enough to live on
>   happily,
> You can always borrow a loaf of barley-meal from the Jews.
> That's surely a thousand times better than at
>   the crack of dawn,
> To gird your loins and say "Sir" to one no better
>   than you.[3]

But the non-panegyric poet was the exception rather than the rule, and despite such liberal-minded poets as Ibn Yamin, most poets in the classical period depended upon patrons for their living and hence upon panegyric.

Nor was panegyric considered a totally servile art. The poet was not merely a parasite upon his patron's name and fame. Nezami 'Aruzi says of 'Unsuri, for instance:

> How many a palace did great Mahmud raise,
> At whose tall towers the moon did stand and gaze;
> Whereof one brick remaineth not in place,
> Though still re-echo 'Unsuri's sweet lays.[4]

As the art of panegyric became more and more widespread many poets employed their art in the praise of the kings and emirs who were by no means worthy of praise, thus contributing to the degradation of this type of poetry. Indeed, a few poets became ridiculously servile. Zahir of Faryab (d. 1193), for example, says:

> Imagination puts nine thrones of heaven beneath its feet;
> That it may imprint a kiss on the stirrup of Qizil Arsalan.[5]

Even greater servility is demonstrated by a court poet of Shah 'Abbas (1588-1629). The poet, Shater Abbas Sabuhi, who wanted to be in the king's hunting party, arrived late and missed the departure, whereupon he wrote with extreme self-depreciation:

> In the morning I came to your quarters,
> You had already left for hunting;
> You had not taken the dog—why were you gone?[6]

Panegyric thus often grew into something quite removed from its original function of immortalizing the deeds of a deserving patron; it led many poets to lies and complete self-degradation.

Because of the servile and restrictive conditions under which most classical poets wrote, a cohesive body of satire could not and did not form. However, some critical work was written and did survive. Often personal ill-reward gave rise to such critical verse.

The story of 'Obeyd-e Zakani, for instance, shows satirical bitterness finally replacing servility in the search for kingly favor. 'Obeyd-e Zakani supposedly wrote a scholarly work on rhetoric, intending to present it to the king. But since jesters were often more welcome in the courts than poets and scholars, the courtiers told 'Obeyd that the king had no need for such rubbish. So 'Obeyd composed a fine panegyric, which was again turned down on the grounds that the kind did "not like to be mocked with lies, with exaggerations, and with fulsome flattery of poets."[7] Thereupon, 'Obeyd said, "In that case, I too will pursue the path of impudence, so that by this means I may obtain access to the king's most intimate society, and may become one of his favorites." The result was 'Obeyd's satirical verse:

> I have neither rank nor position in the courts of the time,
> Since neither jester, pimp, nor buffoon am I.
> I am neither hypocrite nor double-crosser like Mercury and moon,
> So I am not honored in the way of Nahid and Ormuzd.[9]
> Seeking virtue, no silver or gold have I,
> Since I steal not endowments and accept not bribes.[10]

Several other poets also dared to vilify an emir, governor, or judge directly. Mir Abd al-Haqq, for instance, writes a poem which is difficult to translate because of the pun on *khar* ("ass"):

> A man from Golpaigan went to the royal camp
> To become a judge; Sadre [the governor] was not in accord.
> The man gave him an ass as a bribe and received the position.
> If it were not for this ass the judge's seat would have been vacant.[11]

In a similarly ingenious way Mohammad 'Abduh, a Seljuq poet, censures the practices of the officials and people of the *Divan*:

> They ask me: "Why do you flee from the people of the Divan?"
> I say because I know well that only fools [divane] associate
>   with the devils [divan].[12]

Here the pun on *ahl-e divan* ("the officials") and *divan* ("demons") cannot be reproduced in English.

It was not only the poets, however, who ventured to criticize; the court jesters, who played roles much like those of Shakespearean fools also expressed unflattering opinions. The numerous stories about Talhak and Mahmud are cases in point. 'Obeyd-e Zakani quotes one:

The wife of Talhak gave birth to a child. Sultan Mahmud asked him: "What have you got?" He said: "What can be the children of the poor? A girl or a boy." The Sultan asked in amazement: "What else do great men get?" He said: "O my master, they get someone who is a calamity and a destroyer of people's lives."[13]

Unfortunately, even the jesters were often not brave enough to be entirely outspoken. 'Unsor al-Ma'ali warns the courtiers: "However dear you may be, you whould not forget your position and you must not speak contrary to what he [the king] desires. Whoever contradicts his master meets an untimely death. It is foolishness to beat an iron bar."[14] Rumi has a beautifully satirical poem in his *Mathnavi*, too, which further illustrates the point:

> The Shah was playing chess with Daklqak: he [Dalqak]
>   checkmated him: immediately the Shah's anger burst out.
> He [Dalqak] cried: "Checkmate! Checkmate!" and the
>   haughty monarch threw the chessmen, one by one, at his head,
> Saying, "Take [it]! Here is 'checkmate' for you, O scoundrel."
>   Dalqak restrained himself and [only] said, "Mercy."
> The prince commanded him to play a second game: he
>   [Dalqak] was trembling like a naked man in bitter cold.
> He played the second game, and the Shah was defeated:
>   [when] the time and moment for saying "checkmate, checkmate"
>   arrived,
> Dalqak jumped up and ran into a corner and in his fear
>   hastily flung six rugs over himself.
> There he lay beneath [several] cushions and six rugs,
>   that he might escape from the Shah's blows.
> The Shah exclaimed, "Hey, hey! What have you done? What
>   is this?" He replied, "Checkmate, checkmate, checkmate,
>   checkmate, O excellent Shah!
> How can one tell the truth to thee except under cover,
>   O wrathful man who art wrapped in fire.
> O thou, who art defeated [by me], while I, defeated by
>   thy Majesty's blows, am crying 'checkmate, checkmate'
>   under thy house-furnishings?"[15]

Indeed, the poets who did dare to speak out often met with tragic ends. Helali of Astarabad lost his life simply because of a quatrain he had addressed to the tyrant, Uzbek Emir 'Ubeyd-ullah Khan:

> How long will you plunder and take away
> The property of the orphans?
> You sack and rob the Muslim's goods;
> If you are Muslim, infidel am I.[16]

Other instances of cruelty abound: the tongue of Akhtar the Georgian was cut out by order of a Qajar Prince, Suleiman Khan, because of his sharp speech; Farrokhi Yazdi, who ended his life in prison in 1939, literally had his lips sewn up with needle and threat on the order of the governor of Isfahan in 1904 because he had written a "patriotic poem" on the subject of democracy; and Mirzade 'Eshqi, another revolutionary poet of the turn of the century, was assassinated by government agents.

Occasionally poets were lucky enough to get away with their criticism. Mulla Shiri, an Indian poet, satirized the great Akbar in the following lines, yet managed to preserve both his tongue and his life:

> Our king this year has claimed to be a prophet;
> God willing, next year, he will be God.[17]

Mulla Shiri's was not the standard fate, however; many poets, to be safe, chose to criticize only rulers who had died or been dismissed from office. Akhti, the despotic emir of Tirmez, choked and died while drinking, whereupon Adib Saber wrote this quatrain:

> O Akhti, the day you drank wine was the day you hurried to hell.
> One hundred thousand bravos to that day when you drank wine!
> You died, but the world came to life after you:
> You are damned, but blessings be upon the mode of your dying.[18]

Likewise Yaghma of Jandaq criticizes the notorious prime minister of Moham-mad Shah, Hajji Mirza Aghasi. Hajji was well known for his foolish policies; his only two concerns in office were wells and artillery, and even on these two subjects he displayed ignorance. Once, for instance, he insisted on using camels instead of mules to transport artillery. When the camels, not being fit for such endeavor, began falling down the hillsides, Hajji, in his ridiculous determination, had metal shoes made for them. It is just this silly figure that Yaghma rebukes when he writes:

> Not a single dirham was left for the kingdom by Hajji;
> Whatever there was, it was spent on cannons and wells.
> Yet not a drop of that water reached the farm of the friend,
> Nor did grief by that cannon reach the enemy camp.[19]

Despite prevailing conditions that restricted the full development of political satire in the classical era, various satirical writings were produced in a number of different modes and styles. The excerpts cited thus far—those of 'Obeyd-e Zakani, Helali, Adib Saber, and Yaghma—may be classified as "direct criticism" in that they attack a specific ruler or patron. One of the most famous satires of this type is the "Satire of Sultan Mahmud" by Ferdausi.

The direct attack was only one form of political satire, however. Indirect methods, born largely with the emergence of the Sufis and arising from a different poetic sense, were also effective. The Sufi poets expressed a completely different attitude toward poetry and the poet's role than did the panegyrist poets. Most of the early Sufis were artisans who earned their living by working with their hands. The idle and servile life of the court poet was distasteful to them. The Sufis' austerity and immaterialistic view of life contrasted sharply with the out-

look of the poets of the Ghaznavid period, for example, who were forever preoccupied with royal parties, beautiful slaves, and wine. And perhaps the most
significant difference of all was that the Sufi poets often took upon themselves
the task of guiding and reforming people. This, the Sufis' perception of their
societal role, led inevitably to a much different sort of poetry. The Sufi poets
used a simpler language, even favoring local dialects, in order to accomplish their
reformative task; they disliked the pompousness of courtly poetic styles. Khaje
'Abd-ullah Ansari, for instance, translated the *Tabaqat al-Sufiyye* of Suleimi into
the Herati dialect, and Baba Taher wrote his quatrains in the dialect of Hamadan.
Sana'i in one of his *qasides* bitterly criticizes the emirs and kings and their parasitic
poets:

> Leave poetry and concern yourself with religion:
> Since this increases your humility, and that your arrogance.
> Granted you gained magical art, but "magic will not
>   succeed"
> Significations without deceit are the words of the prophets;
> Deceit without signification the fantasies of the poets.
> Never will you see sincerity and truth in a poet's nature—
> Nothing but beggary, falsehood, and denial after denial.
> How long will you insist that you append yourself to
>   the train of the Sultan in order to succeed?
> Go on, seek the fortune of the Sultan; as for us,
>   we will keep our misfortunes and our faith.[20]

'Attar expresses a different view of poetry. He values it highly, while Sana'i
seems to deprecate the art. But the outlooks of both 'Attar and Sana'i derive
ultimately from a common source. Both poets respond to the poetry prevalent
in their day as a vehicle of corruption, lies, and deceit. Thus, in a spirit similar
to Sana'i's, 'Attar censures the poets who have so degraded the art:

> Poetry has been called the best of all things;
> What position can be greater than this?
> But in our age poetry has fallen to ill-fame;
> The mature ones have gone, leaving the raw,
> So words no longer have value.
> This is no time for praise, but for moral wisdom;
> My heart is dulled by patrons and the undeserving.
> The gloom of patronage has darkened my soul;
> Wisdom is ever enough patron for me—
> This is an endeavor worthy of my soul.[21]

A further difference between the Sufi and the court poets was that the religious
beliefs of the rulers often gave the Sufis, like the saints, a special privilege to
criticize them and occasionally to save people's lives. The strong sense of religion
among the populace enhanced this position for the Sufis. This special position
of the Sufis accounts for such reports as that of Timur's visit to Sheikh Safi
al-Din of Ardabil, the ancestor of the Safavid kings. The Tartar conqueror asked
the saint to request something, whereupon the sheikh asked that the lives of

ten thousand prisoners who were accompanying the emir be spared. Timur found this an acceptable request and agreed to save as many people as the *khaneqah of the saint* would hold. Fortunately the *khaneqah* had two doors, so all the prisoners were able to enter one door and go out the other. Timur kept his promise, and in this way all the prisoners were saved.

The Sufis' special conception of poetry and social duty, combined with the privilege of greater freedom often afforded them by the ruling class, allowed them to develop a new sort of critical poetry and prose. It was often a poetry or a prose mingled with an advocacy of saintly virtues—the saintliness thus forming a cover for quite-pointed attacks. Sa'di, for instance, who was greatly respected by the Mongol Abaqa Khan, was able to advise and indirectly criticize the ruler:

> The king who looks after his subjects,
> The tax he levies is worth his guardianship.
> If he is not a shepherd of the people, be it a poison in his throat,
> That whatever he receives is an unjust *jizyeh* on the Muslims.[22]

A story related about Baba Taher also illustrates the point. The author of *Rahat al-Sudur* (Peace of hearts) writes:

> I have heard that when Sultan Tughril Beq came to Hamadan, there were three elders of the saints, Baba Taher, Baba Ja'far, and Shaykh Jamsha. Now there is by the gate of Hamadan a little mountain called "Khidr," and they were standing there. The Sultan's eyes fell upon them; he halted the vanguard of his army, and he alighted, approached them, and kissed their hands. Baba Taher, who was somewhat crazy in his manner, said to him, "O Turk, what wilt thou do with God's people?" "Whatever thou biddest me," replied the Sultan. "Do rather that which God biddeth thee," replied Baba; "Verily God enjoineth justice and well-doing. The Sultan wept and said, "I will do so."[23]

This type of criticism clearly is much different than that of the satirical attack. It contains no *hajv*, as in Ferdausi's verse, but rather advocates ideal social justice and, by implication, criticizes its absence. This method of criticism is also connected to "the crazy saint" phenomenon. Baba Taher in the passage above was described as "somewhat crazy in his manner." This characterization stems from the belief that associated supernatural power with a kind of saintly "craze" or "madness." This belief, of course, has a long history in many societies and cultures; withal, it gave such "crazy saints" the freedom to criticize whomever they deemed worthy of attack and, simultaneously, self-protection from censure. These "crazy saints" were thus known for their not-so-crazy wisdom. Rumi in the *Divan-e Shams* advises us to "hear the truthful word from the madmen,"[24] and the madmen's wisdom is indeed so great that it often outstrips the wisest of the wise. Ibn-Yamin also illustrates the point:

> Once Solomon the prophet, upon whom be peace, asked a madman:
> "How do you find this glorious kingdom which I have inherited
>   from my father?"

How wonderful was the answer: "Since the kingdom is not forever,
Your father flogged a dead horse for many years;
And you are catching the wind day and night."[25]

As in the more "sober" Sufi writings, this madness serves as a cover, as a safe vehicle for pointed attack and for the venting of cynical views toward life and sociopolitical corruption. Many examples of such criticism have been attributed to "crazy-saint" figures like Bohlul. These figures were then used by the poets, as 'Attar does here, as mouthpieces for expressing their social attacks:

> One day the drunken Bohlul
> Climbed the throne of Harun.
> The royal guards beat him such
> That blood from his every wound gushed.
> Being beaten soundly, he opened his mouth:
> "O Harun, the king of the world!
> I sat for a while on this throne,
> And behold me thus inflicted with wounds!
> You who have sat a life-time upon it,
> Joint by joint they will separate your body.
> I paid for sitting a mere moment dearly;
> What will be forthcoming for you?"[26]

The secret of indirect criticism, then, is that it allows the ruler or patron addressed free choice in either acknowledging or ignoring the implied censure of his activity. It is not an art of accusation, nor is it inspired necessarily by a poet's personal insult at the hands of his patron. Rather, it is an art of implication that raises disturbing questions concerning royal policies and actions—questions that the addressee may either attend to or ignore.

Not all indirect criticism addresses a particular person, however. Often the object of attack is the general social and political corruption of the day. The books known as The Mirror for Princes such as Qabus-Name, Siyasat-Name, several chapters of the Gulestan, etc., are meant to praise the just rulers and to censure despotic kings and emirs as a general class. But if the criticism is general, the message is exact. Sa'di writes in the Gulestan, for instance:

> An unjust king asked a devotee, "What kind of worship is best?" He replied: "For you, the best thing is to sleep half the day so as not to injure the people for a while."

> I saw a tyrant sleeping half the day.
> I said: "This confusion, if sleep removes it, so much the better;
> But he whose sleep is better than his wakefulness,
> Is better dead than leading such a bad life.[27]

Another instance is found in an earlier poet, Anvari, who, despite spending most of his life writing panegyrics for emirs and kings, was able to rebuke them:

> Have you heard what a fool once told a man of wisdom

That the governor of our town is a shameless beggar.
The other asked, "How is this possible? A button on his jacket
Is provision enough for us for months, nay, for years!"
He said: "O poor one, here lies your mistake:
Do you know from where so much wealth and provision comes?
The pearls of his necklace are the tears of my children;
The rubies and carnelians of his rein are the blood
   of your orphans.
He that has even his drinking water from us,
If you look to his marrow, he is made of our bread.
Asking is begging, whether you ask poll-tax and tithe.
Give them ten names; they are still the same.
Since asking is nothing but begging,
Then whoever asks is a beggar, be he Solomon or Croesus."[28]

Sometimes general criticism was framed in the fictional context of the poet's experience. Khaju-ye Kermani (d. 1231), though he sets the scene of his poem in the time of a fictional emir, bitterly attacks the Mongol officials of his own time:

> Once an emir died in Isfahan;
> He was one of those who had gained kingship in Iraq.
> I saw him being carried on the shoulders of bath-attendants.
> "What," I asked in amazement, "have they seen in him?
> Carrying corpses is a separate profession;
> Every profession belongs to a special class."
> My interlocutor sighed and said,
> "Bath attendants have always carried dirt!"[29]

To convey its message this type of criticism often employs the example of specific individuals—it is not confined in its references to nameless rulers. One technique along these lines was to eulogize the justice and statesmanship of the ancient kings, creating a pointed, albeit a direct, contrast to contemporary royal practice.

Sometimes, however, a poet would criticize rather than praise the ancient kings, thus creating an indirect parallel to the rulers of his day. This technique was a favorite of Sa'di, who in the *Gulestan* often attacks a royal figure of the past and advises his present patron to pursue a more just and righteous course. We find another fine example of this technique in the work of Amir Hosaini, who recounts the famous story of Alexander and Diogenes. Although set in the distant past, the story contains a biting criticism of the men in Hosaini's own day who boast of their high positions:

> Look at this wonderful story,
> That one day Alexander chanced to pass,
> With all his army, with all his splendor and glory,
> A ruin out of which came an old man.
> An old man—nay, a shining sun,
> Came to the eyes of Alexander.
> He asked, "Who is this? Who is this? How can this be?"
> He rode to that grave-like ruin, and
> The old man went not away.

Since he did not look at him, Alexander angrily told him,
"You who have become a ghoul of this ruin,
Why are you sitting there so forgetfully?
Why do you not pay respect to me?
Is not my name Alexander?"
The old man shouted back to him,
"All this is not worth half a grain of barley to me;
You are neither the head nor the tail of the world—
You are a seed from the sowing of man.
My two slaves, who are greed and desire,
All day long, they are your masters;
How then could you be an equal to me?
You are the slave of my slaves."[30]

We thus see that within the class of "indirect criticism" are found a variety of styles and techniques, united by the fact that they present their message in a manner that allows its target to either accept it or dismiss it. One may question whether these methods rightfully can be called "satire," since many of the examples cited lack the ironical twist and the overtone of mockery usually associated with the genre. It is perhaps best to regard them as didactic rather than pure satire—on the one hand such indirect writing exposes and attacks the arrogance and vanity of emirs and kings; on the other hand it aims to teach both the reader and those whom he attacks a lesson in being ethical. Such double intent causes the work to differ from ordinary satire yet remain fundamentally of the same class.

Another method of political criticism, which lies perhaps between the direct and indirect modes, is that of animal fable. This form, with a long history in Iran and used extensively by classical writers, has remained popular in Persian literature to the present day. Three outstanding modern examples are "The Little Black Fish" by Samad Behrangi, the play *Shahr-e Qesse* by Bizhan Mofid, and "The Dogs and Wolves," a poem by Akhavan Thaleth. But in this chapter we will limit ourselves to the works of satire written before the Constitutional period.

First, let us consider animal fable as a vehicle of sociopolitical satire in classical Persian poetry. The *Manteq al-Tair* (The conference of the birds) of 'Attar, in the section on the eagle who prefers royal company to anything else in the world, contains an interesting satirical piece on courtiers. Another important example is found in Nezami's *Makhzanul-Asrar* (The treasury of secrets):

Intent on sport, Nushirwan on a day
Suffered his horse to bear him far away
From his retainers. Only his Wazir
Rode with him, and no other soul was near.
Crossing the game-stocked plain, he halts and scans
A village ruined as his foeman's plans.
There, close together, sat two owls apart,
Whose dreary hootings chilled the monarch's heart.
"What secrets do these whisper?" asked the King
Of his Wazir; "What means this song they sing?"

> "O Liege," the Minister replied, "I pray
> Forgive me for repeating what they say.
> Not for the sake of song mate calls to mate:
> A question of betrothal they debate.
> That bird her daughter gave to this, and now
> Asking him a proper portion to allow,
> Saying: "This ruined village give to me,
> And also others like it two or three."
> "Let be," the other cries; "Our rulers leave,
> Injustice to pursue, and do not grieve,
> For if our worthy monarch should but live,
> A hundred thousand ruined homes I'll give."[31]

In the "Story of the Jackal Who Fell into a Dye Vat and Pretended to Be a Peacock Among the Jackals," Rumi, in the *Mathnavi*, likens the Pharaoh and his claims to being God to an arrogant jackal:

> A certain jackal went into the dyeing-vat, stayed in the vat
>   for a while,
> And then arose, his skin having become parti-colored, saying,
>   "I have become the Peacock of 'Illiyyin."[32]
> His colored fur had gained a charming brilliance, and the sun
>   shone upon those colors.
> He beheld himself green and red and roan and yellow,
>   [so] he presented himself to the jackals:
>
> "Prithee look at me and at my color: truly the idolator
>   possesses no idol like me.
> Like the flower garden, I have become many-hued and lovely:
>   Bow in homage to me, do not withdraw from me.
> Behold my glory and splendor and sheen and radiance
>   and color! Call me the pride of the World and the
>   Pillar of Religion!
> I have become the theatre of the Divine Grace, I have
>   become the tablet on which the Divine Majesty is unfolded.
>
> "O jackals, take heed, do not call me a jackal: How should
>   a jackal have so much beauty?"
> Those jackals came thither en masse, like moths around
>   the candle.
> "Say then, what shall we call thee, O creature of [pure]
>   substance?" He replied, "A peacock [brilliant] as Jupiter."
> Then they said to him, "The spiritual peacocks have displays
>   [with the beloved] in the Rose-garden:
> Dost thou display thyself like that?" "No," said he.
>   "Not having gone into the desert, how should I read
>   [the valley of] Sina?"
> "Dost thou utter the cry of peacocks?" "Nay," said he.
>   "Then, Master Bu'l-'Ala ["Father of sublimity"],
>   thou art not a peacock.
> The peacock's garment of honor comes from Heaven:
>   How wilt thou attain thereto by means of colors

and pretenses?'"

"Thou art even as Pharaoh, who bejewelled his beard
  and in his asinine folly soared higher than Jesus.
He too was born of the generation of the she-jackal and
  fell into a vat of riches and power.
Every one who beheld his power and riches bowed down
  to him in worship: He swallowed the worship of the idle
  mockers.
That beggar in tattered cloak became miserably drunken with
  the people's worship and feelings of amazement.
Riches are a snake, for therein are poisons; and popular favor
  and worship is a dragon.
Ah, do not assume a virtue [which thou dost not possess],
  O Pharaoh: Thou art a jackal, do not in any wise behave
  as a peacock."[33]

Finally, one of the best-known animal fables in Persian, a staple of children's
literature for generations, is 'Obeyd-e Zakani's *Cat and the Mice*. It is a mock-
heroic poem, parodying the style of the *Shah-Name*; beneath its guise of animal
characterization it is an obvious sociopolitical satire, the meaning of which the
poet himself admonishes us to find. At the end of the book he writes:

This is a story both weird and wonderful,
A souvenir from 'Obeyd-e Zakani:
Dear heart, accept the moral of this story
And you will live happy all your days.
Having heard the ballad of the Mice and the Cat,
Meditate well its meaning, my dear son.[34]

Cat and the Mice offers no particular person as referent for the santrimonious
and tyrannical cat. But the cat strikingly resembles Mobarez al-Din Mohammad the Mozaffarid, at whose hands the gentle and art-loving patron of 'Obeyd-e
Zakani, Abu Ishaq Inju, met his end in 1356. Mobarez al-Din has been described
as "brave and devout, but at the same time cruel, bloodthirsty, and treacherous,"[35] and Hafez derogatorily called him *mohtaseb*—"chief of police"—in his
ghazals. It has been reported that his son, Shah Shuja', by whom he was
eventually blinded and imprisoned, asked his father if he had killed a thousand
people with his own hands. Mobarez al-Din thought awhile and said, "Just over
eight hundred, to be exact."[36] On another occasion, two prisoners were
brought to Mobarez al-Din while he was saying his prayers. Between two prayers,
Mobarez took his sword, cut off their heads, and returned to his devotions undisturbed. Compare this story with an incident in 'Obeyd's poem:

. . . The cat killed and ate the mouse
And then padded delicately off to the mosque,
Washed his hands and face, wiped them carefully
And recited a rosary like any Mullah:
"Creator God, behold, I have now repented;

Henceforth my teeth shall not rend another mouse.
In expiation of this innocent blood I'll give
Two maunds of bread in alms to the poor."
He prayed so submissively and abjectly that
Soon the tears were rolling down his cheek.[37]

We might note that Hafez's poetry contains a mocking reference to a contemporary sheikh and poet, 'Amad al-Din Faqih, who had a cat trained to follow him to the mosque. It is not unlikely that 'Obeyd fashioned his cat after the cat of Hafez's verse, adding to his depiction a biting satire on the hypocrisy of the sheikh.

O gracefully-moving partridge who walkest with so pretty an air,
Be not deceived because the Cat of the ascetic hath said its prayers![38]

The *Cat and the Mice* brings us to yet another method of sociopolitical satire. 'Obeyd's work is simultaneously an animal fable and a parody of Ferdausi's great epic. It derives its satirical quality not only from the parallel between the cat and the sanctimonious ruling class but also from its belittling of the great "Book of Kings." The very substitution of mice and cats for citizens and kings is a harsh statement on the disintegration of ruling-class ethics and behavior. The technique of pardody is thus in itself a type of sociopolitical satire.

'Obeyd-e Zakani in his treatise *The Ethics of Aristocrats* provides more parody in the form of political satire, though this time without the accompanying technique of animal fable. Parodying such books on ethics as *Akhlaq-e Nasiri*, 'Obeyd divides each chapter of his work into two subsections: "the abrogated practice" (*Mazhab-e Mansukh*) and "the adopted practice" (*Mazhab-e Mokhtar*). The "abrogated practice" deals with traditional views on such subjects as justice and virtue, setting forth the ideals that every book on ethics highly recommends. The "adopted practice," however, is 'Obeyd's satirical addition; this section sets forth the practices of "our great masters" in the present day, practices that are of course exactly the opposite of the "abrogated" ideals. The satire emerges from the contrast. The following is the latter section of 'Obeyd's chapter on justice—justice having been described in the "abrogated" section as "one of the four virtues":

But the view of our contemporaries is that this quality is the worst of all attributes and that justice brings forth much loss, a thesis which they have proved with the clearest of proofs. They say: "Punishment is the bulwark of kingship, lordship and mastership." Unless a man is feared no one will obey his orders, and all will feel themselves equals. Thus the order of affairs will be disrupted and the administration will be undermined. One who practices justice (God forbid) and refrains from beating, killing, and fining his subjects, and who does not get drunk and make an uproar and quarrel with them, will not be feared by anyone. Such kings will not be

obeyed by their subjects, and children and slaves will not heed the words
of their parents and masters. Consequently, the affairs of the country will
lapse into chaos. This is why they have said:

> Kings for gaining one of their objects
> Will sacrifice one hundred subjects.

They say: "Justice bequeaths adversity." What proof can be more convincing than this that as long as the kings of Iran such as Zahhak the Arab
and Yazdigird the Sinner who now honor the best seats in hell along with
the other potentates who arrived after them, practiced injustice, their kingdom prospered and flourished. But when the time of Khosrow Anushiravan
arrived, he followed the counsel of feeble-minded ministers and chose the
way of justice. Before long the pinnacles of his palace fell into the ground
and the sacred fire in the temples, which were their places of worship, was
extinguished, and all traces of their existence vanished from the surface
of the earth. The Caliph of the faithful and the establisher of the laws of
religion, 'Umar Ibn Khattab (may God rest his soul in peace), who was
well known for his justice, used to make bricks and eat barley-bread, and
as they relate, his (patchwork) robe weighed seventeen maunds; whereas
Mu'awiyya, by virtue of his injustice, usurped the kingdom from 'Ali (may
God ennoble his face). Nebuchadnezzar did not establish himself as a king
and did not get exalted in both worlds, until he murdered twelve thousand more. Chengiz Khan, who now despite his enemies is the leader and
guide of all the Mongols, ancient and modern, in the deepest compartments
of hell, did not attain the rulership of the whole world until he shed the
blood of thousands and thousands of people.[39]

Another method used by 'Obeyd-e Zakani for satirizing the corruption of his
countrymen appears in his definitions, which remind one of Ambrose Bierce's
Devil's Dictionary. This method is closely allied to the use of aphorism as a satirical technique, which has been discussed in chapter two. In his Treatise of Definitions, 'Obeyd succinctly describes the Turks, who are apparently synonymous
with the Mongols, as well as the ubiquitous bureaucrats. The satirical "punch"
comes from the conjunction of titles and definitions not normally equated, resulting in a brief but accurate depiction of practical reality. The following are excerpts:

> Gog and Magog: The Turkish tribes when they set out for a country.
> The Infernal Guards: Their leaders.
> Famine: The result of their advent.
> Plunder: Their profession.
> Earthquake: When they suddenly descend upon a place.
> The Constable: He who robs by night and demands payment from
>   the shop-keepers by day.
> The Judge: He whom all men curse.
> The Advocate: He who falsifies truth.
> Bribery: The helper of the helpless.
> The Lucky Man: He who never sees the Judge's face.[40]

'Obeyd'e Zakani's importance does not end with these works. He is indeed
one of history's greatest sociopolitical satirists. In all his works he attacks the

corruption, the faithlessness, the arrogance, and the sham piety of men in power, and he does so with both an amazing range of technique and an impressive originality of subject. In spite of his direct or contextual references to the events and manners of his own time, his satire, like that of Jonathan Swift, is timeless. His courtiers and politicians are universal figures, and his hypocritical sheikhs with their doctrinal rancors against opposing sects describe a human type found in any place and time of religious hatred. And behind his amusing and sometimes grotesque depictions, we find in 'Obeyd, as in Swift again, a sad and bitter man. He calls to mind Hafez's pessimistic remark that

> A man in this early world cannot be found;
> A new world must be fashioned, and a new mankind.[41]

'Obeyd's only solace was, in fact, his satire and his humor. 'Abbas Eqbal in his introduction to 'Obeyd's works writes:

> Upon reading *Resale-ye Delgosha* ("The Joyous Treatise"), one realizes that in the time of 'Obeyd and perhaps forty or fifty years before him, there were some wise and learned men who, in spite of their learning and accomplishments, decided to play the jester or the buffoon on account of the social conditions around them and because of their encounters with the rulers and powerful men of their day. They would laugh at everything and criticize corruption and dishonesty through the medium of satire and irony. Among them one can mention the great scholar Qotb al-Din of Shiraz; Moulana Qazi 'Azud al-Din Iji, the author of the famous book *Al-Mawaqif;* the well-known poet Majd al-Din Hamgar; Sharaf al-Din of Damghan; and Sharaf al-Din of Dare-gaz.[42]

Abbas Eqbal here refers to the method of indirect criticism that was discussed earlier—that of playing the "sagacious fool." When 'Obeyd prefers to become a "jester or buffoon," he is in fact embodying this method.

Mention of the *Resale-ye Delgosha* introduces yet another method of political satire employed by 'Obeyd as well as other writers of classical Persia. The *Resale-ye Delgosha* is a collection of humorous and satirical anecdotes that spotlight some aspect of contemporary social conditions. Anecdote, or short story, thus becomes another mode of social and political satire. The stories of the *Resale-ye Delgosha* can be divided into three main categories. First, there are stories that were already popular in 'Obeyd's time, but which 'Obeyd adapts to accommodate his satirical message. The story of the eggplant and the Sultan is a gem:

> They brought an eggplant dish before Sultan Mahmud when he was hungry. It pleased him. He said, "Eggplant is a tasty dish." A court favorite gave a lecture in praise of eggplant. When the Sultan was full, he said, "Eggplant is really sickening." The same court favorite made an exaggerated speech on the offensiveness of eggplant. The Sultan said, "O fellow, you no longer praise it?" He replied, "I am your favorite, not a favorite of the eggplant. I must say that which pleases you, not the eggplant."[43]

The second category consists of stories related by 'Obeyd about buffoon figures like himself and their relationship to the contemporary rulers. Here are two brief examples:

> One day Sultan Abu Sa'id, being drunk, made Mowlana 'Azud al-Din Iji, a great theologian, dance in front of him. Someone said: "O Mawlana, you do not dance according to the rules!" 'Azud al-Din answered: "I dance by decree, not by the rules!"[44]

> Atabek Solqhur Shah would transcribe a Koran [verse] by his own hand every Ramazan, and send it with some other gifts to Mecca. He had been doing this for several years. One year Majd al-Din [Hamgar] was present and said: "You are doing well—you don't even read it, you send it to the house of its Lord!"[45]

The third category of 'Obeyd's sketches address the tyranny and corruption of his time in a more straightforward way. For example:

> A certain person asked his Holiness 'Azud al-Din "How is it that in the time of the Caliphs, people would often claim to be God or a prophet, and now they don't?" He said: "These days people are so oppressed by tyranny and hunger that they think neither of God nor the prophets."[46]

And here is another anecdote, this about khaje Shams al-Din Saheb Divan, a hideously ruthless tyrant, who killed his own son because the child had been playing with his beard:[47]

> An Isfahani peasant went to the house of Khaje Shams al-Din Saheb Divan and told the chamberlain, "Tell your master that the Lord is waiting for you outside." Khaje summoned him and asked, "Are you the Lord?" The man answered, "Yes." "How?" asked Khaje. The peasant replied, "Formerly I was the Lord of the village, the garden, and the house. But your agents have forcibly taken the village, the garden, and the house, so I am only 'the Lord'!"[48]

These stories graphically depict the social conditions of the time and constitute an important part of 'Obeyd's satrical works. Whether preexistent or invented by 'Obeyd, they combine to expose the conditions of the time more accurately than any formal history. Some of the stories may even have been of popular origin, created as representations of the injustice the people had experienced. Thus, the stories constitute a contemporary folklore very similar to that which is evolving in Iran today.

Let us conclude this chapter with one last work that illustrates yet another method of political satire and that brings us up to the Constitutional Revolution. *Rostam al-Tavarikh* (The Rostam of histories), ostensibly a narrative covering a period from the fall of the Safavids in the early eighteenth century to the reign of Fath 'Ali Shah in the early nineteenth century, is actually a beguiling mixture of history and satire. Mohammad Hashem 'Asef, who calls himself *Rostam al-Hokama* or "the Rostam of philosophers," unlike other Persian historians, talks about the most private incidents in the lives of various kings, emirs, and members of similar social strata. He describes the corruption of the government officials and depicts scenes of intrigue and bloodshed in such a matter-of-fact tone that they positively reek with sarcasm and satire. His work may not have been intended as satire, but its language and style nonetheless are such that history comes to function in that capacity. The satirical element is largely produced by the frequent mismatching of style and subject. Mohammad Hashem 'Asef employs the serious and rather florid language used by most historians in Persia (and elsewhere), but the "historical" details he includes in his work are often obscene, trivial, or comically gruesome—they are not relevant to the historical recording of serious events and affairs. The *Rostam al-Tavarikh* is full of such arresting descriptions as:

> May we take refuge in God! Suddenly those bloodthirsty slaves ran and unsheathed their swords, and plunged them into the swollen bellies of the emirs, wazirs, and officials—bellies which had been pampered in great bounty and wealth and out of which were brought tons and tons of fat. And the walls were colored by their blood. . . ."[49]

Though the event described is tragic, and though bloodthirstiness comes from the slaves and not from the officials, the details of the description itself—the pampered bellies and the tons of fat—consciously or unconsciously serve to satirize the high-blown emirs and wazirs.

Not all of Hashem 'Asef's accounts are so comically gruesome. Some receive their satirical quality from the contrast of an outlandishly decadent subject and a straightforward, unassuming narrative tone. A story from the time of Shah Sultan Hosain illustrates, for instance, the absurd arbitrariness in the practice of so-called justice. The story begins when one of the Safavid emirs, Mohammad 'Ali Beik sees a beautiful woman returning from the public bath. After forcing her to his house, he rapes her. The event causes a great uproar, and the emir is brought before the king for punishment. The chief mulla, the royal astrologer, and the court physician are then charged with the duty of trying him. But when it is discovered that the woman is a Sunnite, the whole prospect changes. At this point, Hashem 'Asef begins to describe the splendid court and especially the bejewelled throne, all of which creates an amusing contrast with the king himself, who is extremely simpleminded. Although Mohammad Hashem does not state it directly, he makes it quite clear that there will be no justice this day—for the idiotic king is totally reliant upon the judgments of his three officials:

> After hearing the story, the Mulla Bashi asked: "To what tribe or sect does this woman belong?" They said: "She is from Dar-e Gazin, and all the inhabitants there are Sunnites."
> Mulla Bashi laughed and said: "As Mohammad 'Ali Beik himself has said, this happened when he was out of his mind and almost unconscious. There is no responsibility upon a mad or unconscious man, since God has said: 'For one who loses his senses, there is no blame on him.'"

The chief physician said: "His physiognomy indicates that his dominant humor is sanguine. Excessive semen is created by his body, and if it is not disposed of, it rebels, and the vapors go to his head. These make him a stranger to wisdom, and he acts worse than a madman."

The chief astrologer said: "The sign of this great Pahlevan is Venus. Venus presides over people of luxury, pleasure, good living, singing and dancing. One whose sign is beneath this star will have no self-restraint in his pleasure-seeking and his merry-making. And because of heavenly influence, outlandish and strange modes of pleasure-seeking will come to this great man."

An emir asked, "Has anything happened to the members of the woman's body as a result of this dealing?" Another emir said, "What defect do you expect would result? This woman has never tasted such a pleasure in her whole life, and she will never again experience one like it."

The great minister then said, "In fact, Mohammad 'Ali Beik is a great, handsome and wise Pahlevan whom no one can rival in power and splendor. And it is not wise to annoy him on account of this trivial sin." And in the luminous presence of that illustrious king, he consoled Mohammad 'Ali Beik, and asserted before the Master of Iran that Mohammad 'Ali Beik was a faithful servant who alone could equal a thousand men in bravery, yet that it seemed that he had been afflicted with the disfavor of the royal grace.

That chosen one of the kings thus asked, "How can we redress this?" The minister said, "You could give him a complete robe of honor." The king said, "To contradict the majority rule is not wise. Because all of the members of our royal state support Mohammad 'Ali Beik, how then could we be indifferent to him?" So Mohammad 'Ali was clad in robes of honor.[50]

We see from the foregoing that classical Persian literature offers many examples of sociopolitical satire in a wide variety of methods and forms. Not all strike us, perhaps, as pure satire; the restrictions upon artistic expression were such that satire often had to hit its mark in a very generalized or heavily disguised way. The satire is nonetheless present, whether in a direct or circumvented form; and the presence of the spirit of discontent, which gives rise to satirical expression, is obvious. It was indeed ready to spring forth even more forcefully with the coming of the Constitutional Revolution.

Notes

1. *Gulestan*, ed. Mohammad Javad Mashkur (Tehran: Eqbal, 1965), p. 50.

2. *Qabus-Name*, ed. Gholam-Hosain Yusefi (Tehran: Bongah Tarjume va Nashar-e Ketab, 1966), p. 191.

3. A. J. Arberry, *Classical Persian Literature* (London: George Allen & Unwin, 1958), pp. 310-11.

4. Browne, *Literary History*, 2:120.

5. Ibid., 2:78.

6. Hosain Nurbakhsh, ed., *Dalqak-ha-ye Mashur-e Darbari* (Tehran: Ketabkhaneh Sana'i, 1976), p. 73.

7. Browne, *Literary History*, 3:232.

8. Ibid., 3:233.

9. A god and goddess in the Zoroastrian pantheon.

10. Ehsan Yarshater, *She'r-e Farsi dar Ahd-e Shah Rukh* (Tehran: Tehran University Press, 1955),

p. 204.

11. Quoted by 'Ali Akbar Dehkhoda in *Amthal va Hekam* (Tehran: Amir Kabir, n.d.), 1:308.
12. Quoted by Z. Safa in *Ganj-e Sokhan*, 2:79.
13. 'Obeyd-e Zakani, *Kolliyat*, ed. A. Eqbal, p. 337; cf. pp. 311, 318, 338, 340, 343.
14. *Qabus-Name*, p. 198.
15. Rumi, *Mathnavi*, trans. R. Nicholson, 5:210.
16. Quoted in Hosain Beik Shamlu, *Ahsan al-Tavarikh*, ed. A. H. Navai (Tehran, 1978), p. 294.
17. Quoted in Shibli No'mani, *She'r al-'Ajam*, trans. Ali Javahir Kalam (Tehran, 1965), 5:44.
18. Browne, *Literary History*, 2:334.
19. Browne, *A Year Amongst the Persians*, Century Publishing, London, 1984, p. 127.
20. *Divan-e Sana'i*, ed. Mazaher Mossafa, pp. 337-38. For "magic will not succeed?" see *Koran*, 20:72.
21. *Mosibat-Name*, ed. Nurani Vesal, p. 47.
22. Sa'di, *Kolliyat* (Tehran: Eqbal, 1937), p. 79.
23. Browne, *Literary History*, 2:260. For "Verily God enjoineth justice and well-doing" see *Koran*, 16:92.
24. *Divan-e Shams-e Tabrizi*, ed. Foruzanfar (Ghazal, 1649) (Tehran: Amir Kabir, 1984).
25. Quoted by Shibli No'mani, ed., *She'r al-'Ajam* (Persian translation by Fakhr Da'i Gilani), 2:248.
26. *Mosibat-Name*, p. 117.
27. *Gulestan*, p. 86.
28. *Divan-e Anvari*, ed. Sa'id Nafisi (Tehran: Piruz Publications, 1957), p. 339.
29. Quoted in Z. Safa, *Tarikh-e Adabiyyat* (Tehran: Tehran University Publications), 3:92.
30. Quoted in Shibli No'mani, ed., *She'r al-'Ajam*, 5:168-69.
31. Browne, *Literary History*, 2:404.
32. I.e., the peacock of heaven.
33. *Mathnavi*, trans. R. A. Nicholson, 3:43-45.
34. Quoted in Arberry, *Classical Persian Literature*, p. 276.
35. Arberry, p. 297.
36. Quoted in Mohammad Mo'in, *Hafez-e Shirin Sukhan* (Tehran, 1961), p. 231.
37. Quoted in Arberry, *Classical Persian Literature*, p. 297.
38. See my article, "Tanz va Enteqad dar Dastan-e heyvanat," *Alefba* 4 (1974): 16-18.
39. 'Obeyd-e Zakani, "Resala-ye Akhlaq al-Ashraf," in *Kolliyat-e 'Obeyd-e Zakani*, ed. P. Atabaki, pp. 231-14. A *maund* (or *man*) is normally three kilograms. See also my translation of *The Ethics of the Aristocrats and Other Satirical Works* by 'Obeyd-e-Zakani (Piedmont, Calif.: Jahan Book Co., 1985).
40. Ibid., pp. 359-60.
41. *Divan-e Hafez*, ed. Mohammad Qazvini, p. 321.
42. *Kolliyat-e 'Obeyd-e Zakani*, pp. Ka-Kb.
43. Ibid., p. 321.
44. Ibid., p. 343.
45. Ibid., p. 322.
46. Ibid., p. 318.
47. Browne, *Literary History*, 3:21.
48. *Kolliyat-e 'Obeyd-e Zakani*, p. 330.
49. *Rostam al-Tavarikh*, ed. Mohammad Moshiri (Tehran, 1969), p. 6.
50. Ibid., pp. 109-112.

Mulla Nasreddin and Ghaffar Vakil. *From Azerbaijan, 1 (1906).*

أفرب برتمسنانانغب سکرده وابن قرستا نرآبادميوذهاند باین ترق بعض هاي كوينده كه سلانها خوابيده اند لاالهالا الله الكلام!!! اقرا خزا نفست!!!

The cemetery of deceased newspapers. *From Azerbaijan 6 (30 March 1907).*

Giving away the Caspian Sea to the Russians. "What is the use of this salt water? Why should I bother about it?" *From Azerbiajan 2 (1906).*

The government on the tree of the nation. *From* Sazerbaijan, *3 (1906).*

The governor and the electorate, before and after the election. *From Hasharat al-Arz*, 2 *(1909)*.

"Autocracy." *From Azerbaijan 4 (1906).*

تبریزده بی‌کار آدم تاپولماز

"They say no one is idle in Tabriz." *From Azerbaijan 3 (1906).*

The starving poor and the rich. *From Azerbaijan 5 (1906).*

نكمه ايله وروب يغمالیز

باصمافيتوده جنك بايد انداخت
شیخا — ای واه بر استقلال وطن

England surreptitiously by guile and Russia openly by force combine to expell Mr. W. Morgan Shuster from Persian and prevent his financial reforms. *From Buhlul 34 (22 December 1911).*

Russia presents its second ultimatum to Persia. In the background are seven others. *From Shayda 5 (2 Muharram 1330 [25 December 1911]).*

Iranian prime minister contemplats selling Azerbaijan so that he can live in luxury when retired. *From Azerbaijan 4 (1907).*

The Myrmidons of the former Shah Mohammad 'Ali attend and report on a Constitutional meeting. *From Hasharat al-Arz 12 (8 June 1908).*

Britain and India. *From Mulla Nasreddin 6, no. 34 (23 April 1909).*

The cover of *Hasharat al-Arz*, 12 (1909).

The landlord dividing the harvest. *From Azerbaijan (1906).*

People running away from the newspaper seller in Bokhara. *From Mulla Nasreddin.*

English tourist collecting antiques. *From Mulla Nasreddin 5 (16 February 1908).*

A cartoon from *Ayina-ye Ghaib-numa*, July 4, 1907.

6

Political Satire in Modern Persian Literature
Satirical Newspapers

> Once [General Pakravan] came to see me while I was
> in prison. . . . He said, "Politics is all dirt, lying, and
> viciousness; why don't you leave it to us?" What he said
> was true in a sense; if that is really what politics consists
> of, it belongs exclusively to them.
>
> —Ayatollah Khomeini

The press at the turn of the century effected a turning point in Persian literature. Many writers who had theretofore depended for their living upon various patrons were no longer compelled either to write panegyrics or to play the sycophant. Rather than kings and princes, the common people became the writers' patrons; and during the Constitutional Revolution writers and poets played a crucial role in urging their countrymen to struggle for a democratic government. Poetry, with its roots deep in Persian culture, combined with journalism, became an amazingly effective medium for satire and political propaganda. Especially during the reign of the despotic Mohammad 'Ali Shah, the newest poetic compositions would be printed in various journals and recited publicly, doing much to sustain the freedom-fighters' morale.[1] The poet in this period was no longer the parasitical writer of panegryic whom *Hajji Baba of Ispahan* mockingly defines: "A poet, that is to say, nothing but a homeless wanderer without a nest who can visit one thousand homes; a vain-talking, churlish and shameless beggar who carries his house upon his back; a seller of lies who is tasteless and spoiled; a flattering knave who deceives everyone and whose death everyone asks of God."[2] Rather, the poet had become someone deeply committed to the political and social welfare of the people. E. G. Browne in his introduction to *The Press and Poetry of Modern Persia* stresses this point when

136

he says, "If one collects the poems written since the beginnings of the Persian revolution, it will be a poetic history of the movement."[3]

Indeed, many of these new poets became national heroes. Some, like 'Eshqi and Farrokhi of Yazdi, went so far as to sacrifice their lives for the national cause. Others, like Ashraf Gilani, who ended his days in a lunatic asylum, although perfectly sane, suffered in other ways. The names of Bahar and Saber also revive the memory of the fervent and steadfast men who struggled for freedom. As a result of the poets' new outlook and role, poetic style changed dramatically. The florid language of poetry and prose, which had already begun to change in the nineteenth century, became even simpler—better suited to journalism and other popular forms of writing. At the same time such new forms of literature as drama and the novel were imported from the West. These new forms, as well as traditional genres, were employed in the writing of satire, which flourished to an unprecedented degree during the Constitutional Revolution with the advent of Iranian freedom of speech.

In order to understand political satire in modern Persian literature, one needs to have an idea of the relationship between such writing and the number of newspapers available that are willing and able to publish it.

Printing was introduced to Iran around 1835, and the first newspapers began to appear in the 1880s. According to Browne's *The Press and Poetry of Modern Persia*, 371 periodicals related to Iranian affairs appeared in Iran or abroad prior to 1912. All but 6 such publications were in Persian. Thirty-nine of them appeared between 1880 and 1900, and the remaining 332 were published between 1900 and 1912. This amazing number of publications shows the significance of the press to the Constitutional Revolution.

The First World War was a period of struggle between Iran and British and Russian forces; shortly afterward, Reza Shah came to power. His autocratic reign (1926-41) witnessed an incredible decline in the number of newspapers, only about 50 being published in this period. Additionally, all opposition papers were slowly but surely eliminated. The official position on newspapers was that they should not be political but rather nationalistic and educational.

This was quite in keeping with Iranian tradition—a free press did not come into being until the later part of Mozaffar al-Din Shah's reign (1896-1907). Mozaffar al-Din granted the Iranian Constitution in August 1906, and prior to that time only seven papers (*Akhtar*, *Qanun*, *Hekmat*, *Sorayya*, *Parvaresh*, *Habl-al-Matin*, and *Irshad*) were able to criticize the Persian government and to urge reform. All seven, notably, were published abroad. Those published in Iran, despite their billing as "national papers," were nothing but government propaganda organs, lacking any semblance of freedom of expression. The foreign press, not lacking in such freedom, was able very successfully to vex and outrage Iranian officialdom. E'temad al-Saltane, the Minister of Culture, relates in his *Ma'athir va'l Athar*, for example, how Naser al-Din Shah would grow irate over the material published abroad. One day he saw a copy of a satire by Sheikh

Hashem of Shiraz, printed in Bombay, and he was beside himself with rage. The minister told him about the censorship of the press practiced in some European countries, and the Shah immediately implemented the practice in Iran.[4]

Later, with the establishment of a free press, came a sharp increase in the number of journals and newspapers printed both abroad and in Iran. A free press did not mean, however, that one could write whatever one chose; it merely meant that a publication permit could be issued to private citizens as well as to government agents. When the number of papers published abroad increased, and especially when *Habl al-Matin* of Calcutta and the *Sorayya* of Cairo criticized the government bitterly and pressed for reform, Persian material published abroad was banned in Iran. Mirza 'Ali Asghar Khan Atabak A'zam, the prime minister, explained the prohibitions in this manner: "A newspaper published abroad, being far from governmental sources, cannot contain truthful information and for many reasons cannot be free from lies, inaccuracies and misunderstandings." At the same time, demonstrating his supposed good intentions, he added: "But if the Iranian journalists residing abroad would come to Iran, in accordance with the rules observed by all other nations, they will be allowed to publish in Iran."[5]

In addition to these remaining restrictions, the Persian press was still primitive due to inexperience and lack of facilities. The writers for the most part did not have a clear picture of the western democracy they were constantly advocating, and they often resorted to traditional moralizing and sermonizing methods. Their language at first was florid, archaic, and unsuitable for journalism. However, the sincerity and fervor of the writers, along with the relative freedom of the press, overcame such obstacles in an amazingly short time, and the years that followed the proclamation of the Constitution witnessed a tremendous outburst of political-literary activity.

The development of modern political satire in Iran has thus been linked at every stage to the political situation there, which in turn has dictated the degree of free expression possible at any given time. Because of this correlation, the Persian newspapers outside of Iran have always played a vital role in the battle for freedom of expression.

One of the first satirical newspapers outside Iran was *Shah-Seven* (The king lover), which appeared in Constantinople in A.H. 1306 (1888-89). It vehemently attacked the autocratic government of Iran. Browne writes of *Shah-Seven*, "It was published secretly, and the issue was limited to three hundred copies which were placed in envelopes like letters and sent with various precautions to statesmen, theologians, merchants, and others in Persia. Often in order to conceal the place of publication, they were first sent to Paris, London, etc., to be forwarded thence to Persia."[6] *Shah-Seven* contained many news items satirically critical of the government, and one of them is cited by Browne:

> The British Counsel at Hamadan has sent an official communication to the Government in which he complains that there is a public bath in the neighborhood of the Consulate, and that the Consulate is sorely troubled

by the filth thereof, and by the infection which emanates from it, by reason of which two of its employees have died; and requesting that the Government will either close the bath, or provide a more suitable place for the Consulate.[7]

In Iran itself, only two satirical newspapers were published before the declaration of the Constitution—*Ehtiyaj* [Need], published in Tabriz in A.H. 1316 (1898-99) under the editorship of Ali Qoli Khan, known as Safaroff; and *Tolu'* [Sunrise], published in Bushahr in A.H. 1318 (1900) under the editorship of 'Abdul-Hamid Khan Matin al-Satane.[8] The former, who would become the editor of the satirical paper *Azerbaijan*, was bastinadoed by order of the governor of Tabriz, and his paper was banned after the seventh issue.

Apart from regular newspapers, a number of *Shab-names* (nocturnal news-sheets) were secretly published and circulated among the liberals in the pre-Constitutional period. One of these irregular publications came from the pen of the aforementioned 'Ali Qoli Khan in 1892. Browne cites one of his amusing and sarcastic news items, which is more social than political, about the mud in the streets of Tabriz: "A string of camels sank in the mud, and disappeared from sight. They afterwards reappeared in the bed of the Aji River (distant about one parasang)."[9] These secretly printed "nocturnals" began circulating among the intellectuals during the reign of Naser al-Din Shah. Some of the writings of Malkum Khan and other Iranians, either abroad or within the country, were received by courtiers and even given to Mozaffar al-Din Shah. Three publications of a satirical nature, *Lisan al-Gheyb* (The tongue of the unseen), *Ruzname-ye Gheybi* (A newspaper from the unseen) and *Gheyrat* (Zeal), were all mimeographed and published by a secret society around 1901 and 1902. The first two papers were directed principally against the pro-Russian policy of then—Prime Minister Atabak 'Azam, while the last, along with a fourth secret publication called *Hammam-e Jenniyan* (The bath of the Jinns), criticized the tyrannies of Zell al-Sultan.[10]

Circulating such publications, of course, involved great risk. One of the above *Shab-names*, which opposed the Persian government's loans from Russia, was found by Mozaffar al-Din Shah in the hands of a courtier, Mowaqqar al-Saltane, who had intended to put it secretly on the desk of the king. The courtier was bastinadoed and the author, Sheikh Yahya of Kashan, was sent into exile in Ardabil. A second accomplice, a theologian of some repute, Mirza Hasan Rushdieh, took sanctuary in the house of a great *mujtehed*, Sheikh Hadi Najm Abadi, and it was only because of the kindheartedness of the king that no harm came to him.[11]

Before leaving the pre-Constitutional period, let us consider in more detail the lives and work of two writers and reformers of that time—Malkum Khan and Mirza Agha Khan of Kerman. Although they came from very different backgrounds, both of them were involved in journalism and both occasionally wrote satire. Their writings are perhaps the best of their kind in this period.

Malkum Khan (1827-1908) was from an Armenian family of Isfahan; he was converted to Islam and served in the Persian government, eventually becoming the envoy to England. He preached reform and founded a society called "the Religion of Humanity." He pressed for the introduction and adaptation of western types of government, thereby displeasing Naser al-Din Shah, and was sent into "exile" as the ambassador to England. It was in London that Malkum began to publish his famous newspaper, *Qanun* (Law) (1890-93), excoriating his home government. Malkum died at the age of eighty-one in Europe, and while there were instances of dishonesty in his life that make him subject to criticism, he was nonetheless, as Yahya Aryanpur writes, "an ambitious, brave, learned, and intelligent man, who despite his love of money was deeply patriotic. Despite the criticisms directed against him, it cannot be denied that Malkum played an important role in awakening the Persians."[12]

Unlike Malkum, there is nothing in the life of Mirza Agha Khan of Kerman (1852-96) to attract censure. Mirza's father belonged to a Sufi sect in Kerman, and Mirza left that city because of its tyrannical governor, going to Isfahan and later to Istanbul. There, for quite some time contributing to the Persian paper *Akhtar*, he tried to disseminate his ideas of reform, pan-Islamism, and nationalism. The assassination of Naser al-Din Shah in 1896 by Mirza Reza of Kerman sealed the fate of Agha Khan, since the assassin was a follower of the famous philosopher and propagandist, Seyyed Jamal al-Din Afghani, with whom Agha Khan and two of his friends were closely connected. The three were extradited to Iran, the Seyyed remaining in Istanbul. Mirza Agha Khan and his two friends were beheaded in Tabriz in 1896.

Both Malkum Khan and Mirza Agha Khan wrote satirical treatises on various subjects, though these did not constitute the bulk of their work. While in government service, Malkum was understandably reserved in his criticism, but once outside his attacks were merciless. The following is a short excerpt from his *Resale-ye 'Adalat* (The treatise on justice):

> Every wretch who possesses a patch of ground or a bit of wealth, he [Amin al-Sultan] must strip bare with a thousand lying promises in accordance with that variety of swindling known in government terminology as "an offering to the presence" [*taqdim-e Huzur*], and then, with a filthy scrap of paper known as "the universally obeyed decree" [*farman-e Jahanmuta'*], he appoints him as governor of some wilderness or other, until a few days later he is dismissed with ignominy, and some other idiot is found to take his place.[13]

Malkum's approach is, for the most part, that of direct criticism tinged with sarcasm and satire. He lacks the coherence and control of a master satirist like Dehkhoda, whose work we will discuss below. The opening section of one of Malkum's essays, *Usule Mazhab-e Divaniyan* (The principles of religion for government officials) illustrates again his style of unrestrained attack—once more against Amin al-Sultan, the prime minister:

For what purpose has the Lord of the world created the land and people of Iran? So that a few irreligious scoundrels might enjoy themselves. What is the blessed name of these scoundrels? The trustees of the exalted Iranian state. By virtue of what accomplishment have these noble trustees gained such a privilege? By virtue of the fact that they have made Iran poorer, more wretched and desolate than any other place in the world. What virtues must they possess to proceed with their sacred mission?

First, they must not be ashamed of any disgraceful matter. Second, they must sincerely and faithfully be the enemies of learning and the promoters of the utmost vileness [literally, "cuckoldry"]. Third, they must attain a point of disinterestedness where they can equitably choose as the first among them that villain who by virtue of his innate despicability and lunacy is to be preferred to the rest of them [i.e., Amin al-Sultan]. What is to be the task of that blessed personage?

All honorable and enlightened persons in the kingdom he must vilify, humiliate and persecute with every kind of atrocity. He must put to work around the throne all his brothers, relatives and hangers-on, in particular the least worthy among them, and gather into his own hands all the necessities of the life of the king, in such manner that that auspicious person cannot take a step or even breathe without his permission.[14]

Mirza Agha Khan, like Malkum, was often directly critical of the Persian government. *Salar-Name* and *Sad Masale*, for instance, were both written as works of direct political propaganda and criticism, though the former contains much satire as well. It was originally called *Name-ye Bastan* (The book of the ancients), and it was meant to be a sort of supplement to the *Shah-Name*, adopting its same rhyme and form. Mirza Agha Khan completed it while in exile in Tarabozan; after his execution, one of his classmates versified the rest of its sections, from the beginning of Islam to the time of Mozaffar al-Din Shah. Both volumes were published in Shiraz in A.H. 1316 (1898), but the edition omitted a number of Mirza Agha's dangerously nationalistic poems, which expounded his criticism of the king.[15]

Mirza Agha Khan also wrote a book entitled *Rezvan*, an imitation of Sa'di's *Gulestan*. This work, which is yet to be published, criticizes the government and its corruption through brief and witty anecdotes. The following may serve as representative samples:

A tyrant king asked a philosopher: "It has been said that the Holy Prophet did not have any shadow. How can this be explained logically?" The philosopher replied: "I wish God had no shadow, so that people could rest."[16]

***

. An Iranian member of parliament saw a thief being taken for execution at the court of the king, whereupon he said: "This thief should indeed be killed, since he wanted to steal without an official uniform and without having a government post. . . ."

***

A king said to an ascetic: "You must have had a great soul to forsake the world." He answered: "Yours must have been greater, since you deserted the next world and the joys of heaven!"

***

The Shahanshah of Iran asked the British Ambassador: "Why is it that the roads in Iran are so badly built and so inaccessible?" He said: "Because the only engineers in this country were asses and mules. . . ."

***

Imam Jum'a of Tehran was seriously ill. They brought Dr. Tholozan[17] to see him, and he prescribed drinking old wine. The Imam refused, saying that if he drank wine he would go to hell. The doctor said: "If you don't, you will go sooner."

There are also satirical verses in *Rezvan:*

> You call wine unlawful, and the blood of the people lawful
> And yet you are desirous of reaching Heaven.
> I am amazed that with this ugly soul,
> You could desire union with the *peris* of Paradise.

In this pre-Constitutional period, then, many poets and writers believed strongly in the writer's sociopolitical commitment. Malkum Khan and Mirza Agha Khan both shared—and argued for—the idea of a writer's social duty and role. Malkum in his *Traveler's Narrative*, for instance, satirizes Iranian writers who would rather merely banter with florid and senseless words than impart ideas. Agha Khan more straightforwardly writes that the "people of Iran do not yet know the power of poetry by which a nation can be revived, thoughts elevated, courage increased in the heart, and the moral standards of the society improved." Every starving beggar of a poet who exaggerates and employs a complicated style is, in Agha Khan's estimation, a "poet laureate." "The stupid Qa'ani who did nothing but play with words is given the title of 'philosopher.' This tasteless sycophant has completely sacrificed the nobility of praise and the dignity of panegyric, and poets have made their 'noble art' a means of begging, exaggeration, vain talking, or nonsensical invectives. . . . In fact," he continues, "the Persian poets are less than dogs and more numerous than they," whereas the true purpose of poetry is "to illuminate minds, to dispel superstitions, to remind the forceful, and to inculcate the love of country and a sense of patriotism."[18]

THE CONSTITUTIONAL PERIOD AND LATER

At the turn of the century, nationalistic poetry was spreading throughout the Middle East; ideas similar to those of the Persian writers were expressed by Arabic and Turkish writers as well. In Egypt in 1910, for instance, 'Ali al-Ghayati published a collection of patriotic poems entitled *Wataniyyati;* it created such a sensation that the poet had to flee to Istanbul. The outraged British officials, whose politicies were the subject of al-Ghayati's criticism, even brought two men to trial who had contributed prefaces to the book. Both were convicted and imprisoned for three months. One of the two, Sheikh 'Abdu'l-'Aziz, emphasizes in his preface the sincerity and originality of the poet's feelings, and the other, Ferid Bey, dwells upon "the influence of poetry on the Education of Nations."[19] Both prefaces bear a striking resemblance to the aforementioned essay of Mirza Agha Khan on the social responsibility of the poet. The Persian literature of the time was a special blend of patriotic and satirical poetry, and in order to find its source of inspiration, one must turn to the satirical literature that was published in the Azeri Turkish newspapers of the Caucasus.

The Caucasus was occupied by the Russians in the early years of the nineteenth century, but its cultural ties with Iran continued almost unbroken until the 1920s and the establishment of Communism. Satire, which enjoys a long tradition in Azerbaijani literature, gained a new momentum at the turn of the century. Writers such as 'Abdu'l-Rahim Haq-verdiev, Najef Beik Vazirli, Mohammad Sa'id Ordubadi, Jalil Mamed Quli-Zade, and Taherzade Saber made their appearances on the literary scene. The last two were responsible for the publication of the well-known satirical journal, *Mulla Nasreddin*, which exercised a decisive influence on the course of satirical journalism in Iran.

The development of journalism in Azerbaijan precedes that of Iran by seven or eight years. The first newspaper, *The News of Tiblisi*, appeared in Russian in 1828. A year later the same newspaper was published in Georgian, then in 1830 in Persian, and in 1832 in Turkish. The period from 1905 to 1920, just before Azerbaijan became a Soviet Republic, was the golden age of Azerbaijani journalism, and it witnessed the appearance of many satirical papers. Since most of these newspapers were read in the northern parts of Iran and very often became models for Iranian writers, a list of Azerbaijani satirical papers may be appropriate here. There were 405 journals and newspapers published between 1832 and 1920 in Turkish, Persian, Russian, and a few other languages—140 of which were in Turkish.[20] Of these, the following fifteen were satirical: published in Baku were *Babay-e Amir* (weekly, illustrated, 1909-10); *Mazaly* (weekly, illustrated, 1914-15); *Palanduz* (weekly, 1910-11); *Tuti* (weekly, illustrated, 1914-17); *Charikh-chi* (weekly, 1911-12); *Shaipur* (weekly, 1918-19); *Mash'al* (weekly, 1919-20); *Mirat* (weekly, illustrated, 1910); *Ari* (weekly, illustrated, 1910-11); *Bohlul* (weekly, illustrated, 1907-9); and *Kalniyat* (weekly, illustrated, 1912-13). Appearing in Tiflis were *Kashkul* (monthly, 1883-91); *Tartan Partan* (weekly, illustrated, 1918); and in Erivan, *Lak Lak* (weekly, illustrated, 1914). Finally, the most influential journal of all was *Mulla Nasreddin*, a weekly illustrated paper published in Tiflis from 1906 to 1917. The editor, Jalil Mamed Qoli-Zade, went to Tabriz in 1921 and published eight issues of *Mulla Nasreddin* but, due to police interference, left Tabriz for Baku, where he continued to publish the journal until 1929. In addition to these fifteen Turkish papers, some that were published in Azerbaijan had Persian or Arabic supplements. *Kashkul*, for instance, contained articles in both Persian and Turkish, and *Ershad* had a supplement in Persian written by the Persian poet and journalist, Adib al-Mamalek.

The satirical newspapers published in Iran itself were both fewer in number and shorter in duration than those published in Azerbaijan. They had, however, a remarkable influence in shaping public opinion. Below are listed the papers, either partially or entirely satirical, that were published in the first two decades of the twentieth century: *Sure-e Esrafil* (Tehran, 1907), containing "Charand Parand" (Nonsensical talk) by 'Ali Akbar Dehkhoda; *Azerbaijan* (Tabriz, 1907), published in both Azeri Turkish and Persian, containing interesting color cartoons and reminiscent in many ways of *Mulla Nasreddin*; *Nagur* (Isfahan, 1908-9), containing the satirical column entitled "Zesht o Ziba"; (Ugly and beautiful) *Te'atr* (Tehran, 1908), which discussed various sociopolitical matters in the form of satirical dialogues; and *Nasim-e Shomal*, written and published by Seyyed Ashraf of Gilan almost singlehandedly. This last journal originated in Rasht in 1907 and continued its publication in Tehran for several years thereafter; in it Seyyed Ashraf translated and adapted a great number of Saber's poems from *Mulla Nasreddin*. Finally, to complete this list one should mention *Hasharat al-'Arz* (Tabriz, 1909); *Chante-ye Pa Berahne* (Tehran, 1911); *Jangal-e Mowla* (Tehran, 1911); *Sheikh Choghandar* (Tehran, 1911); *Jarchi-ye Mellat* (Tehran, 1910); and of course *Kashkul* (Isfahan, 1909) and *Bohlul* (Tehran, 1911).

None of these papers, however, met with the success of *Mulla Nasreddin*, even though they shared the same political and cultural conditions that fostered it. After the defeat of the Russian army in Manchuria in 1905 and after the disturbances of the same year, a certain degree of free expression was granted to the press—a liberty that coincided among the Muslim peoples of Tsarist Russia with the movement of the Young Turks and with the Constitutional Revolution in Iran. It was a time of great historical change—leading to the creation of many journals and papers, among them, *Mulla Nasreddin*. *Mulla Nasreddin* began publication in April 1906 in Tiflis, at that time the capital of Transcaucasia and a crossroads of cultures, races, and ideas. It was there that the exiled, largely liberal Russian aristocracy met with the Muslim intelligentsia and with socialists of various stripes. But the extraordinary success of *Mulla Nasreddin* was not primarily due to these circumstances, shared, as indicated, by many other papers. Rather, *Mulla Nasreddin*'s great success was due primarily to the genius of its writers. Not only did the publication include the work of Jalil Mamed Qoli-Zade, a well-known satirist, playwright, and short-story writer, but Saber's talents also graced the journal. Other contributors were the poet 'Ali Nazmi, the dramatist 'Abdurrahim Beik Haqverdiev, and the novelist Mohammad Sa'id Ordubadi. Two German artists, Schmerling and Rotter, contributed cartoons full of verve and caustic humor.[21]

It was the Azeri poetry of Saber, whose satirical poems were regularly published in the journal until his death in 1911, that contributed most to *Mulla Nasreddin*'s tremendous impact upon the satirical press of Iran. Alesio Bombaci writes of Saber that he combines the wrath of Juvenal with the sarcasm of Béranger and the humanism of Nekrasov.[22] His originality of thought and form, coupled with his steadfast, sincere, and humane personality, marks him as a truly great poet.

His poetry fully reflects the aspirations of the liberal Muslims of the Middle East, both then and now. Further, the vivid realism of his poetry reflects the hardships of his own life as well as the corruption, superstition, repression, and ignorance prevalent in his society. In his own life, Saber faced the opposition of the officials and various clerics, and suffered greatly as a consequence. He had to publish his poetry under different pen names, one of which was "Weeping and Laughing"[23]—an accurate description of his life.

The satirical work of Saber embraces a wide variety of subjects, ranging from the defeat of the vainglorious czarist armies by Japan to scenes of social and domestic life at home. The butts of his satire range from Emperor Wilhelm of Prussia to Mohammad 'Ali Shah of Iran, from Sultan 'Abdul Hamid of Turkey to very minor officials and ignorant mullas. Saber's most fruitful years were those from 1905 to 1911, a period which coincided with Iran's Constitutional Revolution. Due to this fortuity of timing and also to his personal interest in that country, Saber wrote many poems on Iranian events, many of which were published in *Mulla Nasreddin*. The struggle between the reactionaries and the Constitutionalists, the social corruption in Iran, the nature of the totalitarian government of Mohammad 'Ali Shah, and many other aspects of the Revolution are all depicted in the bitingly satirical poems of Saber. Mohammad 'Ali Shah was one of the poet's favorite targets. Saber depicted the monarch as a ruthless, hypocritical, and miserly tyrant. In one poem he mockingly exposes the boastful Mohammad 'Ali Shah by donning his voice:

> I am the glorious King, Iran is mine;
> Rey and Taberestan, all are mine.
> If Iran prospers or lies in ruin, all is mine!
> What is Constitutional Law? The decree is mine!
> Glory, splendour, dignity—all are mine!
>
> If my father granted you your rights,
> It was because he was a mulla, tolerant and upright,
> Unaware of political wrongs and rights.
> So now, my countrymen, don your coat of lice!
> Robes of honor, throne of gold, are mine!
> Glory splendour, dignity—all are mine![24]

Mohammad 'Ali Shah, who never approved of his father's liberalism, was indeed one of the most corrupt and ruthless kings of the Qajar dynasty. In another poem Saber depicts him as a man who has put Iran up for auction, including the royal treasures, the provinces, and the country's heritage.[25] And after the king has shelled the Parliament and killed off a number of Constitutionalists, Saber in another highly sarcastic poem congratulates him on his great "achievement" in silencing the opposition! After Mohammad 'Ali has been defeated and has taken refuge in the Russian Embassy, Saber, with a fine ear for sarcasm, expresses himself with mock despair:

My heart aches for that poor, fatherless Sire.
May the Iranians burn and roast in fire!
Bad news I fear: forsaking the throne, he has fled,
Taking refuge in the Consulate, the king of Iranians!
But noble of blood never have been the Iranians.

Why should the Iranians be so untrue?
Why should they reject the ways of the past?
Should they, like "new Ottomans," be so vile and depraved?
. . . .

May God destroy the Iran of Iranians!
But noble of blood never have been the Iranians.

For not even three years were his pleasures spent,
Undisturbed he could never enjoy his crown and life,
So that under his justice the people might happily strive,
And in peace might they prosper, the Muslim Iranians.
But noble of blood never have been the Iranians!

What had he done, this fatherless orphan, to you?
Out of his conscience, what did he do to you?
By deceit and device, everyone made him confused.
Let the soul depart from the body of the Iranians!
But noble of blood never have been the Iranians.

Did he not honorably show his respect to you?
Did he not grant the Constitution to you?
Did he not kiss the Koran and make his vow to you?
So why did they not rest assured, all the Iranians?
But noble of blood never have been the Iranians.

This beautiful country housed nobles in the past—
Noblemen, good elders and youths of renown,
Khans who regarded the King as "shadow of the Lord";
Now men like Yefrem have become the Khans of the Iranians![26]
But noble of blood never have been the Iranians.

O my friend, why interfere with the affairs of the King?
Why observe him so closely or watch him with such intent?
One who is King surely knows what he must do;
Is it possible to entrust such affairs to the common Iranians,
When noble of blood never have been the Iranians?

The Shah knows what he takes, and what he returns;
Sometimes he robs a pocket, or skins alive one or two,
    here and there.
He may sever heads, plunder homes, kill and pluck out eyes,
But let the cries of the Iranians rise to heaven.
Slaves to the King always have been the Iranians;
Noble of blood never have been the Iranians![27]

Such then is the biting satire of Saber's verse—bitter, terse, and with a touch of humor that deepens, rather than lightens, the dead-seriousness of his message. He is clearly the type of poet who greatly values free expression and believes that it is the poet's responsibility to awaken and encourage the people. When the Russian Azerbaijan became a Soviet republic, Saber was glorified as a great revolutionary poet; had he lived to witness the eventual suppression of the press under the Soviets, however, he would have deeply lamented its sad end.

The immense popularity of Saber and of *Mulla Nasreddin*'s other writers led of course to much imitation. In *Mulla Nasreddin*, for instance, the Mulla was represented by a humorous and sometimes cynical character called Mulla Da'i or Mulla 'Amu, and this character pervaded every feature of the journal. He signed the poems, answered the letters, advised the youth, and parodied the viewpoints of the establishment. He was even present in the cartoons, always peeping from the corners. This ubiquitous character was adopted by such journals as the weekly *Azerbaijan*, which began its publication in 1907 in Tabriz. *Azerbaijan* presented the figure of Hajji Baba in Mulla Da'i's role, and the imitation was seeminly quite conscious—the cover of the first issue of *Azerbaijan* shows Hajji Baba standing before the Mulla, listening to him like a faithful pupil.

Similar characters appear in other Persian satirical weeklies, among them *Hasharat al-'Arz* (Tabriz, 1908), *Sheida* (Istanbul, 1911), *Bohlul* (Tehran, 1908), and *Sheikh Choghandar* (Tehran, 1911). The device was even taken up by such famous writers as Dehkhoda; in his column in *Sur-e Esrafil* entitled "Charand Parand," a column that contained some of the most telling examples of his satire, he would sign his name by such fictitious titles as "Damdamki" (Whimsical), "Mulla 'Aynak 'Ali," and "Kharmagas" (Gadfly). The device enjoyed such popularity perhaps because of its deep roots in the Persian satirical tradition, combining as it does the technique of caricature with that of the "wise fool"; but if in fact the cause of its popularity is rooted in classical tradition, *Mulla Nasreddin* nonetheless heralded its modern application.

Individual poems of Saber were also frequently translated or imitated by writers of the Persian press.[28] His famous poem that begins, "However the nation is plundered, what do I care?" was imitated in Persian by Mirza Mehdi Khan, the editor of the newspaper *Hekmat*, and the rendition appeared in the weekly *Azerbaijan* (number 10). Below is a literal translation of Saber's poem, followed by the first few couplets of the Persian imitation. As one can see, the Persian adaptations of Saber's lines are often quite free. They are generally longer, too—Saber's original poem of fourteen couplets being expanded in this particular rendition to fifty-two. Unfortunately, moreover, much of the terseness, the beauty, and the tone of Saber's original is lost in the process. The original:

> However the nation is plundered, what do I care?
> Should she be begging from the enemy, what do I care?
> Let me be full; I have no concern for others.
> If my country, if the whole world, goes hungry, what do I care?

Don't make any noise, lest the sleepers wake up;
I wouldn't want the sleepers to wake up.
God help me, if even one or two are up;
Being safe, I don't care if the whole world is torn up.
   However the nation is plundered, what do I care?
   Should she be begging from the enemy, what do I care?
Don't remind me of the world's past;
Don't talk of the glory of the past!
For the present, bring bread and stuffed eggplant:
Why foresee the future? Life hurries by!
   However the nation is plundered, what do I care?
   Should she be begging from the enemy, what do I care?

Let our countrymen keep on wandering around,
Let them sink in the whirlpool of ignorance;
Let the widow burn in poverty's fire—
Only let me know prosperity and glory!
   However the nation is plundered, what do I care?
   Should she be begging from the enemy, what do I care?

On the world's stage, every nation makes progress;
At every stage, every station, each one makes progress.
In my bed, under blankets, if I think of progress,
Then perhaps in the realm of dream, I will make progress.
   However the nation is plundered, what do I care?
   Should she be begging from the enemy, what do I care?[29]

The adaptation:

> If Iran is gone, what do I care?
> If she is ruined, what do I care?
> If the Pamirs and Fergana are gone
> As well as the province of Bedakhshan,
> What do I care!
>
> If the Russians bought
> The forests of Mazandaran,
> What do I care?
> If their warships are anchored
> At Anzali, what do I care?
>
> If the British have become
> The guardians of all the cities,
> One by one, what do I care?
> If they have bought
> All the border-guards,
> What do I care? . . .

Clearly, the details of thought and image that create the intense crescendo of Saber's sarcasm are largely lacking in the Persian rendition. The adaptation employs Saber's basic motif, but only to create a poem of simpler, lighter, and perhaps less heartfelt emotion.

When we come to other translations of Saber into Persian, a similar situation exists—though perhaps to a lesser degree. The translations tend to be longer than the originals and thereby lose some of the tightness and intensity of Saber's style. The most important translator of Saber's work was Seyyed Ashraf of Gilan, who translated and published many of Saber's poems in his weekly journal, *Nasim-e Shomal.* Ashraf was an important satirist and journalist himself, and he and Saber were very much alike in their sincerity, their spirituality, and their devotion to the welfare of the poor and of the common people. In foresight and breadth of vision, however, the Persian could not compete with the Azeri poet, nor could he equal Saber's literary genius. Ashraf's own style tends to be journalistic and without substantial literary merit.

Ashraf's use of Saber's work varies greatly, too. Sometimes his translations are faithful and exact, other times quite free. The following "translation" by Ashraf falls somewhere in between these two extremes. It appeared early in 1909 under the title of "I Am Selling," and it is a relatively free translation of the poem mentioned earlier in connection with Saber, in which Mohammad 'Ali Shah auctions off the provinces, the treasures, and the heritage of Iran. In Ashraf's Persian version, Mohammad 'Ali Shah has been replaced with the famous reactionary Mujtehed, Sheikh Fazlullah Nuri, though he is still quite clearly an auctioneer of the goods and valuables of Iran. Characteristically, Ashraf's version is twice as long as Saber's poem; the original consists of thirty-six lines and Ashraf's of sixty-eight. Below is Saber's original poem, translated from Azeri by Dorian Rottenberg, followed by the first five stanzas of Browne's translation of Ashraf's rendition:

> People won't be silent, uncle, when they hear the tale;
> Bah! It doesn't matter, does it, what sneers it may entail?
>
> Write it down on paper on a wall to nail:
> I've opened here in Rey[30] a new tremendous sale!
>   Dirt cheap, the wares my shop displays for sale;
>   Come buy! The whole of Rey today's for sale!
> But what is more, I do not sell that article alone,
> But with the Jami-Jam, Rey's subjects, Kubbad's[31] throne,
>
> Although I'm somewhat hindered, I must own,
> By certain Young Iranians[32] well-known.
>   But never mind them—wholesale and retail,
>   Come, buy, the whole of Rey today's for sale!
> What shall I do with all that bric-a-brac?
> So many cares it brings, it sure will break my back.
> That "Salty Water"[33]—not much use, alack!

I'll better sell it all before the sky looks black!
  The palace of Shiraz, the heritage of Rey today's for sale!

  Come, buy! The whole of Rey today's for sale!
I hate the light—I offer gloom for sale,
I love to see Iran under its veil.
I want to leave the city—deserts, hail!
I'd be a khan—being a shah seems stale.
  Sabzivar and Meyaneh's for sale![34]
  Come, buy! The whole of Rey today's for sale!
My will is mine, my words, my home as well,
My honour, self-respect, the shame into which I fell.
My wealth—who else but me its fate may spell?

My Qajar crown and state today I sell.
  Whose business what goods I display for sale?
  Come, buy, the whole of Rey today's for sale!

Instead of being constitutional shah,
A publicly elected guiding star,
The army's puppet—not a sovereign by far,
Instead of always saying Oh! and Ah!
  I'd drink wine as a khan—my crown today's for sale!
  Come, buy, today the whole of Rey's for sale![35]

I Am Selling

(1)

Hajji, the market's brisk, the bidding high;
Here comes the auctioneer! Who'll buy? Who'll buy?
  I'm here the Persian land to sell or pawn,
  The pride and honor of each Musulman,
  Both Qum and Rasht, both Qazwain and Kashan,
  Yazd, Khwansar, every city of Iran.
All's up for auction at a figure fair:
Come, gentlemen, where is a bidder, where?

(2)

Of Liberals I am the stalwart foe:
I'd like to kill them all, as well you know!
I represent Shaykh Fazlu'llah and Co.,
Brokers, who hawk Religion to and fro,
  Here is the carcass. Gentlemen, draw near!
  Who'll buy? Who'll buy? Here comes the auctioneer!

(3)

My countrymen I loathe and execrate;
My country is the object of my hate!
I represent our Monarch wise and great,
Who to my hands commits the Nation's fate!

'Tis time for breakfast. Put this business through!
Who bids? Who bids? Come, Sir, a bid from you!

(4)
At Shahr-i-Naw behold the patroits' post!
Scattered at Karach is the Cossack host!
Well may I rave, or e'en give up the ghost!
Let's sell the land to him who offers most!
    What offer for this richly-wrought brocade
    With gold enwoven? Is no offer made?

(5)
Who wants these trumpets, drums and flags to own?
Who'd make the Lion and the Sun his own?
Who'll make a bid for Persian Jamshid's throne?
Kay's crown, Jam's sceptre in with these are thrown!
    For this fine horse and for this bridle rare,
    Who'll make a bid? Where is an offer, where?[36]

Seyyed Ashraf wrote, of course, much original satire in addition to his translations and imitations of Saber, and a few words should be said about him as
a journalist and as an original author. As a journalist, he was incredibly hard-
working and devoted to the patriotic cause. For many years he managed to write
and print his weekly journal, *Nasim-e Shomal*, first in Rasht and then in Tehran.
His life affords a rare example of a journalist dedicating his life to the welfare
of the common people. Sa'id Nafisi, a long-time friend of Ashraf, comments
on the popularity of his paper despite its various technical and literary demerits:

[*Nasim-e Shomal*] was neither spectacular nor well-printed; its editor was
neither a senator nor an M.P. nor an ex-minister. So why did the people
like it so much? The newspaper was in fact so well-known that people would
call its editor, Seyyed Ashraf Gilani, Mr. Nasim-e Shomal. On the day that
it was to be distributed, several groups of children, aged ten to twelve years,
would gather in front of the printing house, every one proud to be a dis-
tributor of *Nasim-e Shomal*. Then they would leave with huge bundles of
the papers . . . .

The popularity of *Nasim-e Shomal* can only be attributed, then, to the heartfelt spirit and dedicated ideals behind its publication. Nafisi continues:

There was not in fact a day in which *Nasim-e Shomal* did not create a
sensation in Tehran. Many cabinets were seriously annoyed by it, but what
could they do with this unworldly, devoted, and penniless Seyyed? There
was no use in imprisoning him, for he would not sit still even in prison.
He had an extraordinary memory, so that whatever he composed, he could
remember and recite later on. He had no need for pen and paper. Ashraf
entered the journalistic scene when the struggle between the Constitutionalists and the Royalists was at its peak, too. He wrote poems criticizing
Mohammad 'Ali Shah, Amir Bahador and their friends, and these poems
became extremely popular. No one was more effective than he in reaching
the public. Ashraf's value to the Persian Constitutional Revolution is
equalled, perhaps, only by that of its great leader, Sattar Khan. Ashraf even

took to arms in Qazwin, and with the army of Mohammad Vali Khan of
Tonkabon, took part in the freeing of Tehran.

The liberalism and tolerance in Ashraf's attitude were amazing, too. One
could say anything to him and see not the slightest sign of partiality in
him. He was full of witty remarks, and he knew many wonderful tales. He
was a storehouse of feeling and sympathy. He would never begrudge anyone,
yet he would vilify and satirize everyone—and how wonderfully at that!
If only someone like him could do the same with the people of our own
day!

Ashraf's end, however, was sad. He died in abject poverty in a Tehran lunatic
asylum in 1933. Sa'id Nafisi again says of him:

> He lived a bachelor all his life. At the end he met the consequences that
> are part of the lives of great men. He was taken to a lunatic asylum, and
> was given a room facing the backyard. . . . I never discovered the insanity
> in this great man! He was the same as he always had been.[37]

As with Saber, satire for Ashraf was a useful tool for reform. His collected
poems, which have been printed several times in both Iran and India under
the title *Bagh-e Behesht*, (Garden of Paradise) consist mainly of satirical poems
dealing with sociopolitical problems and with the difficult lives of the people.
And because the aim of his verse was to awaken a critical social awareness, its
language was simple and readily accessible to the common man. The simplicity
of his language and his liberal use of such popular forms as the *tasnif* may well
account for Ashraf's enthusiastic reception by his audience.

The butts of Ashraf's satire fall into the same classes as those attacked by
his contemporary satirical poets: reactionary divines, repressive and tyrannical
officials, the king himself, ignorant and superstitious people, and the newly elected
members of Parliament who had so quickly forgotten their promises to the electorate. The main body of Ashraf's poetry can be divided into two categories: poems
that ponder the past glories of Iran and lament her present degradation, and
poems that satirically depict current sociopolitical conditions and urge the reader
to strive for reform.[38] The following poem exemplifies this latter type. The poem
employs a familiar method in which criticism of the poet's liberal views is placed
in the mouth of an imaginary reactionary. In this as well as his other poems,
Ashraf uses imaginary names such as "Kharab 'Ali Mirza," echoing the picaresque
tradition of coining ridiculous names for one's target(s):

> "O Ashraf, be no longer over-bold! Be not so insistent
>   about the Constitution!
> I am an adversary and enemy to all the people; I will not
>   unite with any one;
> I am a Reactionary, a Reactionary, a Reactionary!
>   Do not thou preach Constitutionalism!
> O little minstrel, arise, strike the harp and the lute!

O little cup-bearer, give wine quickly!
If the Empire is lost, to Hell with it! Prate not
　of the Turk and the Empire!
I drink for wine the blood of the people; I eat
　for roast meat the flesh of the people;
I have no fear of torment and retribution; do not put me
　off with threats of to-morrow's Resurrection!
Put not thy trust in the words of the Franks; talk not of
　the maxims of the schools;
Do not find fault with such as love the ancient ways;
　do not exult in the awakening of the Nation!
What can I do? The enemy is sharp-witted. He has
　broken into this garden and meadow:

All Sawujbulagh is topsy-turvy. Weep not over the
　people's condition!
If Urumiyya is gone, Khurasan is enough; if that too goes,
　Isfahan is enough;
If naught else be left, Tehran itself is enough! O Ashraf,
　work no further mischief![39]

Not only Ashraf and his *Nasim-e Shomal* but *Sur-e Esrafil* and its contributors
are also indebted in many ways to Saber and *Mulla Nasreddin*. *Sur-e Esrafil* was
a Persian weekly; its first issue appeared in Tehran on 30 May, 1907, and it was
discontinued on 20 June 1908, three days before the shelling of the "Majles"
and four days before its editor, Mirza Jahangir Khan, was put to death by order
of Mohammad 'Ali Shah. Three more issues were produced by 'Ali Akbar
Dehkhoda at Yverdon in Switzerland, but the paper did not last long in exile.
Sur-e Esrafil resembled *Mulla Nasreddin* in many ways. It did not have such sug-
gestive cartoons, but it did contain a series of satirical essays by Dehkhoda which
resembled the satirical writings of Saber and Jalil Mamed Qoli-Zade. Dehkhoda
had spent some time in Austria and in the Balkan countries in the company
of Persian Ambassador Mu'avven al-Doule Ghaffari, and he started a new trend
in the Persian satirical tradition. Although he wrote some poetry, his greatest
achievement was his prose. His slender volume of satirical essays alone—collected
under the title "Charand Parand"—distinguishes him as a remarkable and original
satirist.[40]

One of the satirical methods Dehkhoda used, which resembled the techniques
of Jalil Mamed Quli-Zade, was to create a very naive or ignorant character for
his feuilleton; another, to affect naiveté while writing. In December 1906, for
instance, Quli-Zade published a short story entitled "Freedom in Iran" in which
he describes an ignorant Iranian worker in Baku and his reaction to the
declaration of the Constitution. Like many thousands of his countrymen, this
man, Karbalay Mohammad 'Ali, has come from Persian Azerbaijan to find work
in Baku, where he has also acquired a second wife. His meager income is not
sufficient to enable him to send money to his first wife at home. It is in the
midst of this financial predicament that he hears that the Shah has granted the

Constitution to the people and that the Iranian consul has asked everyone to gather in the mosque. Mohammad 'Ali describes the event: "There men prayed for the Shah who had granted Persia a Constitution. . . . Now, please God, there will be enough money. All my countrymen greatly rejoiced and wanted to throw their caps in the air, saying that tomorrow the Consul will gather us all and start to distribute the Constitution among us."[41] Indeed, Mohammad 'Ali soon asks someone to write a letter for him to Iran, requesting his share of the Constitution!

Dehkhoda describes a similarly credulous young man in one of his essays. The young man's name is Azad Khan Karandi, a Kurd who imagines religion to be something concrete, just as Jalil Mamed Quli-Zade's Azerbaijani worker had thought of the Constitution. Azad Khan comes to Tehran looking for work, again like Mohammad 'Ali, and he is hired by a succession of employers. While in the service of a high-ranking cleric, he hears that his master has misappropriated some funds that had been entrusted to him for safekeeping. People bellow, "The faith is lost!" Then, while in the employment of a pawnbroker, he sees the wife and daughter of his master seduced away into the harem of a dignitary, and people again bellow, "The faith is lost!" He hears the same outrage on yet another occasion when Salar al-Doule takes his beloved, a handsome young boy, with him on a pilgrimage to Mecca. All these exclamations make Azad Khan wonder what faith is: in one case it is money, in another it is women, and in a third it is a homosexual paramour. And since he has none of these, Azad Khan sadly concludes, "I see now that since I cannot get faith, I will surely go to hell!"[42]

Another satirical trick used by both Dehkhoda and Quli-Zade is to address a letter of advice to a fictitious author, in which the admonition not to reveal this or that incident that the government has censored from the press is a shield for the author's satirical intent. Quli-Zade, for instance, published the following letter in *Mulla Nasreddin* (21 April 1907),[43] addressed to the fictional Damdameki, one of Dehkhoda's pen names:

> Damdameki, are you really mad? Why were you not afraid to write all that to me? Are you bored with your life? What would you say if I were to put your letter on the pages of [this] journal? Try to understand that the people of Baku would pelt you with stones and stop buying my paper.
>
> Can you imagine for a moment if I could write that owls have put their nests in the public reading rooms of Baku? Could I possibly write that the Baku Philanthropic Society interests no one, and that its members are ignorant idlers? And that the streets of Baku are infested with begging Muslims, women and children?
>
> Just think, Damdameki, if I could write that on the 9th of April two distinguished Muslim town councillors pointed their pistols at one another and exchanged dreadful curses. . . . And if I could announce in this journal that on the 28th Safar, several Baku men in Bibi-Hybat[44] smashed one another's heads so furiously that some of them are still bleeding. . . . What is the matter with you, Damdameki—are you mad, or what? Can I describe how in the month of Rabi'a'l-Awal, thieves who had come from various

parts placed certain Baku townspeople on donkeys and displayed them throughout the city, while they set free the local thieves who had been arrested, because they were kinsmen of the town councillors?

So consider, Damdameki, whether I can afford to describe all that which you want me to repeat in my journal. How would you justify yourself if I really wrote all that?[45]

Likewise Dehkhoda printed a letter in *Sur-e Esrafil* (number 5, June 27 1907), addressing his friend "Damdami," another fictitious author. The similarities to Jalil Mamed's letter in terms of subject, tone, and style are obvious, though Dehkhoda's sarcasm is perhaps even more biting:

> If I were to write about all I knew, I would write about many things. I would mention, for example, that if someone examined the accounts of the British bank, he would find over five million tomans there belonging to the Persian government. . . . I would mention too that the project of the Tabriz highroad, on which a Belgian specialist wasted five months' work and several thousand tomans from the treasury of our wretched country, has disappeared from the desk of the ministry and ascended to heaven. . . . And have I explained yet why forging documents, a criminal act everywhere else, is encouraged and approved in Persia? . . . But one cannot speak about this anymore. My beard did not turn white in a flour-mill, and I was not born yesterday.
>
> Be assured, Damdami, I will never write about all that. . . . Why is it my business that Nasr al-Doule, son of Qavam, boasted in the presence of Tehrani worthies, "I drink the blood of Muslims and I shatter the honor of Islam. It is I who with bullets and cannon fire have destroyed seventy-five men and women of the Qashqa'i tribe?" What has it to do with me that after this speech the Tehrani worthies shouted, "Hurrah!" and "Long live Qavam!"[46] No, you cannot jump over your own head. But on the terrible day of judgment, all that shall be reckoned and they shall answer to me for all.[47]

Another technique used by both Quli-Zade and Dehkhoda is called *goriz-zadan*, a technique whereby the writer cites a story, proverb, or general statement and then applies it to current social or political events. The satire arises from the incongruity of application. The following example by Dehkhoda, in which opium-eating is equated with the consumption of white bread, forces an analogy between two opposite qualities—one harmful and one healthful—where no real analogy exists at all. The very ridiculousness of the comparison, though, serves to emphasize the corruption of current conditions, and the use of folk stories, sayings, and proverbial maxims conduces to the *reductio ad absurdum*. Here is Dehkhoda:

A Cure for Opium-Eating

After several years traveling in India, seeing the invisible saints,[48] and acquiring skill in Alchemy, Talismans and Necromancy, thank God I have succeeded in a great experiment; no less than a method for curing the opium-habit! If any one in any foreign country had made such a discovery, he would certainly have been mentioned with honour in all the newspapers. But what can one do, since in Persia no one recognizes merit?

Custom is a second nature, and as soon as one becomes habituated to any act, one cannot easily abandon it. The only curative method is to reduce it gradually by some special procedure, until it is entirely forgotten.

To all my zealous, opium-eating, Muslim brethren I now proclaim the possibility of breaking the opium-habit, thus. First, they must be firmly determined and resolved on abandoning it. Secondly, one who for example, eats two *mithqals*[49] of opium daily should every day diminish this dose by a grain [*nukhud*] and add two grains of morphine in its stead. One who smokes ten *mithqals* of opium should daily reduce the amount by one grain, adding instead two grains of *hashish* [Indian hemp]. Thus he should persevere until such time as the two *mithqals* of opium which he eats are replaced by four *mithqals* of morphine, or the ten *mithqals* of opium which he smokes by twenty *mithqals* of *hashish*. After this it is very easy to substitute for morphine pills hypodermic injections of the same, and for *hashish* "curds of Unity."[50] O my zealous, opium-eating brethren, seeing that God has made matters so easy, why do you not save yourselves from the annoyance of men's foolish chatter, and the waste of all this time and money? Change of habit, if it be effected in this way, does not cause illness and is a very easy matter.

Moreover great and eminent men who wish to make people forget some evil habit act in precisely this way. See, for example, how well indeed the poet says that intelligence and fortune are closely connected with one another. For example, when our great men consider that the people are poor and cannot eat wheaten bread, and that the peasant must spend all his life in cultivating wheat, yet must himself remain hungry, see what they do.

On the first day of the year they bake the bread with pure wheat-flour. On the second day in every hundredweight [*kharwar*] they put a maund of bitter apricot stones, barley, fennel-flower, sawdust, lucerne, sand— I put it shortly as an illustration—clods, brick-bats and bullets of eight *mithqals*. It is evident that in a hundredweight of corn, which is a hundred maunds, one maund of these things will not be noticed. On the second day they put in two maunds, on the third three, and after a hundred days, which is three months and ten days, a hundred maunds of wheat-flour have become a hundred maunds of bitter apricot stones, barley, fennel-flower, sawdust, chaff, lucerne and sand, and that in such fashion that no one has noticed it, while the wheaten bread habit has entirely passed out of men's minds.

In truth intelligence and fortune are closely connected with one another!

O my zealous, opium-eating brethren! Assuredly you know that man is a little world, and has the closest resemblance to the great world; that is to say, for example, that whatever is possible for man may happen also in the case of animals, trees, stones, clods, doors, walls, mountains and seas; and that whatever is possible for these is possible also for men, because man is the microcosm, while these form part of the macrocosm. For example, I wanted to say this, that just as it is possible to put a habit out of men's minds, even so is it possible to put a habit out of the minds of stones, clods, and bricks, because the closest resemblance exists between the microcosm and the macrocosm. What sort of a man, then, is he who is less than even a stone or a clod?

For example, the late *mujtehid* Hajji Shaykh Hadi built a hospital and settled on it certain endowments so that eleven sick persons might always be there. So long as Hajji Shaykh Hadi was alive the hospital was accustomed to receive eleven patients. But as soon as Hajji Shaykh Haddi departed this life, the students of the college said to his eldest son, "We will recognize you as the Master only when you spend the hospital endowments on us!" See now what this worthy eldest son did by dint of knowledge. In the first month he reduced the number of patients by one, in the second by two, in the third by three, in the fourth by four; and so in like fashion until the present time, when the number of patients has been reduced to five, and gradually, by this excellent device, these few also will disappear in the course of the next five months. See then how by wise management it is possible to expel habit from the minds of every one and every thing, so that a hospital which was accustomed to eleven patients has entirely forgotten this habit without falling ill. Why? Because it also forms part of the macrocosm, so that it is possible to drive a habit out of its mind, just as in the case of man, who is the microcosm. —"Dakhaw."

If 'Ali Akbar Dehkhoda and Jalil Mamed Quli-Zade shared a number of techniques, we must acknowledge the distinctive style and personality of each. A frequent mode of Dehkhoda's work is parody—a mode that Jalil Quli-zade did not exploit to the same degree. Dehkhoda's classical training in both Arabic and theology enabled him to parody the pompous, Arabicized language of the clerics with a special skill. In one of his essays he describes the manner in which an Arabic letter is received by the writers of *Sur-e Esrafil*. These writers, being no Arabic scholars, give it to a learned theologian, who translates it into incredibly stilted Persian. Thus Dehkhoda criticizes the artificial language of the Persian clerics, along with of course the biased and reactionary views it is used to express. The relationship of Quli-Zade and Dehkhoda differs, however, from the relationship of Ashraf Gilani and Saber, a relationship that also involved imitation and close exchange; for although Ashraf translated and adapted Saber's verse quite freely and wrote original work, too, he nonetheless remained largely dependent on Saber for the development of his own reputation and style. Quli-Zade and Dehkhoda, on the other hand, while frequently imitating one another, made their respective literary marks essentially as independent writers.

Still another Persian satirical weekly that owes a great deal to *Mulla Nasreddin* is *Azerbaijan*. *Azerbaijan* was one of the oldest satirical weeklies of Iran; according to Browne, it was the second satirical paper to be published, the first being *Tulua*', which appeared in Bushehr from 1900 to 1901. *Azerbaijan* appeared in Tabriz in both Turkish and Persian under the editorship of 'Ali Quli Khan, also known as Safaroff, and it is considered by some to be the second most important newspaper of the Constitutional period. Kasravi in his *History of the Persian Constitution* considers it such; he says that when Sattar Khan, the champion of the Revolution, saw its first issue, tears of joy filled his eyes because it was the only journal comparable to *Mulla Nasreddin*.

The story of Safaroff is an odd one. He was punished for his support of democracy, but then for a time became the head of Mohammad 'Ali Mirza's secret police in Tabriz.[52] After the proclamation of the Constitution, however, he expressed his repentance and joined the Constitutionalists. He consequently established *Azerbaijan* in 1907[53] in imitation of *Mulla Nasreddin. Azerbaijan* did not agree with its predecessor in all respects; occasionally Safaroff would in fact write versified retorts to some stance taken in *Mulla Nasreddin.* The interconnection of the two journals is, however, obvious. *Azerbaijan*'s Hajji Baba figure is a case in point. Further, *Azerbaijan*'s imitation of *Mulla Nasreddin* was often quite conscious. Like *Mulla Nasreddin, Azerbaijan* contained interesting and colorful cartoons. Technically and artistically they were second only to those of 'Azim 'Azim-Zade and the Germans Rotter and Schmerling in *Mulla Nasreddin* itself. On the whole, again like *Mulla Nasreddin, Azerbaijan* followed a liberal policy. Each issue contained short satirical news items, an editorial, and occasional humorous political verse either in Azeri Turkish or in Persian. The following is an excerpt from one such poem, commenting upon the German intrusion into the internal affairs of Iran. It is sarcastically entitled, "An Offering of Thanks and Welcome to the Honored and Revered Guests[54]":

> O newly-arrived guest of Persia, welcome!
> O Germany! Your place is on our eyes: welcome!
> Persia is like a well-filled table with foreigners for guests;
> O guest unbidden to this table, welcome!
> Thanks be to God; The morning of union hath appeared;
> The nights of separation have come to an end: welcome!
> To take captive the bird-like hearts of your unhappy lovers
> With the snare in your hand and the grain in your apron,
>   welcome!
>
> Claiming to be the protector of Islam and the Muslims
> Thou hast entered the gang of thieves: welcome!
> But, since your competitors have carried off all
>   that there was,
> I am afraid that disappointment may be your portion:
>   welcome!
> Islam was friendless and helpless; now
> A hundred thanks, it has found a guardian like thee:
>   welcome!
> I know thee well, O libertine of many spells!
> The Devil sings the praises of thy cunning: welcome!
> Thy favour ever embraces Islam; we are unable to voice
>   the thanks which are your due: welcome!
>   . . . .
>
> Cunning prompted thee to extend the hand of friendship
>   to the Turk;
> Thou didst whisper into his ear the verse of loss: welcome!
> Then, on the pretext of friendship for the Sultan of Fez,
> Thou didst hasten towards Tangier: welcome!
> The injury which Morocco experienced from such a friend
>   as thee
> It had never experienced from the enmity [of another]:

welcome!
Having finished with the affairs of these two, without delay
Thou didst appear in the land of Persia: welcome!
To shear the heads of a handful of innocents
Thou bringest in thy hand a sharp razor: welcome!

. . . .

Wantonly, with pretexts of College and Bank,
Thou hast attained thy secret object: welcome!
Our cry of lamentation still rises to heaven
On account of the Russian and British Banks: welcome!
In short it seems that we have now no option
Save to submit to the orders of the Franks: welcome!
Yet the circling heaven remains not in one position;
Say, "Despair not of God!" Welcome!

[Signed: M. J. Kh.]

Hasharat al-'Arz (The insects of the earth), another satirical weekly of the Constitutional period, was influenced by both *Mulla Nasreddin* and *Sur-e Esrafil*. It began its publication on 18 March 1908 in Tabriz, under the editorship of Mirza Agha Bluri, and continued for fourteen issues before the civil war there made further publication impossible. Only one issue, that of July 1909, appeared during the latter half of the Constitutional Revolution.[55] The lines under its front-page masthead seem to predict its fate. There it is stated: "This is a political and responsible newspaper which speaks in the language of animals. At present, except for holidays, it will be published four times a month, and will be suppressed."

Hasharat al-'Arz consisted of four pages, the first and fourth of which, in color, were devoted to political cartoons. The journal's debt to *Mulla Nasreddin* is evident in its "mad wanderer" figure, called Ghaffar Vakil—a character belonging to the class of *Azerbaijan*'s Hajji Baba and of the Mulla himself. Ghaffar Vakil wrote editorials in *Hasharat al-'Arz* that resemble Dehkhoda's "Charand Parand" column, thus revealing the journal's further debt to *Sur-e Esrafil*. *Sur-e Esrafil* lent *Hasharat al-'Arz* much moral support, too. In its issue of 15 April 1908, *Sur-e Esrafil* announced the publication of *Hasharat al-'Arz* as "the rise of an auspicious star on the horizon of the Persian press." It wrote further: "This is one of the outcomes of this period in our history which will advance good characteristics and praiseworthy virtues." *Sur-e Esrafil* commented too on the journal's fine prose and poetic styles, its realistic approach to many issues and problems, and its skillful and tasteful color cartoons. And *Hasharat al-'Arz* directed substantial attention to *Sur-e Esrafil* in turn, mentioning or answering it many times. The following poem, addressed to "Kablai," i.e., "Kablai Dakhov," a pen name of Dehkhoda, can serve as an example:

O experienced and wise old man, O Kablai!
O brave, witty and pure of heart, O Kablai!
I have a wise counsel for you, O Kablai,
Whether you take it or not. . . .

If Iran is immersed in unquietness,
If the court is corrupt, treacherous and ruined,
If the mother of the nation endures foreign rape;
None are of any importance—comb your beard, O Kablai!

If the Ottoman army invaded Iran,
And if the country became thus a lair for ghouls;
If national zeal left the poor or the rich,
All these are hearsay for me, O Kablai!

The friend whom I know causes world-wide distress;
He prospers with our ruination.
He makes vows hundred-fold, yet remains the same,
Breaking his vows over wine.

But what is it to you if Iran lies in ruin,
And officials are bent for corruption?
Or if Shapshal[56] has closely befriended the Shah,
Foreigners filling his confidential places?

Though in Tehran Amir 'Azm recently became
Constitutionalist, and swore upon the Koran.
Yet returning to Gilan, he forgot his oath,
And burned the houses and the town.

But if the governor of Kerman tyrannizes the
   people,
He is a prince!—he shall suffer no inquisition.
So ask him for carpets and rugs, O Kablai,
To furnish your rooms and your closets.

Say, what purpose have all these murmurings
   from you?
Who will heed your voice and your warnings?
Not a single God-fearing man, O Kablai—
So in this world, in this time, save your breath,
   O Kablai!
My poor man, O Kablai! [57]

Three last Constitutional weeklies deserve mention. The first is *Estebdad*
[Autocracy], one of the oldest journals of the Constitutional period, published
secretly in Tehran in 1907. *Estebdad*'s most striking satirical technique was to
proclaim itself a mouthpiece of autocracy; as it explained in its very first issue:
"This journal is called 'Autocracy' and until one thousand persons write letters
to us, its name will not be altered. . . . When there reaches us one thousand letters
from men of learning, the journal will be renamed 'Constitution.' Otherwise,
like thousands of people, it will strongly support 'Autocracy!' " The second weekly
is *Bohlul*,[58] first published under the editorship of Sheikh 'Ali 'Eraqi and later,
in 1911, of Asadullah Khan Parsi. An interesting episode concerning this journal
occurred in connection with its cartoons—the paper was once suspended because
the red color of its cartoons was considered revolutionary![59] This was, of course,

only one of many excuses concocted by the authorities to halt its publication, which they were able to do, in fact, frequently. *Bohlul* managed to publish thirty-four issues in all; its eventful history was directly related to its role as the voice of the Democratic party. Another journal, *Sheikh Choghondar* (The Reverend Beetroot), although the two were similar in style, was *Bohlul*'s middle-of-the-road competitor. The following is an example from *Bohlul*:

> They say a group of ignorant fools
> Clamour for the martial law,
> So that as in the time of the ex-king,
> All the nation shall be Cossacks' slaves.
> Like the family of 'Ali in Umayyad hands,
> They would let the government lay
> The yoke of servitude on their necks,
> And arrest anyone with Constitutional bent,
> Or anyone possessed of sagacity.
> They would thus close the doors of happiness
> To the men of the Democratic party.
> If *Bohlul* accepts this practice,
> Every wise man will censure its immaturity.
> But suppose they be insensitive, like beasts,
> This group of uneducated common men?
> The wise man will surely not fail to recall
> That an ass becomes tired of being without rein![60]

Let us turn now briefly to the sociopolitical cartoons that so frequently and importantly contributed to the satirical periodicals of the Constitutional Era.

On the basis of composition and quality of printing, the cartoons in *Azerbaijan* and in *Hasharat al-Arz* surpassed those in the weeklies of Tehran in 1907. A.L.M. Nicholas, the one-time French consul at Rasht, writes in *Revue du Monde Musulman:*

> It is very amazing that the capital should be the city least advanced in illustrated journals and that their cartoons should leave so much to be desired. If Baku with its far superior *Mulla Nasreddin* dominates the scene, Tabriz, though to a lesser degree with *Azerbaijan*. . . represents a progress not expected from a provincial paper. I do not mean from the point of view of design, which is frankly bad, but composition of picture, grouping of personages, and dominant ideas, from which almost the whole matter emerges. On the contrary, the journals of Tehran are still in the infancy of this art. For instance, what can be more childish than a picture in *Ayene-ye Gheyb-Nema* (Mirror Showing the Unseen), No. 12, which represents men with two faces, addressing themselves on the one side to the Shah and on the other to the nation?

Nicholas adds the following in favor of the Tehrani cartoons, however:

> Despite all this, even if they lack the qualities absolutely necessary for a journal with cartoons, they never fail to accomplish their chosen task. They are perfectly sincere and have an exemplary loyalty. What they say is the exact thought of the population.[61]

The history of *Ayene-ye Gheyb-Nema* is quite interesting. It began its publication on 4 July 1907 as a fortnightly paper under the editorship of Seyyed 'Abdul Rahim Kashani, and it was among the very few newspapers that were opposed to the Constitution. It ceased publication in 1908, starting anew with a changed policy during the second Constitutional period in July 1911. It now defended the Constitution. The journal number discussed by Nicolas above is from the earlier period when, even despite its anti-Constitutionalism, it tended to favor discipline, reform, and law. Its editor was pragmatic, proposing many courses of moderation and compromise between conflicting views, seemingly afraid of decisive action. The cartoon alluded to by Nicholas shows Mohammad 'Ali Shah on the throne, flanked by his ministers and *ulema*, who "have nothing at heart but the good of the state and the nation."[62] The two-faced hypocrites are on the righthand side, and the caption reads: "The picture of the hypocrites who want to create differences between the state and the people, so that they might remain on the seat of autocracy."[63]

Ayene-ye Gheyb-Nema was lithographed, and its printing and illustration were both very crude. Some of its cartoons resembled the antipapal cartoons of the Lutherans in the sixteenth century, which often depicted the devil giving birth to the papacy.[64] In the issue dated 23 February 1907, for instance, there are three strange-looking "enemies" of the Constitution. One gives birth to cats and dogs and bears this inscription: "This heretic wanted to bring six million people into perdition—how I was punished! Dust is upon my head. Where should I go? No city accepts me. Out of my love for autocracy, one hundred autocratic beasts are born from me every day." Another monster in the same picture has four horns—"heresy, love of autocracy, betraying the nation, and selling the country." He claims that for a few days he managed to sow seeds of discord between the Shah and the people, but advises his children not to do the same, since nothing will come of it.[65] Such cartoons are typical of *Ayene-ye Gheyb-Nema* combining verbal and visual aspects to produce the desired effect.

Thus, the journals of the Constitutional era represent more than any other type of publication the major satirical vehicle for the poetry and prose of the period. In the decades following the Constitutional period proper, the popularity of these journals fluctuated; except for the years of relative freedom between 1941 and 1953, it was most often in decline. Political satire for the most part suffered a dramatic reversal because the expression of political ideas—even in disguised form—grew increasingly dangerous. Consequently, the satirists were forced either to turn their attention to the safer grounds of purely social criticism and comedy of manners, or to take refuge in the guarded symbolism of modern Persian poetry. After the flowering of the Constitutional period, we witness with helpless regret the stifling of substantial satirical talent.

Let us then briefly survey the situation in Iran in the periods following the Constitutional era of 1906 to 1911. The first of these periods consists in the years leading up to the First World War when Russia and Great Britain kept the press under firm control, a control removed only by the coup d'etat of 1921, by the coming to power of Reza Khan, and finally by the transference of king-ship from the Qajars to the Pahlavi dynasty in 1925. This period, 1911 to 1925, marks the end of relative freedom of expression in Iran and, with Russian atrocities in Azerbaijan in the north and British aggression in the south, it was a tumultuous time for that country. Puppet cabinets followed one another, and the liberal movements of Khiabani and Kuchek Khan were quenched by treach-erous means. The Russian October Revolution of 1917 came as a godsend to Iran, relieving it for the time being at least of the depredations of that superpower. During this period a dozen or so satirical journals were published, but only rarely were they able to be as outspoken as their predecessors. As social change snowballed and as contact with the West and western writers grew, social rather than political satire gained momentum, and a great interest in topical problems was displayed. Iraj Mirza's witty criticism of the submissive position of women, Bahar's many sociopolitical satires, and Farrokhi and 'Eshqi's vehement attacks on corruption and social injustice are examples of a new social awareness and mark the thematic concerns of the poetry of these years.

The next post-Constitutional period is the era of Reza Shah's reign, which began in 1925 and ended with his abdication, under pressure from the Allied Forces, in 1941. This period marks an even sharper decline in political satire than the preceding one. Reza Shah's regime strove to weaken or to destroy all possible sources of opposition, and newspapers were considered to be among them. One hundred twenty-five newspapers and forty periodicals were being published when Reza Shah came to power,[66] while toward the end of his reign the total number had dropped to fewer than fifty,[67] a number that included official publications as well. Further, those few of the fifty that were satirical could not publish anything political.[68] In fact, if the newspapers of the previous decades had been instruments of incessant political polemic, in this period writers assiduously avoided political issues and addressed themselves instead to economic, cultural, and social problems of a neutral nature. Often the newspapers claimed that all diverging and differing viewpoints concerning state affairs were incorporated into the officially expressed ideas.[69] Translated, this becomes: "The police supervised all the publications, and all articles and advertisements had to be approved in advance."[70] The truth is, editors had taken a hint from the fate of 'Eshqi, an outspoken poet and the editor of the banned journal *Qarn-e Bistom*, who was assassinated in his own home in 1924.

The next period, which begins in 1941 with the occupation of Iran by Russian and British forces and ends in 1953 with the fall of Dr. Mosaddeq's nationalist government, was full of upheavals, yet rich in journalism and political writing. Although controlled by the Allied Forces from 1941 to 1946 and by a martial-law regulation that gave the military governor through 1948 the right to suppress the newspapers, there was still considerable freedom of expression, and the press thrived in an unprecedented way.[71] The previously banned Tudeh (Communist) party claimed quite a large following among newspaper editors in the 1940s, and in 1943 it formed a coalition called "The Freedom Front." An opposing coalition was formed by the pro-British Seyyed Zia al-Din Tabatabai and several other nationalists. But since a suppressed newspaper could appear in this period under the name of another, properly licensed one, the government's control over the press was considerably weakened. In less than a year the number of newspapers and journals published in Iran rose from 50 in 1941 to 464. Elwell-Sutton in his "Iranian Press, 1941-1947" gives a list of 433 Persian journals, along with 31 newspapers and weeklies in Turkish, Armenian, Kurdish, English, French, Polish, and Russian, which appeared from 1941 to 1947. Of them only 9 were partially or completely satirical. Among these were *Arjang* (The sacred book of Manicheanism), *Omid* (Hope), *Towfiq* (Success), *Hallaj* (The cotton-carder), and *Nasim-e Shomal*, all of which had actually begun publication shortly prior to 1941. Four others, *Hardanbil* (The easygoing one), *Qalandar* (The Sufi beggar), *Yu Yu* (The yo-yo), and *Baba Shamal*, came later. In the following five-year period, which saw the nationalization of the oil industry under the rule of Dr. Mosaddeq, the journals *Chalangar* (The ironsmith), *Luti* (The rogue), *Shab-Cheragh* (The world-seeing lamp), *Nushkhand* (The smirk), *Dad va Bidad* (Justice and injustice), and *Hajji Babi*, began publication.

The period following the abdication of Reza Shah until the American coup d'etat of 1953 that reinstated the Shah achieved new heights of social satire. Comparing it to the period immediately following the Constitutional Revolution confirms the view of Jahangir Dorri, who writes: "The study of the history of satire shows that this art flourished usually during a turning point in a people's life."[73] This timespan was of decisive importance in Iranian history, and the satirical journals *Towfiq*, *Chalangar*, *Baba Shamal*, and *Hajji Baba* were the outstanding periodicals of those years.

Towfiq was founded by Hosain Towfiq in 1927, and he remained the editor until his death in 1939. *Towfiq* was not originally a satirical journal, but in the fifth year of its publication it obtained permission to print cartoons, whereupon it adopted a humorous aspect for about a year. The humor was discarded for an interval of several years, then in 1938 was taken up again. A crucial turning point for *Towfiq* came after the abdication of Reza Shah. Mohammad Sadr-e Hashemi describes its transformation:

> As various political parties sprang to life *Towfiq* became one of the leftist newspapers and one of the most interesting and most widely read weeklies of Tehran. In this period it abandoned its old, flattering style and began criticizing political affairs and the government in a most vehement manner. Though it was suspended several times by the police, it did not forsake its new policy. In brief, *Towfiq* became a political and critical journal in the real sense of the term after 1941, and this was by no means comparable to its past.[74]

Towfiq's son, Mohammad 'Ali Towfiq, became the editor after his father's death, serving until 1953; he was then succeeded by three grandsons, Hosain, Hasan, and 'Abbas. More than the other two grandsons 'Abbas wrote numerous satirical pieces[75] under various pen names, and managed the journal for several years. A number of contemporary humorists and satirical poets, notably Abul-Qasem Halat (b. 1915) and 'Abbas Forat (b. 1894), wrote for the journal. The former, who served for some years as editor-in-chief of Towfiq, collected his poems under the title Fokahiyat-e Halat (Tehran, 1946), and the latter's poetry also appeared in the same year under the title Divan-e Forat-e Yazdi. Given its wide social concerns, Towfiq's humor and satire were influential and weighty, and for many years it served as a school for young Iranian satirists and cartoonists. A recent work on the Iranian press has characterized it as "the most serious in the garb of humor."[76] Unfortunately, Towfiq was closed down in the early 1970s, supposedly because of a pertinent pun upon the word Hoveyda (the name of the former prime minister who was executed after the Revolution).

Another consequential paper of considerable artistic merit was Chalangar [Locksmith], which was published by Mohammad 'Ali Afrashte, one of Iran's most talented modern satirical poets. Born in 1908 in Rasht, Afrashte had to work for his living from childhood onward and many times changed professions. The result of these early hard times was a thorough familiarity with the lives of various classes of people and a profound sympathy toward the poor and oppressed. As an artist, Afrashte responded to all social influences and events, and his profoundly touching and powerful satire—which included both stories and plays—was written both in Persian and in his native Gilaki dialect, and both of them became extremely popular. During the reign of Reza Shah, Afrashte wrote satirical poems dealing with social problems, but after 1941 he joined the Iranian Communist (Tudeh) party, read his verses often at party meetings, and participated actively in the social and literary life of the country. The first collection of his poems, entitled Ay Gofti! [How well said!], was published by the Tudeh party in 1945.[77] The title poem, which is one of his best-known works, contrasts the outlook of the rich and poor on a snowy day and shows what a chasm of difference separates their respective worlds. Afrashte began publication of Chalangar in February 1951 and continued it until Dr. Mossadeq's overthrow in August 1953. Work on the journal required all his strengh—he often took upon himself the task of printing it—and it appeared under various titles: Jajrud, Shabcheragh, Rangin Kaman, Arzesh-e Kar, and Solh-e Donya. Whenever one was banned, the journal appeared under the next title, always indicating its links with "the accursed and offensive Chalangar."[78]

The major part of the literary material of Chalangar deals with the sociopolitical life of those years. It contained interesting sections: interpretations of various political events of the previous week, a prognosis of the future by "the famous astrologer Sheikh Ebrahim Gilani," and "In the Circles of Tehran," which ridiculed government policy. The paper often sided with the most radical factions in Iran; not only was it bitterly opposed to Anglo-American presence there, it also chided the nationalist government for its lack of decisive action and positive reform.

Chalangar's office, located in Afrashte's home, was once burned down by goons hired by the Shah's court, and the journal was eventually banned after twelve issues. Then, under various editorships, of which Abu Turab Jali's was the finest, eleven more issues appeared (the last on 13 August 1953) before the final return of the Shah to power.

After the coup Afrashte emigrated to Bulgaria where he wrote poems and stories on Iranian themes and actively contributed to Bulgarian Turkish-language publications and to the Bulgarian satirical paper *Stershel* [Hornet]. While seriously ill, Afrashte, under the pseudonym Hasan Sharif, published a novel in Bulgarian entitled *The Shah's Nose*.[79] He died on 6 May 1958 in Sophia.

Another important satirical paper was *Baba Shamal*, which came out from January 1943 to the end of 1945 and from the end of 1947 to March 1948. Its editor was Reza Ganje'i, born in Tabriz, who had his training as an engineer in both Tehran and Germany. Returning to Iran after the overthrow of Reza Shah, Ganje'i began the publication of *Baba Shamal* in Tehran with the help of a group of young writers who shared his dissatisfaction with the government.

As the masthead of *Baba Shamal* declared, it was an independent journal, unaffiliated with any party or group. Ganje'i was very critical of the cabinets that succeeded one another without carrying out any substantial reform. He frequently lashed out at the ministers and the deputies of the *Majles*, as well as at the British and Russians, still important factors in the politics of Iran. In spite of all its criticism *Baba Shamal* managed to become a very influential paper, one whose criticism, according to its editor, "would topple a cabinet and bring in a new one."[80]

Ganje'i had a remarkable familiarity with classical Persian literature, and it was through parodying or imitating well-known poems that he often effected his political satire. In contrast to *Towfiq*, whose satire had somewhat serious political overtones, *Baba Shamal* concentrated on political satire in the form of verses, notes, and topical interviews. Cartoons were one of the most interesting features of *Baba Shamal*, and following the old tradition of satirical papers, "Baba Shamal" himself appears in most of them. He is depicted as a cunning old man with a beard and felt hat. Accompanied by his dog, he is shown looking over a fence, through a window, and so on. One cartoon shows Tabataba'i, a member of the *Majles*, digging up a corpse. Baba Shamal asks why he, a good Muslim, is disturbing a grave. Tabataba'i answers, "What's to be done, the Majles has summoned just such a prime minister."[81]

The last important satirical paper of this period was *Hajji Baba*, edited by Parviz Khatibi. It was an independent paper resembling *Baba Shamal* in many ways. Published during the Mossadeq period, it was fiercely anti-British and reflected the prevailing nationalist sentiment. In a period of three years and a few months 174 issues of *Hajji Baba* were produced, but it was banned as a result of the coup in August 1953. Khatebi, who had been tried and condemned three times for being disrespectful of the royal family, was jailed for six months.[82] Though thenceforth political satire took on a gloomy aspect, Khatibi managed to publish one of his several satirical books, *Shahr-e Hert* [City of chaos], in 1954.

In many respects *City of Chaos* recalls the *History of the City of Glupov* by Saltykov-Shchedrin. Of course, Khatibi's work does not rise to the level of satirical fantasy and genial power of the Russian novel; its earthiness, however, the music of its sarcasm, and its biting criticism remind one of the Russian master. Dealing with generally lighter subjects than *Glupov*, *City of Chaos* paints a uniformly sordid picture of Iranian life. Khatibi writes about the indifference of the administration to the hopes of the people, the embezzlement of public property, the self-interest and corruption of the wealthy ruling class, and the powerless and voiceless press. It is hard for him to witness the pursuit of literary careers by those rascals who, "not having anything in their own heads," continue to hang on to a leader and "at the expense of the dead . . . to gain fame and world renown."[83] Various types of people in different professions are attacked and criticized. Khatibi describes the activity of a "master tailor" who dexterously steals some material, drags the customer into endless fitting sessions, and makes a suit that ultimately does not fit. Of more serious consequence is the performance of a doctor who operates with great aplomb in a rare field of medicine in which he has no appreciable skill.

Jahangir Dorri in his work on Persian satire comments on Khatibi's *City of Chaos*:

> With splendid reserve the author writes, "I ask that you understand the references to individuals and situations in this book are not drawn from Iran, but from the 'City of Chaos,' and that this city has no connection to the city in which I reside." Compared to European literature, the composition of the *City of Chaos* is close to *The Book of Snobs* by Thackeray, though the satire of the English writer has broader social scope and a greater singleness of purpose. The pamphlet has a high value, and it may be said of it that it continues the accusatory line in Persian literature. Khatebi in his turn catches up and carries further the torch of Iranian satire, not permitting the extinction of the fire of social protest in Iran.[84]

The years from 1953 onward constitute the final period in our survey; it was during this time that the press came gradually under complete government domination once more, where it would stay until shortly before the 1979 revolution. A Press Law was passed in July 1955 which made it illegal to criticize the royal family or any person appointed by the king.[85] Since the cabinet members and all other top officials were royal appointees, the government was effectively protected from criticism. Satirical newspapers, of course, suffered accordingly. After the folding of *Towfiq* in the early 1970s, several of its contributors joined with Dawalu, an experienced cartoonist and an old hand in the field of Iranian journalism, to publish the weekly *Caricature* in 1968. This, along with another comical journal, *Khandeh* (Laughter), was the only journal of this nature during the last years of the Shah's reign, both carefully avoided touchy political issues.

Although they were not essentially satirical publications, a number of other journals and newspapers introduced humorous and satirical columns. When the weekly *Tehran Mosavvar* (The illustrated Tehran) was being published, for example, it ran a column called "Kashkiat" (Nonsensical talk), written by Manuchehr Mahjubi. Later, however, the paper, forced to discontinue it, replaced it with another column called "Fozul Aghasi" (The arch-meddler) by Naser Khodayar. Iraj Pezeshkzad, meanwhile, a talented novelist and satirist, was writing a column called "Angarib" (In no time) for the journal *Ferdausi*. The same writer was responsible for a much more famous column entitled "Asimun va Rismun" (From here and there) for the same journal from 1954 to 1958. These very witty sketches of the contemporary literary scene in Iran were collected into one volume and published in 1977 under the same title.[86] Modern poetry was then in fashion, and every poetaster was expecting to become a bard of consequence in no time. Iraj Pezeshkzad parodied not only the latest in poetry, comparing it with the works of classical masters in a lighthearted way reminiscent of Swift's *Battle of the Books*, but also the most ridiculous of the contemporary histories, dramas, and novels. In the introduction he wrote to these sketches many years later, Pezeshkzad states that his main purpose was to "criticize the chaotic literary scene, existing at the time, as well as the lack of responsibility and nonsensical assertions on the part of some writers."[87]

Another talented satirist, Khosrow Shahani, whose works of fiction will be discussed in a later chapter, for many years wrote a satirical literary column entitled "Dar Kargah-e Namad-mali" (In the workshop of a felt-maker) for *Khandaniha*.[88] Hadi Khorsandi, a satirist of considerable verve and originality, who has become one of the most reputable satirists outside Iran since the advent of the revolution, began his career on the daily *Ettela'at* (Information) about 1970. While in Iran, Khorsandi's satire was not political but social; with a sharp and cynical sense of humor it mocked and condemned many questionable manifestations of the so-called affluent society. His work pointed the way for many other satirists to follow.

The very short-lived period of freedom of expression after the 1979 revolution —a topic to be explored in this book's postscript—produced numerous satirical newspapers, but one by one they have been closed down, with most of their writers fleeing the country. Today, it is outside Iran that many of these same satirists are living and writing. Iraj Pezeshkzad is politically active in Paris; Hadi Khorsandi has been publishing the satirical weekly *Asghar Agha* in London for the past seven years; and *Ahangar dar Tab'id* (The blacksmith in exile) is also being published in London by several former writers of *Chalangar*.

Notes

1. In Tabriz, where a dialect of Turkish (Azari) is spoken, the poems of Mirza 'Ali Akbar Saber, the Caucasian poet, were recited. See Arayanpur, Az Saba ta Nima, 11:56.

2. This passage is from the translation of *Hajja Baba of Ispahan* into the Persian by Mirza Habib of Ispahan, who has occasionally added to the original and made it even more critical of his own countrymen. For this edition see *The Adventures of Hajji Baba of Ispahan*, translated into Persian and ed. D. C. Phillott (Calcutta 1905), chap. 39.

3. Browne, *Press and Poetry*, p. 3 (Persian Introduction).

4. Aryanpur', *Az Saba to Nima*, 1:250.

5. This notice was published in the *Official Newspaper of Iran* 99 (18 Dul Qa'eh 1901); Mahmud Nafisi, *Sokhan* 25, nos. 7 and 8 (January 1976): 820. 1318 [1901]).

6. Browne, Press and Poetry, p. 106.

7. *Ibid.*, p. 107.

8. Mohammad Sadr-e, Hashemi, *Tarikh-e Jara'ed va Majallat-e Iran (Isfahan, 1948-193), 3:154-56.*

9. Quoted in Browne, *Press and Poetry*, p. 108.

10. Aryanpur, *Az Saba to Nima*, 1:318.

11. See Hashemi, *Tarikh-e Jara'ed*, 2:202-3.

12. Aryanpur, *Az Saba ta Nima*, 1:391.

13. Quoted in Hamid Algar, *Mirza Malkum Khan, A Study in the History of Iranian Modernism* (Berkeley and Los Angeles: University of California Press 1973) p. 275.

14. Ibid., p. 197.

15. Browne, *Persian Revolution* pp. 409-14.

16. An Iranian king was often called "The Shadow of God."

17. A French doctor at the court of Naser al-Din Shah. These examples are from a MS. of Rezvan that is in possession of Dr. M. I. Rezvani.

18. Quoted in Nazem al-Eslam Kermani, *Tarikh-e Bidari-ye Iranian* (Tehran: Intisharat-e Novin, 1983) p. 141.

19. Browne, *Press and Poetry*, p. xxii.

20. Nazim Akhundov, Azarbaijanda Dovri Matbu'at, 1932-1920 (Baku 1965).

21. Nazim Akhundov, *Azerbaijan Satira Journalari (1906-1020)* (Baku: Azerbaijan SSR Elmler Adakemiair Nashriati, 1968), pp. 16-68. See also 'Abbas Zamanov, *Saber va Mo'aserin-e-u*, trans. Asad Behrangi (Tabriz: Intisharat-e Shams, 1979).

22. Quoted in Ahmet Caferoglu, *Azerbaycananin mizah sariri Ali Akber "Sabir"*, (Ðogumunum 100 yili munasibetiyle). Turk kulturur, Ankara, no. 3., p. 15.

23. See introduction to *Hop Hop-Name*, ed. 'Abbas Sehhat (Baku: Azernesr, 1962), p. XVII.

24. Ibid., pp. 140-41.

25. Ibid., pp. 190-91

26. Yefrem (or Yeprem) (1868-1912) was a famous Armenian leader in the Iranian Constitutional Revolution. He was born in Armenia, and after a few years of imprisonment in Siberia, he managed to escape to Iran.

27. 'A. A Saber, Hop Hop-Name, pp. 195-97.

28. For a study of Saber's influence on his contemporaries see *Az Saba to Nima*, by Yahya Aryanpur, 2:20-76.

29. Hop Hop Name, pp. 1-2.

30. The old city which lies south of Tehran. Here, it stands for all Iran.

31. Jamshid and Kaygubad, two famous kings in Persian mythology. The Jam (chalice) of Jamshid was known for its magical quality.

32. Political group opposing Shah.

33. Caspian Sea.

34. Two cities in Iran.

35. *Azerbaijanian Poetry*, ed. Mirza Ibrahimov, (Moscow: Progress Publishers, 1969), pp. 230-31.

36. Browne, Press and Poetry, pp. 215-16.

37. All these passages are quoted by Yahya Aryanpur, Az Saba ta Nima 2:63-64.

38. See Franceszek Machalski, La Litterature de l'Iran Contemporaine, (Warsaw: Zaklad Narodo Ossolimskich, 1965), 2:56.

39. Translated by Browne, Press and Poetry, pp. 193-94.

40. We should also acknowledge Dahkhoda's academic contributions. In his later years he did indeed become one of the greatest scholars of Iran. Among his achievements is a huge encyclopedic dictionary whose publication was completed only a few years ago, many years after the death of Dehkhoda. The project had taken him more than forty years to complete.

41. Quoted by Yahya Aryanpur in Az Saba to Nima, 2:88.

42. Dehkhoda, in Sur-e Esrefil, no. 6 (6 June 1907), pp. 6-7.

43. The Journal Mulla Nasreddin and Its Influence on Political Satire in Revolutionary Persia, 1905-11, translation of two Russian articles on the subject, Central Asian Review, 3, no. 1 (1960), p. 19.

44. Bibi-Haybat is a quarter of Baku.

45. Quoted in Persian translation by Yahya Aryanpur in Az Saba to Nima, 2:90.

46. Qavam was one of the ruthless lords of Shiraz who were bitterly opposed by the Constitutionalists.

47. Sur-e Esrafil (Tehran, 1982) pp. 49-50.

48. The Abdal ("Substitutes") and Awtad ("Pegs") are two classes of the Rijalu'l-Ghayb, or "Men of the Unseen World," who play an important part in the cosmogony of the Mystics. [Browne's note.]

49. The mithqual=4.60 grammes, and is divided into 24 nukhud ("peas"), each of which consists of 4 grains or barley-corns (gandum). [Browne's note].

50. Dugh-i-Wahdat, or Banjab, is a mixture of hashish and curdled milk similar to asrar, habb-i-nashat, etc. Buq-i-Wahdat ("The trumpet of unity") is the name given by hashish-smokers to a paper funnel through which the smoke of the drug is inhaled. [Browne's note].

51. Translated by Browne, Library History of Persia, 4:472-74.

52. Bastani Parizi, Na-ye Haft-band (Tehran, 1971) p. 145.

53. I have in my possession 14 issues of Azerbaijan but Browne had, with some omissions, nos. 1-22.

54. Azerbaijan, 11 Oct. 1907, translated in Browne, Press and Poetry. pp. 257-59

55. See Browne's Persian Revolution, p. 45. According to Mohammad Sadr-e Hashemi, in Tarikh-e Jara'ed va Majallat-e Iran, 11 numbers of this journal were published in the journal's third and final year.

56. Shapshal was the Russian tutor of Mohammad 'Ali Mirza, and an accomplice in some of his later reactionary moves.

57. Hasharat al-'Arz, no. 8 (1908).

58. Bohlul was a wise man who pretended to be a fool (see Chapter 5)

59. Sadr-e Hashemi, Tarikh-e Jara'ed va Majallat-e Iran, 1:38.

60. Ibid., 1:37.

61. Revue du Monde Musulman, (Nov.-Dec. 1907):553-54.

62. Ibid., p. 554.

63. Ibid.

64. See Matthew Hodgart, Satire, p. 49.

65. Revue du Monde Musulman 4, (1908):845-47.

66. U.S. Army Area Handbook for Iran, prepared by Foreign Areas studies Division, the American University, Washington D.C., May 1963, p. 338. Ali Nowrouz in his article, "Registre Analytique Annoté de Presse Persane, "Revue du Monde Musulman 60, (1925):35-62) says that from 7, November 1919, until 21, April 1923, 318 newspapers and journals were published.

67. Elwell-Sutton, "The Iranian Press, 1941-1947," Iran, Journal of British Institute of Persian Studies, 1, (1968) 65-104.

68. There were ten satirical papers: Khande (Laughter, 1927); Ayene-ye Iran (The mirror of Iran, 1929); Khorsihd-e Iran (the sun of Iran, 1923;) Ruzname-ye 'Ankabut (Spider's Journal, 1925); Omid (Hope, 1929); Zanbil (Basket, 1930); Nahid (Venus, 1924); Hallaj (1927); and Morravvej (The propagator, 1941).

69. Roger Lescot, "Notes sur la presse Iranienne," *Revue des Etudes Islamiques* Cahiers 2-3 (1938):261-64.

70. *U.S. Army Area Handbook*, p. 338.

71. Ibid., p. 339.

72. Ewell-Sutton, "The Iranian Press," pp. 65-104.

73. Jahangir Dorri, *Persidskaia Satiricheskaia Prosa* (Moscow: 1977) p. 129.

74. Sadr-e Hashemi, *Tarikh-e Jara'ed va Majallat-e Iran*, 2:14.

75. For an example of his satirical works, see "The Tail of the Cat" which has been translated in chapter 3.

76. Masu'd Barzin, *Matbu 'at-e Iran (1345-53) (1944-74) (Tehran, 1965), p. 118.*

77. This book was reprinted in 1979 in Tehran by *Nashr-e Kargar.* Another edition of his poems in Persian and Gilaki was edited by M. Beh-Azin in Tehran in the same year. A comprehensive edition of the Persian works of Afrashte was published by Nusratullah Nuh in 1970 in Tehran as *Majmu'e-ye Asar-e Muhammad 'Ali Afrashte, Sha'er-e Tuda'i.*

78. Dorri, *Persidskaia Satiricheskaia Prosa*, pp. 133-34.

79. Ibid., p. 131.

80. Gholam-Hosain Javaheri-Vajdi, *Numuni-ha-ye Tanz-e Mo 'aser*, (Tehran: Alhar-e Iran, 1970).

81. *Baba Shamal* (1944):p. 1, quoted by Dorri, *Persidskaia Satiricheskaia Prosa*, p. 138.

82. *Hajji Baba*, 210 (18 April 1980):3.

83. Parviz Khatebi: *Share-e Hert* (Tehran, 1942), pp. 80-83.

84. Dorri, *Persidskaia Satiricheskaia Prosa*, p. 156.

85. See *U.S. Army Area Handbook*, pp. 355-59.

86. Iraj Pezeshkzad, *Asimun va Rismun*, 3rd ed., (Tehran: Ketab-ha-ye Jibi, 1977).

87. Ibid., Introduction.

88. *Khandaniha* was edited twice a week for more than forty years until its editor Amirani was executed after the revolution of 1979, and it closed down.

Two cartoons from the *Collected Poems of Muhammad 'Ali Afrasheta*. *Top*, The ruffians supporting the Shah are financed by the British and Americans. *Bottom*, "At last water came to our street, but the colonel diverted to his garden."

دکتر صدقه (خطاب به ما) میلدی یا فوتت کنم رو پشت بوم سوتت کنم؟
ما ــ فوتم نکن خودم میلم ــ سوتم نکن خودم میرم

Dr Mosaddeq addressing the Shah, asking him to give up his position as commander-in-chief. "Give it to me or else I'll huff and blow you to the roof top." "Don't huff and puff me away, I am going. Don't blow me to the roof top, I am leaving." *From Hajji Baba 169 (June 1953).*

Dr. Mosaddeq and the British. *From Hajji Baba (1953).*

7

Poets Who Contributed to Satirical Newspapers

I am a poet, and my duty is to write poetry,
To write and express every good or evil that I notice,
To describe the sun as bright, the day as pale,
  and the night as dark,
Crooked as crooked, slanting as slanting, and even
  as smooth
Then, o my friend, why do you frown at me?
There is no fault in the mirror; you see your own face.

—*'Ali Akbar Saber*

The careers and lifetimes of several eminent Iranian poets, who also wrote a large number of satirical verses, spanned two or more of the periods examined in chapter six. Some of these, for example, Afrashte and Ruhani, are primarily known as satirists, while others, like Bahar, 'Eshqi, and Farrokhi Yazdi produced only occasional pieces of satire.

Mohammad Taqi Bahar (1880-1951), known as Malek al-Sho'ara Bahar, is a poet who during his long and productive life witnessed many political changes. These changes are reflected quite clearly in his poetical works. Bahar's father Saburi, who was the Malek al-Sho'ara (poet laureate) for the shrine of Imam Reza in Mashhad, died when Bahar was eighteen. The young poet, becoming the head of his family, impressed Mozaffar al-Din Shah with a traditional panegyric *qaside*, and thus received his father's title and stipend. Before long, however, Bahar developed from a provincial panegyrist into an outspoken political poet and published his early poems in the paper *Khorasan* in 1909. In the following year, the revolutionary leader, Haydar Khan 'Amu Ughli, came to Mashhad

175

and aided Bahar and his friends in organizing the Democratic Party there. Meanwhile, Bahar began the publication of his own newspaper, *Now Bahar* (New spring). "This paper," E. G. Browne writes, "had a special importance on account of its extreme boldness and fiery denunciations, especially against the Russian aggressions."[1] This led to complaints from the Russian legation in Tehran, and the paper was suppressed. Bahar resumed its publication under the name *Tazeh Bahar* (Early spring) in November 1911, but a few months later this was also suppressed, and Bahar was banished to Tehran.

The years from 1911 to 1925 were the most turbulent of Bahar's life. In this period he suffered repeated banishment, imprisonment, and threats on his life. Bahar had written in his paper bitterly satirical and vehemently patriotic poems condemning Mohammad 'Ali Shah's despotism and the Russo-British aggressions, but in order to avoid further troubles he directed his later attacks toward religious superstition instead of politics. He urged the emancipation of women and wrote on other such modern issues. In 1914, however, having been elected to the third *Majles* (Parliament), Bahar resumed publication of *Now Bahar*, which continued for some years. With the advent of the First World War, Russo-British intervention became even more blatant in Iran, and life for the pro-German Democrats became even more difficult. The October Revolution enabled the Democrats to reorganize their party, but before long they split hopelessly into two rival groups, while the British, who had been dominating the scene, helped Reza Shah come to power. Reza Shah then began for a time to seek support in setting up a republic. Bahar, who had served in the fourth *Majles* by this point, found himself in the fifth *Majles* also, now in the opposition party led by the well-known cleric and politician, Seyyed Hasan Modarres. Modarres regarded the growing power of the upstart general as a serious threat to the parliamentary system. Bahar and his friends, despite continual harassments, supported their cause in the best way they could, and Bahar eloquently voiced the opposition's viewpoint when the *Majles* was presented with the proposal to depose the Qajars. He was elected to the sixth *Majles*, but finding it an almost powerless, rubber-stamping body, he resigned and thus brought his active political life to an end.[2]

In the years from 1925 to 1941, Bahar, like many other poets and writers, avoided political issues as much as possible and devoted himself to scholarly and academic work and to reflective rather than topical poetry. He was not, however, left in peace; several times he suffered incarceration and banishment because of his former associations and activities. Of these times he gives vivid and sad accounts in his prison poems. Eventually, though, he managed to pacify the authorities with some half-hearted panegyrics, and after 1941, the atmosphere being freer, Bahar attempted to revive the old Democratic party. He republished his *Now Bahar*, as well as a book entitled *The History of Persian Political Parties*. He was also elected to the fourteenth *Majles*. But by this time he was old and ailing, and the years of his fiery political career had passed.

Despite periods of political abstinence, Bahar's long years of political struggle resulted in a large body of satirical and topical poetry. Politically Bahar's most interesting period is the early one that ended in 1925 and in which he most outspokenly displays his democratic ideals. On the one hand he is deeply committed to the revival of the past glories of Iran, but on the other he urges the elimination of superstitions and the adoption of European lifestyles. A modern Persian critic, Professor A. H. Zarrinkub, defines Bahar's place in the national literature:

> Bahar's poetry, despite all its traditionalism and adherence to the manners of the past, represents his own age—an age whose leaders regarded the acquisition of Western civilization as well as the revival of national traditions essential for the revival and survival of the nation. Combining these two was considered possible only in an atmosphere of freedom, the kind of freedom liked and accepted by bourgeoise classes. And if in this period there exists a poetry reflective of the voice of the nation as a whole, it is that of Bahar; because the poetry of 'Eshqi or 'Arif is neither pure nor reflective of all aspects of national life, and the poetry of Iraj, though more modern in spirit, represents neither the national ideals nor the various aspects of the nation's life.[3]

Thus, while the freedom sought by Bahar is akin to the freedom advocated by poets like 'Eshqi, Bahar was a more comprehensive poet; yet his ideal of freedom differed somewhat from the freedom envisioned by a poet such as Farrokhi, who remained all his life a socialist.

In the early satirical poetry of Bahar, two subjects stood out: depiction of the autocratic behavior of Mohammad 'Ali Shah and his criticism of British policy in Iran. Bahar occasionally satirized the Russians, too. In a poem that ingeniously parodies a *ghazal* by Hafez, for example, he personifies Russia as a cruel and irrational beloved who eventually will force its lover to desperation and reckless action.[4] But because of the Russians' presence in Mashhad, opportunities to criticize them were few, so most of Bahar's early poems attack either Mohammad 'Ali Shah or the British. In a long *mosammat* entitled "From the Mouth of the Deposed Shah," for instance, Bahar humorously describes the monarch's feelings, frustrations, and misunderstandings of the Constitutionalists' attitudes.[5] In a *qaside* which Browne has translated as "A Critical Tribute to Sir Edward Grey"[6] Bahar criticizes the British policies in Iran that have paved the way for further Russian aggression—not only in Iran but possibly even in India. He concludes the poem with these lines:

> Headstrong and rash you wrought a deed of shame
> Which stolid Turk and vagrant Arab blame.
> Woe to that judgement cool, that reason bright,
> Which now have put you in so dire a plight!
> All hail that judgement, hail that insight rare,
> Of which, men say, you hold so large a share!

In another long *qaside*, written upon the occasion of Iran's intended division into two spheres of influence, British and Russian, Bahar's vituperation of Great Britain is expressed in a series of curses:

> O Britain, may you wander helplessly in this world,
> Bereaved of Asia, deprived of Europe.
> May you be forced out of the Sudan and Egypt,
> And your fragmented heart severed from Cape and Boer lands.
> With a shattered hat, a tattered dress, and empty-handed,
> May you go begging to America!
> May you give Lali and Haftgel away,
> May your heart burn with grief for the wells of Naftun.[7]
> When you think and recall the refineries of Iraq,
> May your heart be a furnace and your eyes shed blood!
> And when Abadan and its oil tankers haunt your memory,
> May the waves of sorrow engulf you in their sea![8]

The *qaside* goes on to enumerate the mischief wrought by Britain throughout the entire world and to expose its nineteenth-century policy of dividing people against themselves, and then ruling and plundering them.

"The Assembly of Asses" is another of Bahar's poems worthy of note. Here Bahar gives vent quite bitterly to his heartfelt disgust at people's ignorance and lethargy over political issues. The poem was written in 1922, when Qavam al-Saltane had resigned the premiership and disorder was increasing everywhere. Ephemeral cabinets were succeeding one another, while Reza Khan, whom Bahar suspected of encouraging the chaos, remained withal the minister of war. Tehran and especially the *Majles* were frequent scenes of uproar; hence the title of the poem. The Bahar mocks this phenomenon of using a mob of ignorant people as a means of gaining political power. This was just before Reza Khan formed his first cabinet and sent Ahmad Shah to Europe, having already arrested and exiled Qavam al-Saltane:

> Tehran has become an assembly of asses—
>   the assembly of asses, may it live long!
> The asinine nature from now till Resurrection—
>   the asinine nature, may it live long!
> The irrational soul of this ass of a nation,
>   everyday becomes more ass-like, may it live long! . . .
>
> If the Arabian horse dies of grief, let him die—
>   in a race that fools shout, "May the ass live long!"
> If you ask for railroads, they will leave you half-dead;
>   in our pastures, let horses and asses live long!
> In a place where learning and ignorance are equal,
>   let learning be dead and the other live long!
>
> If someone says that 'Ali conquered the stronghold of Khaybar,
>   instead of 'Ali, they'll shout "Long live Khaybar!"[9]
> And if one praises Khouli, Senan and Shemr,[10]

the people will yell, "Yes, long live them all!"
For he who shouts, "Down with someone" today,
   tomorrow, being bribed, will shout, "Long live the same!"

In a rose garden where the nightingale is reproached
   by the raven, die, rose and sweet basil! Thorns and thistles, thrive!
May insightful people of sound mind die anon;
   but the weak, sallow government, may it live long!"[11]

Another biting and bitter poem is "Nush-e Janat" ("Good for you" or "Bon appétit"), written in 1929. The occasion of this poem's creation is quite extraordinary. As is explained in the *Divan* of Bahar, Major Mohammad Khan Dargahi, the powerful chief of police of Reza Shah, was an extremely ruthless and ambitious man. He used his official position for personal gain, slandering anyone against whom he harbored a grudge. In fact, Dargahi was the cause of Bahar's imprisonment, hence Bahar celeebrates Dargahi's reversal of fate in the following poem. Dargahi had built a new prison, Zendan-e Qasr, which he asked Reza Shah to inspect. His scheme was apparently, during the inspection, to lock up the king in one of the cells, thus achieving power himself through a bloodless coup d'état. But Reza Shah, aware of this plan, ordered Dargahi beaten and made the first inmate of his own new prison. Bahar celebrates the downfall of his longtime enemy:

O Mohammad Khan, you have fallen into the police prison—
   good for you!
You have lost your newly attained power and prestige—
   good for you!
You were beaten in the presence of Pahlavi,
   A just reward for your good deeds!
You were lashed and lashed, but put up a face—
   good for you!
You maliciously laid traps in people's paths,
   but at last you fell in—good for you!
The arrow you shot from treachery's bow into the hearts of the
   innocents, has struck your own heart now—good for you!
For years you sat on the seat of tyranny, but finally
   you stood before the tribunal of justice—good for you!
For a while you were the light of the nation's eyes;
   now but a flickering lamp in the raging storm—good for you!
Now you pay for your deeds of the past six years—
   good for you!
Whatever you'd extorted, you gave all away—
   good for you!
And now since you repay your stealth and your lust,
   whatever you stole or lusted for is good for you!
You pretended friendship with Jahad Akbar;[12]
   you betrayed him, and boasted of it—good for you!

O my poetry, be an abyss to hide the treachery of the time;
Forever may you suffer because of Jahad—good for you!

Not all of Bahar's poems are so blatantly satirical and bitter. Indeed, some of his political writings are noteworthy not for their satirical qualities, but for their subtle ingenuity in evading censorship restrictions. When Reza Khan was enlisting support for the creation of a republic, Bahar and two other poet-journalists, 'Eshqi and Kuhi-ye Kermani, were associated with Modarres's opposition party. Since censorship would not allow any criticism of Reza Khan, Bahar conceived the idea of writing under the guise of a *movashshah*, a type of acrostic poetry that if read in a special way will give a totally different meaning than the surface reading conveys. One such antirepublican poem by Bahar is a thirty-six-line *mosammat*, which on its face favors the idea of a republic, but by taking the first words of the first three lines and combining them with the entire fourth line, a *ghazal* can be extracted that is bitterly critical of the republican idea.[14] Bahar did in fact send this poem anonymously to a rival journal, *Nahid*,[15] which was strongly pro-government, and the unsuspecting editor published it!

Another example of Bahar's ingenuity is a short prose work again written acrostically and published under the name of Kuhi-ye Kermani in Kermani's paper, *Nasim-e Saba* (The morning breeze). If only the first few words of every line is read, it becomes a criticism of Reza Khan, poking fun at an incident that had occurred a few days before the piece was written—Reza Khan had forgotten the names of some of his ministers, and so could not introduce them to the *Majles!* The official in charge of censorship did not catch the hidden message in Bahar's short article. When it was published and its trick discovered, Kuhi, not Bahar, had to take refuge in the *Majles.* (Taking sanctuary in Parliament was like taking refuge in a holy shrine, from which no one could be evicted.) Eventually, Kuhi's safety was guaranteed by Reza Khan and he was able to come out. The following is a translation of the piece. It is impossible to reproduce in translation the compactness and subtlety of Bahar's original, the first word only from each line serving in the original to form the acrostic meaning. But the basic idea and technique can nonetheless be conveyed:

> **The** desire of the Persian nation is to be saved from
> **illiterate,** feudal noblemen, and to trust its destiny to
> **Reza Khan,** the great and wise leader of Iran,
> **who** has no peer. One other than he
> **could not** lead us to the free destiny of European nations, and
> **introduce** us to the modern world, where the leader and
> **his ministers** are elected by the people to be responsible
> **to the Majles,** for if a nation cannot decide her own destiny,
> **how** could she have an independent life? And if she
> **could** not rely upon her leader and his Majles, then how could
> **he be** able to civilize his nation and to make her
> **an able** 20th century nation with the pride, among nations, guided by
> **president?** Then could she abolish the monarchy, build, and form
> **the police** to protect the people! But the foreign hand
> **does not** allow the savior of Iran, does not

allow the general of the nation, to lead
us to prosperity, to the fulfillment of our ideals and to the
freedom of reformative action. O nation, heed not the intrigue and
expression of deceitfully garbed ideas by foreign powers
so that you will be able to decide your own good and bad;
we ask you not to be fooled. Thus we wrote, but whether we
wrote or not, the nation must always strive to perceive
our meaning—to not be deceived by the appearance of
ideas, as the provincial telegrams have shown, nor to read behind
acrostically hidden meanings.
    Let the reactionaries call us heretics;
    Relaying the message is the duty of the messenger.[16]

Acrostics were not, of course, the only method used to evade censorship. Allegory, animal fable, and the assumption of simplistic and innocent attitudes toward political affairs were also employed. We might mention here one poem that came from the pen of Kuhi-ye-Kermani, in which he imagines himself the party responsible for various political wrongdoings. While trying to defend himself on these charges, in the guise of self-satire, he criticizes the views and actions of many corrupt politicians. He employs this technique of self-deprecation in another poem, too, in which he likens himself to a former prime minister, Zuka al-Molk Foroughi:

> O people of the Iranian land, what qualities
>   for Prime Minister do I lack?
> I am faithful and religious, and, besides,
> I have glasses just like Zuka al-Molk.
> If my beard is somewhat scantier than his,
> Then my glasses at least are better than his!
> If he understands nothing of the ministry,
> Then like him I too of understanding am free.
> If he forms alliances with Great Britain,
> And creates connections for his own gain,
> Then I will befriend Great Britain too;
> The Ministry is clearly my lawful lot! . . .
> So if I am elected to exploit the people,
> I will grow fat and stout-necked as Sulaiman[17] . . .
> Then I will execute strange-natured deeds,
> And offer the nation my lies and deceit.
> I will speechify Parliament and traitors betray,
> To the pillages I'll seem an eternal foe;
> That among them I'm worst, the people won't know.[18]

Among the important contemporary poets, mention should be made of both 'Eshqi and Farrokhi Yazdi. These two were revolutionary poets whom the government of Reza Shah could not tolerate. 'Eshqi was finally assassinated by two unidentified government agents in 1924, an event that created an uproar in Tehran. His funeral was attended by thousands. Farrokhi, who published the journal *Tufan* [Storm], was also not a man to be silenced, so he ended his days in prison in 1939. Both 'Eshqi and Farrokhi in their writings represent different degrees of liberalism—from nationalistic socialism to Communism. Two other important poets, Iraj Mirza (d. 1926) and 'Aref of Qazvin (d. 1934), should also be mentioned. Their allegiances were somewhat different than those of 'Eshqi and Farrokhi. Iraj Mirza, coming from an aristocratic Qajar family, was quite outspoken concerning social reform, but politically he did not go so far as to risk his life. 'Aref, bitterly opposed to the Qajar rule and fervently nationalistic, was critical of the existing sociopolitical conditions, but he favored the presidency of Reza Khan.[19] Therefore, his sympathies were not with the opposition party. Whatever the degree and particular nature of their stances, though, all of these four poets wrote occasional satirical pieces that deserve consideration.

The poetic output of 'Eshqi (1893-1924) is comparatively small, and not all his poems are of equal merit. Some of his satirical poems, like "Khar-Name" [Book of asses], or "Abru-ye Mellat" [The dignity of the nation], are mere invectives. In his articles and plays his language is more dignified, yet as a whole his work here lacks artisitic value. One of his notable satirical poems, though, is the "Story of Kaka 'Abedin and Yasi'," which humorously depicts Britain acting behind the scenes in the creation of the republic. According to a Kurdish story, Yasi kept robbing the headman of his village, Kaka 'Abedin, of his syrup, despite the latter's attempts to prevent the thefts. One day Kaka decided to sprinkle water on the way to his house so that the footprints of the thief would appear. Yasi, however, was riding a donkey and is once again successful in his stealing. He leaves only his fingerprints on the syrup jar, at which the bewildered Kaka exclaims:

> The trace of Yasi's hands, but the feet of a donkey;
> My poor confused mind is in complete disarray![20]

Yasi is, of course, the hand of British intervention. In another poem 'Eshqi mocks Iran's search for freedom via the help of Great Britain—a search that ended with the pact of 1919 by Vosuq al-Doule, establishing total British dominance in Iran:

> Once in a den of thieves, a man was stripped naked—
> Shoes from his feet, hat from his head.
> He ran all day and long after dark,
> And he reached a village at midnight.
> Entering the house of the village master,
> He begged for some food and shelter,
> And for proper clothing for himself:
> "Your humble slave—"
> He had not finished yet his words
> When the master called for his servants.
> "Now that he is a slave of ours," he said,
> "Take him to the market tomorrow for sale."
> When the wretch heard this, he protested in vain:
> "I said that I was your slave to clothe me,
> Not so that you might sell me!"[21]

Farrokhi was quite another sort of poet—powerful and talented, he employed classical *ghazal* and *qaside* forms to convey his liberal politics and ideas. And although there are satirical lines in his poems, his poems are rarely satirical as a whole. The following poem, entitled "Home News," is an exception. It was written in 1922, published in the newspaper *Tufan* [Storm], and was a response to the ministry of the interior's censorship of the news. Because of this censorship, Farrokhi had at first simply left one page blank in his paper, explaining the reason. In the following issue, however, it was stated that in spite of the censorship, a reporter of *Tufan* had received the following news items from "the unseen." These are some of the items printed in the poem:

Home News

Tehran
God be praised that Tehran is like a paradise now!
People are comfortable, in every respect, whether
    high or low.
The wealthy are considerate, kind of heart;
The poor no longer sleep on mats.
    In short, there is no sign of injustice, not at all;
    The news here is not that there is no news!

Kerman
The people of Kerman are secure and at rest.
No injustice is committed, in secret or in the open.
Everyone is pleased with the delegates,
And thanks to the ministers, the city is affluent.
    In short, there is no sign of injustice, not at all;
    The news here is not that there is no news!

Isfahan
Praise be to God, Isfahan is like the Elysian fields;
All hearts are filled with joy over the government's
    fair deeds.
Freedom of pen, thought and speech is so great,
That people are ever talking of the period of
    potentates![22]
    In short, there is no sign of injustice, not at all;
    The news here is not that there is no news![23]

Like Farrokhi, 'Aref of Qazvin (1882-1934) expressed his sociopolitical criticism in the form of lyrical poetry, and he is especially well known for his *tasnifs* (songs), which were recited to the accompaniment of music. He is responsible for a number of satirical poems that he calls *dordiyat* or *motaibat*, most of which are personal criticisms of individuals. He wrote *ghazals* and *qasides* too, which, like Farrokhi's poems, were only partially satirical. Throughout his poems, and especially throughout his *tasnifs*, *ghazals*, and *qasides*, a deep sense of melancholy, cynicism, and nationalism prevails. The following excerpt from a *qaside* addressed to a friend, 'Ali Birang, may serve as an example:

In this country, to whom can one confide his sorrows,
And for whom can one cherish any hope, dear 'Ali?
The Shah, the ministers, the governor and the governed,
All accept bribes and hush-money, dear 'Ali.
The learned and the ignorant enjoy the same rank,
Truthful and traitor the same standing, dear 'Ali.
Look at the "Age of Civilization" and the "Era of Revival,"
Represented by the dandies of Lallezar,[24] dear 'Ali.
The nation, killer of conscience, filled with treachery and
    humiliation,
Works for the aliens and tolerates them, dear 'Ali.
She serves as a porter to the British and valet to the Russians;
The people are without honor, dear 'Ali.
Some receive monthly wages from the British;
Others take pensions from the Russians, dear 'Ali.
So many hurry to the Legations,
Like camel-riders trying to hide by bending, dear 'Ali.[25]
Whatever is left, the Shah takes it to Europe;
Bravo to this King and his master-work, dear 'Ali!
To regain the treasures from his hand would be
To force the talisman from a dragon, dear 'Ali.
Parliament is base, its members criminals and traitors;
The cabinet and the ministers have no honor, dear 'Ali.
May the old heaven break up this depraved society,
And disperse this poisoned atmosphere, dear 'Ali!
A veil covers my eyes, my heart pounds with fear
Living in this pitch-black fortress, dear 'Ali.[26]

The satirical poetry of Iraj Mirza is often closely linked to the work and to the person of 'Aref. Indeed, these two often satirized each other and each other's ideologies. 'Aref, suffering greatly in his youth from the social injustice under the Qajars, had a lifelong hatred of them and missed no occasion to display it. Iraj was a liberal who very often criticized the weak and inexperienced Ahmad Shah, but being a Qajar prince himself, he could not tolerate the extremely bitter attacks of 'Aref. In the summer of 1921 both 'Aref and Iraj happened to be in Mashhad. 'Aref, who had a beautiful voice, sang one of his *ghazals* vilifying the Qajars. Iraj, who was present at the concert, left in an outrage. That same night he composed most of his " 'Aref-Name," a long satirical poem of 515 couplets in rebuke of 'Aref for his political stance and involvement. The poem is not directed against 'Aref entirely; it in fact addresses many topical issues, among them the condition of Iranian women.[27] Iraj also addresses the problem of homosexuality in Iran, citing the lack of access to women as its main cause. He shifts then to another political topic, dividing Iranians into three groups. First he describes the authorities who are the lackeys of the foreign powers and who have no sympathy or interest in the welfare of the nation. These he calls "the willing thieves." The second group he defines, in contrast, as "the forced or un- willing thieves." This group consists mainly of public officials who, having no other means of sustaining themselves on their meager salaries, accept bribes and plunder the people. The third group consists of poor peasants and the rest of the citizenry who neither understand the law nor can appreciate freedom, and so are tyrannized and crushed by the other two groups. All this may not seem an attack on 'Aref, yet it does constitute a satirical answer to 'Aref's more positive sociopolitical positions; for while the political aims of Iraj and 'Aref were often in accord—both, for instance, supported Reza Shah—their attitudes were always quite different. While 'Aref thought and hoped that some good would come of Reza Shah's rule, perhaps some restoration of order, Iraj had no hope for the alleviation of Iran's chaos. Thus, Iraj's rather Byronic cynicism, coupled with his sharp sense of humor, creates a satire in " 'Aref-Name" upon 'Aref's more optimistic thinking. The following is an excerpt from the long poem:

> Come, 'Aref, things have changed.
> Our relationship has grown more strained;
> In the National Theatre I heard you made
> Your inborn stupidity manifest.
>
> Never would I say what you have said;
> My shame is for your shamelessness.
>
> May God visit your voice with the plague,
> So you would no longer appear on stage.
>
> You're a boar, 'Aref; don't pretend to be a deer.
> You are no poet, but only a songster.
>
> Come, 'Aref, let us be friends again,
> Like in one skin kernels twain.
>
> Let me give you some friendly advice,
> So that you may the better enjoy your life.
> What is this political itch of yours?
> Why step on the tail of a snake?
>
> Don't talk of Constitution and lawfulness;
> Rest from justice and fairness awhile.
> Politics is a profession of deceptiveness,
> Not for you and I with our simple artlessness.
> Politicians are crooks and roguish cheats,
> Whenever need be, full of deceit.
> They are always ready for every change;
> From liberal to royalist, they easily convert
> You and I, we are not of such species,
> But victims and targets within misfortune's clutches.
> In this land of ours, don't you know
> Faith and conscience to the high bidders go?
> And the nation's great men in their stupidity
> Have for their own country no sympathy?
> Some take advice from the British now,
> While others with the Russians make vows.

And in their minds, of Iran lies this notion:
That Russia and England own each one portion.
We thus can perceive the state of great men—
Their inferiors in fact are superior to them.
For they are the nation's willing thieves,
They have no way but servitude,
Lest they be left destitute.
Empty-handed, for livelihood they toil and tread;
They struggle even for their bread.
That is why they call the law qanun—
Because its final letter is a nun.[28]
And if they do enter the political scene,
It is merely for work, power and esteem.
We have no commerce, no industry, no roads;
But for Sardar Sepah,[29] there is no hope.
Still others are helpless, and in thrall,
Destitute, they are wanderers all.
They perish in the master's tyranny,
And are trodden beneath the landlord's feet.
Like cows and sheep they are, one and all;
They like neither freedom, nor the law.
So how can these stupid folk know a straw
About democracy, or about the law?
If the nation consists of these three, O wise man,
Why tire yourself beating a cold iron?

These poems must have given the reader a graphic picture of life during the reign of Reza Shah. This period was the beginning of a real decline in political satire; Reza Shah's regime strove to destroy all possible sources of opposition, and newspapers were prominent among them. Editors of newspapers took a hint from the assassination of 'Eshqi in 1924, and all but a very few avoided political issues altogether.

As the era of Reza Shah progressed, gradually all vestiges of criticism, such as that found in the works of 'Eshqi, Farrokhi, 'Aref, Lahuti, and Iraj disappeared; freedom of speech sharply declined. Poets either devoted themselves to meditative and philosophical subjects, or they referred to social grievances in vague and allegorical ways. It was not until 1941, with the abdication of Reza Shah, that newspapers finally were filled with accounts of his injustices. Of the major poets of the period, 'Eshqi was assassinated in 1924; Iraj died one year later; Ashraf and 'Aref, both of whom died in 1934, had grown silent in their later years. Abul Qasim Lahuti, a great and dedicated political poet, after an abortive uprising in Tabriz, fled to Russia in 1922; and Farrokhi was silenced after 1933. He was constantly in prison, dying there in 1939. Among the outstanding traditional poets, only Bahar and Parvin E'tesami (1906-1941) remained.

Under the iron rule of Reza Shah open political satire became something of the past, and only criticism of a very general nature was tolerated. In this respect at least two poets should be mentioned: Parvin E'tesami and Gholam-Reza Ruhani.

Writing in the traditional forms of *qasides*, *ghazals*, and *monazeres*, Parvin
E'tesami was always preoccupied with injustice against women, the poor, and
the socially oppressed. A great many of her poems, such as "Signs of Freedom,"
"The Afflicted Heart," and "The Tyranny of the Rich Is a Thunder for Us,"
display her deep sense of social commitment. *Monazere*, a kind of debate between
two persons or things, was one of her favorite poetic forms. In most of these
poems she covertly refers to the prevailing oppressive conditions of society,
occasionally assuming a sarcastic tone, although most of her poems are not
satirical. "The Thief and the Judge" and "The Drunkard and the Sober" are
two examples that do border upon satire. The latter is an imitation of a poem
from the *Mathnavi* and is translated here:

> A policeman saw a drunkard and grabbed him by the collar.
> The man said: "My friend, this is a shirt, not a rein!"
> The policeman said: "You're drunk; your walk is unsteady."
> He answered: "That's not the fault of my walking; the road
>   is not leveled."
> The other said: "I have to take you to the judge's house."
> The man answered: "Go and come back tomorrow morning;
>   the judge won't be awake at midnight."
> The policeman: "The governor's house is near, let us go there."
> The drunken man: "How do you know that he is not in
>   the tavern?"
> The policeman said: "Then sleep in the mosque until I notify
>   the chief."
> The man said: "The mosque is not a sleeping place for evil-doers!"
> The policeman said: "Then give some money secretly and
>   set yourself free."
> The other said: "The law can't be settled with silver or gold."
> He said: "As indemnity I will take away your coat."
> The other said: "It is threadbare, a mere pattern of
>   warp and woof."
> The policeman said: "You are not aware that your cap has fallen
>   from your head."
> The other said: "It is intelligence that counts; one should not
>   be ashamed of caplessness."
> The policeman said: "You have drunk too much wine and
>   your senses have left you."
> The other said: "Oh you and your vain words! There is no end
>   to this!"
> The policeman said: "The sober should punish the drunken
>   under the law of religion."
> He said: "Yes, so find a sober man in this land—there is none!"[31]

Parvin was only an occasional satirist, but there were other satirical poets who
chose to deal only with very general social problems of their age and criticize
them. Of these, Taqi Binesh, Furat Yazdi, Rahi Mo'ayyeri, and Gholam-Reza
Ruhani were the finest.[32] They contributed to the weeklies, *Towfiq*, (Success)
Omid (Hope), and *Gol-e Zard* (The yellow rose), which were probably the best

satirical papers in circulation at a time when criticism was not only unwelcome but harshly punished. Taqi Binesh, Furat Yazdi, and Ruhani brought out collections of humorous and satirical poems as well,[33] though these collections rarely touched upon political issues. Ruhani was probably the most remarkable of these three, so he may serve to exemplify the group.

Born in 1894 in Mashhad, Ruhani became an employee of Tehran City Hall and the Ministry of Finance for some years. At the same time, he was an active member of several literary clubs. He had a pungent sense of humor and often created graceful puns and wordplay, which make his poems very hard to translate. Sometimes Ruhani employed animal fable to depict social and political conditions. "The Tribunal of Justice" is an example of the use of this technique, each social class being represented by an animal. And sometimes Ruhani simply gave a humorously pointed twist to a common situation, as in "The Petty Thief," where he justifies petty theft committed against a background of poverty and unemployment, holding those bureaucrats responsible who consume people's money without improving the condition of their lives:

> One who robs the country is a delegate and minister,
> But the thief of a pot is arrested by the police.

He ends this long poem with some reflections on former times:

> Your words reminded me of the days of the age of despotism.
> Oh, how wonderful it was! Low prices and plenitude prevailed.
> A maund of bread cost three shahis,[34] and two maunds of butter
>   only two rials.[35]
> It was a period of tranquillity and comfort;
>   every heart was free from care.
> Don't you know that in the past there was only one thief in this
>   land,
> Whereas now in every city and town
>   there are countless thieves protected by law?
> All are "al-Doule" and "al-Saltane,"[36] all are worse than any
>   highwayman.
> If today is the age of freedom, then how wonderful were those
>   despotic days![37]

In another poem Ruhani celebrates the bill for "Abrogation of Titles," which went into effect in 1925. Commenting upon this poem, Munibar Rahman writes, "Formerly the titled class in Persia was very extensive. Ministers, provincial governors, officials and others were distinguished by some high-sounding title or another. Likewise the title of 'Khan' was found in the names of virtually all Persians, high or low, while that of 'Mirza,' preceding a name, signified an educated person and was held by most of the governmental employees." Here is Rahman's translation of Ruhani's poem:

When Khan and Mirza were annulled, both of them took to
　　roaming the plains.
Said Khan to Mirza, "Eminent Sir, we have been fellow travelers
　　for years.
You had your dwelling at the beginning of each name, and your
　　position was next to Aga.
You placed before and I placed after, we choked the name from
　　both ends.
You became my superior and I your inferior; I became attached
　　to the tail, and you to the head.
You were always the postillion of someone; when did you have
　　to stay behind me?
For years we have been a burden to all; we were a double load
　　on their hands.
So people finally took spite against us; a group of fools
　　lost their temper.
They got rid of us and dismissed us with a kick,
Both of us expelled from Aga's front and back,
And taken to roaming the plains.
We are now waiting until the 'Mashhadi' arrives, and until
　　the 'Karbala'i' joins us;
Then all four of us, hand in hand, may together leave
　　the country."[38]

After reviewing the poets of the Reza Shah era we should turn to the reign
of his son, which began in 1941 and ended in 1979. It breaks into two distinct
periods, divided by the 1953 coup d'état. Freedom of expression and the production of political verse and satire in the newspapers that published them vary
markedly in these two periods.

The earlier period, which began in 1941 with the forced abdication of Reza
Shah and ended with the fall of Dr. Mossaddeq's nationalist government in 1953,
was full of upheaval, yet rich in journalism and political writing. This era of
relative freedom of the press was possible at first because of the Allied occupation of Iran and later because of the emergence of a nationalistic, democratic
movement. Furthermore, Mohammad Reza Shah had not yet gained the
dictatorial powers that proved so detrimental to freedom of the press in Iran.

In the first period under consideration, political and journalistic satire thrived.
Poetry was often the medium used in these battles of ideas. Some of the poets
of the era devoted themselves exclusively to satire, and foremost among them
is Mohammad 'Ali Afrashte, discussed briefly in chapter six as the editor of
the journal *Chalangar*. Unlike several earlier poets who only occasionally wrote
satirical verse, Afrashte, devoting his life to political activity, was a poet and
journalist who wrote nothing but satire. Though Afrashte was very popular when
he published *Chalangar*, after the 1953 coup and his escape from Iran he was
forgotten. His works were not allowed to be reprinted until very recently. After
the revolution, when the Tudeh party was still in favor with the Islamic government of Iran, five different editions of his works were published. Three of these
are collections of his satirical poems, and the other two contain his short stories,

sketches, plays, ta'ziyes, and his travel account of Russia.

Chehel Dastan-e Tanz[39] (Forty Satirical Stories) includes most of his sketches and stories published in *Chalangar* from 9 March 1950 to 19 August 1953. The butts of Afrashte's satire are the rich and corrupt landowners, merchants, and officials who exploit and tyrannize the working classes. His socialist ideology, his broad humanity and sympathy for the oppressed, and his hatred of the ruling classes and more particularly Reza Shah and his iron-fisted dictatorship are displayed in these stories. In *Nemayesh-Nameha, Ta'ziye-ha, Safar-Name*[40] (Plays, passion plays, and travels), Afrashte deals with very similar themes. His plays are one- or two-act comedies, and some of them had been performed a few years prior to the publication of *Chalangar*. *Ta'ziye* (passion play) is a new satirical innovation. Employing both the form and style of the *ta'ziye* and some traditional characters of the Persian farce, Afrashte is able to criticize the current political situation. "Ta'ziye-ye Qibla-ye 'Alam" revolves around an alleged coup d'état planned by the CIA and the Shah in February 1952, which was to take place during the Shah's brief absence from the country. The Shah is weary of his rebellious subjects who are constantly pleading for reform. 'Ala, the minister of the court and an old hand in carrying out "the British plans in Iran," wants to silence the leaders of the revolt by bringing in a number of hired club-wielders and thugs. This time they fail, but, as we know, they were successful in returning the Shah to power a year later. Afrashte rightly emphasizes the role of such groups in Iranian politics.

After fleeing to Bulgaria, Afrashte came to know the Bulgarian satirist and journalist Dimitir Belaguov, who knew Turkish. Afrashte would translate his poems and stories into Turkish, and his friend would then convert them into Bulgarian and publish them in the weekly *Stershel* [Hornet]. It was some years later that Afrashte learned Bulgarian and used that language for his later works.

One of Afrashte's works published in Bulgarian is *The Shah's Nose*. The novel covers a period of four days—16 to 19 August 1953—when the Shah flees the country and, with the help of the CIA-paid thugs, returns to power. The Shah finds that all of his statues have been broken, and he orders them to be pieced together and restored. But the nose is missing from one important statue. A ludicrous search is conducted for the missing organ, and numerous people, whose houses contain various possibilities of the "royal nose," are arrested. The search becomes so absurd that people make noses from wood or stone and throw them into the houses of their enemies.[41]

Afrashte is a remarkable satirical poet. He combines both a deadliness of intent and a mordant wit with a gay, bantering tone and a graceful expression. Lack of social justice and rampant corruption constitute the themes of most of his poems. Sometimes he chooses very ordinary, everyday problems and works them into biting satirical verse. In one poem he criticizes the lack of public toilets in such a large city as Tehran,[42] and in another obtaining water for one's house becomes a large problem. Before there was a system of running water in the city, the water came to the houses in filthy gutters. Afrashte describes how, after the people have waited a long time for such water, a colonel in the neighborhood diverts it for the irrigation of his large garden, leaving them to do without.[43] Because of its witty language and numerous topical references, Afrashte's poem is difficult to translate. A short sample from a poem entitled "The Condemned Jackal" will serve instead as an example of his work. The poem is about a farmer who traps a jackal and wants to hang him for stealing his chickens and melons. The jackal retorts:

> The thief of one chicken is hanged, while the thief of ten hamlets
> is the beloved master.
> The thief of one melon is sent to the gibbet while the thief of
> a hundred villages is the honorable Lord.
> The bloodsuckers of thousands of peasants are their highnesses,
> nobles and grandees;
> If you had any talent, reason or virtue, then in your language
> all would be jackals.[44]

Abul-Qasem Halat is another poet of this period who wrote satirical poems before turning more and more to prose sketches. His poems, which had already appeared in various newspapers, were published in a volume entitled *Fokahiyyat-e Halat* [Humorous poems] in 1946. Rather than siding with a particular political party or with one specific ideology, Halat deals with social problems like the backwardness of women, superstition, clerical hypocrisy, and government corruption.

Feridun Tavallali (1921-80) is another significant poet whose collections of satirical poems constitute only a fraction of his work. His most famous satirical collection is entitled *Al-Tafasil* [Detailed accounts] (1952), and it imitates Sa'di's *Gulestan* in style. It contains seventy-five separate pieces of various social and political subjects, written between the years 1941 and 1945 when the author was actively involved in leftist politics. Tavallali's satirical style, like that of Ruhani and Afrashte, is impossible to translate because of its wordplay, specifically, the author's coinage of bitterly satirical names. The difficulty of translation is further increased by his frequent dependence upon styles—archaic styles the mimicking of the *Gulestan* being a case in point.

The second period of the former Shah's reign—the years from 1953 to the revolution of 1979—saw an ever-increasing subjugation of the press to the government. Mas'ud Barzin, a veteran of Iranian journalism, writes, "The decade after 1953, and particularly its first half, was relatively hard and rough for the press of Iran. With what had happened in the earlier years one should not have expected otherwise."[45] The same writer seemingly continues to serve as the mouthpiece of the Shah's regime, saying, "In the last fifty years, there was no decade like the one under consideration, when the press served the government so well, and 'fulfilled its duties' in propagating the government's ideas and programs."[46] It is obvious that under these conditions no opposition paper worthy of the name would be allowed to exist; indeed, the Press Law of 1954 forced the closure of many. There were poets and writers, however, who braved the censorship and continued to produce.

One of these is Mohammad Hasan Husami, a poet from Khorasan who shows that even under very strict censorship, Iranians managed to write political satire. At one time, in order to "prove" that he was ruling a democratic country, the Shah decided to form two official parties. Quickly, however, they were nick-named the "Yes" and "Of course" parties. Husami writes:

> Two parties have been formed in the country,
> Both with the similar names of "People" and "Nation."
> By your life, I am very amazed
> On account of these two parties.
> Since the formation of both of these today
> Was with the help of the government,
> Little by little surely these two
> Will grow strong in our Parliament.
> Each in turn will be the ruling party,
> To be replaced by the other later on,
> So that it will win the race.
> I fear that these parties finally will be
> Another burden on the people.
> And if you think for a little while,
> The purpose of both will be clear:
> > The "Nation" against the "People"
> > And the "People" against the "Nation"![47]

There are also some anonymous poems from this period. They serve the same function as do political jokes, which have always provided an important outlet for suppressed feelings and frustrated hopes.[48] When General Zahedi, who was one of the main participants in the 1953 coup, died in 1963, the following chrono-gram was anonymously sent to my late friend Gholam-Hosain Sa'edi, the well-known playwright and writer. The last line in Persian reads:

> Lahadash "mostarah-e mardom bad"

If each letter of this Persian line is assigned its special numerical value accord-ing to the *jumal* system of calculation and added up, the total is 1963, the year that Zahedi died.[49] Here is the poem in translation:

> Zahedi is dead, may his grave leave no trace,
> A haven for ant, snake, and scorpion.
> May his bones be installed in the depths of Hades,
> To kindle the fires of that horrible scene.
> The poet has said for the date of his death,
> May his last resting place serve as a public latrine.

Looking back at our survey of Persian satire, we see that up until the 1950s and 1960s, poetry was the most often used and most effective means of satire. Later, drama, novels, short stories, and animal fables gained predominance in the field of satire, since those forms, being free from poetic restrictions, allow a more flexible satirical treatment, a more realistic description of detail, and a richer characterization. Modern Persian poetry had nevertheless begun breaking new ground half a century ago, thanks to the genius of Nima Yushij; when this type of verse reached maturity, it opened a new chapter in the long history of Persian poetry. The nationalistic and revolutionary poetry of the Constitutional era brought new ideas and concepts with it, and modern blank and free verse further revolutionized poetic concept and form. Modern poetry is for the most part preoccupied with sociopolitical conditions, although this concern is often cloaked in extraordinarily complex symbolism because of prevailing literary restrictions. Because of government censorship of any and all viewpoints that differed from the status quo; it is obvious that political satire couldn't flourish. One therefore rarely encounters straight-forward pieces of satire in the modern poetry of Iran. One of the rare exceptions is "O Bejewelled Land" by Forugh Farrokhzad, which was mentioned in part in an earlier chapter:

Finally I made it.
I got myself registered
dressed myself up in an ID card with a name
and my existence was distinguished by a number
So long live 678, issued from precinct 5, resident of Tehran
Now my mind is completely at ease
The kind bosom of motherland
The nipple of former ages full of history's glory
the lullaby of culture and civilization
and the rattling of the rattle of the law . . .
Ah
Now my mind is completely at ease

With utmost joy
I walked to the window and fervently,
  six-hundred seventy-eight times,
  drew into my breast air grown thick
with the dust of dung and stench of garbage and urine
And at the bottom of six-hundred seventy-eight IOUs,
atop six hundred seventy-eight applications, I wrote
                Forugh Farrokhzad

. . . .

Living is a blessing, to be sure
in the home of Mr. Fool-son, instant fiddler
and Mr. O-Heart-Heart of the drum, clan of drums,
city of superstar champion—legs, hips, breasts
  and glossy covers of Art,
cradle of the authors of the philosophy, "Hey man,
  what's it to me,"
source of Olympic scholastic games—ay!
a place where from every broadcast you turn on,
  in vision or voice,
there blares the bleating horn of some young ingenious
  genius,

and the nation's intellectual elite
when they gather in adult classes
each has arranged upon his breast six hundred seventy-eight
    electric kebab grills
and on each wrist six hundred seventy-eight Navzar watches,
    and they know
that impotence comes from an empty purse,
    not from ignorance

. . . .

From tomorrow on I'll be able
to invite myself with complete aplomb
to six hundred seventy-eight sessions of a velvet-couched
    organization
in the assembly for gathering and guaranteeing the future
or the assembly for thanksgiving and praise—
for I've read from cover to cover
    the journal of Art and Learning, and the journal of
    Homage and Flattery
and I know the style of "good writing"
I—I have set foot on the field of existence amid the
    creative masses
which having no bread have nevertheless
a broad and open field of vision,
the actual geographical bounds of which
extend in the north to the verdant greenery of
    Target Square
and in the south, to ancient Execution Square
and in the center of town, to Cannon Square[50]

. . . .

And in the shelter of their shining skies,
    in their utter safeness,
six hundred seventy-eight immense plaster swans
in alliance with six-hundred seventy-eight angels
—they too made of earth and clay—
busy themselves from dawn to dark
launching plans for stillness and silence

I've done it, yes, I've done it
So long live 678, issued from precinct 5,
    resident of Tehran,
who in the shelter of perseverance and will
has attained so high a standing as to have settled down
    in a windowsill
six hundred seventy-eight meters above the ground
And she has this honor:
from her perch she can cast herself headlong—
    not by the stairs—
madly into motherland's kind lap.
And her last wish is this,
that in return for six hundred seventy-eight coins
the great master Abraham Sahba[51]

May exalt her life with an elegy that ends in nonsensical rhymes.[52]

As the last example of political satire in this chapter, I would like to quote a poem that was written in Persian and then translated by the poet himself into English. Reza Baraheni (b. 1935), a well-known poet, critic, and novelist, was imprisoned and tortured under the Shah for having given two lectures during a visit to the United States in 1972-73. He later managed to get out of Iran and go to the United States, where he began a vigorous campaign against the atrocities of the Shah. Writing in English and Persian, Baraheni blended his attacks with a very pungent sense of satire in his essays, stories, and poems. In an essay in Persian entitled "The Royal Farsi" he says, "Since we are not allowed to criticize His Royal Majesty's policies or social reforms, I ask permission to criticize only his Persian style." Then in a most ingenious fashion Baraheni dissects the actual speeches of the Shah, equating the ruler's choice of words with a megalomaniacal frame of mind. Of his own personal experiences, Baraheni wrote a work in English entitled *The Crowned Cannibals*, which, despite dreadful accounts of torture and false imprisonment, has a number of humorous passages. Baraheni has also translated a collection of his prison poems into English under the title of *God's Shadow*, from which the following is taken. These poems are not primarily satirical, but a morbid sense of sarcasm often brings them close to satire. The poem below is called "Dr. 'Azudi, the Professional."[53] Doctor 'Azudi was the assistant to Husainzade, one of the most dreaded torturers of SAVAK.

'Azudi is just like
Genghis Khan when he walks
he walks on a pile of fresh corpses

the Khan did not clean his teeth either
the Khan also belched   the Khan
did not take off his boots either   'Azudi
has shattered the mouths of twenty poets today

'Azudi wears a tie   something
Genghis Khan never did
only this splendid detail reveals the prodigious march of history.[54]

Notes

1. Browne, *Press and Poetry*, p. 149.
2. See M. B. Loraine, "A Memoir on the Life of Poetical Works of Malikau'l-sho 'ara Bahar," *International Journal of Middle East Studies* 3, no. 2, (April 1972):140-68.
3. A. H. Zarrinkub, *Na Sharqi na Gharbi Ensani*, (Tehran: Amir Kabir, 1975), p. 311.
4. Browne, Press and Poetry, pp. 288-89.
5. Ibid., pp. 280-82.

6. Ibid., pp. 253-57. The translation is by Browne.

7. Lali, Haftgel, and Naftum are oilfields in southern Iran.

8. M. T. Bahar, *Divan-e Malek al-Sho'ara Bahar* (Tehran: Armi Kabir, 1955), 1:368.

9. Khaybar was a jewish fortress near Medina that fell to the Prophet seven years after Hijra. 'Ali his cousin broke its gate to let the Muslim fighters into the fortress.

10. These were the chiefs of the army of Yazid, who fought with Hosain, the son of 'Ali and the grandson of the Prophet. Hosain and some of his followers were ruthlessly massacred in Kerbala.

11. *Divan-e Malek al-Sho'ara Bahar* (Tehran 1955), 1:368:Cf. Loraine, "A Memoir," p. 145.

12. Jahad Akbar was one of the victims of Dargahi. Mirza 'Ali, who was known by the name of his newspaper as jahad Akbar, was a militant journalist of the Constitutional period.

13. *Divan-e Bahar*, 1:487-88.

14. *Divan-e Bahar*, 1:357-59.

15. The fate of Nahid is interesting to note. *Nahid* was considered the rival paper of *Nasim-e Shomal*, and the latter's writers envied the relative freedom enjoyed by *Nahid*, a freedom possessed because of its pro-government position. *Nahid*, however, did not always abide exactly by the principles laid down for it by the authorities, and so even with its progoverernment stance, met an early end. In a sadly humorous story, *Nahid's* editor, after many suspensions of his paper, likens its fate to that of a famous and outspoken "Luti" (a Robin Hood-type figure, giving generously to the people but also open in expressing his views), who some decades earlier, because of his outspokenness had first lost his ears and then his life. *Nahid* was published irregularly for nine years, and then in 1930 its office was completely destroyed by arson. Though a few issues came out three years later, the year 1930 effectively marked the end of this extremely popular paper.

16. Kuhi-ye Kermani, *Bargi az Tarikh-e Mo'asser-e Iran* (Tehran, 1952), p. 132.

17. Soleyman Mirza was the leader of the Socialists in the fifth *Majles*.

18. Kuhi-ye Kermani, *Bargi*, pp. 50-52.

19. Aref hailed Reza Shah as a liberator, but then he ceased writing and went into silence during the early years of the new monarch's reign.

20. *Kolliyyat-e 'Eshqi*, ed. 'Ali Akbar Mushir-Salimi (Tehran: Amir Kabir; 1965) p. 279.

21. Ibid., p. 401.

22. This line, which has a double meaning, reads literally, "The people are always talking of the age of autocracy."

23. *Divan-e Farrokhi-ye Yazdi* (Tehran: Amir Kabir, 1978). pp. 200-201.

24. A street in Tehran.

25. According to a Persian proverb, a camel-rider may try to hide by bending himself over, but he will be nonetheless visible.

26. *Kolliyyat-e Divan-e 'Aref Qazvini* (Washington D.C.: Dokan, n.d.), pp. 310-13.

27. This section of *'Aref-name* is translated in the present work in chapter 8, "Women and Satire."

28. Nun in the colloquial means "bread," as well as being the name for the letter N.

29. Sardar Sepah, was the name of Reza Shah before he became the King.

30. *Kolliyat-e Divan-e 'Aref Qazvini*, p. 315.

31. *Divan-e Parvin E'tesami* (Tehran, 1954), p. 185.

32. See Machalski, *La Litterature de l'Iran Contemporaine*, pp. 70-86.

33. Gholam-Reza Ruhani *Kolliyat-e Ashar'e va Fokahiyat-e Ruhani* (Tehran: Sana'i, n.d.); *Divan-e Furat* (Tehran, 1946); *Divan-e Taqi Binesh* (Tehran, 1953).

34. A *shahi* was a small coin like penny.

35. A *rial* is one-tenth of a *tuman*. The official rate of a *tuman* is approximately one-eighth of a dollar.

36. "Al-Dowle" and "al-Saltane" were two aristocratic titles.

37. Munibur Rahman, "Social Satire in Modern Persian Literature," *Bulletin of the Institute of Islamic Studies* (Aligarh University) (1957):85-87.

38. Ibid., p. 86.

39. *Chehel Dastane "Tanz,"* ed. Nosrat ullah Nuh, (Tehran: Haidar Baba, 1981).
40. *Nemayesh-Nameha, Ta 'zaiye-ha, Safar Name,* ed. N. Nuh (Tehran: Haidar Baba, 1981).
41. For an account of this novel see the introduction of *Chehel Dastan-e,* p. 4.
42. *Majmu'a-ye Athar-e Mohammad 'Ali Afrashte,* ed. N. Nuh (Tehran: Hadar Baba, 1979).
43. Ibid., pp. 90-91.
44. Ibid., p. 160. The translation is by Munib-ur Rahman in "Social Satire in Modern Perisan Literature," pp. 85-87.
45. Mas'ud Barzin, *Matbu'at-e Iran (1343-53),* Tehran, 1975, p. 13.
46. Ibid., p. 3
47. M. Shafi 'i-ye Kadkani, *Shar'er-e Emruz-e Khorasan* (Tehran: Tus, 1965), pp. 295.
48. Political jokes have always been a part of Iranian culture, and classical examples are to be found in anecdotes by 'Obeyd-e Zakani or those recorded by Fakhr al-Din 'Ali Safi (d. 1530) in his *Lata'ef al-Tava 'ef,* ed. Ahmad Gulchin Mu 'ani (Tehran: Eqbal, 1967).
49. .L(20) + J(8) + D(4) + SH(300) + M(40) + S(60) + T(400) + R(200) + A(1) + H(1) + /M(40) + R(200) + D(40) + M(40) + /B(2) + A(1) + D(4) = 1342. This date is in *Hijri* solar calender which corresponds to 1963.
50. These three locations in Tehran were places of execution.
51. Ebrahim Sahba, a contemporary poet who wrote topical poems and was associated with the Iran-American Society in Tehran. Forugh deridingly changes his name to the Americanized "Abraham."
52. *Another Brith: Selected Poems of Forugh Farrokhzad,* trans. Hasan Javadi and Susan Sallee, (Emeryville, Calif., 1981) Albany Press, pp. 56-60.
53. Baraheni writes, "They called each other 'Doctor'—Dr. 'Azudi, Dr. Hosain Zade, and so on. It was only later I came to realize that by using a university title, they provided themselves, rather unconsciously, with a certain legitimacy to deal with university students and teachers like myself." *God's Shadow* (Bloomington: Indiana University Press, 1976) p. 15.
54. Baraheni, in *God's Shadow,* p. 15.

8

Women and Satire

From a vixen wife protect us well,
Save us, O God! from the pains of hell.

—Sa'adi, *Gulestan*

Slavery of woman, Tyranny of the Shah and
    the ignorance of populace;
Make a story which is hard to describe.

—Abul Qasim Lahuti

The man-woman relationship has always been one of conflict. Except in early matriarchal societies, man has generally dominated woman, but at the same time he has always been in need of her. Man has enjoyed the advantages of physical strength, political power, and wealth, and until recently those of legal status and education, yet his life has never been complete without the presence of woman. This need, threatening both man's sense of pride and his self-sufficiency, has made woman a continuous target of his satire. Doctor Johnson has said, "As the faculty of writing has been chiefly a masculine endowment, the reproach of making the world miserable has always been thrown upon the woman."[1] Therefore, most satirical works about women express a masculine point of view. A little-known feminist of the seventeenth century, Poulain de la Barre, sums up the whole subject in this way: "All that has been written about women by men should be suspect, for the men are at once judge and party to the lawsuit."[2]

The masculine viewpoint most often expressed is one of aggression or victory over women. Sexual jokes, for instance, portray not an act of mutual pleasure but an act from which only the man benefits. In some languages the very words for lovemaking have a derogatory connotation.[3] In societies where women are

198

less emancipated, swear words often have sexual associations. This is true in English of course, but the number of abusive sexual words in both Persian and Arabic seems to be far greater. One might seek to offend a man by verbally abusing his wife, mother, daughter, or sister. Thus, woman becomes a "sexual object" to be guarded and protected by man. Sometimes even references to a man's relationship with his wife or sister is considered impolite. For instance, even today some men in Iran call their sisters *ham-shireh* ("one who has shared milk with me") or refer to their wives as "the children's mother."

In Persian literature there are at least three categories of women to be found. First, there are women in general; second, saintly women; and third, the beloved. The first category is treated with the most obvious and negative chauvinism, incorporating all the usual prejudices that are common in the East as well as the West. The frame tale of the *Thousand and One Nights*, for example, in which *Shahrezad* prolongs her stories to save herself from impending death, indicates the ever-present male suspicion of female infidelity. Similar themes occur in such other Middle Eastern tales as the Turkish *Forty Viziers* and *The Wiles of Women*[4] and the Persian *Tales of a Parrot* and *Bakhtiyar-Name*.[5] The works of many Iranian poets also reflect this negative view of women. The highly misogynous Jami (1414-92) arranges that the hero of his philosophical allegory, *Salaman and Absal*, who represents the human soul, is born magically, not from a woman, so as to be purer than other men. Asadi of Tus (eleventh century) considers finding a husband a woman's greatest art, and in one poem he says:

> Outside of women is green and lush as a tree,
> But inside they have venom as the fruit.[6]

Naser Khosrow (d. 1088) brings in yet another characteristic opinion:

> Since women are imperfect in faith and reason
> Why should men follow their way and decision?[7]

Jami, alluding to the Biblical story of creation, asks:

> Woman was fashioned from the left rib;
> Who has ever seen right come from the left?[8]

According to some nationalistic Iranian scholars women enjoyed a better status in pre-Islamic Iran, and it was as a result of the association with the Semitic Arabs that they became subordinate to men.[9] But such generalizations exalting the Aryans over the Semites are difficult to justify. The custom of *suttee*, cremating the Hindu widow on the funeral pyre of her husband, for instance, was practiced until the last century by the Aryan Hindus. In Zoroastrianism, although a woman can own property and is urged to learn the sciences and the arts, there are many prejudices against her. A religious Pahlavi text says, "Do not be forthcoming with women, so that your toil will not reap repentance and shame. Do not confide secrets to them, so that your toil will not be wasted."[10] Zoroaster, like Moses and Manu, decreed that if a woman bears a daughter the period of purification will be longer than that of one who gives birth to a boy, as the former has brought to the world a source of sin.[11] The fourth-century priest Arda Viraf, in an account of heaven and hell which is not unlike the *Divine Comedy*, describes the terrible punishments meted out to wives who have disobeyed their husbands.[12]

One of the major sources of information about the condition of women in pre-Islamic Iran is the great epic of Ferdausi, *Shah-Name*. Some of his great heroines—Rudabeh, Tahmineh, Gord-afarid, Katayun, and Ferangis—are worthy companions to the heroes of this famous work. But others of the women, such as Sudabeh and Malekeh, are vicious and treacherous. The former corresponds to Phaedra and the latter brings death to her father, an Arab chieftain, as a result of the love she bears for Shapur, the Sassanid monarch:

> When you hear this story all
> It will suit you better not to follow women.
> Do not seek but pious women in the world;
> Ill-faithed women bring shame on you.
> Women and dragons may lie in the dust;
> May the world be purged of these evils.[13]

The advent of Islam changed the status of women. In pre-Islamic Arabia, where murdering infant daughters by burial was common, the call of Islam to consider not only rich and poor but also men and women as equals in the eyes of God, and the statement that "the most virtuous of you is the dearest to God," were significant revolutions. Although women had become the spiritual equals of men, they still had a long way to go socially. Even the *Koran*, which puts women in the charge of men in such matters as inheritance, testifying, and polygamy, states, "Good women are the obedient, guarding in secret that which Allah hath guarded. As for those from whom ye fear rebellion, admonish them and banish them to beds apart, and scourge them."[14]

The seclusion that was imposed upon Muslim women in the centuries to come and that consequently deprived them of many social activities was not propounded, however, by Islam. In the early days of Islam women were in fact freer in their associations with men. For instance, 'Ayesha, the youngest wife of the Prophet, was actively involved in politics after his death, and even fought with 'Ali, the Prophet's cousin, on the issue of succession. Zainab, the daughter of 'Ali, who was brought as a captive to the court of the Umayyad Caliph Yazid after the tragedy of Kerbela, boldly stood up and gave a fiery speech that made Yazid ashamed. It was only later, as a result of further urbanization of the Arabs and the increasing number of female slaves brought from various parts of the Islamic empire, that the Umayyads and Abbasids, following the example of the Sassanid kings and other rulers of the time, confined their women to seraglios. As the nomadic simplicity of the old days was replaced with luxury and often corruption, men grew more and more suspicious of and tyrannical toward women.

Tales of women's untrustworthiness found ever-wider currency, and folk sayings concerning women began to circulate. One advises, "Consult them, but do the opposite."

Such biased views even contradicted some of the basic teachings of Islam. The Prophet had said, "Learning is a duty for every Muslim man and woman," but later views expressed on the education of women were very different. Qabus Ibn Voshmigir, the ruler of Gorgan and Tabaristan (d. 1012) believed that one should not exceed the learning of the *Koran* and the laws of the faith. He said that a woman should not be taught "penmanship."[15] Two moralists and philosophers of later periods, Naser al-Din Tusi (1200-74) and Jalal al-Din Davani (d. 1502 or 1503), both believed that girls should not be taught writing and reading.[16] The latter added: "They should be taught housekeeping, and be sent to their husband's house soon."[17] Mulla Mohammad Baqer Majlesi (d. 1700), the great Shi'ite theologian, even makes the teaching of the *Koran* to girls subject to censorship, leaving out the amorous story of Joseph and Potiphar's wife. Then he adds that one should not allow one's daughter to sit in the upper chamber and watch the passersby, but that she should be married off as soon as possible.[18] It was also commonly believed that the stories of such legendary lovers as Leili and Majnun, Khosrow and Shirin and Vis and Ramin are inappropriate for women.[19]

But not all women were seen to deserve such distrust, and a limited number were considered "good, pious and obedient." Asadi of Tus in his epic *Garshasep-Name* makes one of the characters thus answer the legendary king, Jamshid, who was suspicious of women:

> Delaram said: "O all-knowing and wise king,
> Not every woman will be double-hearted and ten-tongued.
> Not every one has the same temper and character;
> Even the fingers of two hands are not the same."[20]

Sometimes writers set standards to define a pious wife. 'Awfi (ca. 1176-1236) wrote in his *Javame' ul-Hikayat*, "One should know that when God Almighty's blessings come to someone who is imperfect, she will be more exalted than the men of the world. Though their creation has been from the wrong bone and crookedness imbued in their nature, yet there are many women whose two-foot veil is by far more respected and honored than the thirty-foot turban of men. And no blessing is greater for a man than a pious wife."[21] The writer goes on to give examples of such women. In one story a woman succeeds to return to her husband with her virtue unsullied after many incredible adventures. This was, of course, one of the characteristics of the ideal woman.

The poems written on the ideal women somewhat resemble European encomiums, of which the best example is "The Legend of the Good Women" by Chaucer. There he shows the expectations of the men of his age toward their wives. These expectations do not vary greatly between the West and the East. Men wanted their wives to be extremely patient, chaste, and restrained in their conduct and dress. In the lands of Islam it was always suggested that if a woman tolerates an ugly and ill-tempered husband, she will be amply rewarded in the world to come.[22]

Some of these expectations still persist in the Middle East. For instance, virginity is a precondition of matrimony, whereas a man with no premarital relationships is considered to be "slow" or, at best, a "unsophisticated." Awhadi of Marageh (1271-1338) sums up in one of his poems the attitude not only of his contemporaries but that of many generations to come:

> A veiled wife is a candle for the house;
> A coquette is a calamity at all times.
> An unchaste wife is an evil lot;
> Get rid of her soon as she is a pang to the heart.
> A pious spouse fond of obedience and devotion,
> Will be like a kernel in one shell with you.
> If the wife goes out beat her hard;
> If she wantonly displays herself strip her naked.
> If she does not obey destroy her;
> If she brings shame to you, in the dust bury her.[23]

One level above the chaste wife one finds the mother, and still higher is placed the saintly woman. The mother in Islamic tradition has a fairly elevated status, and she is regarded in a totally different light than other women. A well-known saying of the Prophet states, "Heaven is under the feet of mothers." Saintly women and great Sufi women also enjoyed a venerated status, which reminds one of a similar tradition in Christianity. In this religion the Virgin Mary and Eve are placed in two completely contrasting categories. Sin came into the world through the latter; redemption became possible because of the former. Although it obviously does not subscribe to this mythology, Islam nonetheless divides mothers and saints on the one hand, and women in general on the other, into these two categories.

Even under very adverse conditions great and learned women, such as Rabi'a al-'Adawiyya and the famous Babi poet and scholar Quratu'l-ayn (killed in 1852), did appear. Rabi'a al-'Adawiyya (d. 752) was among the greatest of the women of Islam. Despite the views held by many men of her time that women could not reach heights of sainthood, she gained exactly such stature. Her piety and asceticism, in fact, became proverbial throughout the Islamic world. A tyrannical governor of Basra, who was sent by the notorious Hajjaj ibn Yusef, was so impressed by Rabi'a that he repented and became an ascetic himself.[24]

Though Rabi'a's position as one of the greatest Sufis was well established, and 'Attar in his *Biographies of the Saints* ranked her with the Virgin Mary, there was at least one instance of antifeminism expressed by a visitor who was silenced by her witty answer. She was asked, "All virtues have been bestowed on men, the crown of magnanimity has been placed on men's heads, and the girdle of generosity is for them, and no woman has become a prophet, then why do you boast so much?" Rabi'a answered, "All that you said is true, but egotism, self-love, selfishness, and [sayings like] 'I am your Great God'[25] have not come from woman. And a woman has never been a sodomite."[26]

Of the categories enumerated above, the third one is woman as the "beloved" in Persian literature, which is totally different from either type described previously. It is in fact incredible that the poets with such degrading views of women can be so absolutely humbled by and devoted to the "beloved." These poets consider themselves the "dust of her threshold" and a "captive in her beautiful tresses." Of course, sometimes they are referring to the "Divine Beloved" who is beyond any human perception and imagination; but very often their sentiments are directed toward female beauty as well. Even a Sufi poet like Jami, with an unmistakably worldly nature, in some of his poems describes feminine beauties with such gusto and realistic detail, and such an amorous passion, that one wonders how to explain the misogynous views present in his other poems.

This trend in Persian poetry is reminiscent of the courtly tradition in Europe. While the poet treated his wife with a lack of civility, he traditionally humbled himself beyond all limits before his imaginary or actual beloved. Similarly, the Persian poets praised the beauty and coquetry of the beloved, and even evaluated her faithlessness, cruelty, and lack of consideration as attractive qualities. But when considering the issue of women in general, their views were very different.

Surveying the antifeminist literature of the West—from the Sixth Satire of Juvenal to the harsh sayings of the Church fathers (such as Saint Augustine) and their medieval followers,[27] and from the less offensive picture of a shrewd and bossy woman in Chaucer's "Wife of Bath" to the witty and graceful satire of Molière in *Les Précieuses Ridicules* and *Les Femmes Savantes* or Pope's biting remarks in *On the Character of Women*—one finds many similarities to the view of men of the East. In fact, some of the antifeminist and satirical tales included in the *Disciplina Clericalis* of Petrus Alfonsi, the *Decameron*, or the French *fabliaux* are the same as the tales of the *Arabian Nights*, the *Bakhtiyar-name*, and the *Sindbad-Name*.[28] Comparing the antifeminist satirical tradition in Europe and Iran, one finds that for many centuries similar views and often identical stories existed in Europe and in Iran. However, in Iran the feminist movement did not begin until much later than in Europe, and even then it was inspired by Western influences.

The rule of the Safavids in the sixteenth century, characterized by religious zeal and theocratic administration, was certainly one of the factors in preventing women from gaining their rights. One of the great theologians of the time, Mulla Ahmad Naragi, went to the extreme of forbidding women to participate in religious ceremonies. As westernization gained ground at the turn of the present century, the emancipation of women and the lifting of the veil were among the most often discussed subjects. In modern times the Iranian poets often complained of the seclusion of the woman and her lack of participation in social affairs.

As a whole the satirical works concerning women in Iran can be divided into two main periods: one before the impact of the West is felt in the country, and the other afterward, when attempts at the emancipation of Iranian women begin. In the first period a traditional and medieval attitude persists. Women are often depicted as lustful and not worthy of trust, the harems are full of intriguing women, and the men even prefer boys to women. In the second period the attitudes change. The chastity of women is essential, but being veiled does not necessarily prevent her from yielding to temptation. The superstition and ignorance of women are often ridiculed, and they are urged to look up to their European sisters for inspiration. Gradually when, in due course, they become too westernized, their wastefulness, artificiality, and affected mannerisms become the topics of satire.

Descriptions of the infidelity and lustfulness of women abound in classical Persian literature. In a risqué story Rumi describes how a maidservant contrives, by means of a hollowed-out gourd, to lie with an ass. The gourd is used to prevent penetration and possible injury of her by the ass. The servant's mistress, however, who discovers her "in the act," fails to perceive the gourd. On a pretext, she sends the maid on an errand and tries to satisfy her own insatiable lust. The maidservant returns to find her mistress dead, a victim of her own ignorance and lust. Rumi gives the story an allegorical interpretation, saying that lust makes "an ass seem like a Joseph, and fire like light."[29]

Although in most of his stories Rumi is after elucidation of mystical or moral points, most of them are the same antifeminist tales that are found in the medieval eastern or western sources. Here is another story from the *Mathnavi* with a similar sentiment. A *Dalqak* ("jester") explains to a great man of religion why he has married a prostitute:

> One night a Seyyed Ajjal said to Dalqak, "You have
>   married a harlot in haste.
> You might have disclosed this [matter] to me, so that
>   we might have made a chaste [woman] your wife."
> Dalqak replied, "I have [already] married nine chaste
>   and virtuous women: they become harlots, and I wasted
>   away with grief.
> I married this harlot without [previous] acquaintance,
>   in order to see how this one [also] would turn out in
>   the end.
> Often I have tried [sound] intelligence; henceforth,
>   I will seek a nursery for insanity."[30]

On the subject of salacious women many more examples can be given. Bindar of Rey, an eleventh-century poet known for his poems in the local dialect, wittily describes an old woman who becomes alarmed by a sermon when she remembers her past amorous adventures:

> On a pulpit in Rey once a preacher most vain,
> Did deliver a sermon in somewhat this vein:
> Seven members of your body on Judgment Day,
> Will give testimony to what they did, aye![31]

An old woman did beat at her privates and say,
What a braggart you'll turn out to be on that day![32]

Shrewish wives and quarrelsome in-laws also become the subjects of satire.
Among the scenes of marital life described by Persian classical poets there are
two instances that deserve inclusion here. The first is a well-known episode in
the long and adventurous life of Sa'di (1185-1292), as we know it from his own
fictionalized account; the second is a humorous letter written by Qa'ani (1808-54)
to his royal patron, Naser al-Din Shah. Sa'di's story relates his captivity at the
hands of the Crusaders and his ransom by a Syrian friend:

> I had grown weary of the Society of my Damascus friends, and therefore
> made my way into the Jerusalem desert, where I enjoyed the companion-
> ship of the beasts; until the time came when the Franks made me their
> prisoner, and kept me with Jews in a trench at Tripoli digging clay. One
> of the leading citizens of Aleppo, with whom I had been formerly acquainted,
> chancing to pass by recognized me, and said, "Sirrah, what manner of life
> is this?" I said, "What can I say
>
> > I fled from men to mountain and to plain,
> > For I had nothing from mankind to gain;
> > How is my case? Regard me in this den,
> > Where I must sweat with men that are not men."
>
> > Better to hang in chains, when friends are there,
> > Than dwell with strangers in a garden fair.

He had compassion on my condition, and with ten dinars procured my
release from bondage. He took me along with him to Aleppo, and there
made me marry his daughter, adding a dowry of a hundred dinars. Some
time passed. She was a woman always scowling—disobedient and growl-
ing; she began to give me plenty of her shrewish tongue, and made life wholly
miserable for me.

> > A bad wife comes with a good man to dwell,
> > She soon converts his present world to hell;
> > Beware of evil partnership, beware—
> > From hellish torment, Lord, thy servants spare!

Once in a torrent of abuse she said, "Are you not that man whom my
father bought back from the Franks?" I said, "Yes, I am that man whom
he bought back from the Frankish chains for ten dinars, and delivered into
your bondage for a hundred dinars."[33]

Qa'ani, in a letter that is written in an ingeniously rhythmic prose, describes
how the fighting between his two mothers-in-law ends in a fire that leaves him
homeless. At the end, in the tradition of panegyrical poets, he makes an appeal
to the generosity of his royal patron. Here I give a partial translation of this
letter, but with the reader's understanding, that the translation does not do justice
to the beauty and satirical tone of the original:

Now for many years I have been afflicted with two unruly spouses, who are quick in anger and slow in discretion. One calls herself the "Honored Beloved" and the other the "Beautiful Blossom." One has secured a genealogy, tracing herself back to the tribe of Qavanlu, and the other has procured a scroll, establishing her ancestry in the family of Davanlu.[34] Though I have always tried to keep them both happy, every day they start a brawl and every night a quarrel.

I have two shrewish and intriguing mothers-in-law, who are ugly of face, unpleasant in shape, greedy in taste, fearless, and unclean. They are as old as the world itself, and more wicked and bloodthirsty than Hind, the Eater of Livers.[35] It is as if Ferdausi had them in mind when he said:

> 'Tis better both woman and dragon be buried in the dust
> So that the world free from them both may rest.

They are so full of spite and malice that [your Majesty's] servant cannot describe but one of their thousand [schemes]. For instance, the other day, under a womanish pretext, they scattered dust in the arena of wrestling and like two novice champions got engaged in the sport. Before long their faces were black from slapping and blue from shoe-inflicted blows. They left each other pale, blood-stained, wounded, and in great confusion, with their hair pulled and their dresses torn.

The Qavanlu mother, finding herself beaten and defeated, ran to the house of her relatives and chided them for their indifference. Seeing such a hue and cry, they rushed out in her defence armed with sticks and clubs. While clamoring in the Turkish manner and applauding like Arab women, the maidservants with ladles and skimmers scurried to the house. There was absolute chaos and the neighbors came out to watch.[36]

Qa'ani goes on to describe how the Qavanlu wife and her mother threw out their rival's duenna and set fire to her *korsi*, a heating device shared by the duenna and the other mother-in-law, and as a result burned the whole house down.

It was because of such family feuds that 'Obeyd-e Zakani, one of the greatest satirirists of Iran, writes, "Don't seek comfort, peace and happiness in the house of a man who has two wives."[37] 'Obeyd in his "Definitions," a succinct and humorous description of the people of his age, devotes the ninth and tenth sections to "the householder and what pertains to him" and "the true nature of men and women," respectively. Both sections are very revealing:

> The Bachelor: He who laughs at the world's beard.
> The Unfortunate: The householder.
> The Two-Horned [Dhu'l-Qarnayn]: He who has two wives.
> The most unfortunate of the unfortunate: He who has more.
> The Futile: The householder's life.
> The Wasted: His time.
> The Dissipated: His wealth.
> The Distracted: His mind.
> The Bitter: His life.
> The Abode of Mourning: His house.
>
> . . . .

The Kinsman: His deadly foe.
Joy after sorrow: The triple divorce.

. . . .

The Lady: She who has many lovers.
The Housewife: She who has few.
The Virtuous: She who is satisfied with one lover.
The Maiden: A name denoting what does not exist.[38]

Prearranged marriages and injunctions against seeing one's wife until the nuptials are among other subjects of satire. 'Obeyd-e Zakani in his *Resale-ye Delgosha* relates several such stories. Majd al-Din Hamgar, a contemporary poet from Yazd, who apparently finds himself stuck with an old wife after the marriage, is the subject of several stories in this collection of anecdotes. When the poet came from Yazd to Isfahan, he left his wife behind, but she soon followed him. The news of her arrival was brought to the poet by his servant, who said, "Good news! Your lady has alighted at the house." "Good news," replied Majd al-Din, "would rather be that the house alighted on her!" The lady, to whom this speech was reported, reproached her husband for his unkind words that "the world has existed long before you and me and no one has treated a lady in this manner." She quotes a poem by Khayyam that begins:

Days changed to nights, ere you were born or I.[39]

"Before me, perhaps," replied Majd al-Din, "but Heaven forbid that day and night should have existed before you!"[40] In another story a man marries a woman through the importunity of his friends and, as was customary with the Muslims, saw the bride's face for the first time on the marriage night. She proves to be very ugly, or at best perhaps merely "plain-looking." A few days after the nuptials, she says to him, "My life! As you have many relatives, I wish you would inform me before which of them I may unveil. . . ." "My soul!" responds the husband, "if you will but conceal your face from *me*, I care not to whom you show it."[41]

Some poets advise men not to marry. 'Obeyd-e Zakani says, "Do not marry if you don't want to become a cuckold!"[42] Sana'i (d. 1141), whose misogynous views are strongly voiced throughout his *Divan*, believes that a young slave boy can be the man's partner at night as well as a traveling companion. Sana'i says, "The Egyptian Joseph suffered ten years of prison because of a woman. If this happened to a 'friend of God' what will happen to you?"[43] Then the poet recommends that one should be like a cock that does not confine himself to a single hen. Sana'i compares having a slave girl, who is one's own property, with a wife, who is a creditor. The explanation is that in Islam the wife can have her marriage portion whenever she wishes to, and since it is often paid when there is a divorce, the husband is always in debt to her:

Don't marry! Leave aside women in this spring time:
No man marries if he is in his right senses.

> If you are a slave of passion, buy a bondsmaid,
> Beautiful, fair-faced, comely and well-shaped.
> As long as you wish she will comply with your desires,
> When you don't want her, she will be ready cash.
> It is much better to rise in the morning
> To see the face of your own property than that of a creditor.[44]

The views quoted so far picture a society that is plagued with immorality, hypocrisy, and distrust of women. This was particularly the case in the Mongol period and especially among the ruling class of Iran. 'Obeyd-e Zakani in his *The Ethics of the Aristrocrats* gives a vivid picture of this age, which reminds the reader of the satires of Juvenal at the time of Rome's decadence. 'Obeyd in the chapter "On Chastity" writes about the great men of his age, who considered chastity something of the past, and believed that "the ancients have made a great mistake on the subject and have wasted their precious lives in ignorance and error." The aristocrats of the time of 'Obeyd believed that "it is impossible to enjoy life without playing and indulging in vices and forbidden pleasures."[45] 'Abbas Eqbal, a modern Iranian historian, writes this about the later part of the Mongol period (fourteenth century): "The mother of one of the kings was known for prostitution and promiscuity; the wife of another kills her husband in the most hideous way, since he had imprisoned her lover; another king blinds his father with his own hands and commits adultery with his mother; and a fourth monarch forces his enemies to divorce their wives so that he may woo them and write *ghazals* of his love for them."[46]

Three centuries later, we discover still another picture of moral decadence when Iran was in turmoil and the Afghan invasion imminent. The country was ruled at this time by Shah Sultan Hosain (1694-1729), who was so incapable of running the business of state that he left everything to the discretion of his court ministers, eunuchs, and mullas. Even when the Afghan invasion had laid siege to Isfahan, he was not aware of the real situation. An interesting satirical work entitled *Rostam al-Tavarikh*, written by Mohammad Hashem Asef in 1832, contains numerous passages on the amorous life of Shah Sultan Hosain and at the same time depicts the prevailing moral decadence at the court of Isfahan. There is an ironic duality in the life of the monarch as pictured in this book. He is very religious and something of a theologian and scholar, yet he has no scruples about marrying other men's wives. Though the writer, Mohammad Asef, directs his criticism mostly toward the mullas and ministers at the court of Isfahan, he also gives a vivid picture of the condition of women in the royal harem. He writes of Sultan Hosain:

> Day and night he was eager and without restraint in eating and coition. As a test in one day and night he ordered one hundred virgins to be taken into temporary wedlock, in accordance with the *Shari'a* and with their own and their fathers' consent. In twenty-four hours as a result of a great aphrodisiac that Refuge of the Nation and the Land deflowered all those lovely girls and graceful and sugar-lipped sweethearts, and still like an intoxicated

bachelor was eager for more. Then in compliance with the law of the Prophet he divorced and sent them to their homes with legal marriage-portions and with precious clothes and ornaments presented by the Monarch of the World. As this story spread throughout the land of Iran, whoever had a wife uniquely beautiful would willingly and eagerly divorce and send her to the royal court, which is renowned for justice, out of expediency or in the hope of an ample reward. The Matchless Monarch of the World, in accordance with religious rites, would marry and enjoy her, and then he would similarly divorce and dismiss her. The lady, being thus graced with royal favors, would return to her husband with bounty and riches.[47]

The second phase of the satirical treatment of women begins in the nineteenth century, and it is in sharp contrast with the earlier phase. Here the satirist tries to condemn and criticize the backwardness, ignorance, and superstitions of Iranian women, hoping that by doing so he presses them toward progress and self-reform. Very often the achievements and advancements of the western woman are in the mind of the satirist, and sometimes she is offered as a model for her Iranian counterpart. This attitude persists until, as a result of the steady westernization of Iranian women, a new attitude emerges. The criticism of the satirist is then directed toward too much artificiality and senseless imitation of western women.

One of the earliest satirical works that constructively criticizes the manners and superstitions of Iranian women is the famous book, *Kulsum Nane*, or *The Beliefs of Women*,[48] which has been attributed to Agha Jamal Khunsari.[49] A famous theologian and judge of the Safavid period, Agha Jamal was, unlike many *Ulema* of his time, a generous, liberal and extremely witty man. *The Beliefs of Woman* is written in the form of a theological treatise such as those often composed by highly respected *ayatollahs* in order to advise their followers on various religious and social problems. In this satirical little book three experienced and roguish old ladies discuss with Kulsum Nane various questions pertaining to a woman's life and give the most authoritative and "beneficial" pieces of advice.

In a recent edition of the book the editor notes, "One important point to remember is that in *The Beliefs of Women* the writer's intention was not to collect folklore but to ridicule the beliefs and superstitions of the women of his time and more particularly the women of Isfahan. Furthermore, considering the social milieu of the author, one might say that this ridiculing is also directed to that group of people who had accepted a multitude of unfounded quotations as indisputable principles and obvious facts, or at least they outwardly conceded to them, considering themselves amongst the *Ulema*; as if the writer of the book had wanted to say that [such men and women] are of the same leaven."[50]

The *Kulsum Nane* acknowledges that although many women keenly observed religious ablutions, they would forget about them if it meant spoiling their makeup. The writer says:

When you have painted your nails and created patterns on your hands with henna, or painted your eyebrows, it is necessary to forsake partial or complete ablutions [*vozu* and *ghosl*]. . . .

If a woman has a slave-girl at home and she thinks that by going to the public bath she will give her husband the chance to sleep with the girl, she should forsake the complete ablution until the obstacle is removed. Kulsum Nane has said that this could be for a week, and some people believe that it could be for more . . .[51]

The writer humorously notes the discrepancy in the veiling habits that Iranian women observe:

The men from whom one should be veiled include every turbaned man, even though he is less than fifteen years old. The bigger the turban, the more its wearer should be avoided, particularly students of theology in whatever dress they might be. . . . But the opposite group from whom one should not be veiled includes Jewish peddlers, grocers, cloth-merchants, physicians, fortune-tellers, exorcists, minstrels, etc. . . . If the Jewish peddler happens to be a fortune-teller as well, you should associate with him as much as possible! Avoiding him is considered a cardinal sin. If he enters your house, you should respect him and fulfill his desires.[52]

Chapter nine of *The Beliefs of Women*, devoted to the relationship between husband and wife, features the experienced ladies teaching the young women how to dominate their husbands:

The female scholars are unanimous that the bride should behave as an enemy towards her mother-in-law and sister-in-law and they should reciprocate. Though they might be friends at heart, outward animosity is a must. But Bibi Shah Zeinab, quoting her great master, the accursed Iblis, has said: "The bride should do exactly the opposite of whatever the mother-in-law says, and the latter should always complain of her daughter-in-law to her son. Similarly the wife should calumniate her sister-in-law as much as possible. Also it is an obligation for the wife to quote numerous accusations and lies from the accursed Satan to her husband, and whenever the mother-in-law follows and tries to beat her, she should scratch her." Kulsum Nane has said: "Whenever there is a fight between them, they should fiercely bite each other's privates. . . . The wife who is hurt must capitalize on this when she sleeps with her husband, putting the blame on the sister-in-law, so that he would be less friendly with her, and perhaps she should frequent their house less often."[53]

Although *The Beliefs of Women* criticizes the ridiculous beliefs and customs of Iranian women, the author's intention is not to emancipate them to the level of European women, but rather to bring them into conformity with Islamic ideals as preached by the clerics of that period. Though the book has many positive points, the Safavid period was not ready for western ideas of female emancipation. It was not until the turn of the present century that the role of women in society began to change. Even after the Constitutional Revolution in 1906, the fanatical views that kept women in seclusion were only grudgingly modified. The conservatives who opposed the Constitution claimed that its passage "will permit drunkenness, tolerate vices, allow women to go unveiled and abrogate the

Shari'a."[54] When the full-scale education of women became a topic of controversy, some men considered it outrageous—similar to "allowing alcoholic drinks or spreading prostitution."[55] Even some of the liberal Constitutionalists could not bring themselves to allow women to go unveiled or to take part in social activities. These things were considered to be anti-Islam. Keeping this in mind, the reader should realize what stiff opposition was met when such writers and poets as Saber, Yahya Doulat-abadi, Lahuti, Dehkhoda, 'Eshqi, Iraj Mirza, and many others raised the issue of emancipation.

One of the early progressive poets who defends the rights of women is Jelveh of Ardestan (d. 1896). Jelveh, curiously, was a lifelong bachelor who led a life of seclusion. In the following poem he humorously takes up the subject of polygamy:

> One night a girl sweet and fair-shaped,
> Asking a question of her mother said:
> "O Mother, I have a problem
> From which my heart is in flame.
> Why has our Prophet wise allowed
> A man several wives to wed
> But that most sage and learned one
> Of men for women did not grant but one?"
> A deep sigh heaved the mother
> Which made the daughter even sadder.
> And said, "Since the Prophet was a man,
> So he allowed several wives for a man.
> For sure, if the Prophet had been a woman
> Several husbands would be part of the plan.
> O my darling, good women suffer most
> As from womenfolk has never a prophet come forth."[56]

The Azerbaijani poet and satirist, 'Ali Akbar Saber (1862-1911), at the turn of the century made the cause of Islamic women one of the topics of his subtle and skillful satire. As was mentioned earlier, though he wrote his poems in Turkish, he had great impact on the satirical literature of Iran in the Constitutional period. Not only were most of his poems, published mainly in the famous *Mulla Nasreddin*, immediately translated into Persian by Seyyed Ashraf of Gilan, but his poems were also widely popular in the Turkish-speaking regions of Iran.

Superstitious and ignorant women as well as chauvinistic men are the butts of Saber's satire. On the whole, however, he holds men responsible for the degraded state in which women find themselves. The characters he depicts are typical and true to life. In a poem entitled "Don't Let Him Come" a fifteen-year-old girl is hoodwinked into marrying a man as old as her father in the belief that he is much younger. When she finds out that he is an old man, she exclaims her loathing for his white hair, his chimneylike cap, his body odor, and in short the very sight of him:

O Auntie, don't let him come!
The sight of him is hateful, don't let him come!
   O God, it's as if he is not human,
   His face is not like any other man.
   For love of God, he is no husband for a woman.
He is a devil and a swine, don't let him come!
The sight of him is hateful, don't let him come!

   I was too shy to inquire when betrothed;
   "He is young and nice," I was told.
   This could be my husband! Heavens, what a thought!
O Auntie, don't let him come!
His doings are hateful, don't let him come!

   A chimney-like hat does he wear,
   His eyebrows are bespecked with white hair.
   Though he seems as old as my father fair,
He is a swindler, don't let him come!
His doings are hateful, don't let him come![57]

The men of Saber's poems proudly talk of divorcing their wives and getting new ones. In "The March of the Old"[58] we find "an old man who lives like a ram." Having four wives, every year he marries and divorces three or four more. Outwardly he is pious. He wears a beard, puts on an agate ring, as a sign of religiosity and never forgets his prayers or fasting, yet he is a dirty old man who not only pursues young women but makes passes at handsome boys. In another poem, a man from Ardabil has gone to Baku, where he sees so many beautiful "Madames" on the streets and boulevards, in the theaters, and at circuses that he grows bewildered. Becoming convinced that it has been an absolute waste to live in his small and provincial hometown, where he had not been able to see one female face unveiled on the streets, he vows, "I will never mention your name, O Ardabil!"[59]

Women become the subjects of Saber's satire as well. In a poem entitled "Advice of an Old Witch[60]," young brides are instructed in how to make the best of their lives. As no faithful husband can possibly be found, a woman should spend the earnings of her husband on her women friends and be happy with them behind his back. "Complain"[61] is another poem that satirizes prearranged marriages. The illiterate wife of a poet describes her sad life after marrying an intellectual who lives completely in his own world. The wife, coming from a family where not a single book could be found, regards her husband as insane for poring over books and scribbling away at poetry. Saber gives a hilarious picture of the misunderstanding between a couple whose values are at variance.

Topics similar to those treated by Saber are the subjects of the satirical essays of Dehkhoda, some examples of which have already been quoted, in his *Charand Parand*. One not quoted relates the story of a one-time cameldriver, Hajji Mulla 'Abbas, who, after spending all his money to get concubines in Qom, is initiated by a sympathetic mulla into the clergy. Thereafter, Mulla 'Abbas prospers.

Marrying the orphaned daughter of a merchant, he uses her money in the pursuit of his pleasure while giving her no chance of happiness in return. His profession affording him many privileges, his life is occupied solely with exchanging one concubine for another.[62] In another essay, Dehkhoda answers the letter of an imaginary reader of *Sur-e Esrafil* whose name is Asir-e Joval Khanum ("Lady Captive-in-a-Sack")! She has complained that her children die in infancy, and Dehkhoda gives her a ridiculous prescription that is a combination of witch-craft and old, popular herbology. Later to become a lexicographer of great eminence, Dehkhoda even at this early stage of his career shows an amazing familiarity with the idiom as well as the superstitions of Tehrani women.

Between the two world wars the issue of women's emancipation became one of the most often discussed matters. 'Eshqi's "Black Shroud," Lahuti's "Daughter of Iran," and "Women in Iran" by Parvin E'tesami are only three of the poems written on the subject, but most of them are not of a satirical nature. In Iraj Mirza we find an outspoken poet who treats the subject of women's emancipation in a beautifully vivid and spirited style combined with a far-reaching wit and sense of satire. In one poem he describes with great verve how the *Ulema* are horrified to see an unveiled female face painted on the wall of a public bath and how they save Islam from "shame" by fashioning a veil out of plaster for her! In his "Book of the Veil," which was apparently very popular at the time, Iraj describes one of his youthful adventures with a beautiful half-veiled passer-by. His first attempt at seducing her is unsuccessful, lady becomes indignant at the suggestion that she remove her veil. In the course of a long and humorous discussion the poet succeeds in his stratagem by strictly avoiding the subject of the veil:

> I opened my hand over that lovely one.
> As a *mulla* on rice, a pious man on helva.
> But because chastity was in her face
> From beginning to the end she did not open her veil.
> Her two hands kept the veil taut,
> So that her chastity would not be lost.
> After I ate my fill of that sweet cake,
> She said, "May you choke on it!" and raced away.[63]

The difference between outward appearance and actual character is the focal point of Iraj's satire. Though not free from exaggeration, the story represents the type of woman who dons the veil out of habit rather than from any consideration for chastity. A similar duality in action and belief can be seen in many female characters of modern Iranian novels and short stories. Sadeq Hedayat's novel *'Alawiya Khanum* is a graphic picture of the pilgrimage of a group of men, women, and children to the Shrine of Imam Reza in Mashhad. Their characters and language, as well as their ignorance and degradation are depicted with consummate vividness and skill. 'Alawiya Khanum, an outwardly pious but inwardly vicious woman, is the dominant figure of the story. She epitomizes hypocrisy and sanctimony.

Over the last few decades, there has been a marked change in satirical works on women. Gradually, as there was no need to make either the veil or female superstitions the subjects of criticism, Iranian writers began to find fault with new ways of life. The women who sought equality with men in everything were often scoffed at as unfeminine, and henpecked husbands became the pathetic heroes of many comical short stories. Fashionable and extravagant wives who ruin their husbands by slavishly following every new fashion formed another category of satire. Gholam-Reza Ruhani (d. 1985) is a poet and satirist who commented on many social problems, among them extravagant wives:

> It is New Year's Eve and I am in a bad pickle with my wife;
>> Save me from my wife!
> She is my mate and I am a mate to sorrow and strife;
>> Save me from my wife!
> She wants a dress of Georgette crepe or jersey and voile
>> Of the latest style.
> But I have neither a pair of pants nor proper attire;
>> Save me from my wife!
>
> . . . .
>
> Like an ass I am stuck in the mud, and my heart is full of despair,
>> She thinks of nothing but of coquetry and airs.
> She wants Coty perfume to buy for her hair,
>> O God, save me from my wife![64]

Since we have been considering the antifeminist satire written by men, it will not be inappropriate, as we conclude this chapter, to comment upon a few works by Iranian women answering such men. As the number of educated women was limited until a few decades ago, obviously the works of this category are hard to come by. One of them is by an enlightened and talented woman named Bibi Khanum.[65] *The Vices of Men* (1887), which has a pungent satirical tone, is in fact an answer to an earlier work entitled *The Education of Women.*[66] The anonymous writer seems to be a fanatical cleric, and following the medieval tradition, he equates "the pleasure of God with the pleasure of the husband and His wrath with that of the husband." Diligent and devoted service by the wife "will be rewarded by her admission to heaven," while her wrath at the husband will be punished by the fire of hell. Bibi Khanum's answers to such absurdities are scathingly indignant. She writes that "that genius of the world and unique writer of our times" seems strangely bereft of his senses. "He should have first corrected his own vices and then given us advice. One who has no share of existence, how can he inspire life? . . . He regards himself as 'westernized' and 'civilized,' but in fact, he is not even 'half-civilized.' Does he not know that Europeans treat their women like flowers, and the women freely associate with men?" Bibi Khanum points out that Iranian men say that "women should walk slowly, speak softly, and whisper like a convalescing patient." Or they say, "Women should sit respectfully at the table and eat with the tips of their fingers, and should not talk or make any noise." But what if, she asks, "the children are present and they create havoc at the table who is going to stop them? If the woman sits quietly and the kids pour the soup into the stew and then spill the whole thing, who is going to stop them? These polite manners are for European men and women who dine in the dining room and observe every civility."[67]

Bibi Khanum answers every argument raised by the writer of *The Education of Women*, often in the process engaging in humorous wordplay. She concludes that the work is a *Fazihat-Name* [Book of malice] and says that such men as the author are not *rejal* ("men") but rather *rajjal* ("scoundrels"). She ends her treatise with a poetic diatribe on such men and wishes that instead of expressing such high-flown ideas, they would spend some time serving their own people, so as not to feel ashamed "before both men and God."

Another interesting writer of this period, who knew French and was familiar with European thought, is Taj al-Saltane, the daughter of Naser al-Din Shah. An amazing revolutionary in her ideas about social reform, Taj al-Saltane fought corruption and discrimination against women and was even critical of the short-comings of her father. Though it is not satirical, the recently published biography of this enlightened princess is a very valuable document on the emancipation of women in Iran. We read that the author had forsaken her old religious beliefs and was burning with the desire to go to Europe in order to meet "the women who had fought for their rights." She wanted to tell them that "when, overcome with happiness and dignity, you are fighting for your rights . . . cast a glance to Iran where some creatures, wretched and broken, pale and sallow, some hungry and some naked, some crying day and night, but all in the chains of captivity" spend their lives. She says that Iranian women appear either in the "horrible" black veil of the funeral or the white winding-sheets of death. "I am one of those unhappy women who prefers the white winding-sheets to the terrifying funeral dress. Because compared to this life of darkness, death is our bright day."[68]

The Iranian poet, Parvin E'tesami (d. 1941), reminiscing in 1934 when the veil was banned on the past fate of Iranian women, echoed Taj al-Saltane:

> No one like woman did live in the dark for centuries;
> No one like her was a sacrifice on the altar of hypocrisies.[69]

Nearer to our time, Forugh Farrokhzad in numerous poems took up the cause of women and daringly and openly spoke about her innermost feelings of love and passion. She not only revolted against the destiny of women as dictated by men, but she also ridiculed the women who instead of emancipation are lulled into inertia by the wealth of their husbands and forget about their rights. In her poem entitled "My Heart Grieves for the Garden" she talks of her "sister," who, in just this way, has lost all her simplicity and naturalness:

> Her house is on the other side of town.
> And insider her artificial house

with her artificial goldfish;
in the shelter of the love of her artificial husband
beneath the branches of her artificial apple trees;
she sings her artificial songs
and produces natural babies.
Whenever she comes to see us
and the poverty of the garden defiles
   the corners of her hem
she takes a bath of eau-du-cologne—
Whenever she comes to see us
She is pregnant.[70]

For Forugh, such women, who are ready to trade human dignity and rights for the amenities of modern life, are "like zero in addition or subtraction [and] always end up with the same result."[71] In her poem "Mechanical Doll" she describes such women with amazing power and insight:

You can cry out
in a voice utterly false and strange
"I love—"
You can, in the over-powering arms of a man
be a wholesome and beautiful female
with a body like a chamois spread
with large firm breasts
You can, in the bed of a drunk, a vagrant, a fool
defile the chastity of a love.
. . . .

You can be like mechanical dolls
and view your world with two glass eyes
You can sleep in a cloth-lined box for years
with a body stuffed with straw
in the folds of net and spangles
You can cry out and say for no reason at all
with every lascivious squeeze of a hand:
"Ah, how lucky I am."[72]

More than any other contemporary work, the canon of Forugh represents the revolt of modern Iranian women against traditionally held masculine ideas and prejudices toward women. The Shah granted Iranian women some rights, but like most of his reforms these changes were only cosmetic. However, the passage of the Family Protection Law in 1967 was a significant step toward the improvement of the lot of Iranian women. Women were given the right to vote in 1963, but in a one-party system in which elections were often rigged, suffrage had little meaning. The political repression was so great that Iranian women took it for granted that their complete emancipation would come as the natural corollary of a change of regime. But with the upsurge of fundamentalism and the new brand of Islam existing today, they have been deprived of a significant number of rights that previously went uncontested. The family courts, which protected women's rights in marriage and divorce, were abolished immediately after the revolution of 1979. This was perhaps due in part to the tremendous resistance of long-established patterns of male domination. In short, under the rule of the clergy it seems that Iranian women have been set back many decades,. Further, if the present trend continues, the conflict between the sexes in Iran, far from being resolved, will become more intense than ever before.

Notes

1. Quoted in Hodgart, *Satire,* p. 79.
2. Quoted in de Beauvoir, *Nature of the Second Sex,* trans. H. M. Parshley, (London: New English Library Ltd., 1963) p. 13.
3. For instance, in Arabic, *watti, rafatha, hakka,* and *dahaja,* all of which mean to make love, also respectively mean: "to kick," "to swear," "to overcome" (or to attack with a spear), and "to drag someone on the ground."
4. J. A. Decourdemanche, trans., *The Wiles of Women,* trans. into English by S. F. Mills (London: George Routledge & Sons, 1928).
5. Zia al-Din Nakhshabi, *Tales of a Parrot,* trans. Mohammad Simsar (Graz: the Cleveland Museum of Art, 1978). See a MS text by Sir William Ouseley; edited with introduction and notes by W. A. Clouston (Larkhal, Lanarkshire, 1883).
6. Quoted in Naser Takmil Homayun, "Barrasi Moqe'iyat-e Zan dar Tarikh-e Iran," *Farhang va Zendagi* (1975):25.
7. Ibid. p. 26.
8. Ibid.
9. Ibid. Sa'id, Nafisi, *Tarikh-e Ejtema'i-ye Iran* (Tehran: Mu'assieh-ye Muta'at va Tahqiqate Ijtima'i, Tehran University Publications, 1964) 1:29.
10. Quoted in Sadeq Kia, "Sokhani dar bare-ye Zan az Adabiyat-e Pahlavi," *Majalle-ye Danesh-Kade-ye Adabiayat-e Tehran* 4 (Year 5):82.
11. L. J. Larcher, *La femme jugée par l'homme* (Paris: Garnier, 1858), pp. 152-53.
12. Afifi Rahim, Fargard, trans. *Arda Viraf Nameh* (Mashhad, 1963), p. 21.
13. *Shah-Name,* ed. Mohammad Dabir Sivaqi (Tehran: Elmi, 1956), 2:487.
14. Koran, 4:34. Wife beating was widely practiced in Europe in the Middle Ages and even later. In England it was legal until 1660. In France in 1334 a man who had killed his wife while beating her was acquitted on the ground that he was performing his "husbandly duties". See *La femme jugée,* pp. 219-22.
15. Sa'id Nafisi, ed., *Qabus Name* (Tehran: Frughi, 1937), p. 98.
16. *Akhlaq-e Naseri,* ed., Vahid Damgani, p. 257.
17. Jalal al-Din Davani, *Akhlaq-e Jalali* (Lahore, n.d.), pp. 216-17.
18. *Hilat al-Mutaqqin,* lithographed ed. (Tehran, 1898) p. 58.
19. 'Obeyd-e Zakani, *Kulliyat,* ed. Parviz Atabaki, (Tehran: Eqbal, 1964), p. 207.
20. *Garshasep Name,* ed. Habib Yaghmai, 2d. ed., p. 35.
21. Awfi, Mohammad, *Javami'ul-Hikayat,* ed. Banu Mazaher-e Mossafa (Tehran: Bonyad-e Farhang-e Iran, 1974), pp. 663-64.
22. Ibid. pp. 669-71.
23. *Jam-e Jam,* in *Divan-e Awadi,* ed. Sa'id Nafisi, (Tehran: Amir Kabir, 1961) p. 548.
24. Awfi, *Javame' au-Hikayat,* p. 673.
25. A quotation from the *Koran* (79:24) where the Pharoah claims to be God.

26. Farid al-Din, 'Attar, *Tazkirat al-Awliya*, ed. M. Este'lami, (Tehran: Zavvar, 1967), p. 84.

27. Sayings such as "Mulier est hominis confusio" (Woman makes man perish) or "Mulier est sterci saccum" (women is a sack of dung).

28. For instance, the story of a lewd women in the *Mathnavi* (trans. Nicholson, 4:3544-76) who makes love with her lover in front of her husband is the same as the story 9, day 7, of the *Decameron* and "The Merchant's Tale" of Chaucer. See also on the subject, Petrus Alfonsi, *Disciplina Clericalis*, trans. P. R. Quarrie (Berkeley and Los Angeles: University of California Press, 1977) and *The Book of Sindbad*, trans. W. A. Clouston (Glasgow, 1884).

29. *Mavhnavi*, 1337-1429.

30. Ibid. 4:2332-37.

31. The reference is to the *Koran*, 36:64: "On this day we seal up mouths, and hands speak out and bear witness as to what they used to do."

32. Quoted by Abbas Eqbal, *Majmu'e-ye Maqalat* (Tehran, 1972) p. 457.

33. Quoted in Arberry, *Aspects of Islamic Civilization*, pp. 338-9.

34. Two well-known tribal families.

35. Hind was the wife of Abu Sufyan, who according to a vow that she had made, took out the liver of Hamze, the Prophet's uncle, who was killed in the battle, and ate it.

36. *Divan-e Qa'ani*, ed. M. J. Mahjub (Tehran, Amir Kabir, 1957), pp. 10-11.

37. Zakani, *Kolliyat*, p. 207.

38. Ibid., p. 320.

39. See Whinfield, trans., *The Quatrains of Khayyam*, p. 20.

40. Quoted with some changes from Browne's *Literary History*, 3:119.

41. W. A. Clouston, *Flowers from a Persian Garden, and Other Essays*, (London, D. Nutt. 1890), pp. 61-62.

42. Zakani, *Kolliyat*, p. 168.

43. *Divan-e Sana'i*, p. 61.

44. Ibid.

45. Zakani, *Kolliyat*, p. 168.

46. Zakani, *Kolliyat*, p. 38 (introduction); see also Browne, *Literary History*, 3:60 and 166.

47. *Rostam al-Tavarikh*, ed. Mohammad Moshiri, (Tehran, 1969), pp. 81-83.

48. James, Atkinson, *The Customs and Manners of the Women of Persia*, (London: Oriental Translation Fund of Great Britian, 1832). Though it has a different title, this is a translation of *Kulsum Name*.

49. His full name is Jamal al-Din Mohammad ibn Hosain-e Khunsari. For an account of his life, see Browne, *Literary History*, 3:373.

50. *'Aqa'id al-Nisa va Mir'at al-Bolaha*, ed. M. Katira'i, (Tehran: Athar-e Iran, 1970), p. 9.

51. *Kulsum Nane*, ed. Bijan Asadipour, (Tehran: Amir Kabir, 1976), pp. 79-81.

52. Ibid. pp. 93-94.

53. Ibid. p. 34.

54. Mehdi Malekzadeh, *Tarikh-e Mashrutiyat-e Iran* (Tehran, 1948), 3:89.

55. Ahamd Kasravi, *Tarikh-e Mshruteh-ye Iran* (Tehran: Amir Kabir), p. 416.

56. Qutoed by Tabataba'i, Ehsan, *Chante-ye Darvish*, (Tehran: Ketabfrushi Ateshkadeh, 1958), p. 24.

57. Saber, *Hop Hop Name* (Bakr: Azar Nashr, 1962), pp. 142-43.

58. Ibid., p. 216.

59. Ibid., p. 227.

60. Ibid., pp. 33-35.

61. Ibid., pp. 181-84. This poem has been freely translated by Ashraf Gilani in his *Bagh- Behesht* as "Complaints of an Illiterate Bride of Her Husband to Her Sister."

62. *Sur-e Esrafil*, 1, nos. 27-29 (1907); (reprinted, Tehran: Rudaki Publications, 1982), pp. 225-26 and 233-34.

63. *Divan-e Iraj Mirza*, pp. 77-81.

64. Gholam-Reza Ruhani, *Kolliyat Ash'ar va Fokahiyat-e Ruhani* (Tehran: Kitabkhane-ye Sana'i n.d.), pp. 224-25.

65. See Feridun Adamiyat and Homa Nateq, *Afkar-e ejtem'i va Siyasi va Eqtisadi dar Athar-e Montasher Nashodeh-ye Qajar* (Tehran, 1978), pp. 22-27.

66. The Persian titles are: "Ma'ib al-Rijal" and "Tadib al-Nisa" respectively. The latter has been translated into English by E. Powys Mathers in his *Eastern Love*, vol. 3 (London: privately published 1904).

67. The references are to MS 3970 for "Ma'ib al-Rijal" and MS 4850 for "Tadib al-Nisa" at the University Library of Tehran. Cf. *Afkar-e Ejtema'i*, pp. 20-24.

68. *Khatirat-e Taj al-Saltane*, ed. Mansoure Ettihadieh and Sirus Sa'd-vandian (Tehran: Nashr-e Tarikh-e Iran, 1984), p. 99.

69. *Divan-e Parvin 'Etesami* (Tehran, 1952), p. 117.

70. Forugh Farrokhzad, *Another Birth: Selected Poems*, trans. Hasan Javadi and Susan Sallé, (Emeryville, Calif.: Albany Press, 1981) p. 81.

71. Ibid., pp. 40-41.

72. Ibid.

Husband and wife. *From Mulla Nasreddin 1, no. 15 (14 June 1906).*

خانم‌دوستی، امان، نذار که‌آمدا   هست آفت جان، نذار که آمدا

The young girl and her old husband. *From Hop Hop Nama.*

ناز گلینه احترام

گلینه احترام   (بر آیدان سوکرا)

Before and after the honeymoon *From Mulla Nasreddin* 5 (16 February 1908).

Two cartoons on women from *Mulla Nasr al-Din*. *Top*, The young bride. *Bottom*, The husband and his wives.

حاجی جون یا ۱ مام بتو بیست در صد تخفیف میدهیم ؟

The sign says, "a 20 percent discount is given to the ladies with veil." The streetwalker says, "Come, dear Hajji, we give you a 20 percent discount too." *From Baba Shamal 2 no. 134 (10 1947).*

عدل و عفت

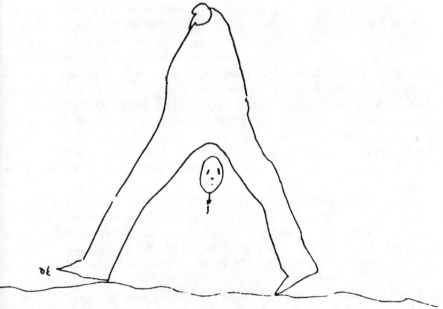

Two views on the position of Women in Iran. *Top, From Ahangar, 1 no 14 (July 1979).*
Bottom, from Bijan Asadipour in Tanz-e Khanagi (Family humor), (1978).

9

Satire in Modern Persian Fiction

Truth is bitter, so I will put it in words of wit;
And present it to you in the forms you know well.

—The motto of the journal *Towfiq*

The novel as a literary form, as well as the short story and drama was introduced into Persian literature at the turn of this century as the result of contact with the West. Stylistically the change from the traditional florid prose style to a simpler and more practical vein of writing was also important in bringing about this development. Two outstanding works mark the beginnings of modern Persian fiction: *The Travel Diary of Ibrahim Beg* by Zeyn al-'Abedin of Maragha, and the translation of James Morier's *The Adventures of Hajji Baba of Ispahan* into Persian. Of the former an account has already been given, and here I shall discuss the latter as a work of fiction which has had a significant impact on the development of Persian fiction.

Morier published his novel in English in 1824 as an alleged translation of the life story of an Iranian friend who had died in Turkey. But in reality it is the result of careful observations that Morier had made during his two sojourns in Iran. Some of the incidents and characters in the novel, such as the Armenian lovers Yusef and Mariam, and the ridiculous rivalry between the court physician and an English doctor who tries to introduce inoculation against smallpox, can be traced to Morier's travel book, which had been published in 1812 and 1818[1]. Similarly, he was inspired by many incidents in the lives of his Iranian friends Mirza Abul Hasan Khan Ilchi, the Perisan envoy to the British court; Hajji Baba Afshar, a medical student who later became the chief physician to Mohammad Shah; and Fath 'Ali Khan Saba, the poet laureate to Fath 'Ali Shah. Morier has woven all these events into a fascinating picaresque novel after the

226

model of *Gil Blas* by Le Sage.

Morier, living at the height of the British colonial age, regarded Easterners as inferior. Being a devout Christian, he bitterly opposed Islam and believed that the only way to "civilize" the Iranians was to convert them to Christianity. He believed it was prudent, in this context, to make the country a British protectorate. Years later he maintained that his intention in writing the novel had been to reform Iranians. "Touching their vanity," he says, "will make them angry. Reflection will succeed anger and with reflection who knows what changes may not be effected?"[2] However, he not only mentions this point several years after the publication of the novel, but also he fails to include it among the reasons given in his long "Introductory Epistle" for writing the book. Apart from his claims of being a "reformist," Morier is basically a satirist, and his novel presents a critical picture of various aspects of Iranian society.

The courtiers and dignitaries with whom Morier associated in Iran were mostly hypocritical and dishonest: Mirza Abul Hasan Khan, who was sent to the Court of St. James, was a paid agent of the British at the time;[3] Mirza Ibrahim Kalantar, the first premier under Fath 'Ali Shah, had turned traitor toward his former master, Lotf 'Ali Khan of the Zand dynasty, and to some extent was responsible for that ruler's cruel death; Hajji Baba Afshar, the physician, was according to some accounts the perfect rogue[4]. With such models there is no wonder that Morier depicted the Iranians unfavorably. However, *Hajji Baba* for many decades was considered by the British a faithful picture of Iranians. A traveler was told, "When you read this you will . . . know more of Persia and Persians than you will if you had lived there with your eyes open for twenty years."[5] Lord George Curzon in his introduction to the book presented it as an exact portrait of Iranians. E. G. Browne was the only critic who pointed out that Morier lived mostly in the circle of corrupt Iranian courtiers and officials and that they were the models for his characters. Browne concluded," . . . let not the reader then, be so far carried away by the charm of Morier's pages to lay down the book in the belief that every Persian is a Hajji Baba, and a Mirza Ahmak, or a Mulla Nadan."[6]

Satire was the most important thing for Morier, and he cared more for it than the plot, incidents, or characters. His pictures of Iranians were caricatures rather than portraits, as they exhibit only defects, distortions, and exaggerations. However, his power of delineation and sense of satire is so fascinating that the reader simply lives in the world of the unbelievably unscrupulous and rascally Hajji Baba. The adventurous career of Hajji Baba takes him through a large cross section of Iranian society, which in turn enables the novelist to present a vividly satirical picture of the various strata.

Hajji Baba, the son of a barber in Isfahan, is a resourceful boy who is captured with his master, a Turkish merchant, by Turkoman bandits. After leading them to plunder his own native city, he succeeds in escaping. Going to Mashhad, he dabbles in different professions, —is successively a water-carrier, a seller of tobacco, a story-teller, and at last a servant to the royal physician. Some clever piece of roguery always enables him to shift from one profession to another. After being involved in the comic rivalry of the royal physician with an English doctor, and in a tragic love affair, wherein he witnesses his beloved's death, Hajji has to take refuge in a sanctuary. Further knavery enables him to escape on a stolen horse from Iran to Istanbul, there to seduce the widow of a Turkish pasha. Jealous compatriots betray his base origin, and he is thrown penniless out of the lady's house. This brings him into contact with the Iranian ambassador in that city; having become his attendant, Hajji goes back to Iran and later accompanies his master on a mission to England.

The Persian translation of *The Adventures of Hajji Baba* was done by Mirza Habib of Isfahan around 1891 from a French translation.[7] He tried to publish it in Istanbul, where he was living, but censorship did not allow it. When Mirza Habib, along with two other Iranian revolutionaries, was extradited by the Ottoman authorities after the assassination of Naser al-Din Shah and consequently beheaded in Tabriz, the book went to his family in Kerman. Some years later the family gave the copy to a certain Colonel Phillott, who published it in India in 1905.

Morier's alleged intention of reform seems very unconvincing in the light of his diplomatic service as the British chargé d'affaires in Tehran,[8] his treatment of Iranian students who were entrusted to his care in London,[9] and his frequently unfavorable remarks regarding Iranians in his travel books. His translator, on the other hand, was a patriotic liberal whose revolutionary ideas brought him many years of exile and hardship. Mirza Habib, being an ardent admirer of 'Obeyd-e Zakani, believed in the use of satire as a means of arousing his compatriots. A modern Iranian critic says, "Mirza Habib has tried as much as possible to turn a novel of colonialism into a story of anti-colonialism."[10] To put it into neutral and apolitical terms, one can say with certainty that the intentions of the author and the translator were greatly at odds. Generally speaking, the translation of Mirza Habib is not very exact. Some passages and interpolated stories that were integral parts of the book are omitted or shortened. For instance, the story of "The Baked Head" in chapter 45 is completely omited and the love story of the Armenians, Yusef and Mariam, has been considerably abridged. Furthermore, many passages have been amplified and many suitable lines of poetry and proverbial sayings are added. Mirza Habib replaces some fictitious names with real names and thus gives an additional touch of realism to the novel.

Politics and religion form the foundation of Morier's satire. He believes dully that Iran has not significantly changed from ancient times, and that the despotic system of government makes injustice widespread in the society. Every official, being tyrannized by his superiors, does the same to his subordinates. Hence, the habit prevails in all strata of society, leading to both hyprocrisy and dishonesty. Morier draws an equally sordid picture of the clerics and Sufis. On the matters of religion and state Mirza Habib not only closely follows Morier's text, but in addition flavors the narrative with his own amplifications. He is often more Catholic than the pope. He fails even to omit the passages where Morier, out of his Christian zeal, speaks irreverently of the Prophet Mohammad.[11] It was not without reason that some of his compatriots accused him of heresy. Hajji Pirzade, a contemporary traveler who met him in Istanbul, wrote, "As a young man Mirza Habib associated with dauntlessly atheistic men and was led astray. He is still fond of playfulness, enjoyment, humor and ribaldry." Pirzade then adds: "If Mirza Habib had some measure of spirituality, religiosity and [attachment to] divine truth, he would have been unique in his age."[12]

The additions to the text by Mirza Habib can be divided into three categories: first, those that are literary in nature; second, documentation; and third, the passages that make the text more satirical. Sometimes the translator is carried away and embarks upon a florid description of a scene or, in the classical Persian tradition, upon the beauties of a particular person. The love scene between Hajji Baba and the Kurdish girl, Zeinab, and the description of the army of winter and the coming of the spring in chapter 5 may serve as appropriate examples. The life story of the poet Asker exemplifies the second kind of addition. He is identified as Mirza Fath 'Ali Khan Saba, the poet laureate to Fath 'Ali Shah. The animosity between the poet and the lord high treasurer results in an ingenious satire. The poet writes a panegyric with a double meaning that is in fact a bitter satire. It abounds high-sounding Arabic words that the lord high treasurer takes for praise, and "he [does] not in the least suspect that they [are], in fact, expressions containing the grossest disrespect."[13] This poem does not appear in Morier's original work, but it is included the Persian version. Similarly, another poem composed on the occasion of the Shah's visit to the house of his chief physician is paraphrased in English, but Mirza Habib cleverly versifies this absurd piece of sycophancy.[14] Relating his story to Hajji Baba, the poet gives a vivid picture of the life of a despotic monarch and of the host of flatterers who surround him. Mirza Habib does not fail to add his own personal touches here and there. Here is another short English paraphrase whose original is provided in Persian, and it carries the absurdities of panegyric writing even further. The poet says, "I compared his majesty's teeth to pearls, and the toothpick to the pearl-diver; his gums to a coral bank, near which pearls are frequently found; and the long beard and mustachios that encircled the mouth to the undulations of the ocean."[15] The poems given in the Persian rendering may not all be genuine works by Fath 'Ali Khan-e Saba, but they blend so well with the narrative that they seem perfectly authentic. All these little details combined with the highly fluent and beautiful prose style of Mirza Habib give the book a genuineness that is quite remarkable.

There are numerous examples of Habib's inserted satirical passages scattered throughout the work[16] Here Mirza Ahmak (Dr. Stupid), the royal physician, comments on the differences between Europeans and Persians. The italicized portions were added by Habib:

Their manners and customs are totally different from ours. . . . Instead of shaving their heads, and letting their beards grow, as we do, they do the very contrary, for not a vestige of hair is to be seen on their chins, and their hair is as thick on their heads as if they had made a vow never to cut it off; then they sit on little platforms, whilst we squat on the ground: they take up their food with claws made of iron, whilst we use our fingers; they are always walking about, we keep seated; they wear tight clothes, we loose ones; they write from left to right, we from right to left; they never pray, we five times a day; *among us the man has the authority, with them authority lies with the woman; we go to the toilet seated, whilst they do it standing; they regard wine lawful, but do not drink too much, we regard it as unlawful, but drink it to excess. . . .*[17]

Between the publication of the translation of *Hajji Baba* and the appearance of the first collection of Mohammad 'Ali Jamalzade's short stories, *Yeki Bud Yeki Na-bud* in 1921, there was a lapse of sixteen years. During this period a number of historical and social novels appeared, but except for occasional passages here and there, they were not satirical. This collection of short stories by Jamalzade (b. 1881), first published in the journal *Kave* in Berlin, is a landmark in the history of Persian fiction. Apart from employing the techniques of the short story, Jamalzade, in his interesting introduction, vehemently criticizes the traditionalists in Persian literature who write for the learned few and ignore the general public by using florid and unrealistic language. Though the work was applauded by the young intellectuals and progressive elements, some reactionary mullas condemned it as a piece offensive to national pride. Its wonderfully graphic and vivid language, however, full of colloquial expressions, served as a model for a later generation of writers.

Of the six short stories in the collection three are distinctly satirical: "Farsi Shakar ast" (Persian is sweet), "Bila Dig Bila Chughundar" (Everyman to his desserts), and "Rajul-i-Siyasi" (The politician). In the first story the writer relates how, upon his return from Europe, he, for no obvious reason, was briefly jailed in the port city of Anzali on the Caspian Sea. There he finds an ordinary Iranian peasant, a dandified and westernized youth, and a pompous mulla who cannot communicate with one another. The high-flown Arabicized Persian of the divine, full of Koranic verses and quotations from the traditions of the Prophet, is as foreign to the poor peasant as is the Frenchified Persian of the young man. "Farsi Shakar ast" is a well-written story with exquisite parodies of the modes of speech of these two notorious types. Their bastardized Persian creates an interesting contrast with the fluent and idiomatic style of the story with its graphic descriptions of the characters. In "Everyman to his Desserts," fate takes a European bath-attendant to Iran, where he associates with the ruling classes. He writes his memoirs, which, as Hasan Kamshad puts it, constitute "a piquant satire on the despotic order, way of life, ruling circles, and class distinctions of the late Qajar times. [They] remind one of some of the saltiest passages of Morier's *Hajji Baba*. It was mainly the remarks made in this story that disturbed religious and state dignitaries in the early 'twenties, when the book was first published."[18] "The Politician" is a humorous account of a semiliterate cotton-carder whose wife forces him to take part in political activities, since their neighbor has been doing quite well as a politician. While rallying with a group in front of the Parliament, the man accidentally becomes their spokesman and is invited inside. This simple incident paves the way to higher positions. The story is a hilarious satire on the political world of Iran and the ignorance, banality, greed, and wickedness of the men who dominate the scene.

Another work of fiction by Jamalzade, *Qultashan Divan* (1946), which may be translated as "The Shepherd of the Chancellory,"[19] is a tragedy blended with satire. Haji Sheikh Mortaza is a dealer in tea and sugar who is elected as a deputy to the first *Majles*, but he resigns after gauging both the degree of corruption and the fact that the deputies want to fill their pockets rather than care for the people. The virtuous and patriotic Sheikh Mortaza and the villian, Qultashan Divan, a ruthless opportunitist, are contrasted as prototypes of good and evil. The latter fails in his stratagem to marry his compromised daughter to the Sheikh's son. Qultashan Divan again appears in the life of the hero during the First World War; paying him a good commission, the villian makes Sheikh Mortaza buy a large consignment of sugar on the condition that the buyer's name not be revealed. Qultashan Divan hoards the sugar in order to make a fortune later on, while Sheikh Mortaza earns all the scorn of his fellow citizens as a hoarder when it becomes scarce, his protestations to the contrary convincing no one. Losing his good fame, he dies heartbroken and in poverty, while his silent partner prospers more and more. The latter even builds an orphanage that makes money. To the lavish parties of Qultashan Divan men of fame and power flock, and when he dies the poets write elaborate panegyrics on his great achievements. No one remembers Sheikh Mortaza, however who had passed away several years earlier.

A bitter irony overshadows the whole story, especially when the roguish Qualtashan Divan becomes the charitable benefactor of Tehran society. Jamalzade with graphic precision depicts not only middle class Iranian society but also the ideas, desires, and frustrations of its characters. As Borecky puts it, "*Qultashan Divan* is Jamalzade's most mature novel. . . . Satire, humor, social criticism and condescending love for the feeble human beings are well weighed throughout the book, and the discontent with the lighter lot of the unjust only strengthens the elegiac tuning of the novel."[20]

In *Rahab Name* (The book of the water channel) (1948), Jamalzade treats a similar theme on a purely satirical and humorous level. He describes the members of six families who inhabit a cul-de-sac in Tehran and get embroiled in a drainage repair controversy. An Iranian student from Europe vacationing back home is authorized by the neighbors to make the necessary repairs. After many comical troubles with various workmen the repairs are completed, and the student pays for them. But the neighbors never pay their share, and as a result the good-intentioned student is unable to return to Europe and finish his studies. The book is concise, to the point, and beautifully descriptive of Persian life and manners. Jamalzade's unrestrained criticism of the national character is once more reminiscent of *Hajji Baba of Ispahan.*

Another remarkable work of fiction by Jamalzade is *Sar va Tah-e Yek Karbas* (All of a pattern) (1956), which, although supposedly an autobiography, after the first chapter is mainly about the life of a friend who is interested in mysticism and ascetic teachings. The book is written with candor, beauty, and humor. Of the stories included in the work some are satirical. Of these "Jahannam-e Ta'assub" (The hell of fanaticism) criticizes the hyprocrisy of the clergy, and "Baj-i Sibil" (Extortion) describes the ruffianism of an army officer.

The other fictional works of Jamalzade include four collections of short stories: *Sarguzasht-e- 'Amu-Hosain 'Ali* (The story of Uncle Hosain-'Ali) (1942), which in 1957 was enlarged to the two volumes of *Shahkar* (Masterpiece); *Talkh u Shirin* (Bitter and sweet) (1956); *Kohne va Now* (Old and new) (1959); and *Gheyr az Khoda Hichkas Na-bud* (There was no one but God) (1960). Some of the stories in these collections are satirical. As an example, from the collection entitled *Shahkar*, "Nov Parast" (The humanitarian) is a classic satire on civilization in the modern world. A famous philosopher and his friend are shipwrecked on a remote island whose inhabitants are primitive but happy people. The philosopher immediately begins to teach them the methods of modern life and within three years ruins their happiness to such a degree that they put him and his friend in a boat and send them back out to sea. "The Secret of Philosophy, or the Dialogue of the Two Mosquitoes" is an animal parable in which Jamalzade lampoons the amazing conceit of mankind. Two mosquitoes, one a heretic and the other a religious sheikh, are having a heated discussion about God and the universe, when a third mosquito, with Sufi inclinations, joins the fight. When they are about to come to blows, the sudden urination of a rat puts a permanent end to their discussion. Their bodies become the provision for two ants, who while enjoying their find, engage in another boastful metaphysical discussion of their own.

The early short stories and novels of Jamalzade are generally well written and to the point and have a close-knit structure, whereas in his later fiction prolixity and a tendency to introduce too many proverbs and colloquial expressions detract from his overall effect. The same can be said of his satire. While his earlier works are marked by a racy, colorful style and a careful delineation of the characters, some of his later works seem to be forced and affected.

After Jamalzade we should consider Sadeq Hedayat (1903-51), who by general consensus is the greatest novelist of Iran. Though Hedayat's fruitful literary career was cut short by his suicide in Paris, he had already produced a large number of novels and short stories. With incredible precision, mastery, and insight he protrayed the lives, aspirations, anxieties, and sorrows of various typical representatives of Iranian society. It is amazing that Hedayat, coming from a traditional and aristocratic background and living most of his life almost as a recluse, could depict such a gallery of characters from all walks of life in such a fascinating and detailed manner. Though his characters are true to type and depicted most naturally, the traces of his distinct personality and thought are discernible in them. An English translator of his works, Henry D. G. Law, explains the reasons for Hedayat's successful creation of characters:

> Firstly his sincerity. After that the magic of his prose. . . . Hedayat does not write objectively; with his "reckless soaring genius" he infuses into each of his tales his own personality, his own mood of pity, indignation, or tenderness: so that you may enter fully into the mind and thoughts of his characters, whoever they may be—seeing them as he sees them. They live and they haunt you long after you have closed the book.[21]

Although the bleak and Kafkaesque world of *The Blind Owl* strangely contrasts with the wine, roses, and nightingales of the *Rubaiyyat*, Hedayat resembles Khayyam, whom he greatly admired, in his thoughts and ideas. However, Hedayat is a romanticist, who is often fascinated with the idea of death, whereas Khayyam is a level-headed realist who lives in this world and wants to enjoy it. Hedayat is a pessimistic materialist who finds consolation in the quatrains of Khayyam from the dark philosophical problems of life that have always tormented the thoughtful person. He is dearly fond of the past glories of Iran, and he regards the dominance of Islam over his country as the harsh oppression of a Semitic culture, hence the criticism of Muslim clerics and their sanctimony, which so prominently figures in his works. Hedayat is an artist who is at odds with his society. He voices his own ideas when he writes of Khayyam that he "wanted to destroy this ridiculous, sordid, gloomy and funny world and build a more logical one on its ruins." And that "Khayyam was weary and disgusted with the people of his time, condemned their morals, thoughts and customs with bitter sarcasm and had not accepted at all the instructions of the society."[22] This clearly explains the use of satire in Hedayat's work.

Hasan Kamshad in his study of Sadeq Hedayat writes, "Satire is one of the prevailing traits of Hedayat's art. Not only in his completely facetious works but in most of his other writings can one trace a melancholy derision."[23] Hedayat's satirical works include *'Alaviya Khanum* (1933), *Vagh Vagh Sahab* (1933), *Velengari* (1944), *Hajji Aga* (1945), and *Tup-e-Murvari* (1947). The collections of his short stories also contain some satirical pieces. In some of these stories, such as "Talab-e Amurzish" (Asking for absolution) and "Mardi ke Nafsash ra Kosht" (The man who killed his passion), a sense of tragedy and satire are blended in a manner typical of Hedayat while a satire may have a tragic twist, it ordinarily does not end in tragedy. However, Hedayat, with what Kamshad calls a "sardonic grin," often obtrudes his sense of satire into a basically tragic story. His narratives linger on the borderline of the two genre and often tilt toward tragedy. For instance, in "The Man Who Killed His Passion" a young schoolteacher, who wants to lead an ascetic life, becomes the disciple of a well-known Sufi, Sheikh Abul-Fazl, and subjects himself to rigorous self-discipline. One day he arrives at the house of the Sufi master to hear a man shouting:

> Tell Ashaykh, tomorrow I will take you to the court. . . . You brought my daughter here as a maid-servant and did all kind of mischief to her. You infected her, and made free with her money. . . .[24]

When more proof of the Sufi's hypocrisy appears, the pious schoolteacher gets drunk and goes out with a prostitute. Two days later it is reported in the newspapers that he has committed suicide for "unknown reasons."

Hedayat's criticsm of supersitition and sham religiosity reveals itself in a more sinister way in "Asking for Absolution," in which a barren and wicked wife who has secretly killed her husband's second wife and her two babies is making a pilgrimage to Kerbela in the hope of divine forgiveness. She doubts that she will be successful in this quest, but a second traveler assures her that all the travelers in the caravan have something on their conscience. He says that years ago when he was a coachman on the Khorasan road he killed a passenger and took his money. Later he gave some of it to one of the Ulema, and he "cleansed" the rest of it. A third traveler asks:

> Have you not heard it said from the pulpit that as soon as the pilgrims specify their intention and set out, they become chaste and purified even if the number of their sins is as many as the leaves of a tree?[25]

In "Morde Khorha" (The ghouls) Hedayat humorously ridicules the false sympathy and mourning shown by relatives at the apparent death of Mashadi Rajab. A bitter conflict ensues between his two wives, who seem to be greatly affected by the event, over the inheritance. But when Mashadi recovers from stroke that he has suffered and returns home, everyone is terrified. One wife throws the money and the key at him that she had stolen while he seemed to be dead; the other wife hurls at him a stolen set of gold false teeth. The story ends with a comment from the first wife, who complains of the inefficiency of the cleric in charge of the burial, saying:

> And this . . . well done! This is how Ashaykh 'Ali works! He left the body on the ground for three hours![26]

The last-mentioned story comes from the collection entitled Zinde-be-gur (Buried alive) (1930) and the two earlier ones from Se Qatre Khun (Three drops of blood) (1932) and are both examples of the earlier writings of Hedayat. Of the stories from a later collection, Sag-e-Vilgard (The stray dog) (1942), which was published after the abdication of Reza Shah and in a more democratic atmosphere, mention should be made of two other satirical offerings. "Don Juan of Karaj" is a light treatment of the dandified and westernized men and women in modern Iran. In "Mihan-Parast" (The patriot) Hedayat paints a fascinating psychological portrait of Seyyed Nasrullah, an official of the ministry of education, who is traveling to India in order to give a talk on the "dazzling cultural progress" of Iran during the "golden age" of Reza Shah. Seyyed Nasrullah is a conceited, boastful, and cowardly man who is so afraid of the sea that he spends all his time worrying about being shipwrecked. His fears put an end to his life and prevent him from accomplishing his "great mission." During a drill, thinking that the ship is sinking, Seyyed Nasrullah has a heart attack and dies. He claims to be well versed in oriental as well as occidental philosophy and quite erudite in ancient and modern sciences. He says that he is fluent in both Arabic and French, and about English he says; "English is in fact French, only they have spoiled the spelling and pronunciation."[27] Seyyed Nasrullah represents the ideal official who prospered during the reign of Reza Shah, and of course, compared to the semiliterate Shah, he must have seemed a paragon of learning. Throughout the story Hedayat's criticism is directed at the cultural and educational establishments under Reza Shah, and most particularly the *Farhangistan* (the Iranian Academy) whose only achievement was to coin new and occasionally ludicrous words in order "to purify" the Persian language. Hedayat's abhorrence of this practice is understandable since he treasured the colloquial and natural language of his people a dearly and he exhibits this fondness in his writings.

'Alaviya Khanum (1933) describes the pilgrimage of a group of simple men and women to the Holy Shrine of Imam Reza at Mashhad. As they travel from Tehran in four carts, Hedayat describes their long journey stage by stage and depicts their differences, quarrels, intrigues, and attitudes toward one another with consummate skill. The eponym of the story is a vicious woman who makes great claims to piety. 'Alaviya Khanum is one of the most memorable characters created by Hedayat, and through her he criticizes the ignorance, superstition, and sanctimony of many Iranians of his time.

The most outstanding satirical work by Hedayat is *Hajji Agha* (1945), which is an even more detailed character study than *Alaviya Khanum*. The story revolves around the life of a "nouveau riche" merchant who invents an aristocratic title for his deceased father as a means of moving into higher social circles. As he tries to gain influence with high officials and to increase his personal wealth, there is no limit to his vicious intrigues. He spies for the police, he misappropriates the funds for the poor, and he becomes the middleman for those seeking high office. Hajji Agha is an admirer of Reza Shah and Hitler and, imagining himself a person of considerable political significance, flees to Isfahan upon the Allies' occupation of Tehran. After the abdication of Reza Shah he returns to Tehran, vilifying the Shah for his tyranny and his extortion of "whatever the country owned," and becomes an outspoken liberal. Upon discovering that the newly introduced democracy is nothing but the old intrigues and corruption he declares, "If this is democracy, then I have been a democrat all my life."[28]

Hajji Agha is an unbelievable miser drawn meticulously in the tradition of Harpagon and Père Grandet. Counting the number of stones from the plums that have been put in a stew, he finds that four are missing and starts a fight over them. He says that God has put the stones in the plums because he knows what cheats and deceits people can be. He beats his wife Zobeyda so badly that she becomes a cripple for life because she bought a few onions. For Hajji Agha money is everything, "his beloved, the cure of [his ailments], his sole purpose in life, and the source of pleasure and fear."[29] He says:

If you happen to have money in this world then you will also have pride, credit, honesty, virtue and everything else. People adore you, you will be considered intelligent and patriotic, they will flatter you, they will do everything for you. . . . The educated engineer takes pride in operating your machine, the architect truckles to you to build your house, the poet licks the dust and writes your eulogy, the painter who has starved all his life paints your portrait, the journalists, deputies, ministers will all stand ready to do your bidding. . . . These scoundrels are all slaves to money. Do you know why knowledge and education are of no use in life? Because when you have got them you still have to serve the rich people. . . .[30]

After money everything is of secondary importance. He changes his ideology to suit the taste of his visitors. With the young intellectuals he talks of progress and of their aspirations. With the Constitutionalists he boasts of his struggles for the right cause; but at heart he is an autocrat who sighs for the "good old days" of the martyred Shah. But he cannot always fool people. Hoping to get elected to the *Majles*, he asks a young and poverty-stricken poet, Monadi al-Haqq,[31] to compose a *qaside* on democracy. The young man exposes Hajji Agha's false piety and patriotism and bitterly denounces him:

It is only natural that you do not know what poetry means, it would be strange if you did. You have never had or seen beauty in your life and if you come across any you fail to appreciate it. You have never been moved by a charming view, by a beautiful face, or an enchanting piece of music, a rhythmical word; a noble thought has never touched your heart. You are nothing but a slave of your belly and your neither parts. . . . Now you can rest assured! I have divorced the craft of poetry. Henceforth the greatest and loftiest poem in my life will be the destruction of you and your kind. . . .[32]

Some critics have found this moralizing passage "affected"[33] and somewhat out of tune with the rest of his otherwise close-knit novel. But this is Hedayat who speaks in the person of the young poet. In a world that is full of tyranny, corruption, and hypocrisy and where everyone seems to play by the "rules," Hedayat wants to create at least one character who stands up for the truth. Furthermore, the effect of this sudden shock on Hajji Agha is well described and interesting in itself. Hedayat also speaks for the younger generation, who wants never to see a government similar to that of Reza Shah. Monadi al-Haqq continues, "For seventy years you have robbed, deceived and made a laughingstock of people. . . . Do you think you will carry this on generation after generation?. . . You are wrong. If the fate of this people remains for one more generation in your hands they will vanish.[34]

Politics and religion play an important part in the novel, but it being mainly a character study of Hajji Agha, his private life is paramount. He holds his office in the vestibule of his house, where he receives his clients—everyone from important dignitaries down to the notorious procurer of the town. From there he can constantly watch his many wives and their activities. His family is a source of worry for him, as he imagines that everyone is trying to cheat him. He deprives his eldest son of his inheritance because after being educated in Europe, the boy has been "corrupted." While undergoing surgery for a hernia, under the influence of anesthetics, Hajji Agha has a dream that forms the conclusion of the story. On the one hand it reflects the misgivings that Hajji has about his family, and on the other it shows his belief that even in the world to come one can get away with wheeling and dealing. He imagines himself dead and being carried to heaven by two angels, but he begs for a last look at his household, only to see his wives are dancing and celebrating his death. His dearly earned wealth is being squandered by his inheritors. In heaven he is made a doorkeeper at the palace of the wife who died because of his ill-treatment, She kicks him out. Upon awakening, he tells his wives that he has had a glimpse of the next world. Asked what his job would be there, he says, "In this world I am your doorkeeper, and in the other world, I was the doorkeeper to the palace of Mademoiselle Halimeh Khatun."[35]

Tup-e-Murvari (The pearl cannon) (1947) is one of the two books that Hedayat wrote toward the end of his life, and it was not published during his lifetime. Of this 150-page typewritten work seven copies were left with his family and friends. But due to its profane and maledictory language and its severe criticism of Reza Shah's reign and Islam, it was not published with the rest of the works of Hedayat. According to Hasan Kamshad:

> Some fragments, taken from the unrevised manuscript of the book, were published in the Persian translation of Vincent Monteil's *Sadeq Hedayat* (pp. 102-27), but it is unfair to judge the book on this mutilated selection.[36]

A few excerpts from the book along with some satirical short stories and essays were published in Berkeley in the 1960's.[37] After the revolution in Iran the whole book was published, but it so infuriated some devout Muslims that they set fire to several bookshops that carried it.

Tup-e-Murvari is the story of a cannon that was captured from the Portuguese by Shah 'Abbas's troops in the battle of Hormoz in 1622. Before Reza Shah set it in front of the Officer's Club in Tehran, it stood in front of the Arg (Citadel) in Tehran, serving as a fertility totem for unmarried women in general and for those who wanted to get pregnant or gain special favor with their husbands.[38] According to Hedayat's story, when Christopher Columbus made his landfall on a Central American island in 1492, he found the natives worshipping this cannon as a phallic symbol. It was covered with the preparation called *cantharides*, whose aphrodisiacal qualities attracted the native women. Columbus killed some of the natives and carried off the cannon, which was in turn stolen by the Portuguese. When Albuquerque invaded Hormoz, he brought it to the island, and later, after the victory of Shah Abbas, the cannon found its way to the Iranian capital. This was how it became a favorite with the ladies of that city.

The story is insignificant and full of anachronisms, but the satire is vehement and manifold. First describing how Shah Baba (i.e., Reza Shah), a ruthless and semiliterate despot, assumes power, Hedayat moves on to a scathing criticism of the Arabs and their conquest of Spain. Arriving at the discovery of the New World by the Spaniards, the author gives an interesting satirical account of the arrogant *conquistadores*, who regard themselves as a privileged race commissioned by God to "civilize" and "Christianize" the world. Describing the occupation of Hormoz by the Portuguese and their subsequent defeat by the combined forces of Iran and England, Hedayat pursues the fateful passage of the cannon among the Iranians, dispensing them their share of his satire.

Unlike most of the works of Hedayat, *The Pearl Cannon* is written carelessly. Apparently put together without revision, it lacks the beautiful and witty style that one finds in his other works. The ideas in the book are familiar: the bitter antagonism of Hedayat toward Islam and Arabic culture and his fondness for pre-Islamic Iran. The criticism of the clergy and the religious establishement is very strong, as are his attacks on European colonialism. Unlike his other works, here his heavy-handed satire is often grotesque and steeped in invective.

Vagh Vagh Sahab, which Hasan Kamshad translates as *Mister Bow Wow*, was written in collaboration with Mas'ud Farzad and published in 1933. In thirty-five narratives, called "cases," the authors cover a wide variety of social and literary matters, from poetry to historical novels, and from Freud to the use of vitamins. The book is a satirical miscellany that comments on literary fashions prevalent at the time and on some aspects of life during the reign of Reza Shah. The emphasis is, however, on the vainglorious poetasters who monopolized the literary scene and whose poetry was the result of petty pilfering from here and there, on the playwrights who flooded the theaters with their cheap and sentimental drama, and on pedantic scholars whose boring works lacked originality. For instance, in "The Case of Forty Daughters, Known as the Top Case," scholars are satirized who edit and reedit the works of the past, adding endless annotations on grammar and prosody without making any real contributions. Most of the cases are written in the form of mock verse that deliberately violates the rules of Persian classical poetry; thus the authors show their contempt for the traditionalists for whom the form was more important than the content. Commenting on the background against which *Vagh Vagh Sahab* was written, Kamshad writes:

> During this period of Hedayat's life, triviality was not only the stimulus for fashionable art and letters but also a dominating factor in the whole pattern of Persian life. Poetry was the strictly guarded domain of a handful of "high-minded dignitaries" whose essential merit was to copy the great classics. Cinemas presented the public with every piece of rubbish Hollywood produced, and the theatre was the scene of cock-and-bull stories mainly about clumsy lovemaking. In the literary field, apart from a few "established" scholars, two groups of upstart novelists and translators had emerged: the first group produced with breathless haste genial stories for the popular papers. The second group, the translators, faithfully followed the direction Hedayat had ironically pointed out to them:

After you have been to a school for a few months and have learnt a few of the foreigners' words so that you can read just the name of the author or the title of an article, you are in a position to push yourself among the distinguished translators. Then try to know who has written the book and what it is about. Having done that, write whatever nonsense comes to your pen and publish it under the name of the well-known orignal writer.[39]

Mediocrity, lack of originality, pedantry, and plagiarism are the main targets of criticism in *Vagh Vagh Sahab*, whether they be in the traditional forms of Persian literature or those that were imitations of western forms. Sometimes the authors parody the style of such literary works, but very often they lampoon the content and the methods used in them. Here is a short example from the beginning of "The Case of a Stormy Blood-stained Love," which mocks the cheap sentimental plays popular at the time:

> Last night I went to see "A Stormy Blood-stained Love."
> It was announced it would begin before long.
> But alas it started very late
> And the people were almost bored to death.
> The play was by a writer of great fame
> Who had put Shakespeare, Moliére and Goethe to shame;
> A tragedy, a comedy and a moral play,
> Social, historical, literary and recreational as well.
> A comic opera and very dramatic,
> In brief, a marvel worthy of any antics.[40]

The cases described in the book represent a wide variety of subjects, most dealing with the cultural life in Iran in the 1930s. Mocking the directives of the Iranian Academy (*Farhangistan*), which wanted to purify the Persian language of Arabic and Turkish words, the titles of the narratives are spelled in the most ridiculous manner in "pure Persian." The subject matter of some of the topics is distinctly popular. For example, in "The Case of King Kong," the impact of such Hollywood products on the mind of the simple man in the street is described. But despite its mocking tone, there is an underlying sense of sadness in "The Case of an Elegy to a Poet." This seems to be a projection of Hedayat's disappointment in contemporary Iranian scholars and critics, and a forecast of what will happen some years later when he commits suicide in Paris. A poet dies and his friends very enthusiastically mourn his death—not only because they are free from his "boring" poetry, but also because a rival has disappeared from the scene:

> If alive, he would be a rival for us.
> Barring progress from all of us.
> So it was good that he breathed his last,
> And we are here to honor the past.
> Now we show our appreciation
> By prolonging our lamentation.
> So that the living will know

How greatly we love those who lie below.
If he were alive, we should swear at him
And never into our clubs would allow him.
But since we are all desirous of progress
Therefore, we express our sorrow at his death.[41]

Another writer of Hedayat generation is Buzurg 'Alavi (b. 1904), who after his education in Germany returned to Iran and became associated with the Communist party of Iran. As a result he spent some years in prison during the reign of Reza Shah and many years in exile, where he became a professor of Persian literature at the University of Humboldt. 'Alavi, who chose his friend Sadeq Hedayat as his model in his early works, followed a different road. Vera Kubickova explains, "From a pessimistic view, colored with romantic individualism, he has worked his way to a socialist outlook, from which the optimistic undertone of his later works derives.[42] Though 'Alavi has some superbly beautiful short stories such as "Gilah-mard" (The man from Gilan) or "Sarbaz-e Surbi"(The lead soldier) and some remarkable novels such as Cheshmhayash (Her eyes), his few satirical short stories are by no means of equal artistic value. Despite the fact that 'Alavi has always been strongly critical of the Iranian bureaucracy and of social injustice, he has only occasionally turned to satire in his writings. Here I will discuss only two of his short stories, "Panj Daqiqa Ba'd az Davazdeh" (Five minutes after twelve) and "Shikpoush" (The fashionable).[43]

The first story, which comes from the collection entitled Nama-ha (Letters) (1952), satirizes the administrative bureaucracy in Iran. The official who issues birth certificates refuses to issue one for the newborn baby of the writer on the grounds that it is five minutes past the offical working hour. Neither complaints to the director nor finding a friend who intervenes proves to be helpful, and the whole affair gets ridiculously complicated, only very easily solved when the writer drops a two-toman bill into the desk drawer of the official.

The second story, "The Fashionable," which is contained in the collection of short stories called Chamadan (The suitcase) (1934), ridicules a Frenchified dandy and dilettante, who pontificates on clothes and manners to the circle of his friends. The narrator, who for the most part of the story maintains a Candide-like naiveté in believing in the greatness and knowledge of his fashionable friend, Mr. Navapur, suggests that he should write an article about his views. The article is written and everybody admires it. It seems that Buzurg 'Alavi in writing this story was influenced by Sadeq Hedayat and Mas'ud Farzad's Vagh Vagh Sahab. Though the article is a commonplace piece of "commercial" writing, paid for by a local tailor, no one discusses its contents, but its style becomes the subject of much talk around town. Each school of thought looks at its style form its own point of view. 'Alavi very successfully parodies the traditionalists, who favor using many Arabic words in their parlance, and the modernists, who are after "pure" Persian. The language of both groups is ridiculously senseless, but they have one thing in common: they do not care for what is written, only how it is written.[44]

After Hedayat and the writers of his generation the short story became a widely used medium in Persian literature. In most of these stories the writers are preoccupied with criticism of the ever-present social problems, a criticism that is very often expressed in satirical form. There are two distinct groups of writers among modern short story writers of Iran. One group is basically made up of novelists and short story writers, and only occasionally does one come across a satirical piece among their works. The other is essentially made up of satirists who have used the short story as a medium of their art. Sadiq Chubak, Jalal Al-Ahmad, Gholam Hosain Sa'edi, and Jamal Mir Sadeqi belong to the first group, whereas Khosrow Shahani, Iraj Pezeshkzad, and Abul-Qasem Halat may serve as examples of the latter. Since it is almost impossible to review the works of all contemporary writers, I will limit my discussion to a few examples of these two groups.

Sadiq Chubak (b. 1916) is one of the most talented and accomplished novelists and short story writers of Iran. He creates his short stories with a remarkable conscientiousness for structure and language and a dedication to the economy of them and incident. He has an incredible familiarity with the lives and thoughts of his characters, who are mostly chosen from the lowest and most deprived classes. Hasan Kamshad adds that "but even there he is not content with the ordinary, commonplace sights, for his sharp, microscopic eyes catch only the ugliest and the most repellent shades of life.[45] The backgrounds of his stories are deprivation, lust, hunger, and loneliness. For instance, one of his best known novels, *Sang-e-Sabur* (The patient stone) (1966), describes the loneliness of a group of people under the bleak and dictatorial reign of Reza Shah, when physical poverty was matched with spiritual intimidation and stagnating intellectual silence. In the gloomy world of Chubak's fiction satirical and humorous characters occasionally appear, but they can never alleviate the burden of misery and corruption. Reza Baraheni comments that "the world of Chubak is like a Shakespearean tragedy which is enlivened by the appearance of the jester but only for a short period."[46]

In some of the naratives in his three collections of short stories, *Khayme Shabbazi* (Puppet show) (1945), *Ruz-e Avval-e Qabr* (The first day of the grave) (1965), and *Chiragh-e Akhar* (The lamp of the last day) (1965), Chubak combines social criticism with a sense of satire. He himself rarely criticizes, rather it is through the characters and incidents that a critical picture of Iranian society is given. In many ways Chubak resembles Anton Chekhov, but his language is much more naturalistic. In "A Bouquet of Flowers," a story from the second collection, a high and corrupt official is being threatened by a series of anonymous letters that reveal his many secrets. He is so scared and distressed that he eventually dies of a heart attack. But the irony is that the letters are written by an insignificant clerk, who puts his hand on the grave of the chief and recites this couplet of Sa'di:

To drink a draught of water after the wicked,
Will be better than living for seventy years or
eighty.

"The Mouse" (Pache-khizak) is another story in this collection with a bitter
sense of irony. In small villages or towns in Iran where people have no way of
entertaining themselves, sometimes very cruel practices toward animals become
a kind of amusement. A shopkeeper has caught a large mouse and various people
suggest ways of putting it to death. Eventually they pour kerosene over it and
set it aflame. The frenzied mouse dashes toward a kerosene tank, which explodes
and destroys the whole village.

Chubak is an artist with a natural aversion to religion, and he often treats
it with a biting sense of satire. In *Sang-e Sabur* Gohar, a young wife who has
been sent away from her husband's house because of a superstitious belief, has
resigned herself to temporary marriages (or *sighas*) in order to feed her child.
As one can imagine, these are arranged by a cunning mulla, Sheikh Mahmud,
who is the butt of Chubak's satire. The plot is complex, and Gohar is the focal
point of the internal monologues that are carried out by several characters in
the novel. It is, in fact, around her fate—an eventual murder at the hands of
a psychopathic killer—that the whole story revolves. Apart from such scenes
as the dialogue between King Anushiravan and a donkey and one between God
and Satan, the novel as a whole is not satirical. Nonetheless the depiction of
some characters, and particularly that of Sheikh Mahmud, borders on satire.

Ruz-e-Avval-e Qabr (The first day of the grave) is the title of another collection
in which Hajji Mu'tamad, a rich merchant, has built a shrine for himself and
has come to insepct it. While sitting all alone in the grave, he thinks of all his
past sins, particulary about a girl whom he had gotten pregnant and then
abandoned. She ended up as a prostitute. His religiosity stems from his ever-
present fear of God, while many doubts that linger at the bottom of his heart.
Being a fatalist, he accuses God of being an accomplice in what he has done,
since everything has been decreed by him. Hajji eventually dies in his own grave.
But when he feels death approaching, he boldly asks God many pertinent
questions that have perplexed mankind for many centuries and that have never
been satisfactorily answered. He asks, "If you are so considerate, why did you
create Satan? And why after so many prophets have the affairs of the world
become worse and worse?[47] In very simple language he asks questions that
Khayyam too had asked. Chubak's criticism is directed at hypocritical devotees,
who lack faith but pretend to be religious.

Another story to be mentioned here is "Esaeye Adab" (Discourtesy), which
appears in the first edition of *Puppet Show* but was removed from the second
edition at the request of the publisher—probably a preventive measure to avoid
government censorship. The story relates how crows have been disrespectful
to the monument of a certain "Shahanshah." The angered ruler of the country
orders his subjects to shoot the crows and daily produce him with

a great body of his defeated "enemies." As a result the crows are forced to leave the land and emigrate abroad. In memory of these events they now all dress in black, and their voices are hoarse from weeping and moaning. Apart from being a political satire, the story is directed against hackneyed literature and its artificial style. Chubak cleverly parodies the language of various contemporary Persian historical novels, and in this respect the story resembles chapter 21 in *Vagh Vagh Sahab*, which is entitled "The Case of Ancient Stories and Historical Novels."[48]

Jalal Al-Ahmad (1923-69), who was born into a very religious family and whose father was a cleric, also chooses his characters from the middle and lower classes. Though his style is very vivid and graphic, he does not have the patience to go into detail in creating his characters. His characterizations sometimes seem like sketches, yet they are full of life. With nostalgic fondness he lays emphasis on the fast-changing beliefs and customs of these people. For him the traditions and originality of a culture are of paramount importance. His approach to Islam is very different from that of Chubak. When he criticizes the devout it is for their fantaticism and senseless religiosity. In "Sitar"[49] a young musician/singer has managed to buy a sitar and treasures it above everything else. When he takes it to the courtyard of the Shah Mosque in Tehran, an enraged fanatic breaks it into pieces. In another story of the same collection entitled "Vasvas" (Scrupulous) a man is so obsessed with ritualistic cleanliness as prescribed by Islam that he spends all his day in the public bath, but at the end his ablution is left for the next day. This story is so imbued with local coloring that outside of religious circles in Iran it makes no sense.

But Al-Ahmad's main criticism is directed against the onrush of modernization and "Westomania"[50] which he thinks has undermined the national traditions and old canons of behavior prevalent in Iran. In the story entitled "The American Husband"[51] he describes a westernized woman from Tehran who marries her American teacher and goes to Washington only to find out that he is in the funeral business at Arlington National Cemetery. The gap of understanding between the American and Iranian is further illustrated when the judge at the divorce court, in referring to her husband's work, says; "After all it's a job," which totally shocks the woman. After returning to Iran with her young daughter, she tells her story to a friend.

The story is told in the first person and, in spite of a somewhat unrealistic plot, has many revealing details. The character of the American, as well as that of the Iranian, is humorously depicted: two cooked turkeys are sent from Los Angeles so that the husband will not feel homesick at Thanksgiving! The Iranian woman in the story is very much a westernized type and the criticism of Al-Ahmad is directed against her. The following passage is representative of the rest of the story. While telling her story to a friend, she wants some cheese with her glass of whisky, and the friend offers her some Ligvan, the best cheese made in Iran:

No, thanks . . . Don't give me any more. It makes me sick. Empty stomach
and whisky . . . What is left at the bottom of the glass will do. A bit of
cheese would be good . . . Thanks! Oh . . . is this cheese? Why is it so white?
It's very salty! Where is it from? . . . Ligvan? Where is that . . . I don't know.
I know Dutch and Danish ones but not this . . . I don't like it, not a bit.
Pistachio nuts will do . . . Thanks! What was I saying? . . . Oh yes, I met
him in the American Club . . . He was very polite . . . First he invited me
to an exhibtition of paintings at the new Abbas-Abad Club. One of those
exhibits where they draw figures without heads, or put heaps and heaps
of paint in the middle of two yards of fabric. He had invited Dad and
Mom too. They were ecstatic . . . Then he invited me to a dance. I guess
it was one of their holidays. I think it was Thanksgiving . . . You don't
know? Thanksgiving is the only thing the Americans have. It is the day
that they give thanks. The same day that they finished off the last of the
Indians.[52]

Another leading contemporary writer of short stories and plays in Iran was
Gholam Hosain Sa'edi (1935-1985). Sa'edi, whose writings are occasionally satirical,
was imprisoned several times and tortured atrociously for his "dangerous political
views" during the reign of the former Shah. By training he was a medical doctor
and a psychiatrist, and he had travelled widely throughout Iran. His work and
his travels enabled him to produce a large gallery of characters from a wide cross
section of Iranian society, most particularly from the lower and middle classes.
Sa'edi pays special attention to dialogue and superbly reproduces the language
of his characters. In some of his works Sa'edi combines a deep insight into human
nature with a remarkable familiarity with Iranian society. He vividly describes
the abject lives of the slum dwellers in South Tehran, the poverty-stricken
peasants in the countryside, and the superstitious inhabitants of fishing villages
in southern Iran. His satirical criticism is directed either toward mullas,
policeman, and government officials, or else toward the whole social system.
Tars va larz (Fear and trembling) (1969), in which the exploitation of villagers
in a remote place in southern Iran by a roguish "cleric" is described, may serve
as an example of the former group, and of the latter the plays *Dikteh va Zavieh*
(Dictation and angle) (1969) and *Ma Namishenavim* (We don't hear) (1970), in
which an absurd educational system and a tyrannical government are
satirized.[53]

Dandil (1968) is a collection of four short stories whose eponymous offering
is one of the best works of fiction by Sa'edi. Dandil is the red-light district of
the small town of Maragheh in Azerbaijan. It is a world of its own with pimps,
policemen, addicts, and prostitutes—a world full of human suffering, deprivation,
and poverty. One of the houses in Dandil is, relatively speaking, larger and taller
than the others, whose proprietor, called "Madame," is seeking a rich customer
for a pretty, fifteen- year-old girl, who has just been brought to the house.
Through the ingenuity of the local policeman a picture of the girl is taken and
shown to an American sergeant from the neighboring army base. The discussion
between the pimp and policeman is typical of the rest of the story:

Asdollah said, "I'm not talking about myself. I'm talking about that guy. They're not poor and starving like us. I swear to God, they're always rolling in money.

"Wherever they go, they spend money like crazy. They pay up and they want to have a good time. But I'm telling you, when he comes here, everything's got to be the way he likes it, because he's going to pay for it all. Just think of it—the guy's a sergeant, but his pay is three times more than our boss gets. Just go to the army base and see the way he's living. It'll surprise the hell out of you. Even the big shots stand at attention for him. So, with a man like that coming here, do you realize how much Dandil is going to improve? You'll have it made, but not the way things are now, with all this filth. . . . Can we bring him in the dark? They're not used to this kind of mess. In their country, the days and nights are the same. . . . In fact, their nights are even brighter then their days. I've seen pictures of their cities.

"The buildings are all glass, and the streets sparkle like crystal. . . . The're rows and rows of banks and every one of them is full of money. They're not beggars like us. They all have private cars. Their whores spend four or five hours a day just playing around in the beauty shops—and you think you're going to bring one of them to Dandil? Well, no matter what, we've still got some pride. . . ."

They do their best to prepare the place for the American and set the table full of food and drinks for him. Amid the curiosity and avid expectation of everyone, he arrives and spends the night with the girl. He leaves in the morning without paying anything. The bewildered procurers urge the policeman to ask for money, but he steps back and answers:

"No, you can't say anything to him. You can't go asking him for money. He is not like you and me: he's an American. If he gets upset, if he's not satisfied, he's going to turn Dandil inside out. He'll kill us all and destroy everything."[54]

Like "The American Husband," "Dandil" is a "story of ideas." In both stories the bitter irony results from the fact that the Iranians' expectations of the Americans are unrealistically high. Written under an unsparing censorship, like many of Sa'edi's works, "Dandil" has an allegorical significance. Though written a decade before the time when the number of American advisors there reached the record high of 43,000, the story clearly indicates the growing resentment toward American involvement in Iran.

"Kay-Kawus, Baldy and Me" is another story in the same collection that satirizes the incredible Iranian bureaucracy and the vanity and complacency of many government officials. Three friends go to a small town on the Persian Gulf to shoot a documentary film for a filmmakers' competition. They have no well-known "star" for their movie, and the town's chief of police, knowing nothing about documentaries, declares their activities to be against regulations. The mayor of the town agrees to help Baldy and his friends in return for their making a film of his election campaign. The two friends are very angry with

Baldy, since, they say, he has compromised himself and received money from the mayor. In the end, however, it is the mayor himself who has been manipulated by Baldy. While the mayor was giving fiery speeches in front of the townspeople, Baldy was shooting with an empty camera! Upon arriving at the airport Baldy gives the mayor a phony address and tells him, "I'll mail you the film."

This story is in many ways reminiscent of the stories in the collection entitled *Shabneshini ba-Shukouh* (A glorious party) (1960), in which Iranian officialdom is satirized. The first story describes a party given on the occasion of the retirement of thirteen officials. Some of them are already dead, but all the same the "honor" of retirement is being conferred upon them. The atmosphere of this gathering and the speeches that are given are hilariously ridiculous. This story, as well as others in the collection, reminds the reader of some of the short stories of Chekhov where the senseless bureaucracy of Tsarist Russia is satirized.

Khosrow Shahani (b. 1929) is a journalist and satirist whose column entitled "Dar Kargah-e-Namadmali" (In the workshop of a feltmaker) in the magazine *Khandaniha* attracted considerable attention for many years. So far he has published five collections of predominantly satirical stories:*Pahlavan-e-Mahalle* (The Hero of our street), (n.d.), *Kur-e-La'nati* (The accursed blindman) (1964) *Wahshat-abad* (The nighmare street) (1969), *Komedi-ye-Iftetah* (The comedy of inauguration) (1967), and *Adam-e- 'Avazi* (The weirdo) (1971). Some of Shahani's stories are similar to those of Aziz Nesin, the famous Turkish short story writer and satirist, who is still very popular in Iran and might have served as a model for this writer. Shahani does not concentrate on characterization and description but rather on humor and social satire. In spite of some occasional stories of tragedy,[55] social satire combined with comedy dominates his writings. Though as a satirist he might occasionally exaggerate, the incidents that he describes are familiar sights in Iranian life.

In "The Comedy of Inauguration" the inhabitants of an underdeveloped area of Tehran dig a well for their drinking water. But it is sealed off by the municipality in order to be opened officially by the mayor. Several months pass until he arrives and opens the well as one of the many projects undertaken by the government for the welfare of its grateful citizens. "The Circular," another story in the same collection, describes the plight of an unemployed worker who travels to various cities of Iran in search of a job. But wherever he goes he faces government regulations that prohibit the unemployed from getting jobs outside their own native towns. He goes to Iraq in order to escape this ever-present "circular," but he is arrested for crossing the border without a passport. On his deathbed, after having given up hope of coping with his bureaucratic enemy, he sees the same senseless regulation overshadowing the lives of his two sons.

A third story in the same collection, "Ham Gasamha" (The confederates), is the story of the writer's trip during the *Nuw-ruz* (New Year) holidays with a friend who is addicted to opium. They arrive in a city where a campaign to deal with drug problems is under way. The friend, who cannot travel without smoking opium, forces the writer to approach various people in order to get some. Eventually a kindly policeman directs them to a house where they are graciously received and served with not only opium but drinks as well. In the evening most of the dignitaries of the town, including the officer in charge of the narcotics squad and the local judge, arrive. Throughout the holidays they gather there each night and have a capital time, drinking and smoking opium and reciting the verses of Hafez. When the writer and his friend want to depart they find out that their car has been stolen from the street. But the judge tells them that they cannot pursue the matter because everyone at the gathering might be implicated. As they leave the town, they see the police chief arrest a greengrocer for possessing a gram of opium.

Bureaucracy is not the only target of Shahani's satire. He attacks a wide range of social problems, but he is careful not to criticize those in power, since such criticism would not have been tolerated at that time. If he occasionally embarks upon political satire, it is very covert and discreet. Shahani may serve as an example of many contemporary Iranian satirists whose works are basically of a journalistic nature. Rasul Parvizi (b. 1920) in his *Shalvarha-ye Vasle-dar* (Patched pants) (1954); Abbas Pahlavan (b. 1937) in his *Shab-e 'Arusi-ye Babam* (The night my dad got married) (1952), *Na-Darwish* (The fake dervish) (1957), *Shikar-e-'Ankabut* (Spider hunting) (n.d.), and *Tashrifat* (Ceremonies) (1970); Iraj Pezeshkzad in *Bu Bul* (1959) and *Asimun va Rismun* (Cheese and chalk) (1964); and 'Abbas Towfiq in his numerous stories and sketches, which were published in his magazine *Towfiq*, follow more or less the same line. While the last two writers' works are predominatly satirical, those of the former two are only occasionally so.[56] There is also another group of satirists who write on the same social subjects, but their works often consist of sketches or essays, though they may occasionally write stories. Of such writers mention should be made of 'Abul-Qasim Payande in his *Dar Sinema-ye Zendagi* (In the cinema of life) (1957) and *Dar Defa' az Mulla Nasreddin* (In defense of Mulla Nasreddin) (1959), and 'Abul-Qasem Halat, a satirical poet and columnist. Halat recently published in four volumes a collection of his work, which he wrote for six years in the Tehran daily newspaper *Kayhan*. The volumes are entitled *Az 'Asre-Shutur ta 'Asre-Mashin* (From the age of the camel to the age of the car) (1978), *Az Bimarestan ta Timarestan* (From the hospital to the mental asylum) (1978), *Zubale-ha va Nukhale-ha* (Scamps and scum) (1978), and *Pabusi va Chapbusi* (Fawning and foot-kissing) (1979). In the introduction to the first volume he writes:

> Someone told me: "You put your finger right on the sore spots!" I said: "It's not because of my art. It's because the sore spots are so prominent that they come right under my finger!"[57]

The number of social evils and the writers who treat them satirically in various journals and dailies is so numerous that all of them could not be enumerated here. Let us bring this chapter to a close with a discussion of several satirical novels by Sa'id Nafisi, Iraj Pezeshkzad and Ebrahim Gulistan. Sa'id Nafisi

(1897-1966) was an amazingly prolific scholar who wrote and edited over one hundred books on Persian literature and history, lexicography, and Russian literature, as well as some translation from French. He also created five works of fiction, of which *Fereshtagan-e Siyah* (The black stars) (second edition, 1949) is a collection of short stories in which "A Pair Of Shoes" and "The Beard" are humorous and satirical. One of his later novels, however entitled *Nimeh-Rah-e-Bihisht* (Halfway to heaven) (1952), presents a large-scale satirical picture of the Iranian ruling class and aristocracy in the late forties and early fifties when American interests were replacing those of the British in Iran.

More than a close-knit and well-structured novel, *Nimeh-Rah-e-Bihisht* is a loose narrative describing the whims and wickedness of the ruling class of Iran. Central to the story is the trial and imprisonment of 'Abbas, an illiterate but clever and patriotic ice-cream vendor whose shop happens to be next to the house of an influential member of parliament. In this house important internal and foreign policies of the country are negotiated and paid for by the customers who want to benefit from them. The only crime of the ice-cream man is that he is a curious observer of events. The annoyed member of parliament arranges his arrest, and his treatment in prison and the mockery of his trial epitomizes the "justice" of the royal courts. A policeman tells him:

> [The courts] are for those who want to get their money from people, or their property, or they want to put an end to the whims of their wife, or to get rid of her. They never form a court for you the penniless. You wretched tongue-tied creature, where would they take you? Do you think that the public prosecutors, lawyers, and judges of His Imperial Majesty's courts have time on their hands so that they will see you? Haven't you heard that our judicial system is respected, independent, and free from everywhere and everybody?[58]

Soon 'Abbas finds out for himself how "independent" the court can be. The animosity of his influential neighbor is enough for an investigating officer to give him a long term in prison as a political activist. That is all his trial amounts to.

Though Nafisi cannot successfully sustain a satirical tone throughout the novel, as he often becomes prosaic and didàctic, there are many interesting passages depicting the follies and vanities of many of his contemporaries. Under transparently ridiculous names he describes a large number of dignitaries and men of letters of Iran: Dr. Manuchehr Idbar (Misery), stands for Dr.Eqbal, a very close friend of the former Shah and for many years the oil chief of Iran. Dr. Dipolmacy (Dr. Siyasi) was the chancellor of Tehran University. Dr. Jahanshah Saleh, also a late chancellor of Tehran University, is called Dr. Ravankah-e Fasid (the Corrupt Diminisher of Soul), and his ignorance of Persian and fluency in English are ridiculed. Seyyed Ahmad Kajravi (i.e., Kasravi), Dr. Lutf 'Ali Ortgar (i.e., Suratgar), and Saria' al-Aman Gurizan-Par (i.e., Badi'a 'al-Zaman Fruzanfar) are only a few of the well-known scholars of Iran whose subtle, and somewhat untranslatable, names are replaced with unflattering characteristics. Sometimes Nafisi evidently cannot resist the temptation to pillory his acquaintances, especially the people with whom he is not on good terms. Seyyed Ahmad Kasravi, Dr. Siyasi, and Muhandis Bazargan (Batangan), now the former prime minister of Iran, may serve as three examples; but often the personalities he depicts rightly deserve his savage caricature.

Chapter 8 in the book, which describes a meeting of professors at Tehran University, is reminiscent of Thomas Peacock's *Headlong Hall* (1816), wherein Wordsworth, Coleridge, and other Romantics are satirized. What Matthew Hogarth writes of Peacock is true of Nafisi's technique as well. "His technique is to collect a representative group of intellectuals at a house-party, and then make them engage in conversation; the ideas they put forward are brilliant parodies of current views on philosophy, politics and literature, close enough to the originals to make them true intellectual history and yet so representative of their absurdity of permanent modes of human thought as to make them of universal satirical value."[59] Perhaps "universal satirical value" does not apply to what Nafisi describes, but his technique is the same, and one must be familar with such characters and must have been through such "academic" meetings in order to appreciate Nafisi's power of description and admirable wit.

In Iraj Pezeshkzad one finds an interesting variety of satirical forms and techniques. Of his aforementioned works *Bu Bul* is a collection of short stories and sketches, whereas in *Asimun va Rismun* he avoids authorial intrusion and allows his characters' own words and actions to create the satire. This collection of essays, poems, and short plays originally appeared under the same title in the weekly *Ferdausi* from 1954 to 1958. Here Pezeshkzad is mainly concerned with the contemporary literary world of Iran, and he revises newly published plays, poems, and works of fiction in the most ingenious ways. The book depicts a strangely chaotic period in the modern literary history of Iran, a time in which free verse and blank verse, as well as unintelligible symbolism and surrealism vied for the attention of the reader alongside the most traditional forms of poetry. Pezeshkzad chooses passages that are suitable for his purpose and transforms them into humorous and absurd short plays or stories. Sometimes he quotes a poem or a passage with a brief comment, and often it is so ridiculous that it turns into a self-parody. *Hajj Mam Jafar in Paris* (1957) is written in the tradition of Montesquieu's *Lettres Persanes* and Morier's *Hajji Baba of Ispahan in England*. Pezeshkzad takes an old-fashioned and traditional Hajji to Paris and through his ideas and superstitions gives a satirical and contrasting picture of two worlds: the modern West and the old East. This novel is basically a comedy that sometimes becomes satirical. The same method is used in a more interesting and much more successful novel entitled *Daijan Napoleon* (1972), which was later made into a television serial.

Daijan Napoleon is the story of the writer's love for his cousin Leila when both were teenagers, and it centers on the events and people who live in several family houses clustered around a larger house belonging to his uncle (Daijan Napoleon). Two characters dominate the story: the uncle whose boundless admiration for

Napoleon has earned him the nickname of Uncle Napoleon, and his servant Mash Qasem. The former is a retired officer who constantly ruminates over his old adventures, battles, and skirmishes with the British troops and insurgent tribes during the First World War. Each day he comes to identify himself more and more closely with Napoleon. Mash Qasem is a Sancho Panza to this quixotic character, and he continually elaborates on the martial tales of his master in order to reaffirm his Napoleonic valor. Ironically, though Mash Qasem's motto in life is "never to tell a lie," he has ready answers for every question, and claims to have taken part in every conceivable event. Uncle Napoleon lives in his own imaginary world, which is constantly reaffirmed by his servant and others. Gradually he comes to believe that he is a person of considerable importance. When British and Soviet forces occupy Iran in 1941, Uncle Napoleon thinks that the British are after him. Out of despair he writes a letter to Hitler and asks for his help. Intertwined with the hallucinations of this comical character are many family intrigues, quarrels, and other events. Pezeshkzad admirably depicts a large number of characters involved in the story. One of these is Uncle Asadullah, a carefree lady's man, who once traveled to America and spent a pleasant time in San Francisco. Whenever he recommends a decisive action in an amorous exploit, he says, "Take a trip to San Francisco." Asadullah is the confidant of the young lover and urges him to circumvent his Uncle Napoleon (who is planning to marry his daughter to a different cousin) by eloping with Leila. But the "trip to San Francisco" never materializes, and Leila is forced to marry the other cousin. The heartbroken lover leaves for Europe to pursue his higher education. Upon his return, however, he meets Mash Qasem at a party. Uncle Napoleon has died, and Mash Qasem has become a wealthy man because of some land speculations. Still repeating his old motto and his wild tales, the former servant has now become the great anti-British "champion."

Comedy and satire blend curiously in this novel, with the former being the dominant element. Some of the characters are satirical but in this respect they vary greatly. From this point of view Uncle Napoleon and Mash Qasem deserve some comment. The pair create an atmosphere of lies and deceit, which may have been indended to represent a microcosm of an autocratic government and its society. One boasts of acts of bravery that were never carried out, and the other tries to validate and perpetuate them with constant affirmation. Uncle Napoleon's claims always seem to suit the demands of the age. It is ironic that although he was a reactionary royalist during the Constitutional Revolution, he portrays himself as a great "champion" of the Constitution.

Criticism of the characters is never expressed directly; nevertheless such an impression remains vividly in the mind of the reader. The humor of *Uncle Napoleon* cannot be summarized in short passages, nor does it depend on verbal wit, although Pezeshkzad is sometimes very witty. The interest of the novel lies in the overall depiction of the characters, their comments on human life, and the author's realistic description of contemporary Iranian life.

Asrar-e Ganj-e Darreh Jenni (The secrets of the treasure of possessed valley) is a film and novel by Ebrahim Gulistan, an outstanding filmmaker and short-story writer now living in England. The film was made in 1971, and in 1974 Gulistan reworked it into a novel. It is the story of a poor farmer who, while plowing his field, finds a burial chamber full of gold and artifacts. He takes pieces of the treasure to the city and sells them to a jeweler, who is the first of many people trying to discover the treasure of the farmer. Dazzled by the glitter of the city, the farmer builds a mansion in his village and decorates it with the most flashy and incongruous pieces of furniture. The jeweler's wife convinces the farmer to take a new wife and marries him to her servant girl. In order to spend his wealth he enlists the help of a young Literary Corps teacher, who supervises the construction of the supermodern mansion and invites artists and painters to celebrate the wedding of his patron. But the farmer's dreams of happiness do not last long—the secret treasure chamber as well as the mansion are destroyed by an explosion set off by a group of engineers who are building a road nearby.[60]

From the outset, when the first caravan of new purchases, kitchen appliances, velvet furniture, and statues of every size and shape reaches the poverty-stricken village, the parable of a poor country like Iran suddenly becoming rich in oil is apparent. The time of the film as well as the novel coincides with the oil price hike and the extravagant expenditures of the Shah in the celebrations of both his coronation and the 2,500th anniversary of the Iranian monarchy. It is the story of an easily acquired wealth that is spent lavishly on the most unnecessary things. Some of the characters of the novel, the jeweler, his wife, the young teacher, and the headman of the village, are caricatures of real types drawn with merciless humor and a remarkable insight. According to Paul Sprachman, who has recently published a study of the novel,[61] it seems to be a heavy indictment of the Shah and his ill-fated prime minister, Hoveyda, who are represented by the farmer and his lieutenant, the Literary Corps teacher. Here is what Gulistan says of the farmer after everything is destroyed:

> He viewed everything on the grounds of the new home as a sign of his own greatness and power, but never realized that the whole landscape represented his real state and identity—in place of the apple and quince orchards, today a field of plaster and cement statues, a kind of Noah's Ark of scattered examples of banality, of unbridled conceit, of worn-out legends, of the power of money and of an ugly, boorish, twisted and futile sensibility. And he could not see that changing the place of things is not the same as changing themselves. He did not realize that moving things around does not mean moving ahead. . . .[62]

The works of fiction covered in this chapter display a variety of satirical trends, ranging from invective and the grotesque to comedy. For example, in *Hajji Agha* Hedayat seems to indulge far too much in simply drawing a despicable picture of his protagonist, who becomes a monstrous personality without any redeeming characteristics. In *The Pearl Cannon* he seems to confuse satire with the use of the grotesque. In some of the short stories of Chubak the weight of tragedy somewhat overburdens his sense of satire. In *Halfway to Heaven* Nafisi allows propaganda to dominate his novel. In the works of Shahani, comedy has the upper hand. If we consider *The Pearl Cannon* mainly as anticlerical invective and works of Shahani satirical comedies, the works represented in this chapter then cover a wide spectrum. While all of them criticize the wrongs practiced in Iranian society and emphasize a need for social change, none of the authors seems to have any suggestions for the future. In other words, we cannot see what the satirists want to *substitute* for the social evils they describe. But after all, in the heat of indignation the satirist intends only to out at the wrongs, not to offer a blueprint for a society to come.

Notes

1. For an analysis of the novel see my article, "James Morier and his *Hajji Baba of Ispahan,*" *Indo-Iranica* Silver Jubilee volume (1970): 163-77.
2. James Morier, *Hajji Baba in England* (London: Macmillan Co., 1895), p. 8.
3. See Isma'il Ra'in, *Huquq begiran-e-Inglis* (Tehran: Amir Kabir, 1969), pp. 17-43. and also the posthumously published book of the same author entitled *Mirza Abul Hasan Khan Ilchi* (Tehran: Javidan, 1981). Also on the subject see my article, "Abu'l-Hasan Khan Ilci," *Encyclopaedia Iranica* (London: Routledge & Kegan Paul, 1983)
4. R. Mignan, *A Winter Journey through Russia, the Caucasian Alps and Georgia* (London: Bently, 1839?, 1:22.
5. C. J. Wills, *In the Land of the Lion and Sun* (London: Macmillan & Co., 1883), p. 3.
6. E. G. Brown's introduction to *Hajji Baba* (London: Macmillan & Co., 1895), p. 12.
7. See the introduction to *Hajji Baba*, ed. M. Jamalzade (Tehran: Amir Kabir, 1969), pp. 13-19.
8. See my article, "James Morier," p. 172.
9. See Mohit Tabatabai, "Sending Students to Europe," in *Shafaq-e-Sorkh*, No. 2393 (Tehran, 1933). Cf. M. Minovi, *Panzdah Goftar* (Tehran: Tehran University Publications, 1954), p. 287.
10. Homa Nateq, *Az mast Ke ber mast* (Tehran: Agah Publications, 1978), p. 102.
11. See my article, "James Morier and His *Hajji Baba,*" p. 168.
12. "Yad dasht-ha'i az Safar-e-Hajji Pirzadeh," *Yaghma* 13, no. 1 (1960): p. 42.
13. James Morier, *The Adventures of Hajji Baba of Ispahan*, ed. C. J. Willis (London: Lawrence & Ballen, 1897), p. 44.
14. Ibid., p. 191.
15. Ibid., p. 44.
16. See Hasan Kamshad, *Modern Persian Prose Literature*, p. 25.
17. *Hajji Baba*, pp. 118-119. Cf. *Sarguzasht-e-Hajji Baba*, ed. M. Jamalzade, Chap. 19.
18. Hasan Kamshad, *Modern Persian Prose Literature*, p. 96.
19. See Milos Borecky, "Persian Prose since 1945," *Middle East Journal* 7, no. 2 (1953): p. 237.
20. Ibid., p. 237.
21. *Life and Letters, Journal*, ed. Robert Herring (London, vol. 63, December 1949).
22. Translated by H. Kamshad from *Tarane-haye-Khayyam*, *Modern Persian Prose Literature*. p. 150.
23. Ibid., p. 161.
24. Quoted in Kamshad, *Modern Persian Prose Literature*, p. 156.
25. Ibid., p. 155.
26. Ibid., p. 156.
27. Ibid., p. 189.
28. *Hajji Agha* (Tehran: Amir Kabir Publications, 1964), p. 85.
29. Ibid., p. 22

30. Quoted in Kamshad, *Modern Persian Prose Literature*, p. 194.
31. The name means "the pronouncer of the truth." Hadayat's choice of names in this work is interesting; he makes use of the picaresque technique of comical names: such as Falakuhun al-Dawla, Sarhang Buland Parvaz, and Banda-yi Daragh, which Kamshad translates as "The State's Catapult," "Colonel Climb-High," and "The Slave of Your Threshhold," respectively. Ibid., p. 196.
32. Ibid., pp. 195-96.
33. A Bausani, *Storia della litteratura Persiana*, (Milan: Nuovo Accademic, 1960), p. 869.
34. Quoted in H. Kamshad, *Modern Persian Prose Literature*, p. 195.
35. *Hajji Agha*, p. 224.
36. *Modern Persian Prose Literature*, p. 200.
37. *Neveshta-hai az Sadeq Hedayat* (Berkeley, Calif. n.d.). Recently a new edition of *Tup-e Murvari* was published by Iraj Bashiri (Mazda Press, Lexington, 1986), but this is neither an authoritative text, nor the annotations are always accurate. However, this is the best existing edition.Mr. Sadeq Chubak has in his possession a handwritten copy of the book by Hedayat, which, if published, will prove to be of great help in illucidation of many points in the work.
38. See Henri Massé, *Croyances et Coutumes Persanes* (Paris: Librairie Orientale et Americaine, 1938), 1:148-49.
39. Quoted in Kamshad, *Modern Persian Prose Literature*, pp. 162-63.
40. Ibid., p. 31-32.
41. Ibid., p.
42. Vera Kubickova, "Persian Literature of the 20th Century," in *History of Iranian Literature*, Jan Rypka et al, eds. (Dordrecht: Karl Jahn, 1968) p. 414.
43. The original title of this story was "Mardi-ke Paltu-yi Shik Tanash Bud" (A man with a fashionable overcoat), but in recent editions the name has been changed.
44. For a discussion of this story see G. M. Wickens, "Bozorg Alavi's *Portmanteau*," *University of Toronto Quarterly* 28 (January 1959), 130-32.
45. Kamshad, *Modern Persian Prose Literature*, p. 128.
46. For an excellent and detailed analysis of Chubak's works see Reza Baraheni, *Qiseh-Nevisi*, (Tehran, Intisharat-e Ashrafi, 1969), pp. 539-713.
47. Sadeq Chubak, *Ruz-e Avval-e Qabr* (Tehran: Javidan, 1964), p. 136.
48. For an analysis of Chubak's satirical stories see Jahangir Dorri, "Satira Sadeka Chubaka," *Narody Azii i Afriki* (Moscow 4, 1979): 106-114. This is translated in *Critical Perspectives on Modern Persian Literature*, ed. Thomas M. Ricks (Washington, D.C.: Three Contenents Press, 1984), pp. 321-29.
49. From a collection with the same name. (Tehran: Javidan, 1948). A sitar is the name of a three-stringed musical instrument.
50. *Gharbzadigi* (Westomania) 1962, is the title of Al-Ahamd's well-known book, which was banned as long as the Shah was in power.
51. Jalal Al-Ahmad, *Panj Dastan* (Tehran: Intisharat Ravaq, 1977), pp. 67-82.
52. Ibid., pp 67-71.
53. For an analysis of Sa'edi's works, see G. R. Sabri-Tabrizi, "Social Values in Modern Persian Literature," *Bulletin of the British Association of Orientalists* 8 (1976): 9-16.
54. G. H. Sa'edi, *Dandil, Stories from Iranian Life*, trans. H. Javadi, J. Meisami and Robert Campbell, (New York, Random House, 1981), pp. 18-19.
55. For instance "Rubabe" and "Mulla Sham'um" in collection *Comedi-ye-Iftetah* the former describes the plight and suicide of a young girl who is forced to marry an old man with several wives, and the latter is about a wealthy Jewish merchant who participates in making unauthorized drugs to which his own children fall victim.
56. The works of these satirists as well as others are not mentioned in this chapter for lack of space. See Bijan Asadipour and 'Omaran Islahi *Tanz-Avaran-e-Ma'asir-e-Iran* (Contemporary satirists of Iran) (Tehran: Athar-e iran, 1970).
57. *Az 'Asre-Shutur ta 'Asre-Mashin*, p. 10.

58. *Nimeh-Rah-e-Bihisht*, 4th ed. (Tehran Goharkhay, 1965), pp. 223-24.
59. *Satire*, p. 222.
60. Paul Sprachman, "Ebrahim Gulistan's *The Treasure*: A Parable of Cliche and Consumption, "*Iranian Studies* 15, no. 1-4, (1982): 155-80.
61. Ibid.
62. Ibid., p. 178. Page 125 of the novel; translated by Paul Sprachman.

10

Satire in Modern Persian Drama

> Comedy accepts the rules of the social game, and satire does
> not; it is a protest against the rules as well as against the
> players, and it is much more profoundly subversive than
> comedy can afford to be.
>
> —Matthew Hodgart, *Satire*

Traditional Persian drama before the introduction of western-type plays consisted
of *ta'ziyes*, which are very similar to European passion or mystery plays, and
such farcical pieces as *baqqal-bazis* and *ru-houzis*, which are full of buffoonery.
Though *ta'ziye* has had a long history, it was not until the nineteenth century
that the *ta'ziye* gained literary importance. At that time, distinguished poets began
to write such plays, and various collections of them were gathered.[1]
Occasionally, a satirical *ta'ziye* can be found, but by nature this type of drama
is not a suitable medium for satire. An example is the *ta'ziye of Ebn-e Moljam*,
which is almost entirely a farcical type of satire, and in which the enemies of
the holy family of Hosain are ridiculed and abused.[2]

Puppet shows (*Kheyme-shab-bazi* or *lu'bat-bazi*) and folk plays of a farcical nature
were apparently in existence long before the *ta'ziye*; Khayyam in one of his
quatrains likens men to the puppets who play on "the board of existence" and
are then dropped one by one into the "box of non-existence."[3] In another
quatrain he talks of a "magic lantern" where the sun is the light, the world is
the lantern, and men are the figures circling it.[4] Of the scripts of such pieces
only the most recent ones are preserved. Although they are not basically satrical,
jesters and puppet masters would sometimes hint at both the wrongdoings of
the governors and the excesses of the clerics.

In the reign of Naser al-Din Shah (1848-96), a number of jesters gained
considerable influence, and foremost among them were Karim Shire'i and Esma'il
Bazzaz. The former, a special favorite of the king, was both dreaded and respected
by the dignitaries of the court because of his pungent remarks. Some of these

jesters gradually introduced criticism of the corrupt officials and of the political situation into the farcical plays they performed for the king. Obviously, though, only a mild type of criticism was tolerated.

One of the most stylish examples of such pieces is *Baqqal-bazi-ye Hozur*, which for some years was performed on *Nuw-ruz* at the court of Naser al-Din Shah. The text of the play was printed for the first time in 1944 in a Persian magazine of drama entitled *Hollywood* (number 18), but since the next edition was never issued, the last act of the play was never published. The author is unknown, but according to Jannati 'Ata'i, he was one of the dignitaries of the court of Naser al-Din Shah and wrote under the influence of Malkum Khan.[5] Yahya Aryanpur in his *Az Saba ta Nima* (2:327) believes that the author was Mohammad Hasan Khan E'temad al-Saltane, whose *Khalse* (the book of dreams) was discussed earlier. Since the latter work was critical of the Qajar king, its publication was forbidden during the reign of Naser al-Din Shah. It is likely that the plays were performed for the Shah, however, but only after the most offensive parts had been deleted.

The plot of the play is trivial. The main action consists of a strategem devised by Karim Shire'i, here included as one of the characters, to procure some foodstuffs from a grocer's shop. The jester makes a bet that he can enumerate so many titles given by the court to various people that the grocer will never be able to write them all down. He then recites two and a half pages of titles, some real and some fictitious, of dignitaries who led parasitical lives at the royal court. One should bear in mind that with each title went a stipend, and thus huge amounts of funds were being wasted. Finally, the titles become so ridiculously funny that the Shah, his sides splitting with laughter, orders a robe of honor to be brought for Karim Shire'i. A "robe" wrapped in silken cloth is produced, but it proves to be the backpack of a donkey. Karim exclaims, "What a great honor! His Majesty has given his own robe to me!" And donning it he says, "Your Majesty, now you must give me a special title to go with such an honor."[6]

It was during this period that western plays, mostly by Molière, were for the first time translated and performed. In 1850, after returning from one of his trips to Europe, Naser al-Din Shah ordered a playhouse to be built near Dar al-Fonun, the first westernized college in Tehran. For many years, because of the opposition of the clerics, this theater could not be used, and even when some plays were finally staged privately, they could not contain any effective criticism of the king or his rule. The first play to be performed was a verse translation of *Le Misanthrope*, which had been published in Istanbul in 1870. *Le Médecin Malgré Lui* was beautifully translated by Mohammad Hasan Khan 'Etemad al-Saltane and printed in Tehran in 1898. Another Molière play was *L'Étourdi* [Scatterbrain], translated as *Ass* in Persian, and which was performed in 1879. The characters of all the plays were changed to Persian characters in oriental settings. In this period and for many years to come the same method was used in the translations or adaptations of Molière's comedies. In this connection mention should be made of *'Arusi-ye Janab-e Mirza* [Marriage of his excellency Mirza] (1903) by Prince Mohammad Taher Mirza, *'Arusi-ye Majburi* [Forced marriage] (1911) by Hosain-Qoli Mirza 'Emad al-Saltana, *Hajji Riya'i Khan* (or *The Oriental Tartuffe*) (1918) by Mirza Ahmad Mahmudi, and nearly all the plays written by Seyyed 'Ali Khan Nasr: *'Avamfarib-e Salus* [A hypocritical demagogue], *Se 'Arusi dar Yek Shab* [Three marriages in one night], *Talab-kar va Bedeh-kar* [Creditor and debtor], and *Qahraman Mirza* (1939). All these are comedies with a tendency toward social satire.

A playwright other than Molière who had considerable influence on the early development of Persian drama, was Mirza Fath 'Ali Akhundzade (1812-78) from Russian Azerbaijan. Akhundzade served for twenty-three years as the oriental translator to Baron Rosen, the general governor of Georgia. Having come to Tiflis from his native Nukha, he became familiar with the dramatic work of Molière, Shakespeare, Gogol, and Griboedov, and it was under their influence that between 1850 and 1856 he wrote his six plays. A devoted reformer and an outspoken liberal, Akhundzade was anxious to introduce European ways of life and democratic methods of government not only to his native Azerbaijan, but also to Iran, the homeland of his father, and the country to which he had a deep attachment. In his plays as well as such nondramatic works as "The Story of Yusef Shah," Akhundzade uses satire as a means of combating superstition, hypocrisy, despotism, and fanaticism. He regarded satire and humorous realism as the best ways to awaken a backward nation that had grown accustomed to wrongdoing, repression, and corruption. He advised those who looked upon the plight of their people with tearful eyes to arise and be strong so that they could regain their rights and the bounties of God from the hands of "dogs and wolves."[7]

Azkhundzade, in a letter dated 25 March 1871 to Mirza Ja'far Qarachedaghi, the translator of his plays into Persian, discussed his purpose in writing *Letters of the Indian Prince Kamal al-Dowle to the Persian Prince Jalal-al-Dowle*. In this book, written in Turkish and translated into Persian in 1863, he criticizes the injustice and social vice connected with the feudalistic governments of the East and the ignorance and sheepishness of the people who were being abused. He uses the Russian word *kritica* and "*kritica* combined with derision" to denote satire, saying:

> Human nature being averse to sermons and morals . . . in the experience of European philosophers nothing is more effective in uprooting vices and evils than criticism, derision and ridicule.[8]

In the introduction to his collected plays Akhundzade says that since a theater was built at Tiblisi in 1848 he thought of introducing "the strange art of drama" to the Muslim world, and he hoped that more and more it would take hold. "My duty," he adds, "was only to lay the foundation and give a sample."[9]

His plays were first published in Russian translation in 1858, and the original Turkish appeared in 1859. Mirza Ja'far Qarachedaghi translated two plays in

1861 and 1863—his efforts greatly admired by the author—and in 1864 published all six of the plays along with the story of "Yusef Seraj Shah." These works had considerable impact on the political thought of the period,[10] and for many years to come served as a model for dramatic satire written in Persian.

In his first play, *Mulla Ebrahim Khalil Kimiyagar* [Mulla Ebrahim Khalil, the alchemist], Akhundzade contrasts a roguish *mulla*, who claims to have discovered an elixir of gold, with a sincere and patriotic poet, Hajji Nuri. In the play "the very respectable people of [the city of] Nukha" who support and encourage such scoundrels are also satirized. In his second play, *Monsieur Jourdain Hakim-e Nabatat va Darvish Mast 'Ali Shah Jadugar-e Mashhur* [Monsieur Jourdan, the botanist, and Darvish Mast 'Ali Shah, the famous magician], the corruption, superstition, and ignorance of the East is contrasted with the learning and advancement of the West. *Khirs-e Quldur Basan* [The bear and the bandit][11] gives a bitterly realistic picture of the life of Azerbaijani peasants and of the plight of women in that society. *Sarguzasht-e Vazir-e Sarab* [The story of the vizier of the chief of Sarab] satirizes the institution of government and the hypocrisy of the officials in a feudal system. Since the city of Sarab is in Iran, the translator, Mirza Ja'far Qarachadaghi, changed its name to Langaran. The fifth play, *Sarguzasht-e Mard-e Khasis ya Hajji Qara* [The story of the miser] is one of the best comedies of Akhundzade and apparently was inspired by Molière's *L'Avare*. In a gallery of fascinating characters, two stand out prominently—Hajji Qara, a cunning, cowardly, and miserly merchant, and Heydar Beyk, one of the few remaining descendants of an aristocratic family. Though the latter is extremely chivalrous, his way of life is nothing but brigandry. These two parasites are flanked by a number of corrupt government officials and honest peasants. The last play of Akhundzade is *Hekayat-e Vokala-ye Morafa' dar Shahr-e Tabriz* [The story of the defense attorneys in Tabriz], which criticizes the corruption of the judicial system and roguery of lawyers. In order to evade the censorship of Tsarist Russia the scene of the play is Tabriz.

The dramatic technique of Akhundzade is interesting in itself. He does not limit himself to the restrictive rules of French classical drama, especially from the standpoint of place and time. The scenes of his plays shift to different localities within the same act and the unity of time is not particularly adhered to. He exhibits in his work the influences of Shakespeare, Molière, and the Russians Gogol, Griboedov, and Ostrovski. The plays of Akhundzade, which are written in simple and lucid Azari Turkish, are full-scale portraits of the customs and mores of the people of Azerbaijan. The writer is very perceptive in depicting human nature. His characters, varied as they are, are fairly well developed, and though their satirical traits are outstanding, they are not mere caricatures, but real human beings. As Aryanpur comments, like Harpagon and Tartuffe and many Gogolian protagonists, his characters still live among us and carry on with their disagreeable activities.[13] Thus, he gives a vivid picture of the Azerbaijani society while laying emphasis on the social wrongs.

The first plays inspired by Akhundzade's works in Persian translation were left in manuscript form for many years, and when they were finally published they were considered to have been from the pen of Mirza Malkum Khan. In 1871 Mirza Aqa Tabrizi, first secretary to the French embassy in Tehran and an ardent admire of Akhundzade, wrote four plays. In 1908, while the plays were being serialized in the Tabriz newspaper *Ettehad* [Unity], Mohammad 'Ali Shah shelled the Parliament, an act which resulted in the closure of all the newspapers. In 1922 three of the plays were discovered in the library of the German orientalist Friedrich Rosen and were published in Berlin as the plays of Mirza Malkum Khan. Under his supposed authorship several translations and editions of the plays appeared in the succeeding years, but it was not until very recently that the original manuscript was found in Baku at the Akhundzade Archives, revealing the true identity of the author.[14] Except for a few points that Mirza Aqa mentioned in his letters to Akhundzade, we have very little information about his life. We know that he knew French and Russian and that he was between thirty and forty years old when he wrote his plays. According to his own account, he taught for some years at Dar al-Fonun and served on political missions to both Istanbul and Baghdad.

The first play in the collection by Mirza Aqa is *The Story of Ashraf Khan, the Governor of Arabestan*, which describes how governorships of various cities are sold by the authorities in Tehran to the highest bidder. *The Story of Shah Qoli Mirza's Travel to Kermanshah* and *The Method of the Governorship of Zaman Khan in Borujerd* both describe how the governors reap the profits of their investments. The former is the farcical account of a cowardly and foolish prince who wants to extort money from the people of Kermanshah, but who falls victim to the ruses of his nephew. The last play, *The Love Affair of Aqa Hashem Khalkhali*, criticizes prearranged marriages and the fact that the wealth of one family prevents the marriage of two young lovers.

Although Mirza Aqa says that he has followed the example of Akhundzade, he is not very familiar with western dramatic techniques. In a letter to the playwright Akhundzade praises his talents but says that "the plays are more for reading than putting on the stage."[15] Then he goes on to give Mirza Aqa a detailed description of what a playhouse looks like and what the characteristics of a play should be.[16] Auguste Bricteux, who translated the first three of Tabrizi's plays into French, remarks that they are not "real comedies in the proper sense of the term, but rather farces (the *Schwanke* as Rosen calls it) or, if we want to use a less uncivil word, sketches or scenes with dialogues: innumerable changes of the scenes make it impossible to stage the plays, whereas they will go wondrously well on the screen."[17] However, the dialogues are very lively and the author captures the peculiarities of each character's speech remarkably well. One interesting example is found in the first act of *Zaman Khan* in which the governor is attempting to extort money from an Armenian tavernkeeper. The latter's Armenian accent and mode of speech are interestingly reproduced.

The themes of the plays are like those of Akhundzade, satirizing mainly the corruption of the government. Bricteux writes:

> They are masterpieces of humor, a kind of comedy which brings to mind the most hilarious pages of Molière in his early works (other works that I have seen are *Doctor Knock* by Jules Romains and *The Inspector General*.) And what is terrible is the fact these irresistible comedies are the result of a sincere presentation of reality. In the adventures of *Ashraf Khan* he has to suffer long days of extortion and blackmail in order to obtain his robe of honor of the governorship; in *The Method of the Governorship of Zaman Khan* money is forced out of an Armenian wine seller and a prostitute. . . . All this could have happened in the Iran of a hundred years ago, and long after that.[18]

Here is a short passage from the second play in the collection. Zaman Khan wants to be an exemplary governor in Borujerd, but his friends urge him to be like other governors. Ferrash-bashi, the chief constable, and his deputy are on hand to help:

Mirza Jahangir Khan. [*To* Khan, *the governor*]. My dear Khan, it's all your fault. The steward is right. You cannot govern like this. No income, nothing. People like you have one hundred tomans as income every day. After all the man who washes the dead is not responsible for sending him to heaven or hell. While you are the governor for a short time, try to save some money and go your way. To hell with the people! One who rules them does not care for them, why should you? These governorships don't last forever. Tomorrow someone might come and pay more and get the job, then you will be left in the corner of your house in Tehran. . . . Jail this, arrest that, use bribery to get some income! How long will this inertia last?

Governor. [*Aside.*] These hangers-on won't let me stay honest. [*Aloud.*] You're right, but this is the fault of Chief Ferrash.[19]

Chief Ferrash. Your Excellency, where have I gone wrong? Where have I failed you?

Governor. What promises have you given me, or what sources of income have you shown me? It's been a long time since you've rounded up any drunks or prostitutes, or stirred up any brawls to get some money. . . . Either you don't know your job or you're not telling me the truth. Which one is it?

Chief Ferrash. [*Aside.*] Surely the memory of the Khan fails him. The day before he was advising me differently. Now he says something else. [*Aloud.*] I don't know what Your Excellency means.

Governor. I have paid my dues to the central government, and the fact is that I am short of money nowadays. Try to find a drunkard, a prostitute, a source of income! This can't go on.

Chief Ferrash. You just allow me to show my services. The day before you were advising me to the contrary. [*He comes out and calls.*] Boys! One of you go and call Sergeant Qasem. [*The* Sergeant *comes and bows.*] Sergeant!

Sergeant. Yes, Sir.

Chief Ferrash. These days the governor is short of money and can't make ends meet.

Sergeant. Then what shall we do, Chief?
Chief Ferrash. Go and see if you can get one of the top prostitutes and get
    forty or fifty tomans out of her.
Sergeant. Which one and how?
Chief Ferrash. Where's the lady from Kashan?
Sergeant. She's gotten married.
Chief Ferrash. What is the Shirazi Beygum up to?
Sergeant. She's come down with clap.
Chief Ferrash. How about Sakineh?[20]
Sergeant. Her? She's gotten old and become a madame.
Chief Ferrash. What is the curly Zivar doing?
Sergeant. These are her golden days. She has become the mistress of the
    stable master, and even the elephant cannot talk to her.
Chief Ferrash. Aha! I've got it! Kowkab Shahverdi-khani! There's nobody
    better. A femme fatale, a crook and a con artist. She knows every trick
    in the book. Have her set up one of those fat cats and then grab him.
    Maybe two or three hundred will come of it.
Sergeant. Yes, Chief, you're right. That's a fine plan.[21]

The strategem works. Kowkab invites an old lover, the wealthy Hajji Rajab,
to her house, and according to their plan the sergeant bursts in upon them,
threatening to arrest her. Eventually she makes him leave, but the next morning
Hajji Rajab sends three hundred tomans to Kowkab to be given to the sergeant.
Of this, half goes to the governor. Meanwhile, Chief Ferrash pays a courtesy
call on the Hajji and receives his share.

One of the early plays in Persian exhibiting western influence was written
by Mohammad Taher Mirza (1835-99), who spent five years at the University
of Al-Azhar in Cairo studying Islamic subjects. He was well versed in English
and French, and apart from writing several historical novels, he translated a
number of works by Alexandre Dumas *père* into Persian. Although he was a
cousin of Naser al-Din Shah and greatly respected by him, Mohammad Taher
Mirza never accepted any official post, devoting his life rather to translating
and writing.

The Marriage of Mirza was published in 1905 after the death of the author.
The story is fairly simple: an old prince's dilemma is whether or not to marry
a beautiful woman of twenty, as he doubts she would be faithful. He consults
two well-known philosophers, but they are of no help on the subject. One is
so absorbed in philosophical argumentation with an imaginary interlocutor that
he pays no attention to Mirza; the second is so nonsensically evasive in his
answers that he might as well have remained silent. The author masterfully
satirizes the pedantry in which philosophers too often wrap their commonplace
thoughts. Eventually, Mirza discovers that his beloved is in love with a younger
man and wants to marry Mirza only for his position. Now he has to choose
between a life of cuckoldry and his dignity. His choice of the former is yet another
satirical flourish added by the playwright.[22]

Production of these early Persian dramatic works had to wait. Prior to the Constitutional Revolution there were neither theatrical troupes nor public playhouses in Tehran. The first professional troupe was formed in Tabriz in 1909 and performed a play there in honor of Sattar Khan at the Garden of Arg. Among the theatrical troupes established before 1921 three were outstanding: "Khayriye" (1912), "Shirqoli Qolizade Reza" (1919), and "Buyuk Khan Nakhjovansky" (1919). These were mostly dominated by Armenians or migrés from the Caucasus, who performed their plays at a private theater called Soleil or at the Aramiyan School. In 1926 a playhouse called Te'atr-e Shir va Khorshid [Lion and sun] was built at the same Arg Garden. Quickly becoming a center of dramatic activity, its opening marked the beginning of a new era in Azerbaijani theater.[23]

The other city noted for its theater companies was Rasht; its first troupe began performing in 1918. One of the most talented actors of Iran, Aqa Da'i Namayeshi, was a prominent figure among them. Most of the plays performed were either imitations of Molière's works or works of Azerbaijani or Armenian playwrights. In Tehran the first troupe was "Sherkat-e Farhang" [Farhang Company], which began its performances in various parks of the city around 1921. A second troupe, which also began in 1921, was "Te'atr-e Melli," which staged plays by Molière and Gogol and a few Azerbaijani works, but did not last long. "Komedi-ye Iran" was formed in 1926 with the help of a number of talented actors and playwrights and lasted for ten years. An interesting feature of this troupe was that the roles of women, which until then had always been performed by men, were given to women. "Iran-e-Javan" [Young Iran] (1932) was the theatrical company that performed the famous comedy *Ja'far Khan Is Back from Europe* by Hasan Moqaddam, a work to be discussed shortly. The last troupe of Tehran was "Komedi-ye Musiqal" (1930), whose director was the well-known composer and playwright, Reza Shahrizad. This troupe was influenced by Caucasian musical comedies; two of the most successful works it presented were the Azerbaijani operettas *Arshin Mal Alan* and *Mashdi 'Ibad*.[24] Most of the plays performed by these troupes, whether of foreign origin or written by Iranians, were satirical comedies. Although there were nationalistic, historical, and didactic works as well, the attempt to reform society through satire and criticism was a foremost consideration. Next, from among numerous plays that were published and performed in this early era of Persian theater, I will review a few playwrights whose work falls into the category of satire.

One of the playwrights of this time is Mirza Ahmad Mahmudi (1875-1931), a graduate of Dar al-Fonun, who worked in the Foreign Office and later in the Ministry of Finance. Throughout his official career he was bitterly opposed to administrative corruption, and suffered imprisonment for his stance. Altogether he wrote seven plays, mostly satirical comedies. Two among them deserve attention. *Hajji Riya'i Khan* or *The Oriental Tartuffe* was written in 1918 when there was a famine in Iran. The play is a poor imitation of Moliére's masterpiece, basically a critique of the contradiction between pretentions and deeds. Hajji Riya'i is not a religious hypocrite like Tartuffe but rather a miser who wants to pass for a great and charitable humanist. While his own family is left unattended, he pays sycophantic journalists to tell the public how he saved many starving families. But very few are fooled by him—both his friends and his servants know his true nature. At the end he pays for his hypocrisy with the life of his son who dies because of a lack of attention and medication. Unlike *Tartuffe*, which is one of Moliére's greatest works, *Hajji Riya'i* is crudely conceived and written. There are several farcical scenes that contrast with the general didactic tone of the play. It has been said the Hajji Riya'i was a caricature of a famous politician who had made huge profits by hoarding grain. When the play was staged at the Grand Hotel of Tehran, the actor playing Hajji Riya'i's part had dressed like that politician and was recognized as him by the spectators.[25]

Ostad Nowruz Pineh-Duz [Master Nowruz, the cobbler] (1919) is a better constructed and written work than the first play. It is a satire on polygamy and the whimsical desire of some Persian men to marry a new wife every now and then. The cobbler, who already has two wives, meets a young widow and borrows some money at high interest to marry her. The two wives, who are forced out of the house by a sudden change in the temper of their husband, plot to come back and catch him on the wedding night before the whole affair goes too far. This play is an admixture of farcical comedy and satire, but the characteristic that distinguishes it from previous plays is that the author for the first time writes his dialogue in colloquial Persian. This was a turning point in Persian drama; previously the formal language had always been used.[25]

Another outstanding playwright of this period was Hasan Moqaddam (1898-1925), who was educated in Switzerland and wrote in French, English, and Persian. For two years he taught Persian at the Iranians' School of Istanbul, and then he joined the Foreign Ministry of Iran. He traveled widely in Europe and North Africa and had an intimate knowledge of French and English literature. He had many great European friends with whom he corresponded, such as André Gide, Igor Stravinsky, and Charles F. Ramuz. Moqaddam was one of the most gifted writers of Iran, whose talents never came to full bloom.

Shortly after the First World War Moqaddam formed a society named Iran-e Javan, which had as it members many western-educated, liberal Iranians. They aimed at bringing their country into the twentieth century. Moqaddam's play, *Ja'far Khan Is Back from Europe*, which was performed at the Grand Hotel of Tehran in 1922, was written in this connection. It satirizes the snobbishness and affected speech used by many westernized Iranians. It skillfully juxtaposes the contradictory modes of life in the East and West and invokes laughter because of the lack of communication between the two. The play was an immediate success. It introduced two expressions into the Persian language: first, the title of the play came to refer to a person who has become so westernized that he snubs his own countrymen; the second, a variant of the first, is the phrase "Ja'far Khan has gone to Europe and has come back as Mr. Jeffrey," meaning that he has even changed his name.

The following is an excerpt from scene 5:

Mashdi Akbar, Ja'far Khan, Carotte (his dog)

Jaf'ar Khan is dressed in a grey coat and trousers, the latest fashion of Paris.
The trousers should be well-pressed, the collar soft, necktie, pochette and
socks of the same color. A rain coat with a belt, a pair of lemon-colored
gloves. A great deal of dust on his shoes and hat. As he enters he has
a small suitcase in his right hand, and the leash of his small poodle in
his left. Behind Ja'far Khan, Mashdi Akbar enters, carrying several
walking sticks, umbrellas, and some other luggage, which he puts down.
Ja'far Khan speaks Persian with difficulty.

> Ja'far Khan. [Putting his suitcase down.] Oh, enfin, we've arrived. But it was
> long! The way was full of dust and "microbes"! [With his handkerchief
> he wipes his shoes and hat, and putting his hat on the table tells the dog.] Ici,
> Carotte! [He looks at his wristwatch.] This morning at fifteen past seven
> we set off from Yengi Emam.[27] It took us exactly eight hours and
> twenty-three minutes to reach here.
> Mashdi Akbar. Well, Sir, God willing,[28] these years have been good to you.
> Ja'far Khan. No, it was not bad. How does it go with you,[29] Mashdi Akbar?
> Are you still alive?
> Mashdi Akbar. By your leave, we are still here. God be praised, our master
> has returned from Europe and God willing he will take a wife for
> himself . . .
> Ja'far Khan. For myself? No, Mashdi Akbar, you are mistaken. No one
> marries for himself. [to his dog.] N'est-ce pas Carotte? [To Mashdi Akbar.]
> Give me my "valise" please.
> Mashdi Akbar. What, Sir?
> Ja'far Khan. Takes the suitcase from Mashdi Akbar and opens it. He brings
> out a number of things and puts them on the table among them a brush, a
> French book, a spray-bottle of cologne, and a comb.] Where is
> Madame . . . Mother?
> Mashdi Akbar. She is coming, Sir.
> Ja'far Khan. [He gives the leash of the dog to Mashdi Akbar.] Hold this, Mashdi
> Akbar.
> Mashdi Akbar. But, Sir, it is unclean
> Ja'far Khan. Carotte unclean? She is cleaner than you a hundred times. I
> shampoo her every morning. Allons, Carotte, allons! [Mashdi Akbar holds
> the leash, but tries to stand far away from the dog.].
> Mashdi Akbar. [Muttering.] What a thing to do! After eighty years of being
> a Musulman, now I have become a dogkeeper!
> Ja'far Khan. The air is too stuffy, it must be full of "microbes"! [He begins
> spraying the cologne around.]
> Mashdi Akbar. By the way, Sir, was there nothing else to bring that you
> brought this dog for us, and even at that a European dog! For instance
> you could have brought a pair of glasses for me.
> Ja'far Khan. Glasses? What for?
> Mashdi Akbar. Sir I have become old. My ears don't hear; my eyes don't see.
> Ja'far Khan. Mashdi Akbar, what age do you have?[30]
> Mashdi Akbar. When the late master, your grandfather, returned from
> Europe with the martyred king[31] —you were not born yet—I remember
> that year the mistress lost two teeth—[He calculates.] Twenty year here

and twenty-five there—This makes fifty-six . . . fifty-six and we have seventeen
  there . . . . I must be eighty or eighty-five years old.
Ja'far Khan. Eighty-five! This is really a bad habit for one's health. You have
  to give this habit up.
Mashdi Akbar. Bad habit?
Ja'far Khan. Yes, if a person wants to live according to the system and rules,
  he has to die after seventy years. This is a very bad habit for one's health.
  [*He comes to stage front and talks to himself.*] I should take a shower, clean
  myself. It's five o'clock. I made an appointment to go to the house of
  Madame Halvapazov.[32]

After incredible scenes of misunderstanding in which the entire group of
superstitious relatives are confronted with the ideas of this dandified youth, Ja'far
Khan decides to forego his prearranged marriage with his traditionally raised
cousin, Zinat, as well as his good position in Iran and return to France:

Ja'far Khan, the Uncle, Mother, Mashdi Akbar, Zinat, Carotte
Zinat. [*Holding the dog's leash.*] I am sick and tired of this dog. It has gone into
  the closet and eaten all our wax, oil, candles and sweets.[33]
Mother. To hell with the sweets! Your husband is leaving! Don't let him go!
Ja'far Khan. [*Very angry to the end of the scene*]. We give up. We give up being
  a minister, being a deputy, we give up a carriage and an automobile . . . .
  We will return to our own heretics,[34] and there we will eat pork and olive
  oil! *Allons, Carotte, allons!* This country is no good for us!
Uncle. Didn't I say that Europe makes people crazy?[35]

Another playwright who was greatly influenced by Akhundzade was Mortaza
Qoli Fekri (1868-1917), who published four plays and acted in some of them.
He was a liberal politician, journalist, and a Sufi of the Safi 'Ali-Shahi order.
Earlier in his life he had served as the governor of Mazandaran, Iraq-e Ajam
and Golpaigan. Being strongly opposed to Mohammad 'Ali Shah's despotic rule,
he gave up his government post and devoted himself to journalism. After the
shelling of the *Majles* he fled the country and for one year wandered in Turkey,
Syria, and the Caucasus. Except for his historical drama, *Cyrus the Great*, his
plays are all strongly critical of contemporary social conditions.

Outstanding among his plays is *Hokkam-e jadid, hokkam-e qadim* [Old and new
governors], which was published and produced in 1915. It is a fairly long play
in three acts with the story spanning twelve years. Muzakhraf al-Molk "His
Excellency, Mr. Nonsense" is a ruthless and tyrannical governor who has spent
nearly forty -thousand tomans in order to get the governorships Sulegan and
Sungar, and now wants to recover double or triple that amount through extortion
and bribery. He is so flagrantly corrupt that the central government is eventually
forced to dismiss him. The second act occurs ten years later when the
Constitutional Revolution has taken place and the whole system has changed.
His son, Jahed al-Molk, has become the governor of Shahristanak. He is

surrounded by several old crooks from his father's office, and he behaves exactly as his father did. People resist him and he too is dismissed. In the third act, Muzakhraf has come to Tehran, trying simultaneously to get his job back and to fight the plaintiffs who are suing him in court. Though people are supposedly protected by democratic laws, money still plays its old role. The court rules in favor of the former governor, condemning his adversaries for the most ridiculous reasons.[36] Though written as a satirical work, the play lacks humor, and its story leaves much to be desired.

On the subject of the Qajar administrative system there is a very interesting and much more humorous play by Zabih Behruz (1889-1971) entitled *Jijak-Ali Shah* (1923) whose subtitle is *Avzaʿdarbar-e Qajar* [The state of affairs in the Qajar court]. The story takes place in three locations: the court of Naser al-Din Shah, the house of Tehran's Beglar Begi (governor), and the house of Emir Davvab, the stablemaster. Behruz wants to show that the same irrational and despotic atmosphere that makes people hypocritical and sycophantic at the courts also exists in lower circles. In other words, when the system is autocratic, every official becomes a tyrant toward his subordinates. Beglar Begi does not care about the numerous plaintiffs who crowd his quarters—he prefers to listen to his friend the poet. After the play opens at the house of Beglar Begi, who passes the most ridiculous judgments on cases brought before him and is praised for his extraordinary wisdom, the play moves to the court of Tehran. The poet laureate at the court recites an incredible panegyric on the king, and the court historian reads the daily report in immoderately florid language. The report says that locusts have destroyed all of the crops of Sistan and Kerman; "His Gracious Majesty" has told the people to eat something else and pray for the Shah's health. In another province some hard-pressed soldiers have revolted and asked for their unpaid salaries. They are ordered to be hanged, because, though they may be starving, the first duty of a soldier is "to sacrifice himself for the Shah."[37] In the second act, the stablemaster, a semiliterate tribal chief with a Turkish accent, who is continuously being teased by the jester Karim Shire'i, becomes an important figure. In the hope of becoming a favorite with the Shah, he tries to write poetry. Having no talents of any kind, he asks his secretary to write a panegyric and, upon the latter's refusal, beats him up. The secretary then writes the poem, but the stablemaster fails to read it correctly in front of the Shah, thus becoming the laughingstock of the court. The poor secretary receives a second beating on this account.

The plot is not very significant, but rather it is the language and skillful imitation of the various modes of speech and style that play an important part in this satirical comedy. Zabih Behruz cleverly parodies the panegyrics of the court poets as well as the prose style of the court historian. The poem written on the Shah, which the stablemaster claims to have composed himself, is in fact written by his secretary, and it is an interesting example of the satirical manipulation of language. When the semiliterate stablemaster reads it in his Turkish accent misconstruing half of the words, it becomes ridiculously offensive.

The Persian ambassador to Belgium affects an unintelligible French accent when speaking Persian, only regaining his native fluency after being properly bastinadoed. Karim Shire'i, the jester, is an outstanding character who has something of the boldness and adroitness of Shakespearean jesters. It is through him that Behruz satirizes the hollow traditions and hypocritical values honored at the court of Tehran. Another interesting character is the court cleric Oqianus al-'Olum ("The Ocean of Learning")—a clumsy hyprocrite who disguises his ignorance by using a sententious and heavily Arabicized speech. He claims to know everything, and when the Shah asks him if he has eaten "Belgium," he says, "Assuredly, Sire, I have eaten it either in Holy Kerbela or Blessed Najaf!"[38]

Behruz, who was educated at the American Schools of Tehran and Cairo, became an assistant to E. G. Browne at Cambridge for five years during the early part of his life. But, mostly he spent his life teaching and writing. In addition to *Me'raj Name*, a parody of the Prophet Mohammad's ascension to heaven, there is a satire in prose and poetry in imitation of Sa'di's *Gulestan* [Rose garden] called *Gandestan* [Foul land]. Recently this work was published for the first time.[39]

The second phase of Persian drama began with the reign of Reza Shah in 1925. He introduced a rigorous program of modernization and reform, which was what many writers, satirists, and reformists were asking for; but he systematically eliminated the democratic institutions that had resulted from the Constitutional Revolution. One of the great disservices that Reza Shah, and later his son, did to Iran during the fifty-three years of their combined reign was to stamp out the budding Iranian democracy. Consequently, under the unsparing censorship and the ruthless dictatorship of Reza Shah, Persian drama followed a different path. Patriotic and historical plays greatly increased in number, concentrating on the glories of the past. Two examples of these are *Maziyar* (1933) and *Parvin dokhtar-e Sasan* [Parvin the Daughter of Sasan] (1930) by Sadeq Hedayat. A number of musical plays were also written, of which the finest were from the pen of Reza Kamal, known as Shahrezad (1898-1937). He was one of the most talented pioneers of Persian drama, and among the many romantic musicals that he composed, *Parichehr va Parizad* (1921), *Shab-e Hezaro Yekom . . .* [Night one thousandth and one] (1928), and *Abbaseh Khahar-e-Amir* [Abbaseh the emir's sister] (1930) are the most famous. A third kind of dramatic production consisted of didactic social comedies that were basically in praise of the new way of life as contrasted with the old. Some of these plays were satirical, but their satire was mild and without any political implication. In staging most of these plays financial problems were often coupled with social ones. Theater-going had not become a very popular entertainment. In spite of the emancipation of women, the actresses, who were mostly Armenians, had a hard time establishing their respectability.

In connection with satirical social comedies, mention should be made of Seyyed 'Ali Nasr (1893-1965), who was also one of the founders of Persian drama. Though he had a busy administrative career and served as the Iranian ambassador to

India, China and the United Nations, among other posts, Nasr never gave up his lifelong love of the theater. Earlier he had helped form the Te'atr-e Melli troupe in Tehran, and a year later had gone to France to study drama. Upon his return he founded another troupe, Komedi-ye Iran, and in 1939 the Academy of Dramatic Arts. Up to the end of his life Nasr was active in the cause of the advancement of theater in Iran, and many of the later playwrights were his students. He wrote and translated from French and English some 100 plays, most of which he staged himself. Of these, thirty-two were his own original works, all except for some historical plays like *Cyrus*, the rest were social comedies. While some of them were mildly satirical, most were didactic, as the translation of some of their titles will suggest: *The Consequences of Polygamy*; *The Consequences of the Illiteracy of Women*; *As Long as We Are Like This, We'll Be the Same*; and *The Faithful Wife*. A typical play by Nasr is *'Arusi-e Hosain-Aqa* (The wedding of Hosain-Aqa) (1939) in which he focuses on social and educational enlightenment and criticizes ignorance and illiteracy.[40]

With the entry of the Allied forces into Iran and the abdication of Reza Shah in 1941, a new phase in Persian drama began that lasted until the CIA-engineered coup d'état of 1953 and institution of the former Shah's dictatorship. In this period, which witnessed the rise and fall of the truly popular premier, Dr. Mosaddeq, many pent-up political grievances found expression in journalism, literature, and drama. The atmosphere of political freedom combined with public support created almost a revolution in Persian drama. "In fact," and as Jannati Ata'i asserts, "modern theater in Iran came into existence in 1941."[41] Political parties sprang up, and in search of an effective means of subscribing public support they vied with each other in attracting writers, poets, and actors. The Persian Communist party, which was supported by the Soviets, attracted many talents. Among them were 'Abdul Hosain Nushin and Mohammad Khairkhah, brilliant actors who also wrote plays.[42] It was partly due to the personalities of these two men and to some of the other performers that the two newly founded theaters, Farhang and Ferdausi, surpassed others by staging a number of European and Persian plays. Unlike the previous period, most of the plays written in these years were political satires, criticizing not only the government but the very foundations of society as well. This heyday of Persian drama however did not last long. After Mosaddeq's government fell in 1953, the atmosphere changed drastically. Mohammad Reza Shah's regime began clamping down on the opposition, leftist and otherwise. Politically invloved actors, including Nushin[43] and Khairkhah were sentenced to prison. Such writers and poets as Buzurg 'Alavi and Mohammad 'Ali Afrashte fled the country.

One of the most interesting satirical plays of this period, one which illustrates the repressive police state of Reza Shah, is *Tup-e Lastiki* [The rubber ball] by Sadiq Chubak, published in 1949.[44] One must have lived under such repression in order to understand fully the pungent satire and vivid realism of the play. Apart from the interesting dialogue of the characters, Chubak, in his stage directions, describes the characters in the most graphic manner. The main figure,

Dalaki, the Minister of Internal Affairs under Reza Shah, is a cowardly and sycophantic figure. When the play opens he is standing in his own house in front of a picture of the Shah addressing it with the greatest humility. Farhad Mirza, his son-in-law, is one of those apathetic types, so cowardly that he must think before he even takes a breath. He continuously glances furtively at everyone from under his glasses, showing great suspicion. Colonel Su Su, Dalaki's brother-in-law, looks like an opium addict, and it seems that "he has been created to affirm other people's statements." Only Khosrow, the son of Dalaki by his first wife, is an outspoken, brave, and liberal young man.

The play opens with Dalaki's discovery of a policeman outside his house asking for his servant, Akbar, who happens to be away for a few days. The continued presence of the policeman in front of the house increases the minister's fear of a possible arrest. His wife urges him to remember all the things that he has said recently in the hope of finding a clue. But Dalaki is too discrete to have said anything. The couple start imagining possible reasons for the "imminent disgrace and arrest of the minister."[45] To his great dismay Dalaki hears that his son has recently started learning Russian in secret. Then Dalaki summons his son-in-law who, is a police colonel; the colonel arrives, but as soon as he finds out that a policeman has been hanging around for a few hours, decides he does not want to get implicated and leaves in a great hurry, feigning illness. The same is true of the other relatives who arrive soon afterword. The fear of the police is so great, and everyone is so suspicious of everyone else, that they are all convinced Dalaki must have said or done something to warrant the policeman's presence. The only person who is not crippled by fear is Khosrow, who urges them to act logically. When the minister has eventually become resigned to his fate and is ready to be arrested, the policeman asks permission to come in. He is very apologetic, and informs the minister that he does not want to inconvenience him, but that he has no other choice. While the policeman's wife was working for a colonel's wife down the street, his son was playing with a rubber ball belonging to the colonel's son. He explains that he has been forced by the colonel's wife to come to get the rubber ball that his son has kicked into Dalaki's garden.

The following excerpt from the play shows that the policeman's presence has frightened everyone except Khosrow, with the result that they try to keep aloof from Dalaki:

> *Khosrow.* Who has security in this damn country? One can't say a word. You're all like cardboard figures. You're all like characters in a puppet show! All his life this father of mine has been frightened by his own shadow . . . . When one man becomes the owner of the lives and properties of the people nothing better can be expected. All of you well deserve what you get!
>
> *Farhad.* [*As if speaking to himself.*] The boy is crazy. There is no one to restrain him. He needs a guardian. . . . What nonsense he talks.
>
> *Khosrow.* [*With sarcasm, he offensively interrupts.*] Sir, you mock yourself. All of you are afraid of each other. The wife is afraid of her husband. The

child is afraid of his father. The sister is afraid of her older brother. All fear, fear, and fear. Is this life? This is death! This is an abomination! Just imagine, in the university all my friends think I am a spy. What for? My father is a minister and everyone's afraid to speak in front of me. The teacher in class is afraid to express his opinions. I wish all of you were idol worshippers and that you would prostrate yourselves in front of the idol from morning to night. At least the idol does not hurt anyone. . . .

Farhad. [*Afraid and with a trembling voice.*] Dear Puran, I am leaving. It is not wise to stay here anymore. Didn't I tell you that this brother of yours has lost all his marbles? If you want to be with your father, there's no problem. You stay, I'm off; I'll send the car for you later. But you have no right to talk of such things. If you answer this boy it's finished between us.[46]

In the last phase of the development of Persian drama, which may be dated from 1953, new elements were introduced. In the 1950s, first Radio Tehran, and later other broadcasting stations in various cities, introduced radio plays as an important part of their programming. Most of these plays were moralistic, romantic, farcical, or satirical, but they very often lacked any literary or artistic value. Professor Yarshater writes of the authors of such works:

> A number of these playwrights continued the broad farcical tradition: their characters achieved humor through exaggerated attitudes, comical dialects, and affected speech. Whereas plays of ideas were rare, maudlin plays abounded. The Broadcasting Service did offer, however, valuable opportunities for actors and playwrights to exercise their talent. In recent years, radio playwrights have managed to broaden their range of subjects and improve their technique.[47]

A further stage of development came with the gradual expansion of the film industry and television networks in Iran. Many novelists and playwrights were able to offer their works to a larger audience. Among the works of prose fiction that were made into movies are Houshang Golshiri's *Shazdeh-Ehtijab*, Chubak's *Tangsir*, and Gholam-Hosain Sa'edi's *Aramesh dar Hozur-e Digaran* [Peace in the presence of the others] and *Ashghal-duni* [The rubbish heap]. The last work was shown in America as *The Cycle* and was favorably received. A number of plays were also made into films—for example, 'Ali Nassirian's *Halu* [The Dupe] (televised in 1964 and filmed in 1969) and Sa'edi's *Gav* [The cow], which was based on his work *'Azadaran-e Bayal* [The mourners of Bayal]. Numerous television plays and serials were also based on Iranian plays and works of fiction. Mention too should be made of Arham-e Sadr, a talented actor and producer, who had his own theater in Isfahan and occasionally made use of television as well. He adapted a number of well-known satirical comedies by European writers and skillfully put them into the context of Iranian life. Using the technique of the traditional *ru-howzi* farces, which gave the actor the opportunity of adding some spontaneous dialogue to the play, Arham-e Sadr became renowned for his pungently witty comments on current affairs.

The upsurge of the Iranian economy in the 1960s served as another impetus for the advancement of Persian drama. Through the efforts of the Ministry of Arts and Culture several drama schools were founded and the writing of plays for television encouraged. A large number of Western plays were translated into Persian, some of which were performed. The Art Festival of Shiraz, the pet project of Farah Pahlavi, lavishly celebrated each summer from 1967 to 1977, also had an impact. In these festivals a number of ta'ziyes were staged, but being performed out of their proper milieu they lacked their desired impact. The performance of many remarkable plays of both East and West was a characteristic feature of the Shiraz Festival. Special attention was paid to staging plays such as Beckett's *Waiting for Godot,* or such avant-garde works as Jerzy Grotowski's *Constant Prince.* No doubt all these plays had their impact on the development of Persian drama, but rather than serving as an impetus for an organic growth from inside, they seem to have been part of an ephemeral vogue. Most of these plays did not relate to Iranian life, and they were often seen and enjoyed by only a small group of the elite who were not at home in their own country to start with. One of the plays that was written under the influence of "the theater of the absurd" is *A Modern, Profound, and Important Research into the Fossils of the 25th Geological Era* by 'Abbas Na'lbandian, which was performed at the Shiraz Festival in 1968 and was later televised many times. Judged by modern western dramatic criteria, it is a successful play, and Professor Yarshater speaks glowingly of it;[48] but most of the Iranian critics who believe in a socially responsible literature and drama do not share his view.

In the 1960s and 1970s, under the changing social conditions and repressive censorship, many Iranian writers became more and more introverted, or, as A. Dastghayb remarks, "turned to their dark opium dreams."[49] Others cultivated the theater of the absurd. In this respect Gholam-Hosain Sa'edi is an exception. Hosain Sa'edi, whose short stories were discussed earlier, is without doubt one of the greatest playwrights of Iran. From 1960 until his dealth in November 1985, Sa'edi published more than twenty plays and film scripts mostly under the pseudonym of Gowhar- Morad. Sa'edi's talent is more fully realized in his drama than in his novels and stories, and he has always confined his works to the context of Iranian society. As his two decades of political activity and nearly one year of harsh imprisonment showed, Sa'edi did not separate his work from his commitment to his country. In his plays Sa'edi presents a wide spectrum of Iranian society. Village and city life receive equal attention in the context of a changing and typically third-world country where poverty, political repression, exploitation, and newly imposed western values are dominant. Changes in the lives of middle- and lower-class urban populations, many social grievances, and the resulting mental disorders are scrutinized with an insight worthy of an able psychoanalyst. His characters are often lonely individuals lost in the wasteland of modern society, their viciousness is not inborn but rather the product of their social milieu.

Satire does not play a prominent role in the works of Sa'edi. Analysis of the human mind, depiction of its workings, and indirect criticism of society are the most outstanding elements of his works. Sometimes, as in his play *Dikte* [Dictation] (1969), where absolute compliance with the status quo is a prerequisite for prosperity and a good life, or in his *Ma Namishnavim* [We don't hear] (1970), where the government's animosity toward the opposition is epitomized, criticism is conveyed in the form of allegory. In these plays the individual events are not satirical, but the overall effect is. On the other hand, some of his plays are unadulterated satire. The following work is a case in point.

Ay bi-kolah, Ay-e ba-kolah [Long A Short A] (first performed and published in 1967) is a satirical commentary on human nature and its workings. An old man has seen a terrifying giant enter a vacant house in the neighborhood. The fear-stricken neighbors, awakened by him, accept whatever he tells them. The most level-headed man in the group is a "man on the balcony" whose teasing but sensible comments are often ignored. It seems that he has been disillusioned by the duplicity presented by the people in the face of their social duties. This duplicity is further evidenced by a doctor in the play, who despite his pretension of responsible behavior does not want his car to be used in fetching a policeman. The first act ends when a poor old woman emerges from the house with her huge rag doll. In the second act a number of bandits enter the same vacant house, and they are seen by the same two men. People are again awakened, but this time they are incredulous. The man on the balcony is ridiculed and abused; the old man is forced to take some sleeping tablets. The doctor takes some tablets himself and gives some to the neighbors. While they sleep happily, the bandits rob their houses. Sa'edi here explores the absurd side of human nature with an acute psychological insight.

Chub-be-dastha-ye Varazil [The club-wielders of Varazil] (first performed and published in 1965) is not basically a satirical play, but it has a satirical overtone. It is a sociopolitical allegory of the third world's dependence on the industrialized powers. The villagers of Varazil are in search of someone to save them from wild boars that destroy their crops. With the help of a certain Monsieur Tavus, they hire two hunters and promise them lodging and food. The hunters kill the boars, but they then in effect replace them by consuming all the meager resources of the villagers. Again, through the good offices of Tavus, they hire two more hunters to drive out the first ones. In the dramatic final scene, the newcomers, who have also depleted the resources of the villagers, take aim at the former hunters, but then suddenly turn towards the shocked and panic-stricken villagers, who run off the stage.

A similar theme is treated in a much more satirical vein in *Khosha be-hal-i bord baran* [Happy are the patient ones]. An old couple decide to be exceptionally kind to their young maid so that she will not leave them. Before long she becomes the virtual mistress of the house and the couple are no match for her. After many humorous incidents, climaxed by the maid's theft of the last of their worldly possessions, they belatedly come to understand the situation. *'Aqibat-e Qalam-*

farsa'i (1976) [The consequences of penmanship] humorously describes the dilemma of a writer who has to produce for a magazine a popular serial full of passion and adventure. He is so desperate for a new story that he asks his servant to concoct a tale. The man's colorlessly mundane notions on sex and marriage in his village fall far short of the writer's expectations, however. An old beggar then knocks at the door. The writer invites him in and, entertaining him with food and drink, asks him to relate an interesting experience from his life. The old man, who has had similar experiences with other writers, makes up a story, and after getting forty tomans, is ready to make it more interesting for more money. The characters are depicted with the remarkable insight and dramatic deftness that is peculiar to Sa'edi's plays. The satirical effect of the play results from the fact that the reality of life and the stories of the writers are strangely at variance, yet the latter are what people crave.

The same collection contains another play entitled *In be-an-dar ya Qaziyeh-ye Namusparastan* [Tit for tat], which is a satirical comedy in one act with two middle-aged men as its main characters. Imani meets Farmani in a sauna bath, and they like each other tremendously. Imani, who plans to catch a girl who has seduced his son, brings his friend into the action as well, and both men await the arrival of the young lovers. Their conversation, which forms the bulk of the play, is fascinating in its uncovering of their double-standard morality. Imani is ready to justify and forgive whatever his son is doing, while he is very harsh in his judgment of the girl who is involved in the affair. Farmani is no better, and they both represent types who set high moral standards for other people to observe. Amusingly enough the girl turns out to be Farmani's daughter, and this brings the two "great" friends to blows.

The word *satire* cannot be easily used to describe some of the works of Sa'edi; perhaps "black humor" would be a more appropriate designation. *Parvar-bandan* [The livestock farmers], (1969) is a case in point. A young writer now is very critical of his country's affairs is "hidden" by his friends on a livestock farm, as several witnesses have testified that the writer has assassinated one of his opponents. However, even though they claim to show every kindness and consideration toward their talented "dear one," this hiding proves to be really a detention. They are joined by the writer's father, uncle, and former professor all critical of his ideas and especially of his "ingratitude" toward his hosts. In the third act the writer is tried by these people, and since he refuses to speak, another person speaks for him. Eventually the "friendly" judge becomes very angry and beats him up, claiming that he is doing this out of "love" for the revolutionary writer. Afterward, while everyone is enjoying a sumptuous dinner, the writer jumps from the window and escapes. One of the "friends" takes a revolver and shoots him. They all return to the table with great gusto.

The Livestock Farmers is typical of the many plays and works of fiction that were written during the last decades of the former Shah's reign. The challenge to the stage artist is to convey his political message without seeming to agitate anyone. To achieve this purpose he combines a parablelike plot with a shrewd use of irony. In Saʻedi's *The Livestock Farmers*, everyone advises the young writer not to rock the boat; similarly in *Dikte* [Dictation] everyone urges the "Failing Student" to take the "dictation" without asking any questions so that like the "Top Student" he will receive prizes and have a prosperous life. Though *The Livestock Farmers* ends in tragedy, its satirical overtone is unmistakable. The compromising and conciliatory attitude of the people who surround the writer when they face the powerful is interestingly ridiculed. The trial of the writer is very much reminiscent of the military trials under the Shah in which the defense lawyers would speak for the political prisoner while his family would plead for clemency on the grounds that the prisoner was young, rash, and ungrateful. Saʻedi's drama explores the dilemmas of the modern state—rebellion versus freedom, and conformity versus control—in such a way that it has universal pertinence. He combines the psychological methods used by Tennessee Williams and the concern for society expressed by Chekhov and Brecht. Like Brecht he forces his audience to discover political connections by surprising them and making them think. And from this emerges his use of satire.

One of the last playwrights of modern Iran to be mentioned here is Bizhan Mofid (d. 1985) whose musical satire *Shahr-e Qesse* (The city of fable) was first staged in 1968 at the Festival of Shiraz. Mofid has based his play on a folk tale and uses animals to represent different types of people in Iranian society. Apart from various animals there are three characters who appear without animals masks: The Narrator; Khaleh Suskeh ("Aunty Beetle"); and Mouse. These two appear as children ranging in age from ten to twelve. Traditionally, in this folk tale the hand of Khaleh Suskeh is sought by various animals who describe what they will do for her if she marries them. But all are rejected except the romantic Mouse, who wins her love. Combined with this children's tale is the story of the elephant who loses one of his tusks in an accident. Since there is no dentist or hospital in "the Wonderful City of Fable," his other tusk is taken out as well. Later on his tusks are fixed to his head and his trunk is cut off in order to make him look like a cow. His sad case represents the person who, in trying to conform to artificial social values, loses his own identity. Woven into the fabric of these two stories are many satirical comments on various aspects of modern Iranian society, ranging from the absurdity of some modern poems to a general trend toward excessive westernization. Mofid writes, "the City of Fable is the painful story of the man whose life is limited by ignorance, superstition, traditions and repressive systems"[50] Unlike some of the plays of Saʻedi, *The City of Fable* is not a political satire. The writer is content with presenting mild social criticism. A short passage from the second scene, where Bear interviews the Narrator to employ her as a maid, is a fine sample of its technique. In the same scene the animals are frantically trying to learn English, since Iranian business life at that time was dominated by foreign firms; without knowing English, one had little chance of getting a good job:

Dog. From morning till night we do our best to learn a few words of English at least. Perhaps it will help us find a job one day.

Narrator. But, Sir, there's no need for English if you become a porter, a driver, a janitor or a grocer.

Monkey. [*To the others.*] It seems that our narrator knows nothing! [*To the Narrator.*] Now you go see Bear, the Astrologer, and ask him if he wants a maid. [The Narrator *hesitates a moment, then goes to* Bear.]

Narrator. Sir, don't you want a maid?

Bear. Well, what should I say? A maid? Not really. But perhaps I could do something for you.

Narrator. Much obliged, Sir.

Bear. . . .I know.

Narrator. May you live long.

Bear. . . .God willing.

Narrator. May your children prosper.

Bear. . . .God willing. Well, now, Miss, do you have a license to be a maid?

Narrator. Yes, Sir, of course. Here is it. [*She produces her licenses one after the other.*]

Bear. Let me see, cooking license?

Narrator. Here it is.

Bear. Diploma of dressmaking and embroidery?

Narrator. Here it is.

Bear. Typing.

Narrator. Here it is.

Bear. Well, weaving?

Narrator. Here it is.

Bear. Now, the certificate of . . .

Narrator. Here it is.

Bear. Now, the diploma of . . .

Narrator. Here it is.

Bear. Well, your measurements. Bust?

Narrator. Thirty-six.

Bear. Waist?

Narrator. Twenty-six.

Bear. Hips?

Narrator. Thirty-eight.

Bear. It's too much.

Fox. Leave it to me. [Bear *and* Fox *consult privately.*]

Bear. By the way, Miss, do you know English?

Narrator. No, Sir.

Bear. Tch, tch, tch . . . too bad.

Narrator. Why?

Bear. It's against regulations.

Narrator. Well, thank you very much. [*She returns to her place.*]

Bear. It's a pity. She was a cute maid.[51]

Another play worthy of mention here is *Majles-e Divan-e Balkh* [The court of the city of Balkh] (1969) by Bahram Beyza'i. This is an extremely long play in which the prevailing corruption of the government officials of Balkh is reflected in a story of the plight of a merchant's family. The main theme of the play seems to be a proverbial Persian poem that is used to describe an absolutely debased city:

> An ironsmith committed a crime in Balkh;
> A coppersmith's head was chopped off in Shushtar.

The original judge of the city is forced to resign and dies of a broken heart. The judge who replaces him has his own brand of justice. He has a box for "the poor" and the contributions to it drastically change the course of justice. The ironsmith of Balkh, who has killed the son of an old woman, manages to find favor with the judge so that a coppersmith is executed in his place. Though the play is satirical, the audience does not recognize that situation or person Beyza'i pillories.

In the last few years contemporary Persian drama has followed the trends of modern drama in the West. Brecht, Tennessee Williams, Beckett, Genêt, Ionesco, and many other masters of modern drama have left their imprint on Persian playwrights. Western influences combined with innovation and experimentation with both popular romance and folk motif give Persian drama vibrant diversity. After the 1979 revolution numerous theatrical groups were formed, and there was hardly a theater in Tehran or any other major cities of Iran without new activity. But the censorship of the Islamic government cut short the life of this fledging art as well as that of the Iranian film industry. In its most extreme manifestation a young poet and playwright, Sa'id Soltanpour, who insisted on staging his own works without the sanction of the government, lost his life in the summer of 1981, though his execution took place under a pretext. Gradually theatrical performances were eliminated altogether. For a time, except for occasional religious representations, no other plays were reproduced or performed. However, more recently, the Islamic government has discovered the great propaganda value of both plays and movies. Several state-sponsored film festivals, which have included titles from third-world countries as well as new Iranian films, have been little more than media for pro-government ideas. True satire of authority is virtually nonexistent in Iran today.

Ironically, the theatrical activities of the exiled Iranian community abroad have been significant. In addition to the production of some earlier works of Sa'edi and Mofid, there have been a good number of new plays produced both in Europe and the United States. *The Trial of Iraj Mirza* by Sadr al-Din Elahi, for instance, may serve as an example. It is a satirical play based on the anticlerical views of the poet Iraj Mirza. After being seen by some three thousand Iranians in London[53] in October 1982, it was taken to Paris in Feburary 1983. The theme of *Khar* [The ass], by Parviz Sayyad is similarly political; it was staged in 1983 by a group formed in Los Angeles and San Jose. *The Mission*, a recent film by the same actor/director, has received very favorable reviews from American critics.[54] Parviz Sayyad plays the role of a former general who has fled Iran and is forced to earn his living as a janitor in New York City. A young Islamic zealot, brainwashed into believing that every former official abroad is a millionaire living in luxury, is sent out to assassinate him. After finding out that, in fact everything is not so black and white, the young Islamic revolutionary is saved from being mugged in a New York subway one night by the general. A friendship develops between them which prevents the young man from carrying out his mission.

The most outstanding satirical play produced outside Iran recently is Gholam-Hosain Sa'edi's *Othello dar Sarzamin-e 'Ajaib* [Othello in Wonderland] (1984). Along with four screenplays this was one of the last works written by Sa'edi before his death in Paris in November 1985. *Othello* is being produced in Tehran, but before coming to the stage it requires approval by a panel of Islamic censors. Not only are the female characters of the play forced strictly to observe the Islamic dress (hijab), but also "brother Othello" is made into an incredible revolutionary who opposes "western values." The interpretation of the actors and the censors is hilariously different. When the latter talk of "the three principles," they are not referring to Aristotelean principles of drama—as imagined by the actors and the director—but rather principles propagated by the present regime of Iran. One of these is the continuation of the war with Iraq and the overthrow of its president. Accommodating such ideals within the framework of the Shakespearean play proves impossible. The language of each character is masterfully representative of the type that he or she represents. *Othello in Wonderland* is a well-constructed and well-written play and a severe criticism of the cultural ideals of the present regime of Iran.

Notes

1. For a list of orientalists who collected ta'ziyes see Abul-Qasem Jannati 'Ata'i, *Bonyad-e Namayesh dar Iran.* (Tehran: Ibn Sina, 1955), p. 31.
2. Ehsan Yarshater, "Development of Persian Drama in the Context of Cultural Confrontation," in *Iran: Continuity and Variety,* ed. Peter J. Chelkowski (New York, 1971), p. 25.
3. Quoted in Jannati 'Ata'i, *Bonyad-e Namayesh,* pp. 52-53.
4. Ibid.
5. Ibid., pp. 28-29.
6. Yahya Aryanpur, *Az Saba ta Nima,* 1:326.
7. Yahya Aryanpur, *Az Saba to Nima,* 2: p. 351.
8. Mirza Fath 'Ali Akhundazade, *Tamthilat,* trans. M. Ja'far Qarachedagi, (Tehran: Kharazami, 1970), pp. 8-9.
9. Quoted in Aryanpur, *Az Saba ta Nima,* 1: 355.
10. Feridun Adamiyat, *Andishe ha-ye Mirza Fath 'Ali Akhundzade,* (Tehran: Kharazmi, 1970); A. Vahap Yurtsever, *Mirza Fethali Ahund Zadenin Hayati ve Eserleri* (Ankara, 1950).
11. The literal translation of th title of the play is *The Bear who overpowered the Bandit.* The above-given title is that of a forthcoming translation of the play into English by the present writer.
12. This play was translated from the Persian by Guy Le Strange and W. H. Haggard (London:

Sampson Law, Marston & Ld., 1882). August Bricteaux translated *The Miser* and some of the plays of Mirza Aga Tabrizi into French, but he thought that Mirza Malkum Khan was the author not Mirza Agha Tabrizi. See *Les Comedies de Malkom Khan: Les mesaventures d'Ashraf Khan, Zama Khan ou le gouverneur modéle; Les tribulations de Chah Qouli Mirza,*Bibliothéque de la faculté d philosophie et lettres de l'université de Liége, 1933).

13. Aryanpur, *Az Saba ta Nima* 1: 356.

14. Mirza Aqa Tabrizi, *Panj Nemayeshname,* ed, H. Sadiq (Tehran: Nashr-e Ayndeh), pp. 5-20.

15. Mirza Aqa Tabrizi, *Chahar Te'atr* (Tehran: Nashr-e Ayendeh, 1977), p. 15.

16. Ibid., pp. 200-15. See also my article on "Mirza Agha Tabrizi" in *Encyclopaedia Iranica,* 1, Fascic 8., (London: Kegan & Paul).

17. *Les Comedies de Malkom Khan* p. 6.

18. Ibid., p. 6.

19. Chief of police, or sheriff.

20. In the original, "Sakineh, the skullcap maker."

21. Mirza Aqa Tabrizi, *Chahar Te'atr,* pp. 61-65.

22. For the text of the play, see Jannati 'Atai, *Bonyad-e Namayesh,* pp. 54-79.

23. For more on the subject, see *Az Saba ta Nima,* 2: 288-91 and Samad Behrangi, *Majmu'e-ye Maqala* (Berkeley, Calif.: 1978), Confederation of Iranian Students, pp. 193-96: "Nakhostin trup-ha-y te'atri dar Azerbaijan."

24. See *Az Saba ta Nima* 2: 292-93.

25. For the text of the play, see *Bonyad-e Namayesh dar Iran,* pp. 84-115; and for a discussion of see Aryanpur, *Az Saba to Nima,* 1: 294-95.

26. *Ja'far Khan Is Back From Europe:* a play by Hasan Moqadam. The Persian text with a French translation by the author and two essays on his life and works, ed. by Hasan Javadi (Oakland, Calif. 1984).

27. A place name.

28. *Inshallah!*

29. *Comment vas-tu?*

30. *Quel age as-tu?* (Che senn dari?)

31. I.e., Naser al-Din Shah who was assassinated in 1896.

32. A humorous name, the daughter of a halva maker in Russified form.

33. All these are ritualistic celebration objects.

34. *Kafer:* heretic, unbeliever.

35. *Ja'far Khan Is Back From Europe,* pp. 8-41.

36. The text of the play is printed by Jannati 'Ata'i, *Bonyad-e Namayesh,* pp. 119-77.

37. Z. Behruz, *Jijak-Ali Shah* (Tehran, n.d.), p. 36.

38. Ibid., p. 63.

39. For the life of Behruz, see an obituary by Iraj Afshar in *Rahnama-ye-Ketab* 14 (1971): also Sa'id Enayat, 'Honar Nevisandegi-ye Behruz," Ibid., pp. 725-27.

40. The text of this play is reprinted by Jannati 'Atai in his *Bonyad-e Namayesh,* pp. 231-56. For Nasr's life and works, see also 'Ali Nasirian's article on Persian theater in *Kaveh* (Munich) 1, no. 3 (July 1963): 188-89.

41. *Bonyad-e Nomayesh* p. 82.

42. See on M. Khairkhah, *Kaveh* 4, no. 4 (January 1967): 255-60.

43. Nushin wrote a number of satirical works among which the most outstanding were *Khan va Digaran* (Khan and others) (pub. 1959) and *Khorus-e Sahar* (The morning rooster) (1947). After the attempt on the life of the ex-Shah in 1949, he was sentenced to three years imprisonment along with several other members of the Central Committee of the Communist party. In prison he wrote a book on Persian drama entitled *Honar-e Te'atr* (pub. 1952). See Buzurg 'Alavi, *Geschichte und Entwicklung der Modernen Persichen Literatur* (Berlin: Akademie Verlag, 1964), pp. 216-18.

44. It is published with *Antari ke Lutiyash Morde Bud,* 5th ed. (Javidan Publications, 1973).

45. Ibid., p. 123.

46. Chubak, "Tup-e Lastiki," in *Antarike Latiysh Morde Bud* (Tehran: Javidan Publications, 1973), pp. 172-74.
47. E. Yashater, "Development of Persian Drama," p. 32.
48. For an analysis of this play, see E. Yarshater, "Development of Persian Drama," p. 37.
49. A. Dastghayb, *Naqd-e Asar-e Gholam-Hosain Sa'edi* (Tehran: Farhang, 1973), p. 71.
50. Bizhan Mofid, *Shahr-e Qesse* (Tehran: Farhangva Honar, 1971) Introduction.
51. Bizhan Mofid, *Shahr-e Qesse* pp. 59-62.
52. Cf. A. A. Dehkhoda, *Amthal va Hikam*, 3: 132.
53. *Asghar Agha*, no. 146, 19 February 1983, p. 8.
54. For instance see Vincent Canby, "The Mission: Exiles from Iran in U.S.," *The New York Times*, 30 March 1983, C21.

Postscript

In the present state of the world it is difficult
not to write lampoons.

—Juvenal

While pursuing the history of Iranian satire we have taken note of various social and political events that had considerable impact on the literature and journalism of Iran, and this study will not be complete without taking into consideration the revolution that took place in February of 1979. The coming to power of the Islamic Fundamentalists changed Iran into a theocratic state beyond the wildest imagination of many Iranians, and subsequent events such as the hostage crisis, the ongoing war with Iraq, and the elimination of various political groups have had far-reaching effects on the social and cultural life of the country.[1]

At the outset of the revolution, when the dam of the Shah's censorship gave way, a torrent of publications poured forth whose variety and number were unprecedented in the modern history of Iran. No precise total of the number of new books and publications for the years 1979-80 is available, but according to one account the number exceeds all those published in the last ten years of the former Shah's reign.[2] These consisted mainly of previously forbidden books, new translations of various revolutionary works, political tracts (whether Marxist or Islamic), and new or previously discontinued newspapers and magazines.

According to a list published in *Keyhan*, one of the Tehran dailies, on 25 June 1979, a total of 222 periodicals of various political tendencies were being published, of which 167 were newpapers and 55 were journals. (This figure includes some Persian publications outside Iran as well.) A total of 18 major newspapers and magazines were already in existence under the Shah; the rest were either new or discontinued publications appearing once again. This sudden influx of newspapers was very similar to what had happened after the forced abdication of Reza Shah in 1941, when one of the most notable phenomenon was the appearance of Azari Turkish and Kurdish publications, which had been banned under that regime. Of these publications eleven were in Azari, one in Kurdish, two in Armenian, two in Arabic, and two in English. Twelve publications were satirical, of which one was in Azari and the rest in Persian.

But the Prague spring of Iranian journalism was short lived. Though the Ayatollah Khomeini, six weeks after his return to Iran, said, "Let them [i.e., the opposition] write or say whatever they want, it will not harm us,"[3] he and his followers could not maintain this stance. Earlier, in August 1979, two opposition dailies, *Ayandegan* and *Peygham-e Emruz*, were closed down, and on 12 August, a fierce confrontation occurred in Tehran between the liberals who protested against the new press laws and the Muslim Fundamentalists.[4] On 21 August, the government banned an additional twenty-two newspapers and magazines that represented the views of various political groups.[5] In the following weeks more papers were shut down, and a fierce fight between the press and the government ensued. Though it severely limited the press, the government still did not gain absolute control. It was in the following months and particularly in the heated atmosphere of paranoia created by the seizure of the American Embassy that numerous publications met their end. It was not only the press that fell victim to governmental intolerance of freedom of speech, but also the Iran's fledgling film industry as well as the flourishing Persian theater.

The fate of satirical papers was not very different from that of the other newspapers. Some were closed during the first few months of the crackdown, and some, because of their mild stand, were given a few more months. Some journalists fled the country and managed to continue the publication of their papers abroad. Three satirical weeklies belong to this catagory: *Asghar Agha*, which has originally appeared as *Taghut* in 1979 in London, is currently being published there by the talented satirist Hadi Khorsandi; *Ahangar dar Tab'id* (Ahangar in exile) is also edited in London by former staff of the *Ahangar*; and *Hajji Baba* was published for a while in 1981-82 in New York by its editor Parviz Khatibi.

The satirical weeklies included in the previously mentioned list of 222 newspapers are: *Ahangar* (The ironsmith), *'Ali Baba*, *Bohlul*, *Hajji Baba*, *Khurus-e Jangi* (The fighting cock), *Kosh Khanda* (Good-humored[man]), *Jigh va Dad* (Scream and shout), *Caricature*, *Mulla Nasreddin* (in Azari Turkish), *Mash Hasan*, and *Shatir al-Sho'ara* (The footman of the poets). To this one should add *Fanus* (Lantern), *Shangul* (The sprightly), and *Yaghut* (Ruby), which was apparently an imitation of Hadi Khorsandi's *Taghut*. Of these, *Caricature* began publication during the Shah's reign and five others (*Hajji Baba*, *Mulla Nasreddin*, *Ahangar*, *Bamshad*, *Bohlul*) were either the continuation of previously banned journals or their imitations. Satirical methods and political tendencies of these papers were quite varied, covering a wide spectrum that ranged from the far right to the far left. Here I will try to give a sample of their views and methods.

One of the least successful and most fiercely militant of these satirical publications was *Jigh va Dad*. Its title was derived from a Persian poem that is quoted on its first page:

> I accuse and incriminate and when they don't agree
> I "scream and shout" that there is no freedom left.

This was a weekly publication, written by hand and then printed in four quarto pages without any date. The front page displays a star of David encircling a map of Iran, inside of which the Soviet Union and the United States are shaking hands. The paper claims to be published by "The Syndicate of the Communists and the Imperialists." The parties of the left, and most particularly the Fada'iyan and Mojahedin, are special targets of slanderous remarks and satirical poems. Although the Shah and his notorious Savak are occasionally criticized, the leftist forces receive a greater share of criticism, being blamed for every event in the tumultuous months after the revolution. From the viewpoint of humor and poetry too, *Jigh va Dad* leaves much to be desired.[7]

On the other hand, *Mulla Nasreddin*, which was not allowed to be published for more than a few months, was very sympathetic to the leftist forces. In its opinion, young political activists like Qotbzade and Bani Sadr, who, upon their arrival in Iran got important posts and for a while were the favorites of the Ayatollah, were the agents of American interests, while the real revolutionaries, like the Fada'iyan and others, were being systematically eliminated. The paper was published in eight pages with interesting poems and cartoons. It was written mainly in Azari Turkish, though some items were in Persian. Apart from the reporting of current events, it had interesting articles about Azari writers of the past. For instance, in no. 3 (16 May 1979) considerable space is devoted to a discussion of the life and poetry of Taherzade Saber, who wrote in the original *Mulla Nasreddin*. In order to show the style of the magazine, here I translate a short piece from the same issue:

Experience

—How is that among thousands of social, economical and political problems of the society the provisional government has decided to pass the press law in order to put an end to the freedom of the press?

—It seems that you are not familar with politics. The so-called provisional government by passing this one-hundred-precent progressive law wants to make an "experiment" for the Constitution.

—Oh, I see. You mean that the provisional government wants to see the reaction of the "reactionary" parties to this progressive law to be prepared for their reaction to the Constitution.

Ideologically very similar to *Mulla Nasreddin* is *Ahangar*, which was modeled on the famous paper published by Mohammad 'Ali Afrashte from January 1951 to August 1953 called *Chalangar* (Locksmith). It was one of the best and most well-written satirical papers of Iran in recent years, but only sixteen issues were published. After the last issue came out on 7 August 1979, a special twenty-four-page edition devoted to the memory of the Constitutional Revolution, it was forced to close, as had been predicted by its editor. Quoting the famous first line of the *Gulestan*, the editor writes, "In each breath [which goes in and comes out] there are two blessings and for each blessing gratitude is due. . . ., Each issue of *Ahangar* which comes out despite the activities of the club-wielders throughout the country and reaches your hands, dear reader, is a blessing, and one should be grateful to the revolutionary masses of Iran for subduing the demon of censorship. . . ."[7] But he has his forebodings for the future, declaring that the imminent passage of the new press law is a sword of Damocles over their heads.

Ahangar was basically a political paper and voiced strong socialist views that often contrasted sharply with those of the government. At the outset *Ahangar*, like its predecessor *Chalangar*, wanted to keep its affiliation with the Tudeh party, but as it was openly critical of the Islamic government and followed an independent policy, the party denounced the journal and denied any ties with it. Like all the newspapers of similar tendencies, at the early stages of the Islamic government *Ahangar* was not at first openly critical of Ayatollah Khomeini, but rather chose his close associates as the targets of its attacks. A growing suspicion is displayed toward the revolutionaries who came from abroad and took over important government posts. It is openly maintained that rightist forces hope to create another dictatorship by making use of the Savak and the army. It is interesting to compare the attitude of *Ahangar* to the elections under the premiership of Dr. Mosaddeq in the early fifties. Perhaps two cartoons from these papers, reproduced on page 305, will make this point clear and show that the political view of the left toward a national government has not changed even after a quarter of a century. In *Ahangar's* cartoon the members of the Bazargan government are waiting for a voter who disagrees with them. They are wielding clubs, brass knuckles, and rubber stamps that read "anti-revolutionary" and "dissenter." In the cartoon in *Chalangar* two goons are guarding the ballot box and stuffing it with votes drawn from the identity cards of the deceased, while the military rule and fire engines keep protesters away. Of course, this is an unjust view of the rule of Mosaddeq, who valued nothing more than democracy and fought for it all his life. It is interesting to note, however, how a similar view appears in *Ahangar* toward Bazargan.

Apart from the political trends outlined above, numerous social problems, ranging from restrictions on women under an Islamic government to the designs that Russia and the United States have on Iran, figure prominently in the journal. It displays an impressive array of satirical pieces in both prose or poetry, combined with an interesting variety of well-drawn cartoons. For instance, no. 16, is a special edition, contains fifty-nine cartoons, four short plays, twenty-six long and short pieces of poetry, three short stories, an article on "The Outstanding Satirists of the Constitutional Era," and a partial translation of the novel by Jaroslav Hask, *The Good Soldier Schweik*, which was being serialized.

Almost two years after being closed down in Tehran *Ahangar* appeared as a biweekly under the editorship of Manuchehr Mahjubi in London in 1981. Any respect it once had for the Ayatollah has by now disappeared, and the paper is extremely critical of the theocratic government of Iran. *Ahangar in Exile*, as it is sometimes called, though published outside Iran and apparently with the support of few of its original writers, has kept its high standard, and it is a remarkably rich and well-written satirical paper. Among the most outstanding contributions to *Ahangar* is the talented poet Isma'il Khoi. He writes in a variety of forms and styles, and so far has published three collections of his poems in London.[8] Here I have translated some examples from *Ahangar* when it was being published in Tehran: part of a poem and a short prose piece in the form of a quiz on a cartoon piece that appears above it. The poem describes the hypocrisy of some so-called revolutionaries who are actually opportunists following the "slogans" of the day:

The Revolutionaries

Hajji Aqa on our street
Has millions clean and neat;
Besides his lands and properties
His safe is stuffed with cash and promissories.
The owner of factories large and great,
He has many assets safely hidden away.
He has recently donned revolutionary garb,
With wild incantations and speeches of fire,
Saying, "Death to Imperialism!
May god save us from Imperialism!"

Mashdi Kazem, brother of Heydar,
Was a well-known profiteer.
He was drunk wherever he went;
Gambling was his game wherever he passed.
Last night I was him, what a change!
How wonderfully he spoke of the new age!
"May the libertine have no eyes to see
Shame be upon the agents of debauchery!"

From Ahanger 10 (7 August, 1979)

Our First Quiz

Above is a picture of the session at which our new and resourceful Foreign Minister wanted to get to know the representatives of various parties and groups and outline the foreign policy of the Provisional Government. As you see they are all seated, mustache to mustache, listening patiently to the Minister who is describing our position in the world. But there were two groups who by the strict orders of the Minister were not allowed in:

reporters and women.

Truly, in this respect the Foreign Office officials did their best and the few women and reporters who had managed to slip in disguise were discovered and kicked out. But since no creature will be left in peace by the members of these two groups, a woman reporter eventually managed to get into this meeting. Now we ask you, dear reader, to locate her among all these mustached men and show her to us and you will get a prize.

A very interesting satirical paper that began publication on 27 July 1979 in London and has gained a significant readership outside Iran is *Taghut* (now *Asghar*

Agha). Hadi Khorsandi, a well-known satirist and journalist who was mentioned earlier in this book, was roughed up in an attack by extremists on the office of one of the newspapers after the revolution. Following this incident Khorsandi went to London and decided to publish his own paper, *Taghut*. Writing in prose and poetry, and even sometimes drawing his own cartoons, he published this weekly four-page newspaper singlehandedly for six months—a remarkable achievement. After twenty-two issues, in January 1980 other satirists joined him, and the name of the paper was changed to *Asghar Agha*. It takes its name from the fictitious satirical character who is given the editorship of the paper.

Taghut, a word coming from the *Koran* and associated with Pharaoh and his reign, came to denote the Shah and his reign after the revolution. Gradually the adjective *taghuti* came to be used not only for the supporters of the old regime, but also for those who opposed the new theocracy. Similarly the expression "the corrupt on the earth"[9] was too indiscriminately employed in the chaotic months after the revolution. By a cynical use of these terms Khorsandi says that he is not a revolutionary in the sense that it is understood in the ruling circles of Iran and that he accepts the inevitable accusation that he is going to be labeled *taghuti* because of his outspoken opposition. In his editorial to the first issue of the paper, Khorsandi says that he does not have the necessary prerequisites of being a revolutionary: he has not lived abroad for fifteen years, nor has he closely followed the route of the Ayatollah Khomeini, nor has he presented himself at the opportune moment to kiss the Ayatollah's hand.[10] The political position of *Asghar Agha* is somewhat more moderate that that of *Ahangar*; however, it is bitterly opposed to the dominance of the clergy and all of the undemocratic measures taken by the government.

Khorsandi, one of the most talented satirists of Iran, displays a variety of techniques and an incredible resourcefulness in his writings. His familiarity with classical Persian literature gives his satire a special richness and depth. Apart from writing numerous satirical pieces of poetry and prose on political events since 1979, he has produced a series of satirical essays through parody and exaggerated style of certain political figures. For instance "The Friday Sermon of *Asghar Agha*"[11], is a witty parody of the particular Persian that Ayatollah Khomeini speaks, and "The Diaries of the President"[12] spoofs the idiosyncrasies of former president Bani Sadr. Satirical names given to the men in power in Iran are worth mentioning: Sheikh Sadeq Khalkhali, the notorious hanging judge of Iran, is called Sheikh Sadeq Drakula. The head of the Revolutionary Council, Ayatollah Montazeri, and his son Skeikh Mohammad, who was killed in the explosion of the Islamic headquarters in Tehran, are referred to as Alexandre Dumas father and son. The latter became famous when he hijacked a plane and took volunteers to Lebanon to fight against the Israelis. Coined after "proletariat," "mullatariat" is an interesting word that has gained currency in *Ashgar Agha* after the coming to power of the clergy in Iran.

Satirical methods employed by Hadi Khorsandi are often very original. He has an incredible repertory of ideas and a razor-sharp sense of humor. He often chooses the funniest and most ridiculous accounts from the Persian press and reproduces them with his own comments. Even to very ordinary quotations his witty remarks add a new dimension. For instance, he notices how the first-grade textbooks have been reformed by making the little girl who appears in the pictures wear a long skirt and a scarf. He draws two pictures of the same girl before and after her change into "Islamic costume," and adds a bitingly satirical poem on the subject.[13]

The following is a short piece from *Asghar Agha* that expounds on the famous saying by Ferdausi: "Don't leave anything till tomorrow, since you don't know what will happen then."

Anecdote

A man had committed adultery and in accordance with the Islamic law he was flogged. The next day the Islamic judge was changed and he had a second adulterer shot instead. The flogged man of yesterday was passing by and thanked God that his adultery had taken place one day earlier. "Had I done it one day later, I would not be here now!" Hence the wise have said: "Don't leave today's adultery to tomorrow."[14]

Another satirical weekly that was being published outside Iran but has now been discontinued, is *Hajji Baba*. It originally began publication during the premiership of Dr. Mosaddeq when the press was free, and it was a liberal paper siding mostly with the policies of Mosaddeq. Its frontpiece announced, *"Hajji Baba* is not affiliated with any group or party." Twenty-six years later, after the revolution, *Hajji Baba* continued publication under Parviz Khatibi, the previous editor, while keeping to its old format and even continuing its old serial numbers. Fifteen issues were published from 25 April to 19 July 1979. The paper came out in Tehran as a weekly in twelve pages full of very interesting poems, prose pieces, and cartoons. One page in each issue was devoted to satirical quotations and cartoons from the old issues. *Hajji Baba* did not show any sign of partisan politics in this period, rather reflecting the general nationalistic fervor and characteristic distrust of the Americans and British. It was also full of praise for Ayatollah Khomeini. But as numerous papers were closed down, a sense of gloom and a fear of the passage of a restrictive press law were felt. The title of an editorial in no. 182 (28 May 1979) reads: "This time, how short was the spring of our life!" Asking whether *Hajji Baba* would close down, the editor writes: "In this second birth . . . we hoped that those who do not like our positions gradually will come to realize that a satirical paper has to criticize. Sound and unbiased criticism prevents mistakes by the authorities. But suddenly everything was changed, and in less than two months the fearful monster of the Press Law dashed all our hopes and enthusiasm into pieces." The forebodings proved correct. It is ironic that on 19 July 1953, after the Shah had returned to power following the overthrow of Dr. Mosaddeq, *Hajji Baba* was closed down for the first time, and Khatibi was arrested. Exactly twenty-six years later, on 19 July

1979, the paper was closed down for a second time. After its closure, *Hajji Baba* resumed publication in New York on 26 October 1979, where it continued for about two years.

Unlike some papers that tried to spare Ayatollah Khomeini and to blame instead his associates for the excesses of the Iranian government, *Hajji Baba* vigorously criticized him as soon as it began publication outside Iran. Between the issues published after the revolution in Tehran and those that came out in New York, not only is a change of heart apparent but also a change of style. In the earlier issues there was a remarkable variety in the forms and techniques of *Hajji Baba*'s satire, and it was much more refined and witty; the satire of the later editions is somewhat crude and borders on diatribe. Here is a translation of a poem from an earlier number on the nationalization of large companies:

> Good tidings, O Hajji, all the banks are nationalized;
> Both the pea and bean are "ration"alized.
> There is a trace of neither fish nor fowl.
> Yet this one in the air and that one in the water are nationalized.
> If you don't find any sign of kindness and love,
> Love is monopolized and kindness nationalized.
>
> . . . .
>
> If there is no trace of the Shah and his company,
> The deprived people of Iran had his crown nationalized.
> If there is not remedy for all our pains,
> The pain has become governmental, but the remedy has been "ration"alized.[15]

Compared to what is being written outside Iran, the political satire published in that country is indeed very rare. If anything at all in this line is published criticizing the current situation, it is either shrouded in an obscure symbolism or is told in the form of either a timeless parable or a historical tale of bygone ages. I will give two examples, one written in the first year after the revolution and the other in 1982.

Sheikh San'an is a remarkable work of satire by Sa'idi Sirjani, which was published in the Tehran literary weekly *Negin* in 1979. It appeared in five consecutive issues as a continuous story before the weekly was closed down, and it was left unfinished. The story was later reprinted outside Iran as a book. The love story of the saintly Sheikh San'an, who falls in love with a Christian girl and subsequently renounces Islam and becomes a Christian, is originally told by 'Attar (d. 1229) in his *Mantiq al-Tair*. In the satirical version of the story Sheikh San'an falls desperately in love with Qudrat Khanum (Lady Power), who has been rescued from the palace of the heathenish "Monsieur" by the followers of the sheikh. First Sheikh San'an entrusts the lady to an "old merchant" (Bazargan), but the followers urge him to bring her into his own house. Written in a fascinating prose interspersed with passages of poetry, the story describes the transformation of a reclusive Sufi shiekh into a power-hungry politician who does not spare any of his opponents. Occupation of the U.S. Embassy in Tehran forms part of the story, and the embassy is called *Hammam-e Jinian* (The public bath of Jinns). The Jinns are strange creatures. They can take the form of any person they like, and they can manipulate everyone. And whatever goes wrong in the country is blamed on them.

The second example, entitled "The Lost Animal," is by Sadeq Hatefi, and it was published in the literary magazine *Cheragh* (Lamp).[16] This curious little parable describes how thousands of years ago two neighboring countries fought for many years. The war continued for such a long time that nobody knew why they were fighting. Eventually people decided to discover the reason for this futile war. It is ultimately determined that the hostilities began over a lost animal, but its identity is not known. At the end, the animal is discovered and awakened by an old man. It is neither a horse nor a camel, as it was believed to be; rather, according to the old man its name is "common sense." At this point the animal wakes up from its sleep, and the old man is shot by an unknown assailant. Dying, the old man shouts to the people, "Please don't let it go back to sleep."

Current political satire in Iran is predominantly anticlerical. As it is difficult inside the country—in fact, almost impossible—to publish anything against the regime once again political jokes with pertinent and biting allusions to current issues are very popular; but this time they are directed against the mullas. As in the last years of the Shah's reign, once again the satirist is forced to transmit his work orally. Though the authors are not known, and their works do not have the wider circulation of printed words, they reach people and serve the satrical purpose.

Outside Iran the number of newspapers and periodicals published in Persian is very impressive. According to some accounts this number is more than forty. Some are political papers of this group or that party, and some, like *Iran Nama* (published in Washington, D.C.) or *Alefba* (published until November 1985 by the late Gholam-Hosain Sa'edi in Paris) are periodicals of high literary and cultural standards. The former is purely scholarly, with no interest in creative writing, whereas the latter, a quarterly of much more liberal tendencies, includes the works of some of the best Iranian writers in exile. Though *Alefba* is not basically a satirical publication, it occasionally includes pieces of satire. For instance, in a trilogy written by Sa'edi himself against the dominance of religion over people's minds, he gives a tragic and at the same time biting account of the trial of an old man arraigned on charges of adultery. The old man, who is eventually flogged to death, is being tried for a deed that had allegedly taken place fifty-six years earlier. But none of the old women who accuse him can remember the incident, and they merely repeat what the religious judge wants them to say. In some other publications there are regular columns devoted to satire. In *Iranshahr* (published in Washington, D.C. until 1984) one page was devoted to satire. Under the title "In the Theater of the Islamic Republic," the most amusing quotations from the Iranian press were reprinted, accompanied by pungent comments.

As in the case of satirical journals an anti-clerical mode dominates individual works as well. Among numerous titles published in the past few years the works of two poets stand out most significantly. M. Sahar (Muhammad Jalali)'s *Hizb-e Tudeh dar bargah-e Khalifeh* (Tudeh party at the court of the Caliph) (Paris, 1985) is a verse drama criticizing hypocritical devotion of the party's leaders to the Ayatollah Khomeini. It is extremely lively and full of humor. Interestingly enough this work was published only a few months before the downfall and the imprisonment of the members of the Tudeh party at the hands of the Islamic government. M. Sahar, who presently lives in Paris, has an unpublished collection of poems on the Pahlavi dynasty. Only passages from this work have been printed in *Ahangar* under the title of "Saltanat-nama".[17]

A more serious and prolific poet whose works are not confined to satire is Dr. Isma'il Khoi, who lives in London and writes for *Ahangar*. Since the Islamic revolution Khoi has published several collections of poems, some of them satirical. Most of his satirical verse has appeared in *Ahangar* under different pen names. Khoi is a talented and remarkable poet, who in a wide range of classical and modern forms, directs his rage at the regime of Tehran. His poetry is full of verve and pungeant witicism.

With these two very recent examples of recent Persian satire we come to the end of this study. This work has presented many examples of satirical talent in Persian poetry and prose, ranging from single poems and parables by poets who were more famous for their other works than for their satire, to complete satirical works in which the author uses various methods and techniques of satire. The classic example is 'Obeyd-e Zakani. But until the beginning of the modern period in the late nineteenth century, there were only a few writers or poets such as 'Obeyd-e Zakani and Mohammad Hashem 'Asef whose works were predominantly satirical.

The turning point was the advent of the press. During the Constitutional Revolution satirists such as Dehkhoda and Ashraf Gilani and satirical papers like *Mulla Nasreddin* and *Azerbaijan* played an important role in the social and political scene. It was a cyclical process: in every period of relative freedom there was a remarkable rise in the production of satirical work. There were three main periods of freedom: the Constitutional period, the period following the abdication of Reza Shah, and the period following the fall of his son. It is interesting to note that of the poets who wrote remarkable pieces of satire in the first period and during the reign of Reza Shah, 'Eshqi and Farrokhi Yazdi were killed by the Shah's agents and Ashraf Gilani ended his days in a lunatic asylum.

Although it is true that under Reza Shah political satire was not tolerated, some works of that nature were nevertheless produced; more often than not, however, mild social criticism was produced. From the abdication of Reza Shah in 1941 until the fall of Dr. Mosaddeq in 1953, there was a period of freedom, and an unusual number of satirical papers such as *Chalangar*, *Baba Shamal*, and *Towfiq* flourished. A remarkable poet-satirist, Mohammad 'Ali Afrashte edited and wrote for his weekly, *Chalanger*, but died in exile after the 1953 coup. Sadeq

Hedayat, who had bitterly criticized the dictatorship of Reza Shah in his *Hajji Agha* and had produced in his hero a graphic picture of changeable men during the age of transition, turned to writing the different types of satire that we see in *Velengari* and *Tup-i-Murvari*. This seems to be the zenith of his satire, which reminds one of mimicking, the style of Mohammad Hashem 'Asef in *Rostam al-Tawarikh*. Hedayat in *Vagh Vagh Sahab* uses a similar method. He lashes out at everything and stands against every kind of domination, dictatorship, corruption, hypocrisy, and compromise. His style becomes very distinctive and more and more anticlerical in his later works of satire.

The return of the Shah to power gradually ushered in another bleak period for satire when harsh or pointed criticism was not tolerated. However, social satire abounds in the works of Iraj Pezeshkzad, Khosrow Shahani, Abul-Qasem Halat, Bizhan Mofid, and many others, as well as veiled political satire in the works of Sa'edi and Feridun Tonkaboni. With the revolution of 1979 an outburst of newly written or fomerly banned material poured forth, but the period of freedom of expression was very short. At present, while political jokes circulating among the people of Iran are their only way of expressing their defiance and dissatisfaction, a significant satirical literature flourishes outside the country in papers published in Persian. This somewhat resembles the Consitutional period, in which the papers published outside Iran which had a definite effect on the course of events inside the country. Whether or not the satirists and writers outside their country will have any influence on shaping of future events in Iran remains to be seen.

Notes

1. See on the subject G. H. Sa'edi's editorial to the first issue of *Alefba* (Paris): n.s., no. 1 (Winter 1983). The translation of this article appeared as "Iran under the party of God," in *Index on Censorship*, February, 1984.
2. Nasrullah Pourjavadi, "Vaza' namatlub-e tulid-e Ketab dar Iran," *Nashr Danish*, 4, no. 6 (1984):2.
3. *Iran Times*, 31 August 1979, p. 6.
4. *Le Monde*, 14 August 1979, p. 3.
5. *San Francisco Chronicle*, 21 August 1979.
6. I have four issues of *Jig va Dad*, which I received in the summer 1979.
7. *Ahangar* no. 53, July 1985, p. 9.
8. For a discussion of Dr Isma'il Khoi's poetry see "Iranian Writers Abroad: Survey and Elegy" by Michael Beard and Hasan Javadi, *World Literature Today*, University of Oklahoma, Spring 1986, p. 259.
9. *Mofsid fi al-Arz*.
10. *Taghut*, 27 July 1979, p. 1
11. This series of articles was published in 1982.
12. This series of articles was published in 1981.
13. Ibid., 16 March 1980, p. 8.
14. Ibid., 9 Feburary 1980, p. 1.
15. *Hajji Baba* 5 June 1979.
16. *Cheragh* 4 (Fall 1982) 207-9.
17. *Ahangar dar Tab'id*, no. 53, July 1985, p. 9.

زیر سرنیزه روزنامه نمی نویسیم...

"We don't write newspapers under bayonets." A cartoon by the famous contemporary cartoonist, Ardashir Muhhases. *From Iranshahr 1, no. 12 (1979).*

Top, "Independence, Free . . . " *Bottom*, "The National Theater presents: the juggler of the revolution." *From Mulla Nasreddin 3 (16 May 1979).*

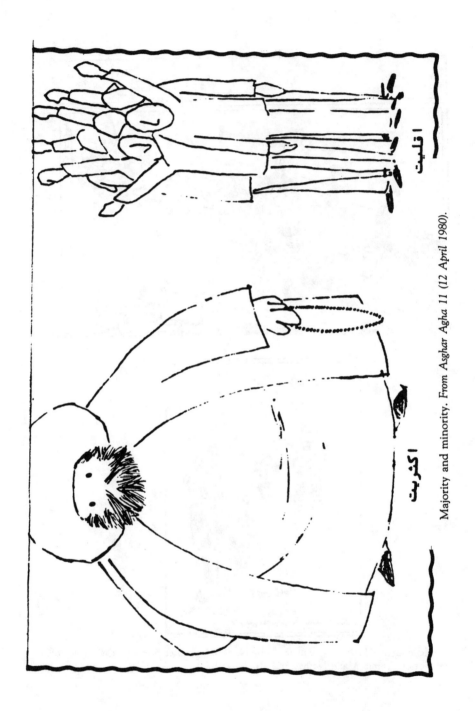

Majority and minority. From *Asghar Agha 11 (12 April 1980)*.

The emblem of Iranian television as seen by the syndicate of the journalists during the rule of the military in the last months of the Shah and later under the directorship of Ghotbzade.

Top, "The authorities have asked the people to report suspicious planes." Khadijeh Khanum: "What is your husband doing?" Answer: "He has been employed by the government to serve as radar." *Bottom*, Dear President, your rescue operations caused us to be transfered to Qom instead of Washington. Please don't rescue us this time or we will end up in Abargu. Timmy, the hostage. (Abargu is a remote town in the central desert of Iran.) *From Asghar Agha 14 (3 may 1980).*

Bani Sadr in front of the occupied U.S. Embassy. The signs on the door and wall read, "All sorts of documents are speedily revealed," and "Closed to the public and to the commander-in-chief [signed] petty commander." Guard: "Last time you said that you were the president, and I didn't let you in. Now you're saying that you are the commander in chief." *From Asghar Agha 7 (23 February 1980).*

شاه! نسبت به بی‌سرپرستها دلسوزی فراوان داشت!

شکوفائی اقتصاد!

Top, "The Shah was exceedingly sympathetic toward the poor." *Bottom,* "The prosperous economy?" *From Shah-name,* a book of cartoons on the life of the Shah, by Iraj Zara'.

A scenario for silencing the press by the Bazargan government. *From Hajji Baba 183 (20 May 1979).*

The Constitutional Revolution, the Revolution of February 1979, and now. *From Ahangar 16 (7 August 1979).*

Top, "He was grateful!" *Bottom*, "The Shah strongly believed in 'Human Rights'." *From Shah-name.*

Top, "Political dodgeball" between Beheshti and Bani Sadr leaving the progressive parties in the middle. On the ball is written, "calumny and slander."
Bottom, "Self-explanatory." *From Asghar Agha 10 (29 March 1980).*

After clashes on the campuses of Iranian universities, "New Academic Disciplines," clockwise from upper *left*: "Physics, Humanities, Surgery, Architecure, Plastic Arts, and [Foreign] Languages." *From Asghar Agha, 13 (26 April 1980).*

اى يا رمبارك بادا   ايشالا مبارك بادا   اى يا رمبارک بادا

عينک مدل آيت‌الله شريعتمداری به‌بازار آمد!

Top, The new parliament is opened. From *Ashgar Agha 10 (29 March 1980)*. *Bottom*, Glasses in Ayatollah Shari'atmadari style. From *Ashgar Agha*, the same issue.

Two leftists views of Iranian elections. *Chalangar's* (December 1951) of Mosaddeq's time and *Ahangar's* (16 August, 1979) of Mr. Bazargan's government

The Parliament was confiscated. *From Asghar Agha 16 (31 May 1980).*

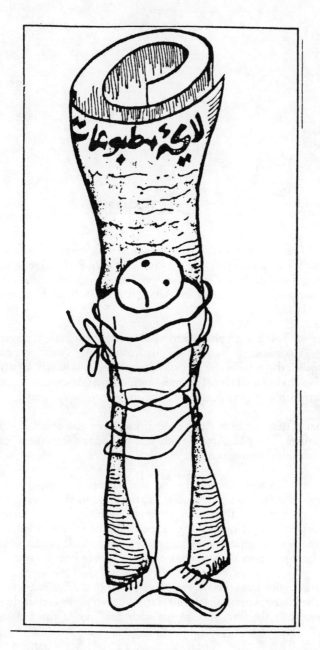

The new press law. *From Mulla Nasreddin 3 (16 May 1979).*

Glossary

Ghazal. The opening section of the *qaside* was eventually developed into a sophisticated genre of lyric or mystical poetry in Persian literature. The subtle language and profound sentiments expressed in *ghazals* reach their zenith in the hands of such masters as 'Attar, Rumi, Sa'di, and, more than anyone else, Hafez.

Mosammat. This is a strophic poem whose pattern runs (aaax, bbax, aaax, bbbax, etc.) According to Rashid al-Din Watwat, the twelfth-century poet and prosodist, this is what the Moorish poets called *movashshah*, in which the *misra'* (or distich) has an internal rhyme. Manuchehri (eleventh century) and Qa'ani (nineteenth century) poets were the masters of *mosammat*.

Motaibat. These are humorous poems that have no paticular form associated with them. The poet Aref Qazvini has coined the term *dordi 'yat* "dregs" for his own humorous poems.

Movashshah. In the Abbasid period the singers and musicians of Baghdad composed songs using colloquial expressions. In the Andolusia, under the Moslems of Spain, these *lahn* or songs, developed into a form called *zajal*, a short poem in strophes. The refined form of *zajal* is called *movashshah*. In Persian poetry *movashshah* is often used for acrostic peoms whose meanings can be discovered by a reference or a clue word at the end.

Mukhams. In this form (from *khams* "five") each of the five lines in the first stanza has the same rhyme. Subsequent stanzas have four lines that rhyme with each other, while the fifth line rhymes with the lines of the first stanza.

Musaddas. This six-line stanza, (from *sadis* ("six") has a pattern similar to the *mukhamas*, with the difference that the first stanza is a six-line stanza and that the last two lines of the second stanza ryhme with the first.

Mustazad. This verse form, or "increment-poem," is an ordinary quatrain, from an ode or *ghazal* whereof each half-distich is followed by a short metrical line. The short line has the effect of a refrain.

```
_____ R
_____ A
_____ R
_____ A
_____ R
_____ A
_____ R
```

Qaside. The *qaside,* a long poem in monorhyme that is often translated as "ode," was a creation of pre-Islamic Arabia. Traditionally it followed a sequence of topics, beginning with a description of the deserted encampment of the beloved and leading to an amatory prelude and the expression of the passion of the poet. Eventually the poem would end in a panegyric to the poet's patron. Derived from this classical Persian pattern, the *qaside* has come to be used for a large variety of subjects. The rhyme pattern of the *qaside,* as well as the *ghazal,* is AABACADA.

Qita' and *mathnavi.* The form of verse called *qita',* which deals with a particular topic, and *mathnavi,* a form devoted to different types of narratives, both are ryhmed as couplets in English: AA/BB/CC and so on. The great mystical work of Jal al-Din Rumi, *Mathnavi,* as well as the Quintet or *Khamseh* of Nazami and many other works in Persian, were written in this form.

Tasnif. A song accompanied by music. It is basically a popular song or ballad, and it is believed to have its orgins in pre-Islamic music.

Bibliography

A List of Satirical Journals in Iran

Ayene-ye Gheyb-nema, a fortnightly illustrated newspaper. Tehran, 1907, under the editorship of Seyyed 'Abdul-Rahim Khan. It renewed its publication in the second Constitutional period in July 1911.

Ayene-ye Iran, a literary, political, and comic weekly published in Tehran in 1929 under the editorship of Amir Jalili.

'Ali Baba, a satirical weekly published in Tehran from February 1945 to August 1946 under the editorship of Muhsin Farzane. It was suppressed several times, but would reappear under different names.

Arzhang, a humorous weekly first published in Isfahan in April 1925 by 'Abdallah Vazirzade. After the change of regime in 1941 it continued for a short time.

Ay Mulla 'Amu, a satirical paper in Azeri Turkish lithographed in Tabriz in 1908.

Azerbaijan, a weekly satirical paper, Tabriz, 1907, under the editorship of 'Ali-quli Khan Sarfaroff.

Baba Adam, published twice a week, Tehran, 1951, under the editorship of Shams al-Din Qaznavi.

Baba Kuhi, published twice a week, Tehran, 1952, under the editorship of Ahmad Shafi'i.

Baba Shamal, a satirical weekly first published 15 April 1943 under the editorship of Reza Ganja'i. It continued until 1947, except for a period between October 1945 and August 1947 when Ganja'i was in Europe.

Bahman, weekly published in Tehran from 1944 to 1947 under the the editorship of Amir Naser Khodayan.

Birjis, a satirical weekly under the editorship of Musavvar al-Sultan Arzhani, published in Tabriz in 1919.

Bohlul, a comic weekly published in Tehran in 1911 under the editorship of Sheikh 'Ali 'Iraqi, and later of Asadullah Khan, called "Parsi."

Bu Qalamun, a small-sized paper printed in Tabriz in 1909 under the editorship of Mirza Mahmud Ghani-zade of Salmas.

Chab Cheragh, a satirical weekly published in Tehran under the editorship of Abu Turab Jali.

Chalangar, a satirical weekly published in Tehran from 1950 to 1951 under the editorship of Muhammad 'Ali Afrashta.

Chanta-e Paberahne, an illustrated weekly paper printed in Tehran from 1904 to 1905 under the editorship of Mirza 'Abdu'l-Muhammad of Isfahan.

Chehrakar, a weekly published in Isfahan in 1952.

Dad va Bidad, a satirical weekly published in Tehran in 1951 under the editorship of 'Ali Asghar Samimi.

Divan-e Balkh, a satirical weekly printed in Tehran from 1951 until 1952.

Dakhow, a satirical weekly printed in Tehran in 1951 under the editorship of 'Abdul-Hosain Farrokhi.

Darvish, a satirical weekly printed in Tehran from 1952 to 1953 under the editorship of Ibrahim Vakil.

Durugh, a weekly printed in Tehran in 1950 under the editorship of 'Ali Asghar Ranjbaran.

Farid, a literary and comic weekly printed in Rasht in 1951 under the editorship of Iran Na'mati.

Gul-e Zard, a literary and satirical weekly under the editorship of Yahya Raihan, printed in Tehran, 1918.

Hajji Baba, a satirical weekly printed in Tehran from 1949 to 1953 under the editorship of Parviz Khatibi. It reappeared after the 1979 revolution and was published for a few months before it was suppressed by the government. After coming out of Iran, Khatibi printed *Hajji Baba* for more than two years in New York.

Hallaj, a satirical weekly founded by Hasan Hallaj in 1919. After being discontinued, it resumed in 1927 and continued until 1931. It reappeared in Tehran in September 1942 and with some interruptions continued until 1947.

Hasharat al-Arz, a satirical weekly published in Tabriz in 1908 under the editorship of Mirza Agha Nala-ye Millat. One more issue of it appeared in July 1909 after the Second Constitution, but it was suppressed by the government.

Hava va Havas, a "jelly-graphed" paper produced in Lahijan from 1907 to 1908 under the editorship of Hajji Hosain.

Hida, a satirical weekly published in Istanbul in 1911 under the editorship of Muhammad Zia al-Din.

Ihtiyaj, a weekly newspaper with some satirical pieces, printed in Tabriz from 1898 to 1899 under the editorship of 'Ali Quli Khan Safaroff.

Intiqad, printed in Tehran in 1922.

Janqal-e Mawla, a weekly satirical paper printed in Tehran in 1911.

Jarchi-e Millat, a satirical weekly lithographed in Tehran in 1910 under the editorship of Seyyed Hosain.

Karikatur, a satirical and comic weekly published in Tehran in 1958 under the editorship of Daolu.

Karikatur-e Istiqlal, a satirical weekly printed in Tehran in 1946 under the editorship of Muhsen Davallu.

Kashkul, an illustrated weekly comic paper printed in Tehran from 1907 to 1908 under the editorship of Majd al-Islam.

Kashkul, a comic weekly lithographed in Isfahan in 1909 under the editorship of the above-mentioned Majd al-Islam.

Kema, a satirical weekly printed in Tehran from 1950 to 1951 under the editorship of 'Ali Asghar Natiqi.

Khayr al-Kalam, a paper with some satirical pieces, printed in Tehran and then in Rasht from 1907 to 1908.

Khurshid-e Iran, a literary and comic weekly under the editorship of Baha al-Din Husamzada Pazagard, published in Tehran from 1923 to 1930.

Kulsum Nane, a satirical weekly published in Tehran in 1949 under the editorship of M. 'Azizi.

Luti, a satirical weekly published in Tehran in 1949 under the editorship of Abul Qasim Lachini.

Matalak, a comic weekly published in Tehran in 1950 under the editorship of Qasim Bastanfar.

Mehdi Hammal, a paper printed in Rasht in 1910 under the editorship of Akbar-zada. Only one issue came out.

Mulla Nasreddin Emruz, a satirical weekly printed in Tehran in 1953 under the editorship of M. 'Azizi.

Nahid, a satirical weekly under the editorship of Mirza Ibrahim Nahid, printed in Tehran from 1923 to 1933. It was suppressed several times in this period.

Naqur, a paper lithographed twice a week in Isfahan from 1908 to 1909 under the editorship of Mirza Masih Tuysirkani. The comic or satirical portion of this paper was called *Zisht va Ziba.*

Nashriye-Salam Alaykum, printed in 1907.

Nasim-e Shemal, a satirical weekly first published in Rasht, 1907 under the editorship of Seyyed Ashraf Gilani. It continued with some interruptions until 1909. Then *Nasim-e Shemal* began its publication in Tehran in 1924 and continued until some months before the death of Ashraf in 1934. From 1935 to 1947 with several interruptions it continued under the editorship of Harirchian Sa'i.

Nasim Saba, a political literary weekly with some pieces of satire in Tehran irregularly published from 1923 to 1934, and then from 1941 to 1944. Its editor and licensee was Husain Kuhi Kermani (d. 1957).

Naw-Bahar, a paper printed in Mashhad twice a week in 1910 under the editorship of Malik al-Sho'ara Bahar. It appeared in Tehran from 1915 to 1923. It reappeared in Tehran in 1943 and ceased publication in 1944.

Nushkhand, a satirical weekly published in Tehran under the editorship of Mehdi Suhaili.

Qalandar, a humorous weekly under the editorship of Murtaza Rafi' that was printed in Tehran in 1946.

Qalandar, a satirical weekly published in Tehran in 1946 under the editorship of Hasan 'Ali Rafia.

Qasim al-Akhbar, a weekly printed in Tehran in 1907 under the editorship of Mirza Abu'l Qasim of Hamadan.

Rah-e Khial, a satirical weekly published in Rasht in 1911 under the editorship of Afzal'ul Mutakalemin.

Rakhneh, a literary and political weekly with cartoons, printed in Tehran in 1951 under the editorship of Isma'il Saberi.

Rouzname-ye Fardvardin, published in Rezaieh in 1911 under the editorship of Mirza Habib

Aghazade and Mahmud Ashrafzade. It has a satirical section in Azeri Turkish called "Daghan Baghdan."

Rouzname-ye Jangal, a weekly published by Gholam-Hosain Kasma'i in Rasht in 1917. It contained some satirical Gilaki poems.

Saihe-ye Asemani, a satirical weekly printed in Tehran in 1942 under the editorship of Muhammad Janabzade.

Sanandaj, a comic and literary weekly published in Sanandaj under the editorship of Ahmad Kamangar in 1950.

Sazesh, a comic weekly printed in Tehran in 1948 under the editorship of 'Ali Akbar Mehdi.

Sepahan, a weekly under the editorship of Muhammad 'Ali Mukarram Habibabadi, Isfahan, 1925. The same editor later published *Rouznama-ye Mukarram* in Isfahan.

Sepida-dam, published three times a week in Tehran from 1946 to 1951 under the editorship of Fath Ullah Mushiri.

Shabcheragh, a satirical weekly published in Tehran in 1952 under the editorhsip of Ahmad Varithian Monfarid.

Shahkar-e Nu, an illustrated satirical weekly printed in Isfahan in 1950 under the editorship of Haj Lutfullah Danishvar 'Alavi.

Shahseven, a "jelly-graphed" paper produced in Istanbul from about about 1888 to 1889. Its editorship has been attributed to Hajji Mirza 'Abd al-Rahim Taliboff.

Shaitan, a comic weekly printed in Tehran from 1950 to 1954 under the editorship of ' Iran Najad.

Shangul, a comic weekly, printed in Tehran from 1943 to 1944 under the editorship of Shayista.

Shar-e Farang, a satirical weekly published in Tehran from 1944 to 1945 under the editorship of Hasan Gulbaba'i and Husain Muharrad.

Shayda, a satirical and illustrated paper printed in Istanbul in 1911 under the editorship of Muhammad Ziyn al-Din.

Shayda, first published in Tehran in September 1946 under the editorship of Muhammad Taqi Pur Hosaini. It was suppressed shortly after publication.

Sheikh Chughundar, a comic weekly paper printed in Tehran in 1911 under the editorship of Abu'l Ma'ali, known as Seyyed-e Ahan-bardar.

Shokuh-e Shah Reza, a literary and comical weekly printed in 1952 in Shah Reza under the editorship of Hosain Shokuh.

Shukhi, a comic weekly printed in Tehran from 1954 to 1957 under the editorship of 'Ali Pazagard.

Shukh va Shang, a comic weekly printed in Tehran in 1951 under the editorship of Hosainquli Haqiri.

Sur-i Israfil, a weekly paper printed in Tehran from 1907 to 1908 under the editorship of Mirza Jahangir Khan. It was *Sur-i Israfil* in which Dehkhoda wrote his satirical essays, *Charand Parand*. After Mirza Jahangir was killed by Muhammad 'Ali Shah in June 1908, Dehkhoda printed three more issues at Yverdon in Switzerland in 1909. The paper was reprinted in one volume in Tehran in 1984.

Tanbih, a comic paper published in Tehran with colored cartoons in 1907 under the editorship of Mu'tazid al-tibba. After the restoration of the Constitution (in July 1909), it was again published until the end of 1911.

Tashwiq, a weekly printed in Tehran in 1907 under the editorship of Mirza Seyyed 'Ali Tabataba'i. It had a satirical column entitled "Sherr-u Virr," which was an imitation of Dehkhoda's *Charand Parand.*

Taza Bahar, a weekly paper printed in Mashhad in 1911 under the editorship of Malik al-Shoara-ye Bahar, which replaced *Naw Bahar* after it was suppressed.

Towfiq, a satirical weekly first published in November 1922 by Hosain Towfiq (d. February 1940). Among its various editors were Parviz Khatibi (1943), Abul-Qasim Halat, and Hosain Bihbudi. In spite of being suppressed several times, it continued until the *coup d'état* of 1953. After being suppressed for a while, *Towfiq* began publication again and continued until 1959.

Umid, a political and comic weekly published in Tehran in 1950 under the editorship of Abul-Qasim Ardalan.

Yeki Bud Yeki Nabud, a comic weekly printed in Tehran in 1950 under the editorship of Muhammad Nasir Darrudian.

Yu Yu, a satirical weekly first published in Tehran in 1930 under the editorship of 'Imad 'Assar. It reappeared 18 February 1944 and with some interruptions it continued until March 1945.

Zanbil, a literary and comic weekly published in Tehran in 1930.

Zisht va Ziba, an illustrated weekly lithographed in Tehran in 1907 under the editorship of Fath al-Mamalik.

Western Sources

Akhundzade, F.A. *Persian Plays: Three Persian Plays.* Translated by Rogers. London: Sampson Law, Marston, Co., 1890.

. *The Vizier of the Chief of Langaran.* Translated from the Persian by Guy Le Strange and W. H. Haggard. London: Kegan Paul Trench, Trubner & Co., 1882.

Algar, Hamid. *Mirza Malkum Khan, A Study of the History of Iranian Modernism.* Berkeley: University of California Press, 1973.

. *Religion and State in Iran 1785-1906: The Role of the Ulama in the Qajar Period.* Berkeley: University of California Press, 1969.

Aqa Tabrizi, Mirza. *Les Comédies de Malkom Khan: Les mésaventures d'Achraf Khan Zaman Khan ou le gouverneur modéle; Les tribulations de Chah Qouli Mirza.* Translated by August Bricteaux. Liége: Bibliothéque de la Faculté de Philosophie et Lettres de l'Université de Liége, 1933.

Arberry, A. J. *Aspects of Islamic Civilization.* Ann Arbor: The University of Michigan Press, 1971.

. *Classical Persian Literature.* London: George Allen & Unwin, 1958.

Aristophanes. *The Complete Plays of Aristophanes.* Edited by Moses Hadas. New York: Bantam Books, 1962.

Atkinson, James, trans. *The Customs and Manners of the Women of Persia, and Their Domestic Superstitions.* Oriental Translation Fund of Great Britain and Ireland, 1832.

Basset, René. *Historical des dix viziers* (Bakhtiar-nama). Paris, 1883.

Bausani, Alessandro. "Il 'Libro della Barba' di Obeyd Zakani," *A Francesco Gabriel.* Universita di Roma, Studi Orientali Publicati a Cur Sculla Orientale 5 (1964): 1-19.

. *Storia della litteratura Persiana.* Milan: Nuovo Accademia, 1960.

Behrangi, Samad. *The Little Black Fish and Other Modern Persian Stories.* Translated by Mary Hooglund and Eric Hooglund. Washington D.C.: Three Continents Press, 1976.

Bennigsen, Alexandre, and Chantal Lemercier-Quelquejay. *La presse et le monuement nationial chez les Musulmans des Russe avant 1920.* Paris: Monton & Co., 1964.

Binyon, Laurence, J.V.S. Wilkinson, and Basil Gray. *Persian Miniature Painting.* New York: Dover Publications, 1971.

Borecky, Milos. "Persian Prose Since 1946." *Middle East Journal* 7 (1953): 235-44.

Browne, Edward G., ed. *A Literary History of Persia.* Cambridge: Cambridge University Press, 1969.

. *The Persian Revolution of 1905-1909.* Cambridge: Cambridge University Press, 1910.

. *The Press and Poetry of Modern Persia.* Cambridge: Cambridge University Press, 1914.

Butler, Samuel, *Erewhon, or Over the Range.* London: Trubner, 1872.

Byron. "The Vision of Judgment." In *The Poetical Works of Byron,* edited by H. Milford. Oxford: Oxford University Press, 1921.

Čapek, Karel. *War with the Newts.* Translated by M. R. Weatherall. New York: Bantam Books. 1964.

Cardonne, Denis Dominique. *A Miscellany of Eastern Learning, translated from Turkish, Arabic, and Persian MSS. at the Library of the King of France.* Vol. 1. London, 1771.

Chelkowski, Peter. "The Literary Genres in Modern Iran." In *Iran under the Pahlavis,* Edited by George Lenczowski, Stanford: Hoover Institution Press, Stanford University, 1978: pp. 333-64.

Christensen, Arthur. *Recherches sur les Ruba'iyat d.' Omar Hayyam,* Heidelberg: Carl Winter's Universitatsbuchhandlung, 1905.

Clouston, W. A. *The Book of Sindibad: or the Story of the King, His Son, the Damsel, and the Seven Vazirs.* Translated from the Persian and Arabic, with introduction, notes and appendix. Glasgow, 1884.

. *Flowers from a Persian Garden.* 1890.

Cook, Nilla Cram. "The Theatre and Ballet Arts of Iran." *Middle East Journal* 3 (1949): 406-20.

D'Andeli, Henri. *Lai d'Aristote: (ou) Aristotle et Phyllis.* Paris: M. Debouille, 1951.

De Beauvoir, Simone. *Second Sex.* Translated by H. M. Parshley. London: The New English Library, 1961.

Decourdemanche, J. A. *The Wiles of Women.* Translated from the Turkish into English by J. Mills and S. F. Mills. London: Whitham, 1928.

Donaldson, Bess Allen. *The Wild Rue: A Study of Muhammadan Magic and Folklore in Iran.* London: Lazac & Co., 1938.

Dorri, Dzh. *Persidskaia Satiricheskaia Prosa.* Moscow: Nauka, 1977.

Elliott, Robert C. *The Power of Satire: Magic, Ritual, Art.* Princeton: Princeton University Press, 1972.

Elwell-Sutton, L. P. "The Iranian Press, 1941-1947." *Iran, Journal of British Institute of Persian Studies* 1 (1968): 65-104.

Empson, William. *Seven Types of Ambiguity.* New York: New Directions, 1966.

Farrokhzad, Forough. *Another Birth: Selected Poems.* Translated by Hasan Javadi and Susan Sallée. Emeryville, Calif.: Albany Press, 1981.

Foreign Areas Studies Division, The American University, Washington, D.C. *U.S. Army Area Handbook for Iran.* Washington, D.C.: The American University, 1963.

Frye, Northrop. *Anatomy of Criticism.* 3d ed. Princeton: Princeton University Press, 1973.

Gelpke, R. "Politic und Ideologie in der Persischen Gegenwartsliteratur." *Bustan,* 4 (Vienna, 1961).

Hanaway, William L., Jr. "Persian Literature." In *The Study of the Middle East,* edited by Leonard Binder, pp. 453-78. New York: John Wiley, 1976.

Heath-Stubbs, John. *The Verse Satire.* Oxford: Oxford University Press, 1969.

Hermes, Eberhard. *The Disciplina Clericalis of Petrus Alfonsi.* Translated by P. R. Quarrie. Berkeley: University of Califonia Press, 1977.

Highet, Gilbert. *The Anatomy of Satire.* Princeton: Princeton University Press, 1962.

Hodgart, Matthew. *Satire.* London: World University Library, 1969.

Huxley, Aldous, L. *Brave New World.* New York: Modern Library, 1956.

Ibrahimov, Mirza, ed. *Azerbaijanian Poetry.* Moscow: Progress Publishers, 1969.

Ishaque, Mohammad. *Modern Persian Poetry.* Calcutta, 1943.

Javadi, Hasan. "James Morier and his Hajji Baba of Ispahan." *Indo-Iranica: Silver Jubilee Volume* (1970): 163-77.

——. *Persian Literary Influence on English Literature.* Calcutta: Iran Society, 1983.

——. "Mirza Abul Hasan Khan Ilchi" in *Encylopaedia Iranica,* I, Fascicle 3, Routledge & Kegan Paul, 1983.

Javadi, Hasan and Sholavar B. "Afrashta." *Encyclopaedia Iranica.* Vol. 1, fascicle 6.

Javadi, H., Ghaffari, F. "Mirza Aqa Tabrizi" in *Encyclopaedia Iranica,* 2, Fascicle 2, Routledge & Kegan Paul, 1986.

Johnson, Edgar. *A Treasury of Satire.* New York: Simon & Schuster, 1945.

Kamshad, Hassan. *Modern Persian Prose Literature.* Cambridge: Cambridge University Press, 1966.

Khayyam, Omar. *The Quatrains of Omar Khayyam.* Translated by Edward Fitzgeral. New York: Everyman Library, 1935.

Kubičkova, Vera. "Persian Literature of the 20th Century." In *History of Iranian Literature,* by Jan Rypka, edited by Karl Jahn, pp. 353-418. Dordrecht, Holland: Reidel, 1968.

Larcher, L. J. *La femme jugée par l'homme.* Paris: Garnier Fréres, 1858.

Law, Henry D. G. "Persian Writers." Special number of *Life and Letters* 63 1949).

——. "Sadiq Hedayat." *Journal of the Iran Society* 1 (1950): 109-13.

Lescot, Roger. "Deux nouvelles de Sadegh Hedayat." *Orient* (1958): 119-54.

——. "Le roman et la nouvelle dans la littérature iranienne contemporaine." *Bulletin d'Etudes Orientales de l'Institut de Damas* 9 (1942): 83-101.

Levy, R. *Persian Literature, an Introduction.* New York: Columbia University Press, 1969.

Lewis, Bernard. *Islam from the Prophet Mohammad to the Capture of Constantinople.* New York: Harper & Row, 1974.

Loraine, Michael B. "A Memoir on the Life and Poetical Works of Maliku'l-Shu'ara Bahar." *International Journal of Middle Eastern Studies* 3 (1972): 140-68.

Lukaćs, Georg. *The Theory of the Novel.* 3d ed. Translated by Anna Bostock. Cambridge: MIT Press, 1977.

Machalski, F. *Litterature de l'Iran contemporaine.* Vol. 2. Warsaw: Zaklad Narodowyim Ossolinskich, 1965.

———. "Principaux courants de las prose persane moderne." *Rocznik Orientalistyczny* 25 (1961).

Massé, Henri. *Essai Sur le poéte Saadi.* Paris: Librairie Paul Geuthner, 1919.

———. "La littérature persane d'aujourd'hui" *L'Islam et l'Occident* (1947): 260-63.

Mignan, M. *A Journey though the Caucasian Alps and Georgia.* Vol. 1. London: Bently, 1839.

Monteil, V. *Sadeq Hedayat.* Tehran: L'Institut Franco-Iranian, 1952.

Morier, James. *The Adventures of Hajji Baba of Ispahan.* London: Oxford University Press, 1959 (first published in 1824).

———. *Hajji Baba in England.* With an introduction by E. G. Browne. London: Macmillan & Co., 1895.

Mostafavi, Rahmat. "Fiction in Contemporary Persian Literature." *Middle Eastern Affairs* 2 (1951): 2737-9.

Nfisi, Sa'id. "A General Survey of the Existing Situation in Persian Literature." *Bulletin of the Institute of Islamic Studies* 1 (1957): 13-25.

Nakhshabi, Z. *Tales of a Parrot.* Translated by Mohammad-e Simsar. Graz: Cleveland Museum of Art, 1978.

Nicholas, A. L. M. *Revue du Monde Musulman* 3 (November-December 1907): 4-5.

Nicholson, R. A. *A Literary History of the Arabs.* Cambridge: Cambridge University Press, 1969.

Nikitine, B. "Le roman historique dans la littérature persane actuelle." *Journal Asiatique* 223 (1933): 297-336.

———. "Sayyed Mohammed Ali Djemalzadeh, pionnier de la prose moderne persane." *Revue des Etudes Islamiques* 27 (1959): 23-33.

———. "Les themes sociaux dans la littérature persane moderne." *Oriente Moderno* 34 (1954) 225-37.

Nowrouz, Ali. "Registre analytique annoté de presse persane." *Revue du Monde Musulman* 60 (1925): 35-62.

Orwell, George. *Nineteen Eighty-Four.* New York: Harcourt Brace, 1949.

Ouseley, William, trans. *Bakhtiyar-name, a Persian Romance.* Edited and with introduction and notes by W. A. Clouston. Lanarkshire: Larkhall, 1883.

Pickthall, M. M. *The Meaning of the Glorious Koran.* New American Library edition, n.d.

Pollard, Arthur. *Satire.* London: Methuen, 1979.

Prochnow, Herbert V. *A Dictionary of Wit, Wisdom and Satire.* New York: Harper & Row, 1962.

Rabelais, François. *Gargantua and Pantagruel.* Translated by Samuel Putnam in *The Portable Rabelais.* Viking Press, 1977.

Rahman, Munibur. *Post-Revolution Persian Verse.* Aligarh: Institute of Islamic Studies, 1955.

———. Social Satire in Modern Persian Literature." *Bulletin of the Institute of Islamic Studies* 2 and 3 (1958 and 1959): 63-91.

———. "Two Contemporary Poetesses of Iran." *Bulletin of the Institute of Islamic Studies,* 8 and 9 (1964 and 1959): 63-91.

Rezvani, M. *Le Theatre et la danse en Iran.* Paris: Maisonneuve et Larousse, 1962.

Ricks, Thomas, M. ed. *Critical Prespectives on Modern Persian Literature.* Washington, D.C.: Three Continents Press, 1984.

Rosenthal, Franz, *Humor in Early Islam.* Philadelphia: University of Pennsylvania Press, n.d.

Rousseau, G. S., and Rudenstine, Neil L. *English Poetic Satire: Wyatt to Byron.* New York: Holt, Rinehart and Winston, 1972.

Russell, John and Ashley Brown, eds. *Satire: A Critical Anthology.* New York: The World Publishing Co., 1967.

Rypka, Jan. *History of Iranian Literature.* Edited by Karl Jahn. Dordrecht, Holland: Reidel, 1968.

Sabri-Tabrizi, G. R. "Social Values in Modern Persian Literature." *Bulletin of the British Association of Orientalists* 8 (1976): 9-16.

Sa'di, Muslih al-Din. *The Bustan of Sa'di.* Translated by G. M. Wickens. Toronto: University of Toronto Press, 1974.

———. *Gulestan.* Translated by Edward Rehatsek. London: G. Allen & Unwin, 1964.

Sa'edi, Gholam-Hossain. *Dandil: Stories from Iranian Life.* Translated by Hasan Javadi, Robert Campbell, and Julie Meisami. New York: Random House, 1981.

Scarcia, G. "'Haji Aqa' e 'Buf-i Kur', i cosiddetti due aspetti dell'opera dello scrittore contemporaneo Persiano Sadeq Hedayat." *Annali dell'Instituto Universitario Orientale di Napoli* 8 (1958): 103-23.

Scott-Waring, Edward. *A Tour to Shiraz.* London: T. Cadell & W. Davies, 1802.

Shafaq, Rezazade. "Drama in Contemporary Iran." *Middle Eastern Affairs* 4, no. 1 (1953): 11-15.

Shaki, Mansour. "An Introduction to the Modern Persian Literature." In *Charisteria Orientalia Jan Rypka,* pp. 300-315. Prague: Ceskoslovenske Akademie Ved, 1956.

———. "Modern Persian Poetry." In *Yadname-ye Jan Rypka,* pp. 187-94. Prague: Academia, 1967.

Shari'ati, 'Ali. *Marxism and Other Western Fallacies: An Islamic Critique.* Translated by Robert Campbell. Berkeley: Mizan Press, 1980.

———. *On the Sociology of Islam.* Translated by Hamid Algar. Berkeley: Mizan Press, 1979.

Soroudi, Sorour. "The Dispute of the 'Old and the New' in Modern Persian Poetry." *Asian and African Studies* 10, no. 1 (1974): 25-38.

Sprachman, Paul, "Akhlaq al-Ashraf." *Encyclopaedia Iranica.* Vol. 1, fascicle 8.

Sutherland, James. *English Satire.* Cambridge: Cambridge University Press, 1967.

Swift, Jonathan. *Gulliver's Travels and Selected Writings in Prose and Verse.* Nonesuch Library, Bodley Head.

Vidal, Gore. *An Evening with Richard Nixon.* New York: Random House, 1972.

Voltaire. *Micromegas.* In *The Portable Voltaire.* New York: Viking Press, 1970.

Vulliamy, C. E. *The Anatomy of Satire.* London: Michael Joseph, n.d.

Wellek, René, and Austin Warren. *Theory of Literature,* 3d ed. New York: Harcourt and World, 1970.

Whinfield, E.H. *The Quatrains of Omar Khayyam.* London: Trubner & Co., 1802.

Wickens, G. M. "Bozorg 'Alavi's Portmanteau." *University of Toronto Quarterly* 28 (1959): 116-33.

. "Persian Literature as an Affirmation of National Identity." *Review of National Literatures* 2, pt. 1 (Spring 1971): 29-60.

. "Poetry in Modern Persia." *University of Toronto Quarterly* 29, no. 2 (January 1960): 262-81.

Wills, C. J. *The Land of the Lion and Sun.* London: Macmillan, 1883.

Yarshater, Ehsan. *Cassell's Encyclopaedia of Literature,* s. v. "Persia." London, 1953.

. "Development of Persian Drama in the Context of Cultural Confrontation." In *Iran: Continuity and Variety,* edited by Peter Chelkowski. New York, 1971.

. *Iran Faces the Seventies.* New York: Praeger, 1971.

. "Persian Letters in the Last Fifty Years." *Middle Eastern Affairs* 9 (1960): 298-306.

Young, Cuyler T. "The Problem of Westernization in Modern Iran." *The Middle East Journal* 2, no. 1 (1948): 47-59.

Persian, Turkish and Arabic Sources

Abu Ishaq. *Divan-e Att'ima.* Edited by Mirza Habib of Isfahan. Tehran, 1983.

Adamiyyat, Fereydun. *Andisha-ha-ye Mirza Agha Khan Kermani.* Tehran: Tahuri, 1967.
. *Andisha-ha-ye Mirza Fath 'Ali-ye Akhundzade.* Tehran: Kharazmi, 1960.

. *Fikr-e Azadi va Muqaddama-ye Nehzat-e Mashrutiyyat.* Tehran: Sukhan, 1960.

Adamiyyat, Fereydun and Homa Nateq. *Afkar-e Ejtema'i va Siyasi va Eqtesadi dar Athar-e Montasher Nashode-ye Dovran-e Qajar.* Tehran: Agah, 1977.

Afrashte, Mohammad 'Ali. *Ay Gofti!* Tehran: Nashr-e Kargar, 1945.
. *Chihil Dastan.* Tehran: Haidar Baba, 1981.

. *Majmu'a-ye Athar Mohammad 'Ali Afrashte.* Tehran: Haidar Baba, 1979.

. *Numayish-name-ha, Tazi'yeha, Safar-name.* Edited by Nusratullah Nuh. Tehran: Haidar Baba, 1981.

Afshar, Iraj. "Jamalzada." *Yaghma* 12 (1948): 337-40.

. *Nathr-i Farsi-yi Mu'asir.* 2 vols. Tehran: Ma'refat, 1951.

Akhavan Thaleth, Mehdi. *Majmu'a-ye Maqalat-e M. Omid.* Tehran: Athar-e Iran, 1971.

Akhundov, Nazim. *Azerbaijanda Davri Metbu'at, 1832-1920.* Baku, 1965.

. *Azerbaijan Satira Journalari, 1906-1920.* Baku: Azerbaijan SSR Elmi Akademisi Nashriyati, 1968.

Akhundzade, Mirza Fath 'Ali. *Tamthilat.* Translated by M. Ja'far-e Qarachedaghi. Tehran: Kharazmi, 1970.

Al-Ahmad, Jalal. *Panj Dastan.* Tehran: Ravag, 1977.

'Alavi, Buzurg. "Sadiq Hidayat." *Piyam-i Naw* 1, no 12: (1943): 25-29.

Al-Isfahani, Abu'l-Faraj. *Kitab-al Aghani.* Bulaq ed., 1886-89.

'Ameli, Shaykh Baha al-Din Mohammad. *Kulliyyat-e Ash'ar-e Farsi va Mushva Gorbe-ye Sheikh Baha'i.* Edited by Mehdi Tohidipur. Tehran: Ketabfrushi Mahmudi, 1957.

Amir-Khizi, Isma'il. *Qiyam-i Azarbayijan va Sattar Khan.* Tabriz: Ketabfrushi Tehran, 1960.

Anvari, Awhad al-Din. *Divan-e Anvari.* Edited by Sa'id-e Nafisi. Tehran: Amir Kabir, 1957.

'Aqayid va Afkar dar Bara-yi Sadiq Hedayat. A collection of articles published in the Persian

press after the death of Hedayat. Tehran, 1954.

Arda-Viraf Nama. Translated by Afifi Fargard. Mashhad, 1965.

Aryanpur, Yahya. Az Saba ta Nima. 2 vols, 5th ed. Tehran: Ketabha-ye Jibi, 1978-7ۊ

Arikbag, Zaffer, and Dundar Akunal. Turk Edebiyatinda Hiciv ve Mizah Şiirleri. Istanbul: Aydinlik Basimevi, 1944.

Asadipour, Bizhan and 'Omran-e Eslahi. Tanz-Avaran-e Ma'aser-e Iran. Tehran: Athar-e Iran in, 1970.

Asef, Mohammad. Rostam al-Tawarikh. Tehran, 1969.

Ata'i, Abu al-Qasem-e Jannati-ye. Bonyad-e Namayesh dar Iran. Tehran: Ibn Sina, 1955.

'Attar, Farid al-Din. Mantiq al-Tair. Isfahan: Ketabfrushi-ye Ta'id, 1955.

. Mosibat-Nama. Edited by Nurani Vesal. Tehran, 1965.

. Tazkirat al-Awliya. Edited by M. Este'lami. Tehran: Zavvar, 1967.

'Awfi. Javami' al-Hekayat va Lavami' al-Revayat. Edited by Banu Mussafa Karimi. Tehran: Bonyad-e Farhang-e Iran, 1973.

Awhadi, Mohammad. "Jam-e Jam." In Divan-e Awhadi, edited by Sa'id Nafisi. Tehran: Amir Kabir, 1961.

Bahar, Mohammad Taqi 'Maliku 'shu'ara. Tarikh-i Mukhtasar-i Ahzab-i siyasi-yi Iran: Inqiraz-e Qajariya. Tehran: Amir Kabir, 1942.

Bakharzi, Abu al-Mafakher-e. Owrad al-Ahbab va Fosus al-Adab. Edited by Iraj-e Afshar. Tehran: Tehran University, 1966.

Baraheni, Reza. Qessehnevisi. Tehran: Ashrafi, 1969.

. Tala dar Mes. Tehran: Zaman, 1968.

Barzin, Mas'ud. Matbu'at-e Iran 1343-53. Behjat, Tehran, 1965.

Bashar Ibn Burd. Divan. 2 vols., Cairo, 1950.

Beh'azin, M. E. Mehman-e in Aqayan. Tehran: Nil, 1978.

Behruz, Z. Jijak-Ali Shah. Tehran, n.d.

Beyza'i, Bahram. Pahlavan Akbar mimirad. Tehran: Sa'ib, 1965.

Bürgel, Christopher. "Lamahat an dowr al-Hija fi al-Adab al-Arabi." Fakr va Fann 17. (1980).

Chubak, Sadeq. Antari Ke Lutiyash Morda Bud. Tehran: Elmi, 1966.

. Cheragh-e Akhar. Tehran: Elmi 1963.

. Khaima-Shab-Bazi. Tehran: Javidan, 1947.

. Ruz-e Avval-e Qabr. 2nd. ed. Tehran: Elmi, 1973.

. Sang-e Sabur. 2d ed. Tehran: Elmi, 1973.

. Tup-e Lastiki. Tehran: Elmi, 1949.

Dabir Siyaqi, Mohammad. Ganj-e Baz-Yafte, Tehran: Khayyam, 1965.

Dastgheyb, Abdol'ali. "Honar-e Tanz dar Neveshtehha-ye Chubak. Payam-e Novin 7 (1962): 1-11.

. Naqd-e Asar-e Gholam Hosain Sa'edi. Tehran, 1973.

Davani, Jalal al-Din. Akhlaq-e Jalali. Lahore, 1864.

Davudi, Nasrullah. Dar Shinakt-e 'Obeyd-e Zakani. Mashhad: Intisharat-e Pegah, 1966.

Dehkhoda, Ali Akbar. Amthal va Hekam. 4 vols. Tehran: Amir Kabir, 1959-60.

. *Charand Parand.* 2d ed. Tehran: Ma'rifat, 1953.

. *Lughat Nama.* Tehran: Sazeman-e Lughat Nama, 1946-83.

Enayat, Sa'id. "Hunar-e Nevisandegi-ye Behruz." *Rahnama-ye Ketab* 14 (1971): 725-27.

Eqbal, Abbas. *Majmu'e-ye Maqalat.* Tehran: Khayyam, 1972.

'Eshqi, Mirzada. *Kulliyat 'Eshqi.* Edited by Ali Akbar Salimi. 3d ed. Tehran: Amir Kabir, 1952.

Este'lami, Mohammad. *Adabiyyat-e Dovreh-ye Bidari va Mo'aser.* Tehran: Entesharat-e Daneshgah-e Sepahiyan-e Enqelab-e Iran, 1976.

. *Barrasi-ye Adabiyyat-e Emruz.* Tehran: Amir Kabir, 1964.

E'tesami, Parvin. *Divan-e Parvin E'tesami.* 3rd ed. Tehran, 1954.

Farrokhi, Yazdi. *Divan.* Edited by Hosain Makki. Tehran: Amir Kabir, 1978.

Farrokhzade, Forugh. *Tavallodi Digar.* Tehran: Morvarid, 1963.

Ferdausi, Abul-Qasem. *Shah-Nama.* Tehran: Brokhim, 1966.

Garshasp-Nama. Edited by Habib Yaghma'i. 2d ed. Tehran, 1938.

Gilani, Ashraf. *Bagh-e Behesht.* Tehran, n.d.

.*Javedana Seyyed Ashraf al-Din Gilani.* Edited by Hosain Namini. Tehran: Ketab-e Farzan, 1984.

Guran, Hiva. *Kushesh-ha-ye Nafarjam.* Tehran: Agah, 1981.

Hafez, Mohammad. *Divan-e Hafez.* Edited by Mohammad Qazvini. Tehran, n.d.

Halat, 'Abul al-Qasem. *As 'Asr-e Shotor ta 'Asr-e Mashin.* Tehran: Gutenberg, 1978.

. *Az Bimarestan to Timarestan.* Tehran: Gutenberg, 1978.

. *Divan-e Khrus-e Lari.* Tehran: Gutenberg, 1973.

. *Pabusi Chapluse.* Tehran: Gutenberg, 1979.

. *Zubale-ha va Nukhale-ha.* Tehran: Gutenberg, 1978.

Hedayat, Sadeq. *Afsana-ye Afarinesh.* Rome, 1977.

. *Alaviya Khanum va Velengari.* Tehran: Javidan, 1977.

. *Hajji Agha.* Tehran: 1966.

. *Neveshtehha-yi az Sadeq Hedayat.* Berkeley, n.d.

. *Neveshtehhe-ye Parakandeh.* Tehran: Amir Kabir, 1965.

. *Se Qatra Khun.* 8th ed. Tehran: Parastu, 1965.

. *Tarane-ha-ye Khayyam.* Tehran: Javidan, 1977.

. *Vagh Vagh Sahab.* Tehran: Javidan, 1977.

. *Zenda Begur.* Tehran: Javidan, 1977

Hoquqi, Mohammad. "Ki Mordeh, Ki be-Jast?" *Jong-e Esfahan* 7 (September-October 1966): 161-228.

. *She'r-e Naw az Aghaz ta Emruz.* Tehran: Ketabha-ye Jibi, 1974.

Howfi, Ahmad Mohammad-al. *Al-Fokaha fi al-Adab.* Cairo, 1966.

Iraj Mirza, Jalal al-Mulk. *Divan-e Iraj Mirza.* Edited by Mahjub. Tehran: Amir Kabir, 1964.

Jamalzade, Mohammad 'Ali. *'Amu Hosain- 'Ali.* Tehran: Ma'refat, 1942.

. *Asmun Rismun.* Tehran: Ma'refat,: 1964

·*Dar al Majanin.* 4th ed. Tehran: Ma'refat, 1965.

. *Rahab-Name.* 2nd ed. Tehran: Ma'refat, 1960.

.*Sahra-ye Mahhsar.* Tehran: Ma'refat, 1964.

. *Sar u Tah-ye Yk Karbas.* Tehran: Ma'refat, 1965.

. "Sharh-i Hal." *Nashriya-hi Danishkada-yi Adabiyat-i Tabriz* 4, no. 3 (1954).

. *Talkh va Shirin.* Tehran, 1964.

. *Tasvir-e Zan dar Farhang-e Irani,* Tehran: Amir Kabir, 1978.

. *Yeki Bud Yeki Nabud.* Berlin: Kaviani, 1922.

Jami, Abdu'l Rahman. "Selselat al-Dhabab." In *Haft Owrang.* Tehran, n.d.

Javadi, Hasan. "Tanz va Enteqad dar Dastanhaye Heyvanat." *Alefba* 4 (1974): 1-22.

. "Tanz va Enteqad-e Ejtima'i dar Adabiyyat-e Farsi pish az Mashrutiyyat". *Ayandeh* 7, nos. 5, 9-10, 11-12 (1981-82).

. "Taqlid-e mozhik ve kenaiye-ye tanz amiz." *Ayendeh,* 12, no, 1-3; and no. 4.

. *Tanz, va Mazhab.* Berkeley: Afra, 1981.

Javaheri, "Vajdi." Editor, Gholam Hosain, *Numane-ha-ye Tanz-e Mo'aser.* Tehran: Athar-e Iran, 1970.

Kasma'i, 'Ali Akbar. *Nevisandagan-e Pishro dar Dastan-Nevisi-ye Emruz-e Iran.* Tehran: Sherkat-e Mu'alefan va Mutarjiman-e Iran, 1984.

Kasravi, Ahmad. *Tarikh-i Hijdeh Saleh-yi Azarbayijan ya Dastan-i Mashruta-yi Iran.* 2 vols. Tehran: Amir Kabir, 1961.

. *Tarikh-i Mashruta-yi Iran.* 16th ed., 2 vols. Tehran: Amir Kabir, 1984.

Kermani, Hosain Kuhi. *Bargi az Tarikh-e Mo'aser-e Iran ya Ghogha-ye Jumhuri.* Tehran, 1951.

Khanlari, Parviz Natil. "Marg-e Sadeq Hedayat." *Yaghma* 4 (1951): 106-13.

. "Nathr-i Farsi dar Dawra-yi Akhir." *First Congress of Iranian Writers* (1947): 128-75.

Khaqani, Afzal al-Din. *Divan.* Edited by 'Ali 'Abdul Rasuli. Tehran: Sa'adat, 1937.

Khatibi, Parviz. *Shahr-e Hert.* Tehran, 1954.

Kia, Sadeq. "Sokhani dar bare-ye Zan az Adabiyat-e Pahlavi." *Majalle-ye Danesh-Kade-ye Adabiyat-e Tehran* 5:4.

Kohan, Guel, *Tarikh Sansor dar Matbu'at-e Iran.* 2 vols. Tehran: Agah, 1981.

Majlisi, Mulla Mohammad Baqir. *Hiliyat al-Muttaqin.* Tehran: Javidan, 1968.

Malikzada, Mehdi. *Tarikh-e Inqilab-i Mashrutiyat-i Iran.* 7 vols. Tehran: Ibn Sina, 1948-56.

Malkum Khan, Mirza. *Majmu'a-yi Athar.* Tehran, 1948.

Maraghi, Zain al- 'Abidin. *Siyahat-nama-ye Ebrahim Beg.* Edited by Baqer-e Mo'meni. Tehran, 1974.

Minovi, M. *Panzdah Goftar.* Tehran: University of Tehran, 1954.
. "Qissa-ye Mush va Gorba." *Yaghma* 10, no. 9 (1957): 405-16.

Mirsadeqi, Jamal. *Qisse, Dastan Kutah, Roman.* Tehran: Agah, 1981.

Mirzaev, Abdul-Ghani. *Abu Ishaq va Fa'aliyat-e Adabi-ye U.* Dushanba: Danish, 1971.

Mo'azzen Naser, ed. *Dah Shab: Shabha-ye Sho'ara va Nevisandegan dar Anjoman-e Farhangi-ye Iran va Alman.* Tehran: Amir Kabir, 1978.

Mofid, Bizhan. *Shar-e Qesse.* Tehran: Farhang va Honar, 1969.

Mo'meni, Baqer. *Dard-e Ahl-e Qalam.* Tehran, 1978.

Moqaddam, Hasan. *Ja'far Khan is Back from Europe.* Persian text with a French translation by the author. Edited by Hasan Javadi. Oakland: Jahan Book Co., 1984.

Morier, James. *Sarguzasht-e Hajji Baba.* Edited by M. Jamalzade. Berkeley: Iran Zamin, 1983.

Mu'arri, Abul 'Ala. *Risala-t-ul-Ghofran.* Edited by Dr. 'Aiysha 'Abdul Rahman, "Bint al-Shati." Cairo: Dar al-Ma'arif. 1965.

Mudarrisi, Taqi. "Mulahiza-ha-yi dar Bara-ye Dastan-Nivisi-ye Nuvin-e Farsi," *Sadaf* 1: 913-20 and 977-91.

Mu 'in, Mohammad. "Chiraghi ka Khamush Shud." *Yaghma* 9 (1956): 294-301.

____ . "Tarjuma-ye Ahval-e Dehkhuda." The introduction to *Lughat nama,* Tehran: Saziman-e Lughat nama, pp. 379-94.

Mostowfi, Abdulla. *Sharh-e Zindigani-ye Man ya Tarikh-e Ijtima'i va Idari-ye Dovra-ye Qajariya.* 3 vols. Tehran: Ketabfrushi Zavvar, 1945.

Muwailihi, Mohammad. *Hadithe'Isa Ibn Hisham, O Fitratan min al-Zaman.* Cairo: Dar al-Ma'rif, 1964.

Nafisi, Sa'id. *Nimeh-Rah-e Behesht.* Tehran: Gohar Khay (Sepehr), 1952.

____ . *Pur-e Sina.* Tehran: Danish, 1954.

____ . *Tarikh-e Ejtema'i-ye Iran.* 2 vols. Tehran: Inlisharate Bonyad, 1965.

____ . ed. *Shahkarha-ye Nthr-e Farsi-ye Mo'aser.* Tehran: Ma'refat, 1951.

Nakhustin Kungira-ye Nivisandigan-i Iran. Tehran: Anjoman-e Ravabet Iran va Showravi, 1947.

Naser, Khosrow. *Divan.* Edited by S. H. Taqizada. Tehran, 1956.

Nateq, Homa. *Az Mast ke bar Mast.* Tehran: Agah, 1978.

Nazimu'l-Islam, M. *Tarikh-i Bidari-yi Iraniyan.* Tehran: Amir Kabir, 1909.

Nesin, Aziz. *Cumhuriyet Doneminda Turk Mizahi.* Istanbul: Ankara Yainlari, 1973.

Nezari, Hakim. *Farhang-e Iran Zamin.* Vol. 6. Edited by Ch. G. Baradin. 1958.

Nizami, Abu Mohammad Ilias. *Kulliyat-e Khamsa-ye Nizami.* Tehran: Amir Kabir, 1972.

No'mani, Shibli. *She'r al Ajam.* 5 vols. Tehran: Ibn Sina, 1947-57.

Nuri-ye Ala, Esma'il. "Arzeshha-ye Ejtema'i-ye She'r." *Arash* 17 (April-June 1968): 83-99.

____ . *Sovar va Asbab dar She'r-e Emruz-e Iran.* Tehran: Agah, 1969-70.

Pahlavan, 'Abbas. *Na-Darwish,* Tehran: Amir Kabir, 1967.

____ . *Shab-e 'Arusi-ye Babam.* Tehran: Amir Kabir, 1962.

____ . *Shekar-e 'Ankabut.* Tehran: Amid Iran, n.d.

____ . *Tashrifat.* Tehran: Amir Kabir, 1970.

Parizi, Bastani. *Khatun-e Haft Qal'e.* Tehran: Dehkhoda, 1965.

Parvizi, Rasul. *Shalvar-ha-ye Vasle-dar.* Tehran: Amir Kabir, 1957.

Payande, Abu'l Qasem. *Dar Cinema-ye Zendegi.* Tehran: Inlisharat-e Tala'i, 1975.

Pezeshk-zad, Iraj. *Asemun va Rismun.* Tehran: Ketab-ha-ye Jibi, 1977.

____ . *Bubul.* Tehran: Nil, 1959.

____ . *Da'i Jan Napoleon.* Tehran, 1972.

____ . *Internasional -ha Bache Poru-ha.* Paris, 1984.

Qa'ani, Habibullah. *Divan.* Edited by Mohammad Javad Mahjub. Tehran: Amir Kabir, 1957.

Ra'in, Isma'il. *Huquq Begiran-e Ingilis dar Iran.* Tehran: Amir Kabir, 1969.

Ravandi, Mortaza. *Tarikh-e Ejtema'i-ye Iran.* Tehran: Amir Kabir, 1977.

Resale fi al-Tanbih 'ala al-Asrar. . . . MS 1933. Istanbul: As'ad Effendi Collection, Suleimanieh Library, ca. 1202.

Rumi, Jalal al-Din. *Divan-e Shams-e Tabrizi.* Tehran: Amir Kabir, 1970.

. *Mathnavi.* Tehran: Nashr-e Kutub-e Akhlaqi, 1942.

Saber, 'Ali-Akbar. *Tahirzada, Hop Hop Name.* Baku: Azernashr, 1962.

Sa'di, Muslih al-Din. *Bustan.* Edited by Abdul 'Azim Qarib. Tehran: Elmi, 1967.

. *Kolliyyat.* Tehran: Eqbal, 1937.

Sadr-Hashimi, Mohammad. *Tarikh-i Jarayid va Majjallat-e Iran.* 4 vols. Isfahan, 1948-53.

Sa'edi, Gholam-Hosain. *'Aqibat-e Qalam Fars'i.* Tehran: Agah, 1976.

. *A-ye Bi-Kolah, A-ye Ba-Kolah.* Terhan: Agah, 1968.

. *'Aza-daran-e Bayal.* Tehran: Agah, 1965.

. *Chub be Dast-ha-ye Varazil.* 2d ed. Tehran: Morvarid, 1971.

. *Dandil: Chahar Qisse.* Tehran: Intisharat-e Javas, 1966.

. *Dikta va Zavia.* Tehran: Agah, 1968.

. *Khane-Roshani.* Tehran: Amir Kabir, 1972.

. *Khosha be Hal-i Bord Baran.* Tehran: Amir Kabir, 1976.

. *Mah-e 'Asal.* Tehran: Ketab-ha-ye Jibi, 1978.

. *Parvar-bandan.* Tehran: Agah, 1969.

. *Shab-Neshini-ye Bashokuh.* Tehran: Amir Kabir, 1960.

Safa, Zabibullah. *Ganj-e Sokhan.* 3 vols. Tehran: Ibn Sina, 1961.

. *Tarikh-e Adabiyyat dar Iran.* 7 vols. Tehran: Ferdausi Publications, 1984.

Safi, Fakhr al-din 'Ali. *Lata'ef al-Tawa'ef.* Edited by Ahmad Golchin Ma'ani. Tehran: Eqbal, 1962.

Safi al-Najafi, Ahmad. *Omar al-Khayyam.* Tehran, 1950.

Saif Farghani, Abu Mohammad. *Divan.* Edited by Z. Safa. 2 vols. Tehran: University of Tehran, 1962.

Sana'i, Majd al-Din *Divan-e Sana'i.* Edited by M. Mosaffa. Tehran: Amir Kabir, 1957.

Shafi'i-ye Kadkani, Mohammad Reza. *Advar-e She'r-e Farsi: Az Mashrutiyyat ta Soqut-e Saltanat.* Tehran: Tus, 1980.

. "She'r-e Mo'aser az Omq-e Ensai Tohist. *Farhang va Zendegi* 9 (1972-73): 32-35

. *Sovar-e Khiyal dar She'r-e Parsi.* Tehran: Nil, 1970.

Shahani, Khosrow. *Adam-e 'Avazi.* Tehran: Ketab-ha-ye Jibi, 1971.

. *Komedi-ye Iftetah.* Tehran: Ketab-ha-ye Parastu, 1976.

. *Kur-e La'nati.* 2d ed. Tehran: Ketab-ha-ye Jibi, 1964.

. *Pahlavan-e Mahalle.* Tehran, n.d.

. *Vahshat-abad.* Tehran: Ketab-ha-ye Parastu, 1969.

Sireshg, M. Shafi'i-ye Kadkini, and M. Azarm. *She'r-e Emruz-e Khorasan.* Tehran: Tus, 1965.

Tabari, Ihsan. "Sadiq Hedayat: Shakhsiyat-e u, Afkar-e u, Jay-i u dar Hayat-e Adabi va Ijtima'i-ye Mu'asir." *Mardum* 5, no. 10 (1947): 42-47.

Tabataba'i, Ehsan. *Chante-ye Darvish.* Tehran: Ketabfrushi Atishkada, 1958.

Tabrizi, Mirza Aqa. *Chahar Te'atr.* Edited by M. B. Mo'meni. Tehran: Nashr-e Ayanda, 1977.

Tabrizi, Yar Ahmad. *Tarab-Khane.* Edited by Jalal Homa'i. Tehran: Amjaman-e Athar-e Melli, 1963.

Takmil Homayun, Naser. "Bar-rasi-ye Moqe'iyyat-e Zan dar Tarikh-e Iran. *Farhang va Zandegi*, nos. 19-20. (Winter 1975).

. "Hajji Morier va qisse-ye Isti'mar." *Alefab* (4 1974).

Tonkaboni, Feridun. *Dah Dastan va Nevashta-ha-ye digar.* Berkeley: Confederation of Iranian Students, 1977.

Tusi, Nasir al-Din. *Akhlaq-e Nasiri.* Edited by Vahid-e Damghani. Tehran: Farnhani, n.d.

Unsur al-Ma'ali Kaikavus. *Qabus-Nama.* Edited by Sa'id-e Nafisi. Tehran, 1937.

Vajdi, Javahiri. *Nomune-ha-ye Tanz-e Mo'aser.* Tehran, 1970.

Vatvat, Rashid al-Din. *Hada'iq al-She'r fi Daqa'iq al-Seh'r.* Edited by Abbas Eqbal. Tehran, 1929.

Yaghma-ye, Jandaqi. *Divan.* Tehran: Itizad al-Saltane, 1866.

Yarshater, Ehsan. *She'r-e Farsi dar 'Ahd-e Shah Rukh.* Tehran: University of Tehran, 1955.

Yasami, Gholam Reza Rashid. "Talibuff va Kitab-e Ahmad." *Iranshahr* 2 (1923): 283-97.

Yegani. *Hakim Omar Khayyam va Roba'iyyat-e-u.* Tehran: Anjuman-e Atharte Melli, 1963.

Yousefi, Gh. H. *Didari Ba Ahl-e Qalam.* 2 vols. Mashhad: Danishgah Ferdausi, 1978-79.

Yurtsever, Vahap. *Mirza Fathali Ahunt Zadenin Hayati ve Eserleri.* Ankara, 1950.

Yushij, Nima. *Arzesh-e Ehsasat va Panj Maqaleh dar She'r va Namayesh.* Tehran: Gutenberg, 1972.

Zakani, 'Obeyd. *Kulliyat-e 'Obeyd-e Zakani. Edited by Parviz Atabaki. Tehran: Eqbal, 1964.*

Zara' Iraj. *Shah-Nama* (a cartoon collection), Tehran, 1979.

Zarrinkub, 'Abdul-Hosain. *Az Kucha-ye Rendan.* Tehran: Ketabha-ye Jibi, 1970.

. *Ba Karevan-e Hulla.* Tehran: Aria, 1964.

. *Na Sharqi Na Gharbi Ensani.* Tehran: Amir Kabir, 1975.

Zarrinkub, Hamid. *Cheshm-andaz-e She'r-e Now-e Farsi.* Tehran: Tus, 1970.

Index